Educational psychology

the instructional endeavor

The

Educational psychology

instructional endeavor

C. M. Charles, Ph.D.

Professor of Education, San Diego State University,
San Diego, California

Second edition

The C. V. Mosby Company

Saint Louis   1976

Second edition

Copyright © 1976 by The C. V. Mosby Company

All rights reserved. No part of this book may be reproduced in any manner without written permission of the publisher.

Previous edition copyrighted 1972

Printed in the United States of America

Distributed in Great Britain by Henry Kimpton, London

Library of Congress Cataloging in Publication Data

Charles, C   M
    Educational psychology.

    Includes bibliographical references and index.
    1. Educational psychology. I. Title.
[DNLM: 1. Psychology, Educational. LB1051 C475e]
LB1051.C3326   1976   370.15   75-43611
ISBN 0-8016-0952-6

TS/VH/VH 9 8 7 6 5 4 3 2 1

Foreword for first edition

This is truly a new kind of textbook in educational psychology. The approach makes crystal clear that the primary concern of teaching psychology to pre-service teachers is that of *changing behavior,* not that of covering a preconceived outline of subject matter.

Trainers of teachers for the public schools are correctly concerned with the complicated problem of what *teaching* is. Probably it would be best if we would stop *teaching* in the traditional sense and stop using the word "teaching." Then we might be better able to provide for students those appropriate learning experiences that are motivating, that meet their needs for growth, and that *do change their behavior.*

A beginning course in educational psychology must provide the same types of learning experiences that young teachers must provide for the boys and girls in their classes. Dr. Charles has arranged the content of this text to easily establish behavioral objectives that the teacher expects to achieve. The movement from *telling,* which has proved to be woefully inadequate, to promoting the *doing* of inherently worthwhile exercises that provide for learning is a welcome modification in textbook preparation. The principles of psychology have not been omitted; innovative ways of presenting them have been added so that new teachers will be able to apply them in their own classrooms.

The exercises provided in this text will be most useful in integrating theory and practice if they are incorporated into teacher training programs that utilize professional semester plans. The excellent writing style in the text helps to accent in a cogent manner the very point of view that Dr. Charles is emphasizing.

A beginning course obviously does not give a teacher comprehensive mastery of learning theory or of the psychology of teaching. But this text can serve as an excellent introduction to the problems that are encountered by classroom teachers. For those who continue to grow, additional courses and seminars are readily available.

I believe that this text provides a badly needed, novel way of involving undergraduate students in crucial subject matter that, far too often, we have only abstractly discussed.

Miles V. Zintz, Ph.D.

Professor of Education
University of New Mexico
Albuquerque, New Mexico

Preface

Educational psychology is a field of study that has to do with learning, remembering, and applying knowledge. It began taking its present form about seventy-five years ago. For many of those years, its great thinkers strove to find out how people learned, remembered, and transferred—or used—knowledge. Despite their efforts, no satisfactory explanations came forth to explain how learning, retention, and transfer occurred.

Educational psychologists no longer concern themselves with theories of *how* learning and transfer occur. Instead, they give attention to the *conditions* that affect learning and transfer.

These conditions fall into the following categories:

maturation the changes that occur with growth and development, that set individuals' limitations and potentialities.
motivation the kinds and degrees of purposes, incentives, and desires that cause people to act.
physical environment the physical space within which learning occurs, including objects it contains and the manipulations made on those objects.
social environment the persons involved in the setting in which learning occurs, including groupings, communication, and interactions.
climate the feeling tone within the learning environment, including emotions, attitudes, values, acceptance, and rejection.

reinforcement the rewards, payoffs, and satisfactions that learners experience in association with their efforts in the learning environment.

Clustered around and within these categories are other activities that play important roles in educational psychology. Those activities include the following:

measurement and evaluation the testing, diagnosing, appraising, and judging of learners, teachers, and educational programs.
psychological services the identification and correction of personal problems that interfere with learning and adequate functioning.

Educational psychologists concentrate on these conditions and activities because they are known to affect learning— how quickly it occurs, how long it lasts, and how useful it remains for the learner. Most important, their findings help teachers do a better job with students. Specifically, educational psychology helps teachers to

1. Know what to expect, and not expect, of learners at different stages of physical, intellectual, social, and emotional development
2. Arrange physical environments that interest learners, attract their involvement, and maximize their intellectual functioning
3. Arrange social interactions that enhance communication and interpersonal relations

4. Establish emotional climates that attend to learners' feelings, interests, attitudes, values, and self-concept
5. Establish success environments that, though challenging, maximize success while removing the stigma from failure
6. Put into effect behavior management systems that increase the amount of on-task, productive activity of learners while decreasing the amount of off-task, disruptive, or counterproductive behavior

7. Diagnose learner needs to prescribe learning situations best suited to each individual
8. Monitor and evaluate learner progress and instructional effectiveness

Whether your interests lie in teaching, educational research, or school psychological services, you will find that educational psychology plays a crucial role. For education today, educational psychology is where the action is.

C. M. Charles

Acknowledgments

The contributions of many people shaped this book. It seems unjust that each one of them cannot be named here, for their numbers include great writers, fine professors, stimulating colleagues, and bracingly frank students. I am in the debt of them all.

Yet, while most must go unnamed, it would be inexcusable not to acknowledge the particular contributions of five colleagues whose critical insights made this book significantly more than it would otherwise have been: Dr. Miles V. Zintz, University of New Mexico, Albuquerque, New Mexico; Dr. Peter C. Gega, San Diego State University, San Diego, California; Dr. George Kaluger, Shippensburg State College, Shippensburg, Pennsylvania; Dr. Richard O. Davis, Edinboro State College, Edinboro, Pennsylvania; and Dr. Joel Macht, University of Denver, Denver, Colorado. My gratitude to them is deep and heartfelt.

Contents

Part I

Psychology and education

explains the development, assumptions, and practices of **behaviorism** and **humanism**, shows how they affect the practice of **education**, and presents an overview of intellectual and psychosocial processes in **human development**, accomplished through chapters

1. Behaviorism and its stars
2. Humanism in psychology
3. Behaviorism, humanism, and teaching
4. Human development

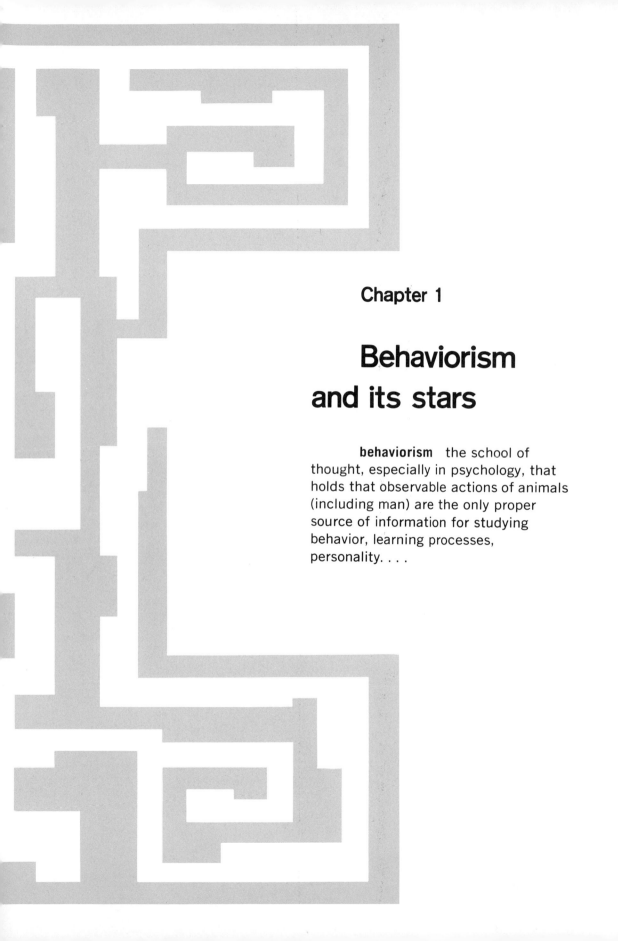

Chapter 1

Behaviorism
and its stars

behaviorism the school of
thought, especially in psychology, that
holds that observable actions of animals
(including man) are the only proper
source of information for studying
behavior, learning processes,
personality. . . .

associationists

Philosophers like to bedevil psychologists with cute tricks. For example, whenever psychologists come up with a new idea in human behavior, philosophers quickly name a half dozen people out of the past who have already considered the idea. They usually begin with Plato or Aristotle, who seem to have thought of almost everything, and then they touch on a few Sophists, Scholastics, Thomists, and what have you, who fill in the spaces between 400 BC and the present.

So it is with most aspects of psychology's great twentieth-century invention — behaviorism. It is true that J. B. Watson pulled behavioristic thought together and gave impetus and respectability to it. He is rightly remembered for doing so. Yet, seeking out the origins of behaviorism sends one leapfrogging back to Aristotle, whose essay "Memory" shows strong attention to *associationism,* a predecessor of behaviorism.

Aristotle pondered over phenomena such as: Suppose you see a stack of hay and you think immediately of a cow, which is not present. What is the nature of the relationship, in one's thought, between the hay and the cow? Or, in a similar vein, between a peach and a pear or a pond and an ocean? Such associations are made, Aristotle believed, because the objects being associated are similar, or opposite, or near to each other.

A curious fact of Western thought is that with the advent of the post-Renaissance Age of Reason, philosophers turned to the ancient Greeks for inspiration and logic. Thomas Hobbes (c. 1650) followed Aristotle's ideas, attempting to reduce human behavior to physical terms. He wrote of fundamental elements of thought — sensation, recall, and sequence — and used terms such as motion, communication of motion, and inertia.

John Locke (c. 1690) introduced the concept of "association of ideas." He believed that ideas come from two sources: sensory experience and mental operations (carried out by each individual).*

George Berkeley (c. 1709) contributed the concept of sign-meaning association. He explained that a sound, for example, might be much more that a simple sensory experience. The sound might have meaning if the individual previously had had experience with it.†

David Hume (c. 1740) added to Berkeley's concept of meaning through association by stressing the importance of contiguity, that is, the "nearness" in time of one senation to another.‡ He felt that associations occurring frequently become firm and habituated and that whenever the antecedent occurs, the consequent is bound to follow.

David Hartley, in his book *Observations on Man, His Frame, His Duty, and His Expectations* (1749), built a theory of associationism that incorporated the ideas of his predecessors. He felt that all mental functioning could be explained in terms of associations, either simultaneous or successive.

Thomas Brown (c. 1820) made contributions that expanded Hartley's theory of associationism. He puzzled over the observation that *A* will remind you of *B* at one time, but perhaps of *C* or *D* at another time. That is, a haystack may remind you of a cow today, but it might remind you of a frosty morning on another day. Brown added the concepts of

*Note the similarity between Locke's idea and those of the great contemporary psychologist Piaget, whose work is discussed in Chapter 4. They did not agree, however, on the role of the mind in motivating behavior.

†The notion of sign-meaning played a crucial role in the learning theory of the contemporary behaviorist Edward Tolman, whose work is described later in this chapter.

‡Temporal contiguity was assigned a major status in the learning theory of Edwin R. Guthrie, whose work is described later in this chapter.

4

frequency, recency, and vividness in associations to explain the relative strengths, life spans, and occurrences of different associations. James Mill followed with *Analysis of the Phenomena of the Human Mind* (1829), in which he brought the theory of associationism to its highest level of development.

With the works of Alexander Bain (c. 1855), associationism took on new dimensions. Bain pointed out that not all sensory experiences that occur together become associated. Rather, factors such as likeness, difference, and cause-effect play crucial roles in association. This notion holds that one must discriminate among sensory items before they are associated. Bain also showed that all motor behavior cannot be explained from the basis of associations, citing as an example the innate reflex movements shown by infants.

The work of Herman Ebbinghaus added yet another dimension to associationism and gave it an experimental, modernistic look. Previous associationists started with associations that they had established in their own minds and then tried to reason backward to determine how they became established. Their approach was logical and philosophical. Ebbinghaus initiated the procedure of forming new associations and later testing their strength. To avoid preestablished associations, Ebbinghaus used nonsense syllables, had subjects associate them, and checked to see how strong the associations remained over periods of time.

From such experiments, Ebbinghaus formulated a "law of frequency," which held that learning (association) increased in proportion to the frequency with which a particular association was made.* He also formulated a "law of recency,"

*This law of frequency is similar to the law of exercise that held such an important place in the learning theory put forth by Edward L. Thorndike some thirty years later.

which held that recently made associations were strongest and that they decayed over periods of time. The graphic representations of the frequency and recency data became famous as "the learning curve" and "the forgetting curve," both of which still receive attention today.

Just prior to the work of Ebbinghaus, biologists had become interested in the motor activity of animals, motivated in large part by Darwin's pronouncements on origins of species through natural selection. That interest resulted in a number of animal study reports. Chief among them was George Romanes's *Animal Intelligence* (1883), which dealt with mental evolution. This work was soundly criticized for explaining animal behavior in terms of higher mental processes. Also important at that time were L. T. Hobhouse's summaries of experiments on animal behavior; those experiments were conducted with animals ranging from cats to elephants.

Animal studies played a key role in the development of the field of psychology, changing its emphasis from what had been a primarily philosophical one to the experimental direction it took in the first half of the twentieth century. This new direction stressed physiological processes and focused on the overt behaviors of animals, both human and infrahuman.

Pavlov

The behavioristic movement in psychology began to crystalize with the landmark discoveries of the Russian physiologist Ivan Petrovich Pavlov. Working in the Institute for Experimental Medicine in St. Petersburg (now Leningrad), Pavlov won a Nobel Prize in 1904 for his studies on the nerves and reflexes of digestive glands. However, it was an accidental discovery in 1902 that immortalized Pavlov in the annals of psychology.

Pavlov had been studying the salivary responses of dogs. In that work, he had constructed a device that permitted the collection and measurement of saliva secreted in response to food placed in the dog's mouth. Pavlov noted that after a few trials, saliva began to flow from the dog's mouth before the food, a meat powder, was actually presented. The salivation occurred when the dog saw the food container, and later when the dog heard the attendant's footsteps.

Pavlov called the salivation response that occurred before the food presentation a *conditioned reflex,* and he used the term *conditioned stimulus* to refer to the stimulus—whether food dish, footsteps, or whatever—that elicited the conditioned reflex. Those concepts continue in use today, except that conditioned reflex is now called *conditioned response.*

Pavlov pursued this new direction in his research with a great deal of interest, attempting to determine how conditioned responses could be established, maintained, and removed. He showed that conditioned responses could be made to occur following a wide variety of conditioned stimuli and that they could be strong and persistent. He found that their formation could be *inhibited* by presenting distracting stimuli simultaneously and that once established they could be removed, *extinguished,* by merely withholding the unconditioned stimulus, the food, for several trials.

In addition to these discoveries, Pavlov established that stimuli could be *generalized* and *differentiated.* As an example of stimulus generalization, suppose that the dog had been conditioned to salivate at the sound of a high-pitched tone; it would also salivate, though not so much, at the sound of a low-pitched tone. Thus, the dog would have generalized the original conditioned stimulus to other similar stimuli.

Stimuli are differentiated in this man-

ner: suppose that several conditioned stimuli produce a conditioned response (salivation). The desired conditioned stimulus can be maintained by following it with the unconditioned stimulus (food). Meanwhile, the undesired conditioned stimuli are not followed with food, and they gradually cease producing the conditioned response.

Pavlov concluded from his research that the key to understanding behavior lay wholly within the realm of physiology. Although he did not formulate an acceptable theory of learning, he nonetheless turned scientific attention strongly toward experimentation with animal behavior, made several discoveries that shaped the development of theories of learning, and added terminology that is still widely used in psychology. Because of this influence, Pavlov is rightly considered a giant in the history of psychology.

Watson

The behavioristic movement in psychology grew with sudden energy in the first decade of the twentieth century. Pavlov's work gave it vitality, but it was J. B. Watson who, more than any other, gave it form and direction.

John Broadus Watson was born on a South Carolina farm in 1878. He failed to distinguish himself academically until he entered Furman University, where he became a scholar of the classics and received a master's degree in 1900. His interest in philosophy took him to the University of Chicago, to study with John Dewey. There his interest in philosophy waned as be became intrigued with the new work taking place in animal psychology. He established an animal psychology laboratory at the University of Chicago and then moved as a professor to Johns Hopkins University in 1908 to continue his work.

To understand the importance of Watson's contributions, we must recognize the nature of psychology at that period in its development. Generally speaking, psychology was still considered to be the science of conscious experience; introspection, or looking within oneself, was the principal means of gathering data. Watson saw two great problems with that situation. First, he considered introspection to be nonscientific, since the data were accessible only to the person looking within himself and thus not open to scrutiny by impartial observers who could be more free from error-producing biases and blind spots. Second, it was obvious to him that introspection and consciousness were not available as techniques for investigating animal behavior. He considered that animal researchers conducted the only truly scientific work in psychology, since they based their conclusions on the behavior of the animals —evidence available to all observers.

Watson popularized this view of psychology in lectures and writings between 1912 and 1914. In his book *Behavior* (cited in Woodworth 1948, p. 68), he wrote:

Psychology as the behaviorist views it is a purely objective experimental branch of natural science. Its theoretical goal is the prediction and control of behavior. Introspection forms no essential part of its methods.

Unlike most of his predecessors, Watson believed that the study of animal behavior could lead to the establishment of all the fundamental principles of behavior and learning, essential to psychology. He recognized that additional concepts might be needed to explain human mental functioning, but felt that those concepts would fit naturally into the basic framework resulting from animal studies.

Watson's ideas made a strong impression on younger psychologists of the day. The current of prevailing thought quickly swung from the concept of consciousness to the concept of behavior, which for Watson and his followers included

these ideas (cited in Woodworth 1948, p. 71):

1. Psychology is defined as the science of *behavior,* not as the science of consciousness.
2. The proper scope of psychology includes both animal and human behavior.
3. The method of psychology rests on wholly objective data—data available to all observers.
4. Concepts fundamental in psychology include those established through observation of behavior, such as stimulus, response, and habit formation.
5. The application of psychological work lies in the practical prediction and control of behavior.

Following World War I, Watson conducted pioneer experimental studies of young children's behavior. He showed how fear, for example, could be associated with objects "not dangerous" to young children through a process of presenting a loud noise in conjunction with an object such as a white rat. He then showed how that fear was generalized to a human face wearing a false white beard. By 1924, he had concluded that such conditioned responses could explain all habit formation. He stimulated great discussion by his claim that given a normal infant and complete control over its environment, he could train the child to become outstanding in any field of endeavor—music, art, languages, mathematics, and the various professions. He wrote:

Give me a dozen healthy infants, well formed, to bring them up in any way I choose and I'll guarantee you to take any one at random and train him to become any type of specialist I might select — doctor, lawyer, artist, merchant-chief and, yes, even beggar-man and thief, regardless of his talents, penchants, tendencies, abilities, vocations, and race of his ancestors. [Watson 1919, p. 10]

Few of Watson's specific ideas are accepted today. Yet, he is considered a monumental figure in the development of psychology. This lasting reputation remains because of his boldness of thought, tough-mindedness, rejection of the mystical, insistence on scientific procedures, and an abiding faith in the

7

power of psychology to contribute to the betterment of human affairs.

Thorndike

Application of psychological inquiry into matters of school learning and education was purely incidental before the time of Edward L. Thorndike. Thorndike, a contemporary of Watson and a student of the Harvard psychologist William James, was one of the first to see the great applicability that psychological research could have for matters of learning in the school setting. He turned his energies in that direction, and within two decades, he almost single handedly remade eductional practice. Because of Thorndike the classical "mind training" curriculum was swept aside in favor of a curriculum consisting of practical studies. Because of him, objective achievement and aptitude testing replaced subjective oral and written examinations. And because of him, great research activity welled up in the pursuit of scientific theories of learning—of its nature, its occurrence, and its transfer to other situations.

Thorndike, born in 1874, was an established writer and authority in psychology by the age of 25. Encouraged by James, he had conducted significant early experiments in learning. From those experiments and numerous others he conducted while a long-time professor at Teachers College Columbia University, Thorndike formulated his theory of learning, which he called "connectionism," and his theory of transfer of learning, which he called the theory of "identical elements."

Thorndike's early experiments were done with animals, mainly cats. He would place a hungry cat inside a box that could be opened by pulling a string or pressing a button or lever. The cat would move about energetically and would sooner or later hit the escape key by accident. Replaced in the box, the cat would again go through numerous movements until hitting the escape mechanism. In this manner the animal learned to avoid acts that were not successful in escaping, while repeating the act that led to escape.

Thorndike noted that the cat would repeat the movement that led to success. If the cat triggered the escape mechanism by accidentally backing into it, that was the procedure that it repeated — it opened the door by backing into the release mechanism.

Such experiments led Thorndike to propose his "law of effect," a crucial part of his theory of learning. The law of effect held that:

Any act which in a given situation produces satisfaction becomes associated with that situation, so that when the situation recurs the act is more likely than before to recur also. Conversely, any act which in a given situation produces discomfort becomes dissociated from that situation, so that when the situation recurs the act is less likely than before to recur. [1905, p. 203]

But obviously for an act to become associated, whether pleasantly or unpleasantly, with a situation, the act had to be repeated in that situation. Thorndike stipulated this phenomenon in a second law, called the "law of exercise." The law of exercise and its sublaws, "use" and "disuse," stated that the more times a response was made in a given situation the stronger it became (law of use). Conversely, prolonged disuse weakened the likelihood of the reoccurrence of the response.

Thorndike turned his attention to human learning in attempts to further define and clarify his theories of learning. The results of this work caused him to make minor modifications in some of his laws. Chief among those modifications was a revision of the law of effect, so that greater emphasis was placed on reward and less on punishment. He felt that reward had a strong positive effect on human learning but that punishment had little or no effect in extinguishing learning.

In short, Thorndike's theory of learning maintained that learning was merely connecting stimuli and responses, hence the name *connectionism*. He considered the mind to be man's connecting system (analogous to a telephone switchboard), but his theory gave no attention to the processes that might occur in the mind. Instead, he focused on the conditions, exercise and effect, that comprise the learning situation. In Thorndike's words:

A good simple definition or description of a man's mind is that it is his connection system, adapting the responses of thought, feeling, and action that he makes to the situation that he meets. [1943, p. 22]

For a good thirty years no serious challenge was mounted against Thorndike's ideas on learning. True, psychoanalytic theory developed by Freud and his followers was causing great excitement in psychological circles, but those ideas never formed into an explanation of learning. Essentially the same was true for Gestalt psychology, which blossomed in the early 1900s, though it provided great insights into the phenomena of perception and perceptual organization. The apex of the Gestalt movement came with Lewin's attempts to develop a "cognitive field" theory of learning, somewhat analogous to the electromagnetic field theory in physics. Lewin used the concept of life space, combined with topological drawings to explain human purposive behavior. Although this notion attracted considerable attention, it too failed to explain learning in an adaquate way. Thus, it remained for later behavioral psychologists to develop theories of learning and transfer that moved significantly beyond the contributions made by the greatest of all educational psychologists, Edward L. Thorndike.

Thorndike to Skinner

When Thorndike died in 1949, there was general feeling that an educational psychologist of his omnipresent stature might never appear again. Indeed, there is still good reason to believe that such will be the case, for the diverse areas of the psychology of human learning have become so complex and sophisticated that any one person can hardly hope to exert significant influence in more than one or two of them.

Nevertheless, we find ourselves with a modern day giant in our midst. Although he has in no way been dominant in the breadth of school learning and curriculum matters that were reconstituted under Thorndike, he has nonetheless provided a simple theoretical explanation for the conditions under which learning occurs. He has carefully amassed incredible quantities of data that support his ideas, he has made direct application of his ideas to matters of school learning, and he has seen his ideas exert powerful influence on virtually all areas of school curriculum and teaching practice. The person responsible for these innovations, B. F. Skinner, is today generally considered to be the world's most influential psychologist.

Before examining Skinner's contributions, let us take a moment to note a few of the significant contributions made by other behavioral psychologists spanning the interval between the peak years of Thorndike and Skinner. We must recognize that in truth a great number of psychologists made important contributions to the development of behavioristic thought. Only four of the most outstanding will be mentioned here — Karl Lashley, Edwin Guthrie, Clark Hull, and Edward Tolman.

Lashley

Karl Lashley, born in 1890, was one of Watson's students who later became a professor at Harvard. Though his approach to psychology was behavioristic, as indeed one would expect from the influence of Watson, Lashley believed that behavior should ultimately be explained in terms of processes occurring in the brain. Yet he ruled out subjective introspection as a means for searching out those processes. He concentrated instead on the physical mechanisms of the cerebral cortex, and he succeeded in demonstrating that the major findings obtained through introspective approaches to behavior could be expressed adequately in objective terms. Objectivity was the key for Lashley. With that condition met, he judged introspective psychology acceptable to behaviorism.

Lashley's studies included numerous brain experiments in which he used rats as subjects. From those studies he found that various parts of the cerebral cortex had equal ability to learn various kinds of performances, such as movement through a maze. This phenomenon, *equipotentiality,* is regularly called to use with humans who have suffered brain damage, with resultant loss of ability to perform certain functions. They can relearn those behaviors, using an undamaged part of the cortex. Lashley did find exceptions to equipotentiality. One such exception included his finding that the visual perception of a shape or pattern could be accomplished only by the rear (occipital) area of the cortex.

Lashley's work in neuropsychology brought the behaviorists and the Gestalt psychologists closer together. He caused behaviorists to give more consideration to the role of the central nervous system in explaining behavior, and he showed that there was much more to learning than could be explained by the reflex, conditioned-reflex paradigm.

Guthrie

Edwin R. Guthrie, like most other behavioral psychologists of the first half of the twentieth century, was strongly influenced in his outlook by J. B. Watson. Yet, far more than that of Watson, Guthrie's work formed itself into a theory of learning. Indeed, his theory was the first behavioristic alternative of substance to the powerful theory of Thorndike.

Thorndike, you will remember, emphasized repeated performance (law of exercise) and reward for performance (law of effect) in his theory of the learning process. Guthrie's work led him to formulate markedly different descriptions about the course of learning.

Guthrie believed that learned responses were fully and completely established in one trial. He stated this idea very simply: "A combination of stimuli which has accompanied a movement will on its reoccurrence tend to be followed by that movement" (1935, p. 26).

Put briefly, Guthrie believed that learning occurred at full strength on the first trial. His conception of learned responses involved only the movements of the organism and had nothing to do with whether those movements were considered successful or erroneous. Guthrie's theory of learning no longer attracts advocates among psychological theorists. As a system, it is too vague, too imprecisely stated. It can be neither proved nor disproved through experimentation. Still, Guthrie made a lasting contribution to the behavioristic position in psychology. His ideas motivated a great deal of serious research. Moreover, he gave attention to practical, everyday activities, showing that psychology need not be a cold discipline, devoid of humaneness and removed from the life problems of human beings.

Hull

Against the soft, vague, and imprecisely stated theories of Guthrie, those of Clark L. Hull stood in stark contrast, fairly bristling with postulates, corollaries, symbolic representations, and

| Input variables (environmental data) | | Intervening variables (traits and conditions of the organism) | | Output variables (behaviors) |

equations. Hull firmly believed that human behavior could be accurately predicted as soon as we learned to identify and quantify data taken in by the organism (the input variables) and specify how they interacted with existing traits and conditions of the organism (the intervening variables). The above diagram is his fundamental scheme for explaining behavior, stripped to the barest essentials.

Until Hull's time most behavioral psychologists had used the stimulus-response (S-R) paradigm to study behavior. That is, the environmental stimuli (S) were manipulated to see what would be the resultant response behavior (R). Hull followed a suggestion by Woodworth that a much more acceptable paradigm would be S-O-R, where O symbolized the organism. He recognized that a given stimulus could produce a variety of different responses in different organisms; therefore, there must be conditions existing within an individual that interacted in various ways with the stimulus presented. Those existing conditions were called *intervening variables,* indicating that they intervened between stimulus and response. Hull used the S-O-R paradigm and attempted to specify and quantify both S and O, so as to more accurately predict R.

Hull's postulates and corollaries reveal the extraordinary degree to which he attended to detail, as well as his attempts to specify thoroughly all variables and their interplay. Many psychologists of the 1940s held out hope that Hull could formulate a comprehensive theory of learning. He had not done so at the time of his death in 1952. Nor has the lead he set been followed by contemporary theorists.

Hull's process of theorizing, with its rigor and precision, left its mark deeply on the course of psychology. His theory pushed aside Thorndike's connectionism and held the forefront during the late 1930s and the 1940s. To date, only Skinner's work equals that of Hull for detail, comprehensiveness, and quantitative empiricism. Hull was exemplary in that regard.

Tolman

Before the time of Edward C. Tolman, behavioristic psychology conceived of the acts of organisms in the sense of reactions. That is, on the presentation of a stimulus, the organism would react to it. Such a conception left the impression that responsive behavior had little meaning except in direct relation to the stimulus and that it was essentially without purpose.

Tolman judged otherwise. He believed that behavior could best be explained and predicted in terms of purposiveness. When he used the term "purposive," he meant behavior directed toward or away from a given object, location, or situation; the individual movements involved in such overall behavior were less important in understanding the behavior than was the goal of the behavior. The goal was not mysteriously mentalistic; it could be objectively identified, and its identification in no way depended on introspection, which Tolman staunchly repudiated as a source of objective data.

Tolman also emphasized the teachability of purposive behavior. He thought of goal-directed behavior as occurring through a tangle of obstacles, paths, objects, and tools. The organism shows a selective preference for easier, more convenient routes to goals, as opposed to those more tortuous and difficult. Because of this selective preference, organisms can be taught to seek out, in a purposive way, the more convenient courses of action. Their behavior is not reflex reactions to stimuli. Rather, it is active seeking out of facilitative means to ends.

In his system, Tolman emphasized what he called "sign learning" as distinct from the traditional "response learning," meaning that in purposive behavior the organism learned to follow signs that lead to the desired goal. According to Tolman, those signs, whether they be objects, ideas, movements, or whatever, were imbued with meaning—they were recognized as conducive to goal attainment; they were markers that guide the way.

Various experiments supported Tolman's beliefs. They showed two important phenomena, at least in higher animals:

1. **Reward expectancy.** Organisms were shown to expect or anticipate gratification in one form or another.
2. **Place learning.** The locations of goals were shown to be learned and retained, even when the organism was forced to reach them along circuitous routes. When given the opportunity, organisms would take the shortest route, even though it had not been followed during previous learning trials.

Perhaps Tolman's most lasting contribution to psychology has been his provision for cognitive processes within his behavioral system. Hull had dealt with intervening variables but had not assigned them purposive, goal-seeking characteristics. With his emphasis, Tolman made behaviorism palatable to a new group of psychologists and educators—those who felt that there was more to learning, especially human learning, than

could be explained through stimulus-response theory.

Skinner

Let not the strong
Be cozened
By *Is* and *Isn't*
Was and *Wasn't*.
Truth's to be sought
in *Does* and *Doesn't*.
Skinner (1962)

"Does" and "doesn't"—there you have the hallmark of the behavioral psychologist. The study of behavior must rest on what organisms do and do not do, and that, in fact, is all one need pay attention to, at least in the strongly put opinion of B. F. Skinner. Of course the scientist attempts to manipulate the "does" and "doesn't." Science, after all, is basically an attempt to predict, control, and explain. Prediction, control, and explanation of behavior can come about only through careful manipulation and observation. Skinner's procedure used in manipulating and observing is one he calls "operationism." Skinner (1945) wrote:

Operationism may be defined as the practice of talking about
1) one's observations,
2) the manipulative and calculational procedures involved in making them,
3) the logical and mathematical steps which intervene between earlier and later statements, and
4) *nothing else.*

Of the world's contemporary educational psychologists, none stands larger than Burrhus F. Skinner. Born in 1904, Skinner majored in English and set his sights on a writing career. When that venture proved less than satisfying, he entered Harvard, undertook graduate study in psychology, and earned his Ph.D. in 1931.

Almost immediately he made his mark on psychological thought. He developed the concept of operant conditioning and did exhaustive experimentation to establish data and set forth principles

12

governing that phenomenon. Rejecting theoretical schools of thought, which he considered worse than useless to the scientist, he concentrated on the observation and manipulation of behavior, first in the animal laboratory with rats and pigeons, then later with human verbal and meaningful learning.

Through the 1930s and 1940s, Skinner amassed incredible quantities of data pertaining to operant conditioning. Then in the 1950s he turned strong attention to human learning and its pursuit in the schools. His article, "The Science of Learning and the Art of Teaching" (1954), stressed the application of operant conditioning procedures, a process now called *contingency management,* to matters of school learning. There he illustrated how human behavior could be shaped rapidly and without aversive threat through the use of principles of positive reinforcement. What teachers needed to do, Skinner (1954) wrote, were these three things:

1. Identify positive reinforcers effective in motivating the efforts of learners.
2. Decide how the reinforcement is to be applied.
3. Develop instructional programs that lead learners step by step, with suitable reinforcement, to the desired end behavior.

These three tasks, Skinner avowed, could best be managed through programmed materials used in teaching machines. He amplified this idea in greater detail in a later article entitled "Teaching Machines" (1958). This article described the nature of programmed instructional materials and the sorts of mechanical devices, the machines, that housed and controlled them. Skinner emphasized that the programs should be so constructed as to lead the learner in virtual 100% correctness on all responses. Constant success was indispensable. When learners made errors in responding to materials, the fault lay with the material, not with the learner.

These two articles aroused great attention, not to mention agitation—much of it bitter—in educational circles. Fears were expressed that the machine would replace the teacher. Many educators denounced programmed learning as cold, stifling, and dehumanizing, and they ridiculed the teaching machine as mind-controlling gadgetry.

Yet, in calmer quarters, Skinner's proposals regarding the shaping of learned behavior stirred hopeful excitement. Management of contingencies of reinforcement gained acceptance. In the years since 1958, programmed learning and contingency management have become a common part of educational practice, used both in academic learning and in the training of students to function socially in the school setting. Teaching machines have almost disappeared. Programmed materials, the true heart of teaching machines, remain, though not in great abundance. Principles of positive reinforcement, and their application in education, are overwhelmingly accepted and used in present-day instruction.

basic ideas

Like many great and powerful ideas, Skinner's notions of operant conditioning are surprisingly simple, clear, and easy to apply. They deserve mention and explanation here.

Behavioral psychologists prior to Skinner had conceived of behavior in terms of stimulus and response (S-R), with some modifications such as the previously mentioned S-O-R paradigm. Simply put, in the presence of a given stimulus, the organism responded, moved in some way. Skinner was dissatisfied with this explanation of behavior. He noted that organisms often moved about when no discernible or identifiable stimuli were present. He suggested, therefore, that two distinct kinds of responses occurred normally in behavior.

One kind of response was already in vogue in psychology, the response occurring in the presence of a stimulus.

Skinner called that type of response an "elicited response," elicited by the stimulus.

A second kind of response was one Skinner called an "emitted response." The movement was simply emitted by the organism. It was not a reaction to a stimulus. Skinner called such emitted responses "operants," to indicate that the organism was, in a sense, taking the initiative and operating on its environment.

According to Skinner, most of the behavior of higher organisms is of the operant type. He found that operants could be shaped by controlling the consequences that followed them. He found, as had Thorndike earlier, that when behavior was followed by consequences desirable to the animal, that behavior became much more likely to be repeated. In common terminology (though Skinner carefully avoids mention of pleasure and satisfaction, for example) we tend to do and repeat what brings us satisfaction.

Skinner used the term *reinforcer* to refer to any situation, object, movement, that increased the likelihood that an organism would repeat an act. He identified two classes of reinforcers—*positive* and *negative*. Positive reinforcement occurs with the *addition* of something, increasing the likelihood of an act's being repeated. Negative reinforcement occurs with the *removal* of something, thereby increasing the likelihood of an act's being repeated.

Both positive and negative reinforcement increase the probability of responses. Note that positive refers to addition and negative refers to removal. They have nothing to do with pleasantness or unpleasantness. Negative reinforcement is altogether different from punishment, although many educators fail to make that distinction between the two when they speak of reinforcement.

Operant conditioning can be summarized very simply. You wait for the organism to emit an operant response that is similar to a behavior you consider desirable. When it emits that response, you reinforce it. For laboratory animals, food is an excellent reinforcer. For humans, praise and affection are effective reinforcers. As the organism continues to emit responses, you selectively reinforce those that more and more closely approximate the desired end behavior.

Through using this simple procedure, Skinner has demonstrated, often before students' eyes, how to quickly and easily shape the behavior of a variety of animals—rats, pigeons, and humans. Teachers routinely use this procedure today to shape their students' behavior. Contingency management is one of those rare ideas, so simple in design, yet so powerful in application, that have truly revolutionized the course of educational psychology.

As you can see from the breadth of application, Skinner has by no means confined himself to the halls of academe. He wrote a novel, *Walden Two* (1948), in which he outlined his conception of a utopian society functioning on principles of operant conditioning. In 1971 he wrote a controversial book, *Beyond Freedom and Dignity,* that had great and continuing impact on philosophical thought. Basing his ideas on the belief that all human learned behavior is shaped through its consequences, he argues that the concepts of "freedom" and "dignity" are no longer useful in modern society. Man is not truly free to choose, he says, because what a person will do in a given situation depends almost entirely on what has happened to him in the past. Skinner has long believed this. Much earlier he had written:

We must expect to discover that what a man does is the result of specifiable conditions and that once these conditions have been discovered, we can anticipate and to some extent determine his actions.

This possibility is offensive to many people. It is opposed to a tradition of long standing which regards man as a free agent, whose behavior is the product, not of a specifiable antecedent condition, but of spontaneous inner changes of course. Prevailing philosophies of human nature recognize an internal "will" which has the power to interfere with causal relationships and which makes the prediction and control of behavior impossible. To suggest that we abandon this view is to threaten many cherished beliefs—to undermine what appears to be a stimulating and productive conception of human behavior. [Skinner 1953, p. 26]

Since, Skinner contends, people are not independent of the controlling influences of the environment, we should capitalize on the condition, not shy away from it. The powerful effects of behavior control are occurring anyway, but unfortunately in a random, haphazard fashion. We must learn to control behavior systematically to produce people who are good and right-minded. We should not limit this conscious control to a few aspects of schooling but should expand it to all of life. That is the way to produce a society of people who are concerned, caring, and productive.

Beyond Freedom and Dignity has made many people fighting mad. The article "Teaching Machines" did the same several years earlier. Whether or not you agree with Skinner regarding the application of his ideas to human concerns, there can be no denying the power that lies in their application. That power, for good or bad, assures that Skinner will never be taken lightly.

References

Guthrie, E. R.: The Psychology of Learning, New York, 1935, Harper & Row, Publishers.

Skinner, B. F.: Beyond Freedom and Dignity, New York, 1971, Alfred A. Knopf, Inc.

Skinner, B. F.: Verbal Behavior, II, Encounter **19**:43, 1962.

Skinner, B. F.: Teaching Machines, Science **128**: 969-977, October 1958.

Skinner, B. F.: The Science of Learning and the Art of Teaching, Harvard Ed. Rev. **24**(2): 86-97, 1954.

Skinner, B. F.: Science and Human Behavior, New York, 1953, Macmillan, Inc.

Skinner, B. F.: Walden Two, New York, 1948, Macmillan, Inc.

Skinner, B. F.: The Operational Analysis of Psychological Terms, Psychol. Rev. **52**:270-277, 291-294, 1945.

Thorndike, E. L.: Man and His Works, Cambridge, Mass., 1943, Harvard University Press.

Thorndike, E. L.: The Elements of Psychology, New York, 1905, A. G. Seiler.

Watson, J. B.: Psychology From the Standpoint of a Behaviorist, Philadelphia, 1919, J. P. Lippincott Company.

Woodworth, R. S.: Contemporary Schools of Psychology, New York, 1948, The Ronald Press.

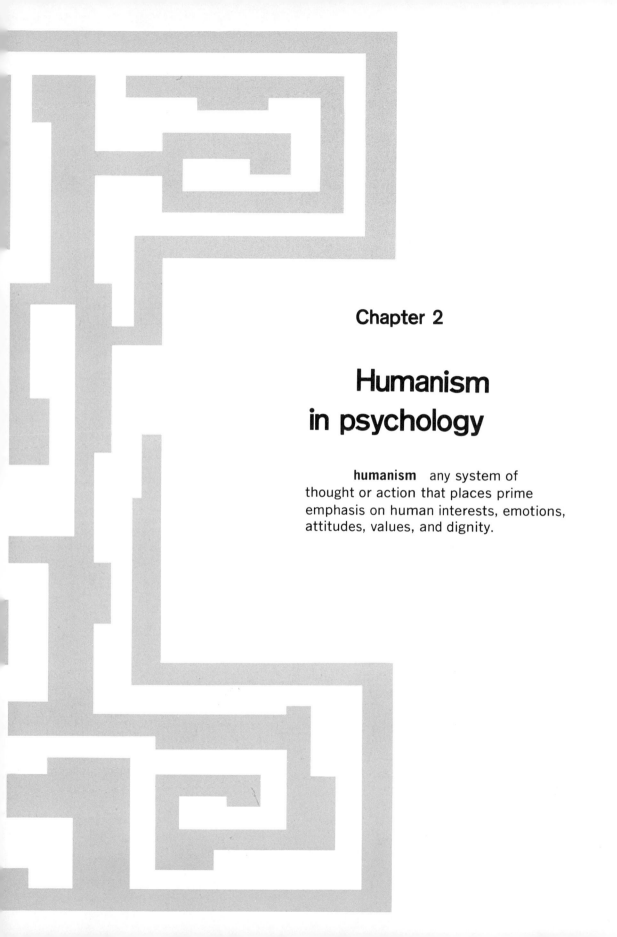

Chapter 2

Humanism
in psychology

humanism any system of
thought or action that places prime
emphasis on human interests, emotions,
attitudes, values, and dignity.

Lives pass, the pendulum swings, the moon waxes and wanes, the tide moves ever in and out. Just as surely, the currents of the mass mind shift. What is true today is false tomorrow. What was sweet yesterday is sour today.

In the past decade, a short ten years, we have witnessed one of the rapid shifts in values that makes the human psyche so intriguing. That shift has occurred in psychology and education, and it has come from an overwhelming acceptance of behaviorism to a startlingly rapid espousal of humanism. Few converts argue against the practical validity of behaviorism. They know it can be applied with great effect in the control of human behavior. Even so, many are turning to humanistic ideas, and they are making the shift for three reasons:

1. They feel that behaviorism explains motor processes adequately, for humans and lower animals. They do not feel that it attends properly to those traits that set man apart from the animals—traits such as values, attitudes, interests, and morals, that define humaneness.

2. They are concerned philosophically and ethically over whether one person should consciously control the behavior of another. Who, they ask, is to determine which is "right" behavior and which is "wrong" behavior?

3. They judge that behahavioristic techniques serve well when applied to the teaching of factual, ordered, step-by-step material, but that they limit imagination, creativity, and work output. They think that its preset procedures restrict learners' horizons and fail to allow potentialities to develop fully.

As a result of these concerns, humanistic thought has leapt suddenly to prominence in psychology and education. At present we see a virtual deadlock in popularity between humanism and behaviorism as theoretical frameworks from which to consider and influence human behavior. In this chapter we will trace the development of humanism, consider why it has become so popular so rapidly, and note the influence it now exerts on the study and teaching of humans.

Humanism, like behaviorism, is a way of explaining and influencing behavior. Humanists readily admit they want to influence behavior. They simply do not want to control it rigidly. They hope to encourage the full realization of human potentialities, whatever those might be for any individual. At the same time they wish to encourage development of a strong sense of morality. They recognize that many human behaviors can be irresponsible and injurious; they want to encourage the acceptance of responsibility and the development of concern for others.

Humanism is predominantly concerned with humaneness. To be humane is to be enlightened and to have compassion for others. Those qualities are uniquely human; they set man apart from the lower animals. Enlightened persons act with wit and wisdom; they are open to ideas; they inquire and appreciate; they know themselves—their abilities, limitations, values, and goals; and they recognize others for their aspirations and accomplishments.

Compassionate persons show tenderness and concern for others. They are disposed toward kindness for people and animals. They recognize their relatedness to others and can share joy, pain, frustration, and misery. They see that to the extent they improve the condition of mankind, so also do they improve their own condition.

The humanistic movement in psychology and education, then, focuses on this humaneness. Enlightenment and compassion are the paths by which human behavior should be known; they are also the great goals toward which humans should strive.

historical perspective

Whatever might have been the ebb and flow of man's humanity in the uncounted millennia before recorded history, it was again the ancient Greeks who formalized humanistic principles and set them into the annals of philosophic thought. Their philosophers established the humanistic tradition during the Golden Age of Greece (600 to 338 BC), basing everything on the unshakeable belief that each individual person had intrinsic worth, not as a vassal, lord, matron, or courtesan, but inherently by virtue of being human. Pericles put the notion this way: "Each single one of our citizens, in all manifest aspects of life, is able to show himself the rightful lord and owner of his own person." Sophocles said, "The world is full of wonders, but nothing is more wonderful than man."

The Greeks held that although human worth implied freedom, such freedom had to be tempered with responsibility. Freedom could not mean license; it could not be anarchy. Always it required consideration of others. The Greeks also established the remarkable code of living by laws. They might have been free and tolerant in their private lives, but in public affairs they lived by the common law. They obeyed laws and people they had placed in positions of power.

Their laws were also humanistic. Although far from being perfectly equitable, those laws were put forth for the collective good of the people, and as they were based on popular consent, they could also be changed by popular consent. Greek law had the prime purpose of helping make life and property secure for members of society.

Athenian democracy at once reflected and supported the Greek concern for individual worth. By 400 BC, Greek aristocrats had relinquished their special political power. No political body stood stronger than the Popular Assembly, which was open to all free, adult, male citizens. Positions of power and trust were assigned by the governed and given to people on the basis of ability alone.

But society, too, can be dictatorial and can, if not restrained, subjugate the individual. It was Socrates who urged individual morality. Oftentimes, he argued, one's conscience may be a better guide to right and wrong than are the demands of society. Atrocities that have been perpetrated through mob action seem to bear out this contention.

Socrates of course greatly influenced Plato and Aristotle, who formalized much of the humanistic conception that has endured to the present day. Aristotle in particular left his mark. He set forth a series of treatises that held man's senses as a prime source of knowledge. Such empiricism, common in modern life, was a revolutionary idea at that time. This knowledge was human-generated; man did not have to rely on the gods or mystics for the knowledge necessary for establishing truths. Aristotle also put forward a system of ethics that focused on individual well being. The goal of every action, he maintained, should be to foster happiness. Such happiness was conceived to have a lasting nature, and it was clearly differentiated from transitory pleasure.

The conquest of Greece by Phillip of Macedonia (338 BC) signaled the decline of Greek humanistic thought. Greece was later to fall under the domination of the Roman Empire and would produce no new works of humanistic philosophy.

The Romans, themselves producers of art and fine laws, complimented the Greeks by adopting many of their customs, literary forms, much of their religion, and in some cases even their language. They maintained schools of philosophy and rhetoric, usually headed by Greek-educated directors. They did not, however, further develop the classical humanism so admirably conceived by the Greeks.

With the advent of Christianity, classical humanism was submerged, save for a few unlikely places in Spain and North Africa. Christian churchmen did not disparage all learning. They believed, in fact, that Christianity reflected the highest level of philosophical thought. They even used Aristotelian logic in attempting to prove theological truths. But classical humanism held no charms for theological scholars. The notion of free men, deriving truth out of their own senses and intellects, seemed threatening to the promise of redemption through faith. Even scholars such as St. Jerome and St. Augustine warned that education was good only as long as it remained subservient to Christianity.

the Dark Ages

Classical humanism faded entirely from western Europe after the barbarian conquests of Rome. Schools disappeared, and the church concentrated mightily on Christianizing the pagans. The social order evolved into kingdoms and serfdoms, the people stagnated under the grip of feudalism, and Europe settled into the Dark Ages. For five hundred years, a handful of monasteries maintained a flickering light of learning, but for practical purposes the five centuries up to AD 900 were a time of educational and philosophical sterility.

Such was not the case everywhere in the world. Some civilizations in Central and South America, though of course unknown to Europeans, reached their peak development. The Chinese, Hindus, and other peoples of Asia produced notable works of art and philosophy. And in the Moslem world, Greek humanism lived on in classical learning.

Islam had conquered the Near East, North Africa, and much of Spain. Classical documents, left from Greek and Roman influence throughout Spain, Egypt, and the Middle East, were collected and preserved. Universities were established, particularly in Spain, and scholars from Arabic, Christian, and Jewish lands studied and taught there. Thus it was that classical scholarship was preserved through the Dark Ages—preserved by those very "infidels" that were to suffer the wrath of the holy wars and at last be driven from Spain in 1492 by the Catholic monarchs, Ferdinand and Isabella.

In the ninth century AD, Charlemagne began to consolidate the small kingdoms of Western Europe. He ordered the establishment of a school in every abbey of his empire—an unheard of pronouncement for that day. He imported monks from Pisa and York to serve as his educational advisors. Instruction in the liberal arts was made available, chiefly to the aristocracy and scholars of the church. Within that tradition rose the intellectual giants of the medieval period—St. Thomas Aquinas and St. Bonaventure.

Although Charlemagne had proposed that learning be made available to the populace, it became in fact almost the sole province of the Scholastics—religious philosophers who strove to prove articles of Christian theology through the use of Aristotelian logic. The Scholastics intended to show the world that the ideas of Christianity were reasonable, not because the church said so, but because they could be deduced logically through enlightened thought. Ironically, it was the failure of that attempt that forced the clerics to relegate doctrine after doctrine from the realm of reason to the realm of faith. Once again, education became viewed as useless, if not downright dangerous for the people as a whole.

the Renaissance

The holy wars helped open the European mind to other places and other people. Conquests and territorial consolidations, such as those of Charlemagne, produced expanded power. Improved shipping and navigation helped open trade routes among lands surrounding the Mediterranean Sea. Those factors served to heighten commerce among peoples of the region. Ideas and books found their way in along with wines, olives, hides, grains, textiles, and dyes. Classical Greek works, long preserved in Constantinople, Alexandria, and the Spanish monasteries, began to turn up in various city states such as Rome, Florence, and Milan, and on to larger centers of population in France and up into north and central Europe.

With these documents and ideas came a reawakening, a rerealization of the role that man could play in his own destiny. Petrarch (1304–1374), more than any other person, rekindled the humanistic fires that became the Renaissance. He studied ancient Greek and Roman manuscripts brought in from Constantinople. Stirred powerfully by the human dignity portrayed in them, Petrarch and his followers turned their attention to the lives of men about them, centering on the dignity of man as a human being. Caught up in this new spirit, thinkers throughout Italy spurred a great revival of the love for learning. This frenzy was by no means restricted to the realms of logic, rhetoric, and philosophy. Monumental advances occurred in the arts and sciences, immortalizing the names of geniuses such as Michelangelo and Leonardo da Vinci.

Renaissance scholars, flamed by the Greek concern for man as man, moved forward to sort out the elements that would allow humans to live better and more responsible lives. The time was ripe for such endeavors. Trade between Italy and other Mediterranean countries was flourishing. Education and training in practical, utilitarian matters, such as language, rhetoric, mathematics, accounting, and even diplomacy, was clearly needed. The theological studies of the Middle Ages could not fill this need. Once again, education turned to the moral philosophy, grammar, rhetoric, history, and ethics of the Greeks. These disciplines became known as the humanities, and those who pursued them, as humanists.* Humanism emphasized learning for the here and now.

Such practical emphasis was bound to produce conflict with the very powerful Church. The Scholastic tradition held that learning had one prime purpose — to prepare one to gain entrance into the hereafter. If learning stressed reason and a questioning attitude, it was dangerous, at least if the questioning attitude were directed toward Christian articles of faith. Skirmishes between various thinkers and the hierarchy of the Church occurred whenever ideas or pursuits ran contrary to established dogma. Artists, though breaking new ground in perspective and technique, encountered little opposition from the Church. Indeed, their contributions often fit in well, since they commonly dealt with religious themes, as in the case of Michelangelo's *David* and *The Last Supper.*

For scientists it was another matter. Burning people at the stake for heretical notions was not only threatened — it was carried out. Leonardo da Vinci, the fabulous pioneer in art, science, and practical mechanics, was forced under threat of public burning to recant his pronouncements about the structure of the solar system. Church dogma had established the Earth as the center of the universe. Scientific findings were not allowed to challenge that belief. Otherwise, science was tolerated and in fact

*This idea survives into the present day. Many people, most notably Robert Maynard Hutchins, believe that educational liberation can best be brought about through assimilation of the "wisdom of the ages." Hutchins presents this collected wisdom in the "Great Books Curriculum"—a curriculum consisting of the study of history's great thinkers, many of whom were classical Greek humanists.

encouraged in some of its practical applications, such as in the development of war machines.

Still, there was no stemming the tide of enlightenment. Renaissance scholars avowed that learning should serve all the people, not just the scholars. They refuted the idea that poverty, misery, and ignorance had to remain the inescapable lot of the masses. They scorned celibacy and seclusion as characterizing the noblest aspirations in life. They cried out that man could and should influence his own destiny, not rely resignedly on the will of God. Christian doctrine, though useful in spiritual matters, was not to be the sole guide to the good life. Scholars now rejected the notion of man as an innately sinful creature — an idea basic to Western thought during medieval times. In its place much was made of man's ability to think and act rationally. Man should prepare for life, they said, not for death.

Although the Christian Church has been portrayed as a formidable obstacle to the humanism of the Renaissance, such was not the case. True, it attempted to squelch thought that ran contrary to established doctrine. Still, on many fronts it encouraged humanistic development, especially in the arts. Ferment was occurring within the Church itself. A new spirit of concern for man-in-life began to develop, and the Church established hospitals, schools, orphanages, and houses for the destitute. This concern for man's well-being grew so strongly that it was, at a later date, to be called Christian humanism. Many churchmen, such as Erasmus, the Dutch priest, avidly spread the gospel of humanism, stressing the value of man and his works.

After a time, strong counterreactions began to stir within the Church. The liberalization of viewpoint, together with a bona fide taint of unseemly worldliness and abuses of various kinds, provoked the rebellion of such priests as Martin Luther and John Calvin. The reformation that followed their outrage produced outrages of its own, particularly against persons not considered true believers. And it cast a pall, particularly in Western Europe, over the humanistic movement. The pietistic reformers rebuilt the concept of man's intrinsically evil nature, discouraged formal learning, and reestablished the notion that the primary purpose of life was to endure an agonizing preparation for death.

the Age of Enlightenment

Although the Reformation greatly dulled the humanistic movement, it by no means snuffed it out completely. Its great resurgence did not occur until recently. Yet it was kept alive, nourished, and even further developed somewhat by various thinkers between 1600 and the present.

Gottfried Leibnitz (1646–1716), for example, established the tradition that a person is not a mere collection of acts, brought in from without, but rather the source of acts. Behavior was not the result of pushes and pulls from external stimulation. It sprang from within the person. It involved purpose, direction, and judgment. To understand the nature of man, one had to consider individuals' future possibilities and their potential movement toward those possibilities.

Jean Jacques Rousseau (1712–1778), the frenetic reformer without a system of philosophy, found ubiquitous fault with society in its dehumanization of man. He contended that civilization, as it existed at the time, corrupted man, was antieducational, and was dogmatically religious. He advocated reason, but despised intellectual arrogance. He saw good in established order, but evil in the corruption that permeated it. Man is born free, he said, but everywhere he is in chains. God, man, and nature

99612

are good. The natural order liberates man's potential. Evil appears when the natural order is subverted.

Voltaire (1694–1778) was the patron saint of the intellectual rebellion that occurred against the established order in the eighteenth century. Incredibly cutting and sarcastic, he simultaneously defended and sliced to pieces the institutions by which men lived in Western Europe. He showed open skepticism for church, government, and the ruling class. He claimed that all men should have the right of freedom of thought and action. Everything around him felt the sting of his pen. Yet he urged freedom of expression for all, making clear that although he might not agree with one's opinions, he would defend to the death the right to express them. Voltaire was truly a beloved philosopher. He was witty and humorous, and no one could stay angry with him for long.

John Stuart Mill (1806-1873) lauded human reason. All thinkers, he said, have the responsibility to investigate for themselves rather than to accept blindly the authority of others. Knowledge is not to be handed down from on high; it is to be gained through one's own efforts and based on experience.

Herbert Spencer (1820–1903) pushed for the development of a code of ethics in which actions would be guided by their consequences. He stressed that pleasure promoted function and that living things took pleasure in doing acts conducive to their survival.*

Henry David Thoreau (1817–1862) lived a life of deep humanism. Although best remembered for his simple-life philosophy described in his reports of life at Walden Pond, he also established,

along with his brother John, a school at Concord. The school gained notoriety for its innovative and progressive methods, such as the use of field trips and motivation of learning through attention to individual student's interests. Thoreau was often abrupt with adults. He found difficulty in tolerating what he considered foolish logic. Yet he was affectionate with children and gentle in his work with them. Not only in his lectures and writings, but in his entire life, he stressed simplicity, civil liberty, and the rejection of violence and dogmatism.

Ralph Waldo Emerson (1803–1882) was a philosopher, theologian, and essayist who made special appeals for bringing forth the highest traits in man. He urged the practice of self-reliance and fearless adherence to convictions. Above all, he would have man remain sincere and steadfast in the love of liberty. He found those traits sadly lacking in the institutions of his time.

humanism and psychologists

At the end of the nineteenth century, the science of psychology began taking form out of the natural sciences and philosophy. Because of Pavlov, Watson, and Thorndike, it grew strongly behavioristic. Yet it was not without its humanists. Franz Bretano (1838–1907), for example, pushed the humanist position into the newly developing field. He conceived of the mind as active and productive, not passively recipient. The intellect, he argued, is ever active in judging, comparing, comprehending, loving, desiring, and avoiding.

William James (1842–1910) was in large measure responsible for the growth of Thorndike's abilities in psychology. But the two did not see eye-to-eye on what should be the nature of psychology. Thorndike conceived of psychology in peripheralistic terms—sensory impres-

*You may remember the prominent place this idea held in the behavioristic theories of Thorndike and Skinner. It also found a place in the pragmatic philosophy of such men as William James and John Dewey.

sions connected to motor responses, without attention to the processes involved in the central nervous system, or mind. James, on the other hand, developed his philosophy and psychology around the notion of free will. Because of his beliefs, he is better remembered as a pragmatic philosopher than as a psychologist. He believed that man functioned on the basis of ideas and that he validated those ideas as he lived them out and saw their consequences.

John Dewey (1859–1952) was greatly influenced by James. Although a first-rate psychologist, Dewey, like James, is best remembered for his contributions to pragmatic philosophy. He also made extensive applications of his beliefs to schooling.

Dewey saw man as an active manipulator of his life and his environment. Knowledge and reality grew out of that active experience. Thinking began with life difficulties, not with premises, and grew as man grappled with those difficulties. That procedure made knowledge functional, rather than merely conceptual; it was concerned directly with the solution of problems. Thought was thus not limited to understanding the world; it also, and more importantly, served to refashion the world. For Dewey, the overriding concern with human development lay in the process of maturing, refining, and perfecting one's ways of interacting with and remaking the environment. Man was therefore eminently active by nature, rather than reactive as the behaviorists believed.

centralist psychology

Behaviorism, which at the turn of the century grew into psychology's giant amongst dwarfs, has been characterized as:

peripheral deals with the *peripheral processes* of sensation and movement without attending to the *central processes* of thought, will, and mental activity.

reactive behavior is seen as occurring in response to stimuli, instead of being initiated from within the desires and interests, for example, of the person.*

molecular behavior is conceived of as consisting of numerous bits and pieces rather than having a global or holistic nature.

Humanistic psychologists disavow all three of these descriptions. First, they see central intellectual processes as lying at the heart of human behavior. Behavior springs from ideas, problems, attitudes, interests, and so forth. Second, they see human behavior as active rather than reactive. Humans do not simply respond to stimuli; they initiate behavior. Third, purposive human behavior does not occur piecemeal. It is integrated, organized, and directed toward a goal. Thus humanistic psychology is "centralist," in the sense that it puts overwhelming emphasis on mental processes—on intellectual activity, values, attitudes, interests, and so forth—and sees them as global and purposive.

In the first half of the twentieth century, three systems of psychology played prominent parts in the development of the centralist notion of humanism. Those three systems were Gestalt psychology, field theory, and Freudian psychodynamics. Each of them will be discussed briefly.

Gestalt psychology

Humanistic-centralistic psychology has been rooted in philosophy, logic, and observation of global behavior far more than it has in discrete empirical findings from the experimental laboratory. That fact helps account for its receiving little attention during the development of psychology as a science. Still, it has had its experimental base, too. Some of the earliest experimentation within the centralist framework was conducted by a

*Skinner modified this view in his description of behavior by adding the concept of "emitted responses," which he called "operants."

24

group of German psychologists, whose frame of reference for considering behavior strongly emphasized the organization of perception. Because of this emphasis, they have been called Gestalt psychologists, and their school of thought, Gestalt psychology. The word "gestalt" translates into English as "pattern" or "configuration." Gestalt psychologists concerned themselves with the ways that sensory information was formed into patterns by the mind and thus made recognizable or comprehensible to the individual.

The basic notion of Gestalt psychology was introduced by Max Wertheimer in 1912. However, it remained largely unknown in this country until 1925. At that time there appeared Kurt Koffka's book, *The Growth of the Mind* (1924), followed by the English translation of Wolfgang Kohler's book, *Mentality of Apes* (1925). Koffka and Kohler visited the United States at the time of the publication of those works, and they helped make Gestalt psychology known throughout the psychological community. Their criticism of trial and error learning, which lay at the heart of Thorndike's connectionism, introduced a disturbing if not particularly threatening alternative to the behavioristic tradition.

Kohler's experiments, in particular, attracted widespread attention. He had done those experiments, using chimpanzees as his subjects, on the island of Tenerife from 1913 to 1917. When he confronted the apes with certain problems, he noted that they did not follow trial and error procedures in solving them. Instead, they seemed to reflect on the problems, decide on a path of action, and then move to the solution of the problem.

One of Kohler's problem situations involved placing a chimp in a cage that had a banana suspended from the top, well out of reach. Also in the cage was a box that could be used as a platform from which the chimp could jump and reach

the banana. To solve the problem, the animal had to recognize the possibility afforded by the box, turn attention away from the goal (banana), move the box into position, and then climb on it and jump.

A second problem situation involved placing fruit outside the chimp's cage, again out of reach. A stick that could be used to reach the fruit and draw it to the cage was placed inside the cage with the animal. To solve the problem, the chimp had to see the connection between the stick and the fruit and use the stick as a tool in obtaining the fruit.

Some of Kohler's animals were able to solve these problems and obtain the fruit. He was convinced that the animals' actions in solving the problems reflected far more than simple trial and error. He called their method of attack "insight," implying that the animals were mentally organizing elements of their perceptual field in such a way that the solutions were "seen" inside the animals' minds. This view emphasized intelligent, purposive behavior, which was from the beginning a basic contention of the humanists.

The principles of learning from the gestalt point of view were best presented by Koffka, in his *Principles of Gestalt Psychology* (1935). Essentially, those principles explained perceptual organization, undoubtedly important in human learning, though hardly satisfactory descriptors of the entire learning process. Still, they have central importance in the humanist-centralist position and therefore deserve brief attention here.

Purposeful, problem-solving behavior necessarily involves organization of the perceptual field. That is, one must first identify significant elements involved in the problem situation. Those elements include important items that can be perceived, people, objects, movements, and processes, for example, on the physical and intellectual levels. Second, one must organize those elements in such a way that they make sense. This organization involves groupings and relationships. Items are grouped on the basis of similarity or nearness to each other. They are further related in terms of cause-effect and means to end.

Gestalt psychologists derived laws that described aspects of perceptual organization. One such law, the "law of similarity," held that items in perception are grouped on the basic of likenesses in color, form, sound, and so forth.

Another law, the "law of proximity," described the grouping of perceptual items on the basis of their being near to each other. That nearness can be either spatial or temporal. That is, their nearness might be physical closeness, or it might be that they occurred at close to the same time.

A third law of perceptual organization was the "law of closure." Closure has to do with completeness. Although the principle applies to the perception of sensory data, it has much more far-reaching implications for ideational perception. Ideas and tasks left uncompleted are dissatisfying to the individual and thus motivating to further action. Closure brings a sense of finality and conclusion. In problem situations, closure is not reached until the problem is solved. Until that time, anxiety exists. On completion, closure, this anxiety gives way to satisfaction.

A fourth law of perceptual organization was called the "law of good continuation." Again, although this principle applied to the organization of sensory data, it figured more significantly in the organization of thought processes. Good continuation provides one with a sense of the means required to attain a certain end, or of the effects that are likely to be produced by certain actions. The principle helps explain what we call interpolation and extrapolation. To interpolate, we fill in missing information between a present condition and a desired end condition. In the case of a problem situation, it would give us clues

at to what we needed to do mentally and physically to move toward the solution of the problem. In extrapolation, we project ahead, making further predictions based on what we already know to be true.

The technical treatments of just how perception is organized may not be particularly helpful to educators. Nevertheless, Gestalt psychology has made a truly significant impact on matters of school learning. This impact has resulted from the conviction that perceptual organization lies at the heart of understanding—of making sense of what we learn. The humanist tradition stresses intelligent, organized, purposive behavior. Such behavior relies on basic conceptualization and understanding. These conditions have not, at least until recently, figured to more than a minimal degree in the work of behaviorists. Yet they have overriding importance in school learning, and for that reason, educational practice reflects the unmistakeable impact of Gestalt psychology.

field theory

Kurt Lewin (1890–1947) was an original member of the Berlin group of Gestalt psychologists, all of whom, interestingly enough, emigrated to the United States. He broke away from that group, not because he differed with them concerning the importance of perceptual organization, but because he felt that mere perceptual organization did not sufficiently explain the driving force behind behavior. Perception does not energize behavior, he felt, though it does guide it.

To explain the driving force behind purposive behavior, Lewin developed the concepts of needs, tension systems, valences, vectors, and boundaries. He saw these factors functioning within a "psychological field" of activity, which he called "life space." Every individual has a life space, within which thought and movement occur. That life space is psychological, not physical, though physical space and objects make up part of it. It includes all persons, objects, places, ideas, and sounds, for example, that make up one's psychological life. No two peoples' life spaces are identical. First, they do not have access to the same contents. Second, the contents that are available pass through each person's filters and are edited and reformed through differences in perception, biases, and values.

In a metaphorical sense, Lewin saw the individual moving about, physically and intellectually, inside the boundaries of the life space. Certain objects, people, and ideas, for example, might have a particularly strong attraction for the person. Those items are said to have a "positive valence." Other items are said to have a "negative valence." One's behavior can be described and predicted through analyzing the interplay of positive and negative valences within the life space.

Learning, for Lewin, meant a change in the life space. Lewin felt that learning could change the life space boundaries by expanding them, that it could change the life space contents by modifying them or adding to them, and that it could change valences within the life space.

Lewin used topological drawings in attempting to show life space boundaries, contents, vectors, and obstacles. His work attracted wide attention in this country, and for a time he had a sizeable following. Since his death, interest in field theory has diminished, and there are few present-day advocates of his theoretical position. Too, cognitive field theory provides relatively little for educators and psychologists whose work depends on practical applications. Although one can easily influence behavior through application of behavioral principles of reinforcement, there is little technique available from field theory that is useful in teaching. Nevertheless,

Lewin made significant contribution to continuance of the tradition that man is rational and purposive, that behavior results from here-and-now factors, and that goals, needs, attitudes, values, and interests play significant roles in human behavior.

psychodynamics

Neohumanists may blanch at the inclusion of Sigmund Freud and his psychoanalytic theory in a discussion of modern humanism. Freudian psychology, for many, deals with lower, rather than higher aspects of the human mind. Indeed, the "third force" humanistic psychology of the 1950s was a repulsive reaction to behaviorism and psychoanalytic theory, the two dominant psychological schools of the time.

Nevertheless, humanistic psychology owes much to Freud's system, which here we will call psychodynamics. True, it dealt with understanding and treating the behavior of "ill" rather than "healthy" persons. True, it highlighted psychologically crippled behavior rather than that of fully functioning people. True, it dealt with repression, phobia, anxiety, guilt, and shame, and the hedonistic antics of the id. Still and all, psychodynamics dealt with the mind and searched into behavior along lines of emotions and the powerful controls they held over behavior.

Psychodynamics is centralist, not peripheralist. If humanism treats of man's goals, aspirations, values, attitudes, and feelings, it must acknowledge its kinship to psychodynamics. It need not explain healthy human behavior in psychoanalytic terms, but it must recognize the other side of the affective coin.

Freud's work began with the mentally ill, his theories attempted to explain how they became that way, and subsequent psychiatric practice rests on the foundations he established in his work. He saw the human passing through various developmental stages—oral, anal, phallic, and oedipal—from birth up to around age 5. Unfortunate experiences during each of those states could cause fixations that, though operating at the unconscious level, could plague an individual throughout life. They could produce fears, anxiety, guilt, and shame, and at a more serious level, neuroses and psychoses that prohibited normal functioning.

Freud saw the mind as playing a pivotal role in human behavior. He conceptualized the mind as consisting of three levels—the id, the ego, and the superego. The id functioned at the unconscious level, constantly seeking selfish gratification. The ego functioned at the conscious level, dealing with reality and attempting to satisfy the needs of the individual. The superego functioned at a conscious, but idealistic level, serving as one's conscience in matters of right and wrong.

Mature human behavior, in the Freudian system, resulted from the interplay of id, ego, and superego. Fixations from childhood stages could produce neuroses that seriously hampered this normal interplay. The task of psychoanalysis was to identify and treat the factors that inhibited normal functioning.

Psychoanalysts have identified a number of stereotyped behaviors that are used to protect the ego from harm. They serve as buffers against facing up to one's real or imagined inadequacies. The following are included among them:

rationalization making excuses for one's behavior, giving reasons, taking a sour-grapes attitude.
reality denial refusing to face up to disagreeable happenings, minimizing them, or pretending they did not happen.
displacement shifting hostile, aggressive impulses away from the intended person or thing and toward a target safer or less threatening.
compensation over-stressing a strength to substitute and make up for a weakness.

regression behaving as if one were at an earlier stage of development as a means of disengagement from threatening situations.
projection assigning one's own inadequacies to others.

We all employ defense mechanisms, and they can be humorous when not used to excess. They become hurtful when they prevent us from facing up to problems that we must deal with in life.

humanism of today

When today's educators and psychologists speak of humanism, they are not referring to classical humanism, Christian humanism, scientific humanism, or any of the other varieties of humanism developed in the past. Instead, they are referring to a new emphasis on influencing behavior, one that uses the avenues of individual values, interests, attitudes, and emotions. This new humanism has at its core the unabashed intent of influencing behavior. Such influence is intended to open up new horizons of thought and action for every person, to stress and amplify those traits that are peculiarly human, and to release the innate potentialities that will allow everyone to function more fully and more humanely.

To grasp the meaning of today's humanism:
1. You must take into account the conceptual traits of humaneness, the self, self-concept, self-actualization, perception, values, attitudes, emotions, freedom, responsibility, morality, and personal meaning.
2. You must recognize the roles that these conceptual traits play in human behavior.
3. You must clarify the procedures that are effective in enhancing these conceptual traits to maximize the level at which each individual can function.

Once you have done these three things, you will have a good notion of what today's humanism is all about. Furthermore, you will have in mind the basic strategies suggested for helping people toward self-actualization and full functioning.

In a subsequent discussion we will explore the key concepts and characteristics of humanism. First, we will examine the thought involved in the recent surge of interest in humanism— a surge that might be called an explosion, since it saw humanism leap from obscurity to a power equal to behaviorism in a scant twenty years. The thought will be shown through the work of three key thinkers. These men are but a few of the dozens who have made significant contributions, particularly in recent years, but their work has been formative and pivotal. These thinkers are Gordon Allport, Abraham Maslow, and Carl Rogers.

Allport

To reset the scene in which today's humanism burst forth, recall the nature of psychology in the first half of the twentieth century. Behaviorism dominated the entire discipline. Freudian psychology drew great attention but was resistant to experimental analysis and was thus shunted aside by the experimentalists who hoped to make psychology an exact science. So far as learning theory was concerned, behaviorism held sway with a vice grip. Neither Gestalt psychology, field theory, nor Freudian psychology presented more than minor annoyances to the powerful giant. Such was the state of the discipline up to and past 1950—to outward appearances a most improbable environment for the growth of humanistic concerns.

Yet seeds were being planted in ground that proved vastly more fertile than expected. Much credit goes to Gordon Allport, a personality theorist who for a time stood almost alone in his insistence that behaviorism could not explain human personality. He was especially adamant in his insistence that Freudian psychology could not explain healthy human behavior. Allport fit naturally into the mold cast much earlier by Gottfried Leibnitz. Leibnitz, you will remember, strongly disagreed with his contemporary, John Locke. Leibnitz saw the human mind as active, manipulative, and self-motivating. Locke saw the mind originating as a blank slate (tabula rasa) and being built gradually as information was fed into it. Leibnitz claimed the mind was active, purposive, and the originator of behavior.

Behaviorists were concentrating on stimuli and responses, disregarding the mind. They conducted their experiments on laboratory animals and based their conclusions on those findings. They considered the basic principles of behavior identical for lower animals and humans. Allport rejected all those ideas. Human behavior cannot be explained by animal behavior, he said. Human behavior is greatly influenced by activities of the mind—perceptual organization, recognition of structure, active problem solving, and purposive goal directed action (Allport 1955). Allport had little support from other psychologists, but his book *Becoming* furnished a rallying point around which the new humanistic movement grew.

Maslow

The humanistic movement took form and received great emphasis from the work of Abraham Maslow (1908–1970). Contact with Wertheimer and Koffka, the great Gestalt psychologists, opened his eyes to the importance of perceptual organization in human behavior. Training in Freudian psychology further established Maslow's convictions about the generating and controlling nature of the mind. A lasting interest in anthropology gave him a cultural perspective that encompassed multiple facets of human behavior. Nor was he insulated from behaviorism—in an intriguing quirk of fate, Maslow became the laboratory assistant of Edward L. Thorndike, the grand behaviorist. Although in strong disagreement with Maslow's ideas, Thorndike promised to support his efforts as long as necessary and urged that Maslow pose well-considered arguments against connectionism.

Maslow was convinced that every human had, as part of the hereditary make-up, an inner nature that consisted of potentialities paired with a drive to realize those potentialities. This inner nature was not evil. It was neutral, but its release resulted in behaviors considered good by adult society. Realization of this nature came about through uninhibited, spontaneous expression of the self. When this free expression was frustrated, denied, or suppressed, sickness resulted. Adults, then, should make it possible for the young to gratify their own needs, make choices, and be themselves. They should not interfere too much—should not try to make the young grow. Rather, they should let them grow and help set conditions for free and spontaneous activity (Maslow 1962).

To explain his notion of drive toward growth, Maslow proposed a theory of growth motivation that he believed true for all people (Maslow 1943). The theory held that as each lower level human need was fulfilled, there emerged a higher level need that the individual sought to meet. Maslow saw these lower level and higher level needs as being arranged in hierarchical order, consisting of the following:

Aesthetic
Self-actualization
Esteem
Love and belonging
Safety
Physiological needs

Starting at the base, physiological needs, one avidly seeks the gratification that promotes normal physical functioning. These needs include such things as air, water, and food. When, and only when, these needs are met, a next higher order of needs—safety from fear, threat, and abuse, for example—is released. As those needs are filled, one seeks love and belonging, then esteem, and on to self-actualization and aesthetic needs.

For Maslow, self-actualization was the epitome of humaneness. When all lower order needs were filled, individuals strove for the development of their potentialities and the expression of their individuality. Such self-actualizing persons become real, genuine, one of a kind. They live by the morals and convictions that they, themselves, have developed. They lead lives that are, for them, the most satisfying possible. They no longer waste energies trying to impress others. They have already become secure in esteem and love. This allows them to turn their energies to the full development of the potentials inherent in the natural self.

Maslow believed that individuals strive for the attainment of each level of his hierarchy of needs and that they take pleasure in doing so. Attainment of these needs produces psychological health. Far from being compulsively driven, in a deprived manner, individuals enjoy growing and moving forward. They find pleasure in acquiring new skills and powers. Psychological growth, therefore, is a process characterized by joyful striving to actualize, put into operation, the highest potentials one has for humaneness, self-direction, and self-reliance.

Rogers

Carl Rogers (1902–   ) is generally recognized as the foremost humanistic psychologist of the day. Now in his seventies, he maintains a very heavy work schedule; his services are sought throughout the world. He became well-known in the 1950s for his work in client-centered therapy. Later, he applied his client-centered ideas to the teaching of school students, and has described his conclusions in the widely read *Freedom to Learn* (1969).

Subsequent to his undergraduate work at the University of Wisconsin, Rogers entered Union Theological Seminary to prepare for the ministry. His study there led to a fascination with psychology, and he moved to Columbia University to pursue this study, working through to the attainment of his Ph.D.

Rogers moved to the University of Chicago, where he organized and directed the counseling center. There he developed and refined his client-centered method of counseling and therapy, which guaranteed his fame. He has since taken greater interest in school learning and teaching and has published several articles on teaching in addition to *Freedom to Learn*. Rogers is presently a resident fellow at the Center for Studies of the Person, in La Jolla, California.

Early in his career Rogers came to believe, like Maslow, that all individuals had internal potentialities that they strove to realize. He believed that those potentialities usually went unrealized, except for the intervention of someone trained to help. The help, however, had to be of a specialized sort. It could not be simply telling another person what to do. Such a procedure would produce dependence rather than the self-reliance necessary for full functioning.

Rogers, working with clients in the counceling center at the University of Chicago, saw that troubled people had the ability to solve their own problems — indeed an ability that far surpassed the ability of another person to solve the problems for them. He judged that counseling and psychotherapy had been overly dominated by the clinician, a condition that did not allow clients to learn how to solve problems independently. To obviate those shortcomings, he developed a counseling technique that accepted, reflected, and clarified the feelings expressed by the client, the person receiving counseling. Because the emphasis was placed on what was said by the client, rather than the counselor, Rogers called the technique "client-centered therapy." The client was not hurried or directed during counseling. The therapist merely helped clients clarify their feelings, so they themselves could work toward their solution.

For many years Rogers has worked with people who, as he puts it, are in the process of becoming. This work has helped him identify traits shown by people who seem to be living life most adequately — people he calls "fully functioning" (Rogers 1962). The following are among the traits Rogers identified:

1. Genuineness — the rejection of facades
2. Concentration on meeting one's own expectations rather than the expectations of others
3. Increased acceptance of oneself and others, recognizing that the self is always in a state of becoming
4. Increased oneness to all ideas, experiences, feelings, thoughts, and memories, both pleasant and unpleasant.

These traits, for Rogers, show that the individual is living in harmony with the inner self, the hallmark of the fully functioning person.

Other humanists mentioned in this chapter stressed their concepts about the nature of man and how learning should occur. Rogers, far more than any other, stressed the "helping relationship" — the functions employed by one person in helping another reach full potential. In writing of the helping relationship, Rogers (1958) described his search for means to accomplish the following acts, which he considered essential in the helping relationship:

1. Behave in a way perceived by other persons as dependable, consistent, and trustworthy.
2. Experience positive attitudes of caring, interest, and respect for the other person.

3. Be strong and secure enough to remain separate from the other person — to allow that person to be deceitful, infantile, or despairing, without advising, admonishing, molding, or fostering dependency.
4. Go fully into the other person's feelings and personal meanings, to see them from the same perspective and to accept them.
5. Behave sensitively enough so as not to be a threat—so as not to subtly evaluate, praise, or punish.
6. See the other person as *becoming,* not to be judged by the past.

Years later, Rogers reiterated those beliefs, with a greater sense of conviction. Speaking of personal qualities that facilitate the learning of others, he stressed that teachers should strive for genuineness as a person, for a prizing acceptance of one's students, for an empathic understanding of how learning appears to the student, and for a basic trust of the student (Rogers 1969, pp. 106-114).

fundamentals of humanism

We have thus far examined the history of humanism, briefly tracing the movement from its beginnings in ancient Greece down to the present day. Throughout the 2500 years of its existence, humanism has consistently focused on the intrinsic worth of the individual.

Beginning in the late 1800s psychology carried forward two widely differing views of the nature of man. One of those views, strongly put by John Locke, stressed the mind as a blank slate, to be filled with information in a passive, receiving manner. This view developed into the school of behaviorism, which placed primary attention on the peripheral processes of stimulus-response behavior.

A second view of man's mind was put forth by Gottfried Leibnitz, who argued that the mind is continually active, operating on the environment and directing man in purposive behavior. That view later developed into the school of humanism in psychology.

To conclude this chapter on humanism, let us reiterate the basic concepts that constitute the fundamentals of the new humanism.

mankind

People are born good, not evil. They may be corrupted, but they are originally trusting and trustworthy, friendly, well-intentioned, and able to direct their own lives. Every individual has worth. Everyone has a rightful place in the overall scheme of things. Everyone deserves respect as a being. We all have the right to live, to be free, and to pursue happiness.

the person

The overt behavior of humans is important, and behavioristic psychology has done valuable work in describing and understanding such behavior. For the humanist, however, those observable behaviors have secondary importance. Of far greater importance are human values, beliefs, attitudes, and feelings. These entities comprise the inner person; they motivate action; they guide; and they cause behavior to be purposive.

the self

Humanists place great emphasis on the self, considered to be the totality of traits that makes each of us unique. The self consists of our physical attributes, behaviors, beliefs, values, interests, talents—in short, everything about us, including what we believe about ourselves. This self is, for each of us, the center of the universe. Humanistic literature is replete with references to the self as originator and guide of behavior. The affective side of the self is far more important than the physical. Whether we can conduct ourselves in humane ways depends on how we perceive ourselves and others, and on the emotions connected with those perceptions.

self-concept

Our self-concepts are the sum of what we believe about ourselves. We may see ourselves as beautiful, wanted, important, secure; and we will tend to act in accord with those beliefs. Or we may see ourselves as ugly, shameful, rejected, unimportant. We will behave in accord with those beliefs, as well, either by withdrawing and resigning ourselves or by overcompensating and using a variety of crippling defense mechanisms. When the self is insecure, we act to protect it.

self-actualization

Actualization of the self is the main goal of life. To be actualized is to function fully — to be authentically without sham and facade, to be gentle and accepting and understanding in relations with others, and to realize to the fullest the potentialities we possess.

Self-actualized people are realistic. They accept themselves and others. They are autonomous, independent, and true to themselves. They see humor around them, but their humor is kind, not cruel. They are creative, in the general sense. Self-actualized people are at the highest level of productivity, interpersonal relations, and psychological health.

freedom

Humans have great capacity for self-direction and self-determination. This capacity unfolds within an atmosphere of freedom. Of all human traits, the ability to make rational choices most fully sets man apart from other animals.

Choice can occur meaningfully only where freedom of choice exists.

Unlike the behaviorists, who see behavior as resulting from external influences, humanists see man as ever able to choose. Unlike Freudian determinism, which holds that much of human behavior comes from unconscious motivation, humanists believe that man usually exercises conscious judgment in making choices. In short, humanists see man functioning for the most part in a life that permits choice. Furthermore, they believe that man functions best, most fully, only in such a life.

goals

Goals play a key role in the humanist's conception of behavior. This is not to assert that all behavior is goal directed. Certainly much behavior occurs as responses to stimuli. And undoubtedly much occurs from unconscious drives of various sorts. Yet, goal-directed actions make up a large portion of the behavior of all higher animals, particularly so in the case of man.

Maslow described classes of goals that seem to motivate much of man's behavior. Those classes are common to all people. They do not change. Within those classes exists a wide range of subgoals. The subgoals may be particular to given individuals, and they may change from day to day. Chief among such goals, from the humanistic viewpoint, are those having to do with psychological growth and the fulfillment of potentialities. The conscious, rational pursuit of such goals best describes behavior that is uniquely human.

values and interests

Values are those things — objects, ideas, ideals, people, and compositions, for example — that one considers important and worthwhile. While they can and do change, they have a stable, relatively lasting nature. They are important in human behavior because they clarify goals toward which individuals strive. They help direct purposive behavior and thus are of great interest to humanistic psychology.

Interests are much like values, except that they tend to be shorter lived and transitory, and they need not be considered particularly worthwhile. One might, for example, be interested in finding, cutting, and polishing rocks without pretending that such an activity had use or importance to others. By the same token, one might value science (think it valuable and worthwhile) without being interested in it. Interests intrigue humanists because of the effect they have on group and individual behavior.

attitudes

Attitude refers to an emotional predisposition to act in a certain way. It can be thought of as an emotional posture, taken automatically when a topic is mentioned. For instance, we want students to have a positive attitude toward school. That means we want them to consider school worthwhile, enjoyable, and deserving of attendance and support. We want students to have a negative attitude toward violence. That means we want them to avoid violence and consider it counterproductive. A positive attitude is an emotional set favoring something. A negative attitude is an emotional set against something. Both are important in understanding and influencing human behavior.

feelings

Feelings refer to sensitivity and emotions. We have feelings of anger, love, hate, jealousy, and affection, for example. Such feelings powerfully affect our behavior. When angry, we do and say things we often regret in calmer moments. Love, hate, and jealousy all have their own effects on behavior. For this

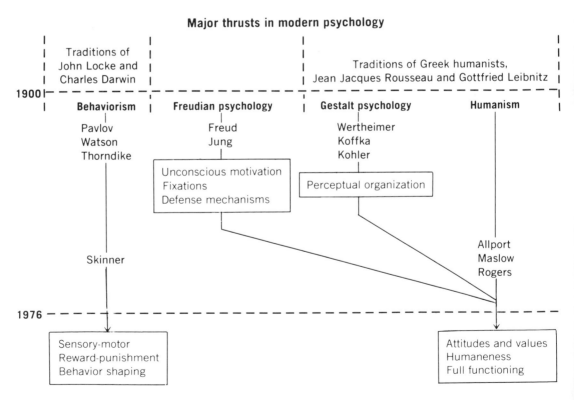

Major thrusts in modern psychology

reason, they hold special interest for humanistic psychologists.

Feelings also refer to the sense of well being and the sense of malaise. Sometimes we are content, happy, and optimistic. At other times we are sad, hurt, anxious, and depressed. Such conditions have a profound effect on the inclination and ability to function. Thus, they too interest the humanist.

To summarize, humanism is the psychology of the individual person, focusing on human traits that affect behavior. It is centralist; it gives major attention to the mind and the emotions. It stresses free will, choice, and responsibility. It searches out conditions that enable people to become fully functioning. It has emerged powerfully in the past twenty years and, as a movement, is still growing rapidly. In some peoples' eyes, it is loose sentimentality. For others, it represents an eminently desirable alternative to behaviorism. For still others, it helps complete the picture of human behavior, well begun but inadequately completed by behaviorists.

The diagram on the opposite page summarizes the major thrusts in modern psychology, examined in Chapters 1 and 2.

References

Allport, G. W.: Becoming, New Haven, Conn., 1955, Yale University Press.

Maslow, A. H.: Toward a Psychology of Being, New York, 1962, D. Van Nostrand Company.

Maslow, A. H.: A Theory of Human Motivation, Psychol. Rev. **50:**370-396, 1943.

Rogers, C.: Freedom to Learn, Columbia, Ohio, 1969, Charles E. Merrill Publishing Company.

Rogers, C.: In Combs, A. W., Chairman ASCD Yearbook Committee: Perceiving, Behaving, Becoming, Washington, D.C., 1962, National Education Association.

Rogers, C.: The Characteristics of a Helping Relationship, Personnel and Guidance Journal **37:**6-16, 1958.

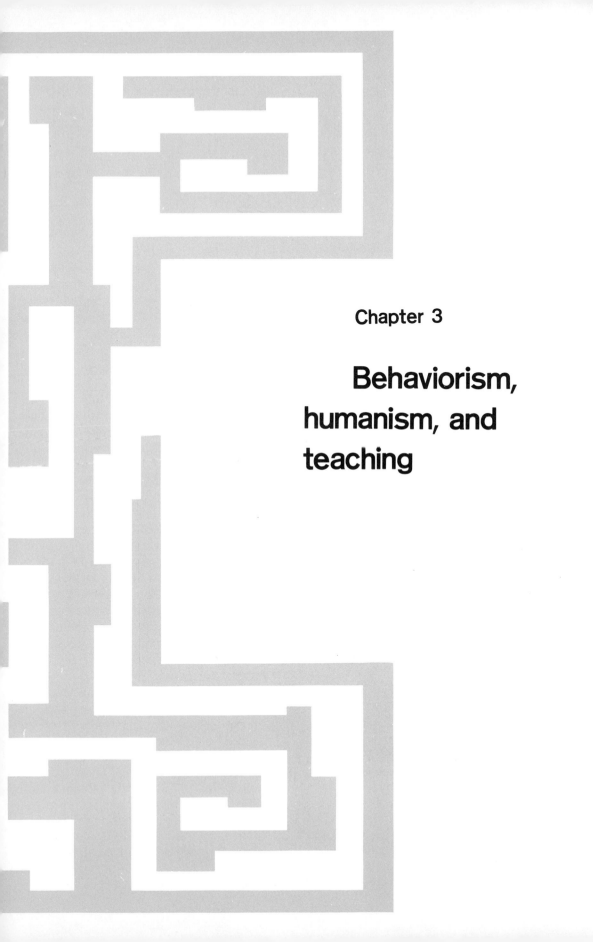

Chapter 3

Behaviorism, humanism, and teaching

Do you believe this?

> What is needed is a new conception of human behavior which is compatible with the implications of a scientific analysis. All men control and are controlled. The question . . . in the broadest sense is not how freedom is to be preserved, but what kinds of control are to be used and to what ends. [Skinner 1956, p. 1060]

or this?

> The function of the child is to live his own life — not the life that his anxious parents think he should live, nor a life according to the purpose of the educator who thinks he knows what is best. All this interference and guidance on the part of adults only produces a generation of robots. [Neill 1960, p. 12]

Do you believe this?

> The hypothesis that man is not free is essential to the application of scientific method to the study of human behavior. The free inner man who is held responsible for his behavior is only a prescientific substitute for the kinds of causes which are discovered in the course of scientific analysis. All these alternative causes lie *outside* the individual. [Skinner 1953, p. 477]

or this?

> I would be at a loss to explain the positive change which can occur in psychotherapy if I had to omit the importance of the sense of free and responsible choice on the part of my clients. I believe that this experience of freedom to choose is one of the deepest elements underlying change. [Rogers 1969, p. 268]

Do you believe this?

> Some teachers view behavior modification simply as tricks to get children to behave and make the teacher's life less troublesome. This is far from the case. Behavior modification is simply effective education. [Becker, Engelmann, and Thomas 1975, p. v]

or this?

> Behavior, it must be understood, is only a symptom; the causes of behavior lie in perceptions and beliefs. Exclusive concern with behavior is not likely to be effective.
>
> Behavior is a product of meaning. The effect of any behavior is also dependent upon the meaning it evokes in the receiver. [Combs 1972, pp. 287-288]

The preceding excerpts reflect two very different notions about the teaching-learning process. You no doubt recognize the first of each pair as behavioristic and the second of each pair as humanistic. If you do, Chapters 1 and 2 were not idle exercise for you. You know what behaviorism and humanism are about, you can recognize their influences, and you know they both exert powerful forces on educational practice. Most importantly, you are ready to begin deciding which strategies from the two camps of thought best suit your own teaching philosophy.

But first a word of caution: from this Aristotelian either-or beginning you might get the notion that teachers jump on one bandwagon or the other — that they either intend to control and shape students' behavior or else leave things open and free wheeling, letting the chips fall where they may. Such is not the case. Far from it.

Go into almost any classroom (well, there are some exceptions) and you will see in operation a combination of techniques for shaping behavior and for allowing open-ended exploration. The teacher will be using reinforcement devices but, at the same time, will be interacting warmly with students and calling on them to make decisions.

The majority of teachers do not give a hang about whether they use behavioristic or humanistic procedures. While most would call themselves humanists, since that sounds better to most ears these days, they are manifestly interested in their students' working actively at worthwhile tasks, with some semblance of order. They will use whatever techniques they find effective in promoting that condition.

That concern helps explain the way things are in most classrooms — an impromptu, commonsense mixing of behavioristic and humanistic influences.

But impromptu and common sense do not satisfy either behaviorist or humanist. Impromptu does not fly because both camps advocate well-considered strategies, not haphazard ones, that produce the effects they cherish. Common sense carries poor credentials because it is too often common and too seldom makes sense. Moreover, neither the humanist nor the behaviorist is overly enthralled when their special potion gets adulterated with a swig of the other. So it is they go on hawking their wares in the school marketplace.

The wares are attractive, indeed. The following are some of the glamor items pushed by behaviorists:

Mastery learning
Success environments
Precision teaching
Contingency management
Diagnostic prescriptive teaching
Computer assisted instruction
Criterion-referenced instruction
Performance objectives
Modularized instruction
Behavior modification

These techniques and strategies carry the banner of excellence and efficiency. Excellence, in whatever form it is conceptualized, is first operationalized — what one *does* or is capable of doing once the condition of excellence is reached should be stated beforehand. These operations constitute the objectives toward which instruction is aimed.

Efficiency comes from the guidance provided by these operational objectives. You know precisely what you want students to become able to do. Materials, instructional techniques, and learning environments are all set to hurry learners along toward the golden objectives. Because the objectives are stated in terms of "can and can't," "does and doesn't," you can easily determine whether and when students have attained them. So there, in a neat package, you have the very model of modern efficiency — clear, unambiguous goals that can be objectively evaluated and toward which instruction can be directly aimed.

Who would argue against the behaviorists' no-nonsense models for getting students there fastest, best, and with least waste motion? Humanists would.

Over in the next stall they are letting us hear it for

Discovery
Self-guided learning
Open experience
Inquiry
Personal meaning
Values and moral development
Interpersonal relations
Decision making
Freedom and responsibility

Not surprisingly, these strategies, for humanists, also bring forth excellence. And as humanistic excellence can only be attained through such procedures, they are therefore the most efficient.

To see the logic of this position, recall what excellence means to the humanist. It means development of the highest human potential. This potential includes not only the learning of facts and skills, which are certainly important as tools for building the higher qualities; it also includes the development of ability to reason, to create, to establish personal meaning, to cherish learning, to select and direct one's own learning, to live by convictions, and to behave responsibly toward oneself and others. That is what schooling is all about; when it does not contribute toward those ends, it does not serve its purpose.

behaviorism—advocates and strategies

To this point our considerations of behaviorism and humanism have dealt with the historical development and the key ideas of each. Now let us see how the fundamental ideas of each are being applied in schooling. To do this, we will survey the works of fourteen contemporary authorities — seven from each camp.

Once more you will see the behaviorist position presented first. This position will be illustrated through the works of Skinner, on contingency management; Mager, on behavioral objectives; Bloom on objectives taxonomy; Popham and Baker, on instructional sequencing; Hunter, on efficiency in teaching; Block, on mastery learning; and Nagel and Richman, on competency-based instruction.

Skinner — contingency management

At the brass-tacks level, almost all the techniques and strategies used in behavioristic approaches tie back to the findings and opinions of B. F. Skinner — recall his work in operant conditioning, discussed in Chapter 1.

Skinner found that animals, including humans, could be controlled to behave in desired ways. That control need not be harsh or aversive — quite to the contrary, Skinner stressed. Organisms will behave to receive gratification. Such gratification may come in many different forms — food, recognition, affection, and praise, for example. Skinner showed that through use of such benign control procedures, desirable behavior can be shaped in school students.

The overall procedure Skinner advocates is called *operant conditioning.* The key part of operant conditioning is contingency management, which, briefly put, means giving the correct "reward" (reinforcer) at the correct time. The correct time is immediately after the student shows desired behavior. Desired behavior can be any act so designated by the teacher; for school students the act usually has to do with the learning of designated material or with correct deportment, manners, for example, in the classroom.

The correct reinforcer may be any one of a variety of things. Widely used are such social reinforcers as recognition, attention, praise, affection, and privilege. When stronger reinforcers are needed, they can include such tangibles as marks, tokens, candy, or even money.

There is probably no teacher in the country who does not use social reinforcers, consciously or unconsciously. Skinner contends that renforcement constantly influences learning. To him it is clear that teachers should use reinforcement in a conscious, consistent way and, in so doing, shape student behavior in ways considered desirable by society.

The majority of schools have one to several teachers who use planned programs of contingency management. These programs also go by the name of *behavior modification. Precision teaching,* a variation, requires that students chart their own progress. Virtually all special education programs for educationally handicapped, educable mentally retarded, trainable mentally retarded, and autistic students make heavy use of contingency management. The technique is a powerful one for influencing behavior. Teachers who have no philosophical qualms about controlling students' behavior laud the technique for the help it gives them in teaching.

Mager — behavioral objectives

Robert Mager's book, entitled *Preparing Instructional Objectives,* was published in 1962. It was one of those small books whose timing seemed divinely inspired. It sold like proverbial hotcakes, and through it Mager made his mark, a deep and lasting one, on contemporary educational practice.

The idea was simple enough. Before preparing instruction, Mager said, you should have the goals of that instruction clearly in mind — so clearly in mind that you can state them in terms others will grasp. Those goals then give form and direction to your instructional methods, materials, and procedures of evaluation. In the preface to his book Mager wrote:

It is assumed that you are interested in preparing effective instruction, and that you have taught, are teaching, or are learning to teach. It is further assumed that you are interested in communicating certain skills and knowledge to your students, and in communicating them in such a way that your students will be able to *demonstrate* their achievement of *your* instructional objectives. (If you are *not* interested in demonstrating achievement of your objectives, you have just finished this book.) [1962, p. vi]

Skinner tells us that truth is to be sought in "does and doesn't," not in "was and wasn't." Mager shows how that principle is applied to instruction. By stating objectives in behavioral terms — that is, in terms of *acts* the student is expected to perform after instruction ends — you can improve instruction in the following ways:

1. Everyone, students and teacher alike, know what the intent of instruction is.
2. The most suitable materials, methods, and activities can be selected for leading to the attainment of the objectives.
3. Everyone can tell when the objectives have been reached.

How do you prepare such objectives? No problem, says Mager (1962, p. 53). You do the following:

1. Describe what you want the learners to become able to *do,* and how you will know when they are doing it.
2. Describe this terminal behavior — this "doing" — in such a way that you
   A. name the act [Mager discusses verbs that acceptably indicate *doing.*]
   B. specify conditions under which the act is to occur
   C. specify the level of acceptable performance.

To illustrate Mager's scheme, here are two examples of instructional objectives, one stated nonbehaviorally (vague) and the other stated behaviorally (precise) (Mager 1962, p. 58):

Nonbehavioral: "To understand the principles of salesmanship." (*Understand* does not indicate what act the student will become able to perform.)

Behavioral: "Given a contract with certain legal terms circled, the student can write a correct definition of each of the circled terms."

Mager adds that if you give your students a copy of the objectives, you may not have to do much else. Primary grade teachers find strong exception to that statement, but in general his point may have considerable validity.

Bloom — taxonomy of objectives

A taxonomy is a classification according to natural relationships. Taxonomies have long been used in the biological sciences to classify plants and animals. The novel application of such a classifying system to educational objectives was the brainchild of a group of college examiners who met in 1948. They felt that a taxonomy would help in the communication of educational intents. They established working committees to develop taxonomies in the cognitive (knowledge), affective (attitude-emotion), and psychomotor (movement) areas, or "domains."

The first of the taxonomies was published in 1956, under the editorship of Benjamin Bloom. It was entitled *Handbook I: Cognitive Domain,* but has become popularly known as "Bloom's Taxonomy."

Cognition has to do with perception, awareness, and knowing. The *cognitive domain* deals with knowledge and its uses. The Taxonomy of Educational Objectives for the Cognitive Domain suggests lower and higher levels of objectives having to do with knowledge and the ways people put it to use.

Bloom's taxonomy consists of six levels of objectives. Each level in turn (except for level 3.00) is comprised of additional sublevels.

Level 1.00 — *knowledge,* in the sense of storing factual information in the mind. This factual information includes specifics, abstractions, and generalizations and ways of dealing with them.
Level 2.00 — *comprehension,* shown through such activities as translation, interpretation, and extrapolation.
Level 3.00 — *application* of knowledge.

Level 4.00—*analysis* of facts, abstractions, relationships, and so forth.

Level 5.00—*synthesis,* or the creative recombining of existing knowledge into new formulations.

Level 6.00—*evaluation* of knowledge and processes, in terms of internal and external criteria.

Though successful from the beginning, the sales of Bloom's Taxonomy spurted with the appearance of Mager's book on preparing instructional objectives. It has gone through numerous printings since 1963. Various attempts have been made to develop school curricula that paralleled Bloom's Taxonomy. Those attempts have been largely unsuccessful. Nevertheless, the taxonomy in the cognitive domain is widely known and used in educational circles. One of its greatest contributions to teachers has been in reminding them of the various levels of cognitive functioning, so they will remember to emphasize the uses of knowledge as well as its acquisition.

Popham and Baker—instructional sequencing

Mager brought the behavioral objective into the world, but it has been James Popham who cajoled it through its adolescence and into a vigorous middle age. There has been no more eloquent and convincing spokesman for the behavioral objective than Popham. He has defended it, lauded it, popularized it, and urged it on others. To help the process along, he has established and directed the Instructional Objectives Exchange (IOX) at U.C.L.A., where thousands of behavioral objectives in many different curricular areas have been collected, refined, compiled, and made available to interested users.

Popham has also carried the behaviorists' banner into the instructional arena. He and his colleague, Eva Baker, published three books in 1970, all having to do with instruction as today's

behaviorist sees it. The books are entitled *Establishing Instructional Objectives* (1970a), *Systematic Instruction* (1970c), and *Planning an Instructional Sequence* (1970b). They describe ways a behaviorist might organize instructional episodes, so as to make learning most efficient. Such organization would include the following:

1. **Specifying behavioral objectives.** In the first step, teachers identify specific, observable behaviors that they hope to establish in their students. They write statements that name the act, the conditions under which it is to occur, and the criterion of acceptable performance. The techniques for writing objectives in this way were introduced by Mager and have since been elaborated by a number of other writers, including Popham and Baker.

2. **Supplying appropriate practice.** Once the objectives have been established, students should have the opportunity to practice the behaviors that are stipulated in the objectives. The practice may be either analogous to the act specified in the objective or identical to it.

3. **Furnishing knowledge of results.** To make rapid improvement, learners must be informed during practice about the accuracy of their behavior. If on target, they should be so notified. If off target, they should be informed of that also, along with what they need to do to improve.

4. **Analyzing and sequencing learning behaviors.** It is a fairly simple, straightforward procedure to write behavioral objectives. It is more difficult to select practice activities and put them in a sequence appropriate to the objectives. Popham and Baker advocate selecting "en route" behaviors that lead to the terminal objective. This done by analyzing the objectives to determine what skills and abilities the learner requires to perform the acts they specify. Practice in those skills and abilities, if not already possessed by the students, con-

stitutes the practice portion of the instructional activity. Each such activity should lead into the next or directly into performance of the terminal objective.

5. **Assuring perceived purpose.** When students see why it is they are asked to work at certain tasks, they are more likely to work diligently and master the tasks. Popham and Baker suggest, as ways of helping students perceive purpose, the use of extrinsic rewards held up as motivation, exhortation by the teacher, explanations of why by the teacher, and questions asked by the teacher that will help students understand why the task is useful.

6. **Evaluating.** Popham and Baker describe both formal and informal means of determining whether students have reached terminal objectives. They stress measuring and interpreting evidence of student performance, and urge that preassessment and postassessment of student behavior be done to give direction to instruction while student progress is being charted. Basically, evaluation calls on students to perform, under controlled conditions, the very behaviors stipulated in the behavioral objectives.

Hunter — teaching efficiency

"Of all the factors important in learning, by far the most important is *your ability* as a teacher to *promote* that learning in your students" (Hunter 1969, p. 1). So begins Madeline Hunter's book *Teach More — Faster!* We now have the psychological knowledge, says Hunter, to produce significantly increased learning in students. And so saying, she explains what that knowledge is and how it can be applied in teaching. Her approach rests on the belief that teachers are made, not born, and that they can be taught how to make learning for their students predictable and successful.

To increase your teaching efficiency, all you have to do is, first, know which factors serve to increase learning and which serve to interfere with it. And second, build your teaching style to emphasize the factors that increase learning and suppress the factors that interfere with learning.

It has been established that the following factors increase the amount students learn in a given period of time:

1. **Motivation.** By employing principles that increase motivation to learn, the teacher can inspire rather than perspire. "Motivation refers to a state of need or desire that activates the person to do something that will satisfy that need or desire" (Hunter 1967, p. 4). That conditions exists within the learner, but we can manipulate the environment to intensify or diminish the internal state of need. Variables known to affect this internal state include feeling tone (pleasant-unpleasant), interest, success, knowledge of results, and relation of the activity to student goal.

2. **Meaning.** Meaning influences the speed with which learning occurs. If you understand what you are learning, you learn it more quickly and remember it longer. Information is meaningful when it fits together — when there are obvious relationships for the learner that cause the material to "make sense." Teachers should always maximize meaning for students.

3. **Sequence.** School learning of facts and skills, for example, usually occurs in short episodes, which combine to reach the desired level of learning. To make learning more efficient, it is essential that the instructional episodes be sequenced so that each one leads into the next. Such sequencing enhances meaning because it makes evident how the information ties together.

4. **Part-to-whole learning.** Learning efficiency is determined by the size of the task. For greatest efficiency, break tasks down into smaller amounts, as long as

you maintain meaning and do not waste time. Consider memorizing a poem. It must be learned one or two lines at a time. The entire poem will be too large to learn without breaking it down into manageable parts.

5. **Practice.** Practice makes perfect, or does it? Hunter says that just any old kind of practice will not suffice. Practice is necessary in school learning, but that practice should be imbued with vividness, guidance, activity, and knowledge of results.

    a. **Vividness.** Attracts learners' attention and holds it (color, excitement, beauty, and movement, for example).

    b. **Guidance.** Suggestions and comments by the teacher that help students attack problems and keep on track.

    c. **Activity.** Student search, discussion, and movement. It causes learning to occur much faster than when the student is a passive recipient of information.

    d. **Knowledge of results.** Active practice alone is not enough. Knowledge of results is necessary for improvement. Learners must know about the accuracy of their efforts and what they need to do to improve. The more precise the feedback, the more helpful it is to the student.

6. **Reinforcement.** Hundreds of experiments have borne out the fact that reinforcement shapes and speeds learning. Principles of reinforcement theory and contingency management have already been discussed at length in this and previous chapters.

Madeline Hunter has for many years served as principal of the Laboratory School at U.C.L.A., and she teaches educational psychology in the teacher education program there. She has written many books and articles and has developed teacher effectiveness appraisal inventories that are widely used by school districts.

Block — mastery learning

John Carroll (1963) devised and presented a "model of school learning" based on careful description of learning tasks and statements of performance criteria on the tasks. He advanced the novel idea that, given analyzed and specified tasks, together with optimal means of teaching the tasks to students, virtually all students should be able to reach criterion if given enough time. Put briefly, Carroll suggested that almost all students could *master* the material to be learned. Some students, however, would need considerably more time to do so than other students.

Carroll said further that if a student were not allowed the time necessary for mastery, the amount of learning could be expressed as a ratio between the amount of time needed and the amount of time actually spent in learning.

Since Carroll was not naive when it came to learners in school, he added other factors to the equation, such as perserverance, aptitude, and quality of instruction.

Benjamin Bloom seized on Carroll's hypothesis and developed it further. He sought ways to circumvent the time factor, since school programs were so tightly bound to time periods, such as semesters. He concentrated instead on the quality of instruction, stressing (1) specific objectives, (2) small sequenced steps, and (3) feedback-correction procedures that optimized quality of instruction for each individual student. The feedback procedures were criterion tests administered frequently, at the end of each small instructional segment. The correction measures were then based on the results of these criterion tests.

James Block (1971) enters the mastery learning picture as the prime popularizer of the technique. *Mastery Learning: Theory and Practice* — the book he edited and helped write — presents the development, basic ideas, and rationale for mastery learning. It also includes research reports of many studies in which mastery learning was implemented in schools.

Block's own article, entitled "Operating Procedures for Mastery Learning," outlines the procedures for putting the technique into use. The basic procedures include the following:

1. **Selecting topics appropriate to mastery learning.** Topics that lend themselves best to mastery learning techniques are those that (a) are sequentially learned and (b) require convergent rather than divergent thinking.

2. **Defining and measuring mastery.** Mastery is usually defined in terms of ability to perform the terminal objectives at an agreed level. The level that has been shown maximally effective lies at around 80% to 85% correctness in the attainment of objectives. The students know beforehand what level they must achieve.

Measurement procedures include summative (terminal) and formative (en route) assessment. The formative measurement is especially important, since it provides for corrections during the learning process.

3. **Providing learning correctives.** En route measurement shows where correction is required for each student. The corrections can then be provided through (a) small group problem sessions, (b) individual tutoring, (c) alternative learning materials, and (d) reteaching.

4. **Orienting students.** Mastery learning ideas and practices should be discussed with students. This assures that they understand they are considered capable and are expected to reach mastery level. They are informed that they will be graded on the basis of their own performance and not in relative terms against their peers. They know that diagnostic-performance tests will be used routinely to pace and guide their learning. They are assured that they will be given all the help they need.

Mastery learning has been implemented at all school levels with thousands of students. Block asserts that when used with suitable topics, mastery learning permits 75% to 90% of all students to reach the same levels of achievement that are normally reached by only 25% of students.

Nagel and Richman — competency-based instruction

Axiom 4

> Competency-Based Instruction equals
> Criterion-Referenced Instruction plus
> Personalization of Instruction.
> Nagel and Richman (1972, p. 57)

Through a series of four axioms and associated explanations, Nagel and Richman make a case for competency-based instruction. They present a strategy that focuses on student competency, that is, on demonstrable ability to perform desired acts. Instruction is aimed at developing that ability. Like Block and colleagues in mastery learning, they see instruction taking the form of carefully planned and controlled learning sequences that give special attention to each individual student.

Nagel and Richman built their strategy to serve as a positive alternative to academic failure. Their concerns were reflected in rhetorical questions presented at the beginning of their book (Nagel and Richman 1972, p. 2):

Are you frustrated when you look around and see some students tuning you out?

Does it disturb you when you see students falling further and further behind the others, when you must go on, for you have no time to remediate an individual student's difficulties?

Would you like to spend a proportionate time working with each student's attitudes, interests, and values within the context of your classroom program?

Nagel and Richman assume that most teachers will answer yes to those questions. They judge that competency-based instruction is the ticket that will get teachers to the land of their dreams.

Competency-based instruction is seen as a "flexible, individualized program that frees both students and teachers to work at their own rates without fear of failure" (Nagel and Richman 1972, p. 1). The strategy fits around and within existing curricula, books, and courses of study. It attends to different interests and different rates of learning. Just how this individualization is accomplished is explained through their four axioms.

Axiom 1 deals with with *time.* It maintains that traditional programs hold time constant, while achievement varies. Competency-based instruction does just the opposite: it holds achievement constant, while time varies. Slower learners are no longer stigmatized. The program is designed so that the slower students continue with work until they reach the same level of achievement as faster learners.

Axiom 2 has to do with *entry and exit requirements.* It holds that traditional programs place the greatest weight on entrance requirements. For example, "Jack isn't *ready* for first grade because he hasn't learned the alphabet." "Joan can't enroll in English 2 because she made a D in English 1." Competency-based instruction places emphasis on exit requirements. It uses entry diagnosis to plan efficiently what each student must do to reach exit level.

Axiom 3 concerns *informing students about your expectations.* If you want students to learn something, tell them exactly what it is. Do not keep them in the dark; do not make them play the guessing game. To do this, you inform them about the explicit behavioral objectives you expect them to achieve. Those ob-

jectives specify terminal behaviors, conditions under which the behaviors are to occur, and levels of acceptable performance.

Competency-based instruction also makes provision for "expressive objectives." These objectives are global experiences, such as listening to a Beethoven symphony, for which behavioral outcomes are difficult or impossible to define.

Axiom 4 states that competency-based instruction is a combination of *criterion-referenced instruction and personalized instruction.* Criterion-referenced instruction is instruction directed at a predetermined behavioral objective. The objective and the instructional procedures are usually the same for all students. Competency-based instruction adds the personalized dimension. The instructor is freed, through use of multiple media and programs planned for each student, to work with individuals and groups, providing guidance, assistance, and remedial help as necessary.

Nagel and Richman feel that instructional "modules" provide the best organizational scheme for this kind of teaching. A module is a packet of instructions, materials, and tests that includes the following:

A clear statement of objectives
Preassessment devices
Alternative instructional activities, materials, and media
Postassessment devices
Remediation activities

Use of the modules by students allows the teacher to spend the majority of time conferencing and working with individual students.

humanism—advocates and strategies

We have seen that behaviorism emphasizes observable acts, in conjunction with stimuli that either elicit the response or reinforce it. In its adherence to that emphasis, behaviorism has followed a straight and narrow path through the years.

Humanism, on the other hand, has followed a broad and winding path, pausing here, rushing there, detouring to the other side of the valley. For humanistic psychology, only one guidepost has remained steadfast to mark the way. That guidepost is the human mind, described in terms of its cognitive and affective functions in motivating and guiding behavior.

This discussion outlines some of the applications to education that have come out of the humanist camp. As you might expect, they are not, generally speaking, so clear-cut and definite as were the behavioral strategies discussed previously. That slight fuzziness has not prevented their enthusiastic acceptance; far from it. The strategies included here have gained widespread recognition and approval in education.

Again, we will examine the strategies through the work of individuals most responsible for their development or popularization. The individuals and strategies are Bruner, on discovery learning; Rogers, on facilitation of learning; Neill, on student freedom; Kohl, on open education; Glasser, on reality attitude; Gordon, on teacher-student communication; and Raths and Simon, on values development.

Bruner — discovery learning

Jerome Bruner, a longtime professor of psychology at Harvard and Oxford, has not become identified as closely with humanistic psychology as have Allport, Maslow, and Rogers. His work, however, fits comfortably within the bounds of the humanistic movement. It has dealt with cognition (knowing) and cognitive processes. Though a colleague of B. F. Skinner at Harvard, Bruner has not followed the stimulus-response route for explaining and influencing human behavior. Instead, he has been concerned with how knowledge is acquired and how it is used.

Bruner rocketed to fame in educational circles following the publication of his small book *The Process of Education* (1962). That book reported the conclusions of a group of scholars from various disciplines who had met to discuss the improvement of science education in the schools. They convened at Woods Hole, Massachusetts, in 1959, under Bruner's direction. Their conclusions about the process of human cognitive learning put forward a new conception of the kinds of learning that should be emphasized for school students.

Basically, their conclusions held that students should learn the fundamental "structure" of the various disciplines. Instead of becoming repositories of factual information, with little idea of how to use it, students should first grasp the basic idea of what a discipline, such as chemistry, mathematics, or history, was all about, that is, how its parts fit together, what kinds of human concerns it met, and what its procedures were for meeting those concerns.

Bruner wrote that to learn structure was to learn how parts were related. The learning of structure had four advantages (Bruner 1962, pp. 23-26):
1. It made the subject easier to understand.
2. It provided an organized pattern into which details naturally fit, greatly aiding memory.
3. It increased transfer of learning, since fundamental principles transfer more adequately than discrete details.
4. It narrowed the gap between elementary and advanced levels of knowledge.

And how is structure best learned? Bruner advocates a "discovery" approach, in which learners find out for themselves how a discipline is structured. In a sense, learners build their own structures and, in this way, grasp the larger meaning and purpose of the discipline.

In his powerful 1961 article entitled "The Act of Discovery," Bruner wrote:

I would urge now in the spirit of an hypothesis that emphasis upon discovery in learning has precisely the effect upon the learner of leading him to be a constructionist, to organize what he is encountering in a manner not only designed to discover regularity and relatedness, but also to avoid the kind of information drift that fails to keep account of the uses to which information might have to be put. It is, if you will, a necessary condition for learning the variety of techniques of problem solving, of transforming information for better use, indeed for learning how to go about the very task of learning. Practice in discovering for oneself teaches one to acquire information in a way that makes that information more readily viable in problem solving.

In 1966, Bruner added:

To instruct someone in [a] discipline is not a matter of getting him to commit results to mind. Rather it is to teach him to participate in the process that makes possible the establishment of knowledge. We teach a subject not to produce little living libraries on the subject, but rather to get a student to think mathematically for himself, to consider matters as an historian does, to take part in the process of knowledge-getting. Knowing is a process, not a product. [p. 72]

The rationale for discovery learning is clear and basic. Learning by discovery makes one more adept at discovery — at learning by and for oneself. That skill is one we all need. It is one we must have if we are to continue as learners once we are away from teachers.

To exemplify the method he advocated, Bruner built a fifth grade social studies curriculum entitled "Man, a Course of Study."* The purpose of that curriculum was to enable children, through a discovery approach, to learn what is "human" about humans, how they got that way, and how they can become more so. Certain techniques for

*Avaliable from Curriculum Development Associates, Inc., 1211 Connecticutt Ave., N. W., Washington, D.C. 20036.

encouraging discovery are stressed in that curriculum. The following are two of them:
1. **Emphasizing contrast.** In this case the contrasts between modern man, primitive man, and the various animals are emphasized.
2. **Practicing informed guessing.** Students make educated guesses about contrasts, similarities, procedures, and reasons for different activities. The educated guesses are then checked against what scholars agree to be the correct answers.

There is disagreement among psychologists concerning the overall effectiveness of discovery learning. It obviously requires more time than expository instruction. Bruner recognizes that everything cannot be learned through discovery. But he is steadfast in his insistence that if we want students to continue as learners outside school, we must give them practice in finding out and structuring knowledge for themselves.

Rogers — facilitation of learning

If I had a magic wand that could produce only one change in our educational systems, I would with one sweep cause every teacher at every level to forget that he is a teacher. You would all develop a complete amnesia for the teaching skills you have painstakingly acquired. [Rogers 1971]

Carl Rogers, the great humanistic psychologist whose works and ideas were summarized in Chapter 2, has had much to say about teaching. Most of it has been derogatory. That does not mean he is a foe of education. Quite the contrary. His writings show an abiding faith in schooling as a prime means of developing full functioning. What he criticizes is the prevailing teaching methodology.

Rogers (1969) says such things as "the outcomes of teaching are either unimportant or hurtful" and "anything that can be taught to another is relatively inconsequential and has little or no significant influence on behavior" (pp. 152-153). He is using the word "teach" in a narrow sense. He is using it to mean that the teachers decide what students should learn and then try to stuff it into their heads.

Instead of teaching, Rogers favors "facilitation of learning." He maintains there is a world of difference between traditional teaching and facilitation of learning. Teaching, he says, has these characteristics (Rogers 1971):

1. The teacher decides what would be good for a particular group of students to learn.
2. The teacher then plans lessons, activities, and materials that will motivate students and get them to learn the material.
3. The teacher decides how to examine the students to see whether they have learned the material.

That, says Rogers, is what *good* traditional teaching is like.

But that traditional teaching produces the inconsequential results that Rogers deplores. It has little effect on learners, Rogers (1969, p. 153) says, because "truth that has been . . . appropriated and assimilated in (one person's) experience cannot be directly communicated to another." Rogers goes on to say, "I have come to feel that the only learning which significantly influences behavior is self-directed, self-appropriated learning."

Does that, then, mean we do not need teachers—that we should simply put learners in a rich environment and leave them to their own devices? Not at all, according to Rogers. Learners must have the help of trained facilitators. But instead of functioning like traditional teachers, facilitators would do the following (Rogers 1971):

1. Continually ask questions of the students, for example, what things interest you? What problems bother you?
2. Having obtained answers to such questions, they help identify resources—people, books, and experiences, for example—that students can use as sources of information about their own concerns.
3. Create a psychological climate that fosters curiosity, allows mistakes, and promotes learning from the environment, the teacher, and other students.
4. Provide classroom activities and devices that involve students and let them make decisions, such as simulations and inquiry.
5. With the students, decide how they can express their learnings and conclusions and how they can participate in evaluating their efforts.

To make this procedure possible, facilitators must have an attitude toward learning that is quite different from that of traditional teachers. The traditional teacher's attitude corresponds to what Rogers calls the "mug-and-jug theory." The teacher's concern is in how to make the mug hold still while it is being filled from the jug. In contrast, the facilitator's attitude revolves around identification of students' interests and concerns, helping them find ways to satisfy those concerns and providing a climate that engenders free and responsible work.

The facilitative attitude maximizes potential for acquiring lasting and pervasive knowledge. It fosters independence, creativity, and self-reliance. Most importantly for Rogers (1969, p. 163), it sets learners on a course of "learning the process of learning, a continuing openness to experience, and incorporation into oneself of the process of change."

Neill—student freedom

A. S. Neill died recently, after serving for fifty years as director of Summerhill School, a private school in Suffolk, England, about one hundred miles from London. The following are a few of the plaudits he earned while still actively working at Summerhill: "A. S. Neill is one of the great pioneers of modern times in the education of the child" (Ashley Montagu — renowned anthropologist, professor, and author). "No other educator whom I know has as much that is stimulating and important to say to American parents and teachers" (Goodwin Watson — distinguished educator and author). "I know of no educator in the Western World who can compare to A. S. Neill" (Henry Miller — acclaimed author of *Tropic of Cancer* and numerous other books). "I wish that every person having to do with children — parents, teachers psychologists, psychiatrists, social workers — might read (his) book" (Carl Rogers — eminent humanistic psychologist). "Neill . . . endeavors to rear children who will become happy human beings, men and women whose values are not to *have* much, not to *use* much, but to *be* much" (Erich Fromm — renowned social psychologist and author).

To have earned him such glowing commentaries (and these are only a tiny sampling) you might suspect that A. S. Neill's school, Summerhill, was a place of great curricular reform and instructional innovation. Such was not the case. The curriculum was completely traditional, as were the methods and materials of instruction. No, Summerhill and Neill earned their fame for another reason — for the great freedom and self-direction that Summerhill students exercised in their lives.

Summerhill students did not have to attend classes. Some went years without doing so, though the classes were always available to them. The students could think, behave, and talk exactly as they wished, so long as their behavior did not do injury to other people's rights or property.

Neill always insisted, and he exemplified that insistence by his own behavior, that students be allowed to live in a truly free and unrepressive environment. He judged that only in that way could they become adults who were self-directing, genuine, and free from guilt and repression. He was convinced that life in such a free environment would not produce a gang of intolerable brats. The evidence bears out his conviction. Students at Summerhill have been notably warm, spontaneous, joyful, and self-disciplined.

How this unorthodox school came to exist and persist, what its organization and functions were like, how the students were treated, and how they behaved in return are all described in fascinatingly readable detail in Neill's book *Summerhill: A Radical Approach to Child Rearing* (1960).

Neill believed that every child was born good, filled with potentialities to love and be interested in life. The aim of education was to help students find that love, interest, and joy for life. That aim could be reached only by emphasizing the emotional aspects of life, along with the intellectual.

Such an emphasis on the feelings and emotions of students requires the abandonment of discipline that is dogmatically imposed from without. Such discipline produces fear, and fear produces hostility. Fear and hostility cripple students' normal growth toward realization of their potentialities.

Summerhill students enjoyed unusual freedom. That freedom, including the absence of aversive threat and control, did not allow the growth of guilt. The absence of guilt removed the ties to authority, thus permitting individuals to become independent and find positive union with the world, rather than submission to or domination of it.

Yet that freedom was not license, indeed could not be license if children were to develop regard for others. Neill forever emphasized that individual respect must be mutual and that this applied to relations between teacher and student as much as between student and student. That mutual respect rested in large measure on Neill's insistence on absolute sincerity on the part of his teachers.

Neill and Summerhill have received their share of criticism. Some critics question whether Summerhill graduates are any more successful in life than other young adults. Others point out that it is the community within the boarding school, not the school program, that produces the effects Neill describes. Therefore, Summerhill can hardly be used as a model for public schools. Moreover, since repeated attempts to establish Summerhill-type schools have met with limited success, it might have been the personality of Neill himself that produced the results in his students.

Granted the possible accuracy of such observations, one fact remains. Few education books in this century have so fired the imagination as has *Summerhill*. Probably none has so well illustrated the practical circumstances that permit students to lead free and responsible lives.

Kohl—open education

Herbert Kohl began teaching fifth grade in a Black ghetto school in New York City. He was immediately struck by the one teaching function that seemed to override all the rest. That function was control, control of the student, and it seemed to Kohl that it was more important to teacher success than all other functions combined.

That overwhelming emphasis on control did not sit well with Kohl. He was troubled that schools were so fraught with power and discipline, that they were so authoritarian. Despite control and discipline (or perhaps because of it) students hated school, were chronic truants, and behaved terribly.

Kohl managed to turn a disastrous beginning into a satisfying conclusion. How he did so is described in his book *The*

Open Classroom (1969). Small, to the point, and easy to read, Kohl's book has had great impact on teachers and teaching. In it, he described how he "opened up" his classroom—how he made the curriculum relevant to students' lives, how he made school an exciting place for students, and how he learned to give up much of his authoritarian power and develop a sense of community with the students.

Kohl is quick to point out that open education is not synonymous with permissiveness. In an open situation the teacher expresses feelings as freely as do the students and seeks to treat classroom problems as situations with which the entire group must come to grips. The open teaching style does not fit the stereotyped picture of the teacher at the front of the room, the grand judge of right and wrong, being cool, collected, and proper, always speaking perfectly correct English. Instead, the teacher behaves as a normal person, genuine, without facade, free to discuss personal goals, confusions, trimuphs, and failures.

To begin the school year, Kohl suggests that teachers tell about themselves, freely and easily. Then students can tell about themselves as well. Afterwards, teachers can show the resources available in the room—supplies, equipment, and books, for example. They can suggest that students add to the environment by bringing things that they care about.

As one plans for instruction, it must be remembered that learning need not be orderly and that it most certainly need not be the same for every student. Therefore, Kohl rejects typical lesson plans that call for specific objectives all students are to attain, that fit activities into rigid time compartments, and that impose a single direction for thought and activities for the entire class.

Instead, he advocates plans that indicate the options made available to students each day, together with means for assessing where students are in their work and where they are going. The teacher can set themes and ask questions, attempting to provide activities that are meaningful to the lives of students. This requires paying close attention to the class, to see who is involved and who is not. This helps determine student interests and abilities and provides a guide for structuring the learning environment.

Kohl recognizes that it is difficult for teachers to change from more traditional teaching to more open teaching. The change is, in fact, quite unlikely unless the teacher has become distressed over classes that are dull, with students who are lethargic or misbehaving.

Still, change is possible. Kohl suggests beginning by devoting a mere ten minutes a day to something different. This requires that there be several interesting activities available from which students can choose. The options are presented to them, and for ten minutes they can do whatever they want (within reason, of course), including the option of doing nothing at all. As the students become able to function in this way, the teacher can gradually increase the amounts of time given over to this type activity.

Kohl cautions that to operate a classroom in this way, as rich an environment as possible must be provided. You want the students to make choices and be responsible for their actions. But they cannot make choices where none are available.

Open classroom teachers, like all others, are expected to keep track of what is happening with their students. This duty is especially crucial for open teachers, because their relaxation of rigid direction and authority makes them suspect in the eyes of many parents and colleagues. Kohl (1969, p. 112) urges teachers to

Document what is happening in your class.
Document what you are trying to do.
Let the students' work speak for the students.

Glasser — reality attitude

Most people who spend their life work in a profession never contribute a single idea that has wide impact in that profession. That does not mean they are not dedicated, hardworking, or expert at what they do. It means that the special combination of conditions necessary for bringing forth a significant new idea rarely occurs.

That fact puts into perspective the uncommon contributions that William Glasser has made to education. Beginning with his practice in psychiatry and then shifting much of his energies to education, he has, in the past ten years, contributed no fewer than three impact ideas to educational practice. These impact ideas have to do with "classroom meetings" as a vehicle for dealing with various school problems, with "eliminating the failure syndrome" that so afflicts students in school, and with establishing a "reality attitude" that places responsibility for self-direction squarely on the shoulders of students.

Glasser cogently presents all three ideas in his provocative book *Schools Without Failure* (1969). Reality attitude comes from a concept developed and explained in an earlier book, *Reality Therapy: A New Approach to Psychiatry* (1965). It is this idea that adds significantly to the humanistic concern for student responsibility, decision making, and self-direction.

Glasser, a psychiatrist since 1957, developed much of his thinking on education as a result of his work with juvenile delinquent girls. He found he could have positive effects on their behavior by working with them in ways that emphasized positive involvement and individual responsibility and allowed no excuses.

The key point in his reality emphasis is that he will not condone excuses for unacceptable behavior. In writing of school failure Glasser asserts:

I do not accept the rationalization of failure commonly accepted today, that these young people are products of a social situation that precludes success. Blaming their failure upon their homes, their communities, their culture, their background, their race, or their poverty is a dead end for two reasons: (1) it removes personal responsibility for failure, and (2) it does not recognize that school success is potentially open to all young people. [1969, pp. 4-5]

Glasser does not go along with the notion of mental illness either. Students who behave unacceptably are not ill, he says. They can remedy their own behavior; it is not outside their control. They are choosing to do what they do. They must be made to see that they are responsible for behaving in ways that bring success. They can either choose to behave in success related ways, or in ways that bring failure and diminish self-worth — ways that lead to suffering, withdrawal, and delinquency. True, each person must work hard and concentrate on self-discipline. But that, after all, is a responsibility we all must face.

How can students make responsible choices that lead to success? Although many can make them on their own, the likelihood is greatly increased through strong emotional involvement with persons adept at making choices. In school, such persons might be teachers, counselors, administrators, or other students. The helping person must be warm and personally interested. That warmth alleviates the loneliness that afflicts the lives of so many students.

The helping relationship must emphasize acceptable student behavior. Instead of considering behavior as resulting from emotion, behavior should be seen as the cause of emotion. Behavior can be changed. Good feelings then result.

To deal with unacceptable behavior, the teacher should do the following things:

1. Get the student to make a value judgment about the behavior in question — about its worth to the student and others.

2. If the student is satisfied with the behavior, he must then suffer the consequences. Those consequences should be reasonable, but by no means should they be forestalled by the teacher.
3. Keep trying. As the student repeats unacceptable behavior, request his value judgment about it. Sooner or later he will begin to doubt whether the behavior is really best.
4. If the student judges that his behavior is not valuable, then ask what he could do that is different. The student himself should be asked to suggest a suitable alternative.
5. Help the student commit himself to the course of behavior he has suggested. Under no circumstances accept an excuse when the commitment is broken. Accepting excuses tells the student that the teacher does not really care. Punishment, but not of a harsh or painful type, comes as the natural consequence of not following through on a commitment.

Students, says Glasser, need teachers who will not excuse their unacceptable behavior. They need teachers who care enough to work with them again and again until at last they learn to live by commitment. Such living by commitment brings forward maturity, respect, love, and a successful identity.

Gordon — interpersonal communication

In 1970, Thomas Gordon published his book *Parent Effectiveness Training,* and by 1974 it had sold over 500,000 copies. Its immense popularity resulted from the direct practical help it gave parents in relating to their children. That help came in the form of ways of talking with youth. It concentrated on what you could say and how you could say it to open channels of communication, keep them open, and use them to increase self-esteem, self-confidence, and creativity.

In 1974, Gordon published a sequel, entitled *Teacher Effectiveness Training*. In it he retained the same basic techniques for communication between adults and youth, modified to attend to the special problems inherent in school learning.

Gordon points out that there is a fine line between teaching that fails and teaching that succeeds. He believes that perhaps the main factor that differentiates between failure and success is the quality of the relationship that develops between teacher and learner. Teacher effectiveness training is Gordon's strategy for developing, through specific styles of communication, such a quality relationship. The relationship is good when it has the following:
1. Openness—permits honesty
2. Caring—each person is valued by the other
3. Interdependence—of each on the other
4. Separateness—allows unique growth
5. Mutual needs meeting—neither progresses at the expense of the other

By and large, the teacher effectiveness training program consists of specific methods for establishing and maintaining quality relationships. Among those methods are communication facilitators and the "no-lose method" for resolving conflicts.

Communication facilitators that Gordon presents are techniques of passive and active listening. They contrast markedly with twelve "communication roadblocks" that teachers typically employ when talking with students. The following are passive listening techniques that aid communication:
1. **Silence.** Pay attention to the student, but do not interrupt or comment. This silence communicates acceptance. It makes the student feel inclined to share more of whatever is troubling him.
2. **Acknowledgement responses.** As the student talks, lean forward, nod, smile, say "uh-huh." These responses show you are paying close attention. They reassure the student that you are interested and willing for the conversation to continue.
3. **Door openers.** When students seem hesitant or reluctant to talk, you can use messages called door openers. For example: "Would you like to tell me more about it?" or "Sounds like you are upset about it." These messages are nonevaluative.

The *active listening technique* is extremely important. It provides helpful feedback to the student. The teacher responds to the student in ways that reflect how the student feels about the situation. Active listening requires that the teacher genuinely accept the student's feelings, realizing that they are usually transitory. It helps students deal with their strong feelings and helps them find their own solutions to problems.

The second technique Gordon advocates, the "no-lose method" of resolving conflict, helps find solutions suitable to everyone concerned and leaves everyone's ego intact. The technique involves six steps:
1. Clarify exactly what the problem is.
2. Jointly suggest possible solutions.
3. Evaluate the suggested solutions, eliminating any that produce negative reactions from any participant.
4. Decide on one of the solutions. The decision should be adopted by consensus but should always be considered tentative.
5. Decide how to put the solution into effect. Identify "what's," "who's," and "when's."
6. Evaluate the success of the solution. If it fails, look for another solution to try.

Gordon spells out these suggestions and numerous others in ample detail. He emphasizes throughout that teachers should practice the techniques until they become second nature.

Raths and Simons — values development

Values have held a prominent place in the conceptions of humanistic psychology. Since behavior is directed in large measure by judgments based on values, they strongly influence attitudes, beliefs, and actions. They furnish our basis for decisions about good and bad, right and wrong, important and unimportant.

Our values, which in totality make up our value system, develop without our knowing it, and most of us live our entire lives without ever knowing just what it is that we do and do not value. Because of that fact and because values can be shaped, several investigators have begun looking into ways of developing and clarifying values. Among such investigators, Louis Raths and Sidney Simon have made notable contributions.

Raths (1963) has urged that teachers help students build their value systems. He suggested that they do so through the use of clarifying procedures, put into effect within a psychologically safe climate.

The safe climate must exist before clarifying procedures will be effective. Students must feel that they can express their deep feelings without being judged or reprimanded. This climate will grow naturally as the teacher shows concern for what each student has to say by listening, responding, and remembering.

The clarifying procedure involves making nonjudgmental statements after students express their ideas. Certain statements elicit more information from the student that others. For example:

Is that what you mean?

Can you give me an example?

Where do you think your idea comes from?

Should everyone think that?

Have you thought of any other possibilities?

A second type of teacher response takes the form of accepting comments. For example:

I see what you mean.

I think I understand better now.

The purpose of clarifying procedures is to encourage students to do these things, showing evidence of establishment of values (Raths, Harmin, and Simon 1966):

Choose from alternative possibilities.

Prize the choice made. Be willing to affirm it publicly.

Act repeatedly in ways consistent with the choice.

Raths suggests listening for students to make comments, such as "When I get. . . ." "What I like to do. . . ." "Someday I'm going to. . . ." The teacher can then follow with questions to determine whether the student prizes the choice and is willing to act on it. Such questions might include:

For prizing: "Are you glad you feel that way?"
"Is that something you really like?"
"Do you tell others about it?"

For acting: "Is there anything you can do about that?"
"Have you done it before?"
"Will you do it again?"

Sidney Simon and his colleagues have devised a number of intriguing strategies to help students clarify their values. Simon, Howe, and Kirschenbaum (1972) have described seventy-nine activities to use with school students. Two examples of their activities are "Things I love to do" and "Personal coat of arms." The first exercise has students list, as quickly as they can, twenty things they really love to do. They then go through the list to decide such things as which ones involve risk, which ones probably will be gone from the list in five years, and which ones their parents would agree to.

The "Personal coat of arms" begins with a picture of a shield, divided by lines into six sections. Students fill in each section, according to directions, with a drawing of something that they value greatly in life.

teaching

The fourteen strategies just examined are valid and reliable. They bring about what they purport to bring about, and they do so consistently. Since they all work, and work well, how does a teacher select among them? Two reasonable bases exist for making a selection. They are (1) one's philosophical stance regarding control of human behavior and (2) one's beliefs about the nature of learners and learning.

The first of these bases, the outlook regarding control, has been discussed previously. You can find excellent, detailed arguments, both pro and con, in the works of Skinner, Maslow, Rogers, and numerous other writers. That matter is one you must decide for yourself in your heart and head.

The second of these two bases, your beliefs about the nature of learners and learning, has also been discussed previously. It would be well, however, for us to see how the different assertions about the nature of man fit together. Such a synthesis has been attempted by William Hitt, in his article "Two Models of Man." The following discussion draws on the considerations Hitt undertook in his article.

nature of learners and learning

Ample reason exists to believe that neither behaviorism nor humanism, by itself, adequately explains human behavior. Both viewpoints have much to commend them. When combined, they furnish a much fuller picture of how humans behave and how they learn. That contention will be supported here by considering the following combinations: behavior-consciousness, information transmitter–information generator, objectivity-subjectivity, rationality-nonrationality, and species similarity–individual uniqueness.

Behavior and consciousness. Behaviorists and humanists have disagreed strongly over which of these two avenues best serves to explain human behavior. There is no doubting the valuable findings that behaviorists such as Pavlov, Thorndike, and Skinner have accumulated. The findings of Maslow and Rogers and the gestaltists also have unquestioned value.

Therefore, it seems clear that both viewpoints serve to explain important aspects of human behavior. Thus, teaching strategies can validly be based on a combination of the two viewpoints.

Information transmitter and information generator. The behavioristic line of considering man's mind goes back to John Locke, who believed that we started with a blank slate and became intelligent in proportion to the amount of information that was fed into us. The humanistic line can be traced back to Gottfried Leibnitz and beyond. It has held that the mind is an active, purposeful organizer and generator of information.

Evidence seems to show that both beliefs have their merits. Creativity, in its various forms, supports the humanists' view. If the mind did not organize and generate, how could new questions and novel ideas come to be? On the other hand, the mind does not generate out of nothing. It must have information on which to operate. Creative ideas do not come from ignorant minds.

Teaching objectives and methods should, therefore, stress a balance of knowledge acquisition and creative production. Both kinds of mental activity play important roles in human behavior.

Objectivity and subjectivity. Behaviorism has played its hand in the objective world — the world of objects, facts, and observable actions. Behaviorists felt that by being objective they could make a science of psychology, a science like biology or chemistry or physics.

Humanism had placed its bet on the subjective world — the world of feelings, emotions, values, and attitudes. Those factors, they believed, explained the motivations and purposive actions that constituted human behavior.

Both these conceptual positions explain a portion of human behavior, but neither explains it adequately by itself. Teachers do well to look for objective evidence of student achievement. Such achievement is basic to the educational enterprise. Yet they would be remiss indeed if they overlooked the powerful effects that emotions have on learning — effects that outweigh the most carefully administered systems of mastery learning and contingency management.

Rationality and nonrationality. Technological and scientific advances have occurred because of man's ability to use rational thought — logic, reason, and scientific argument. Such rational thought is based first and foremost on empirical evidence, which is factual information available equally to all trained, impartial observers.

But much of man's life is nonrational. The realm of metaphysics relies more on intuition and faith than on empirical evidence. Religion, philosophy, and mythology, all tremendous forces in human existence, are essentially nonempirical, as are feelings and attitudes.

Education, then, should not restrict itself entirely to the rational, as it would if it were thoroughly behavioristic. Do not infer that humanism is totally nonrational. Such is far from the case. Yet it does recognize the nonrational bases of human behavior; so likewise should education.

Species similarity and individual uniqueness. The behavioristic position has implied, through its search into behavior, that individuals of the same species are very similar, so far as the factors that influence their behavior. Thus the same principles of operant conditioning, contingency management, and criterion-referenced instruction hold true for all students.

The humanistic position has stressed the uniqueness of the individual by not-

ing and emphasizing differences in the ways individuals organize perceptions, in their value-belief systems, and in their diverse reactions to identical environmental situations.

Both notions, similarity and uniqueness, explain facets of human behavior. Both notions should influence teaching and education. Humanists stress that education should help realize individual potentialities, potentialities that differ from one person to another. Behaviorists have provided strategies that work for all individuals to help them realize their unique potential.

To summarize, evidence shows that both the behavioristic and the humanistic viewpoints explain and influence important parts of human behavior. Education is intended to help each person toward realization of potential. Teaching entails putting into effect the strategies that forward the goal of education. To limit oneself to a strict adherence to either humanistic or behavioristic doctrines in teaching would be to disregard important aspects of human behavior, a disregard that no one in the helping professions would condone.

teaching methods

We have considered at length the admonitions behaviorists and humanists have made regarding learning, teaching, and education. We have seen that both their viewpoints are required for a complete picture of what humane education should be.

To conclude this chapter, we will briefly survey some of the teacher traits and teaching methods that have been used to advantage in working with learners in school.

In the past half century, teaching has undergone a remarkable change. Since earliest times, school teaching had employed one predominant method, lecture-recitation; the teacher lectured and the student recited back what the teacher had said. The teacher was usually a stern taskmaster. If learning did not occur, it was the student's fault, and the teacher made ample use of threat and punishment.

In recent years, many new teaching methods have been developed. Those new methods were accompanied by a different set of teacher behaviors, that relied less on threat, punishment, and cajolery and more on warmth, enthusiasm, and student involvement. Some of those new traits and approaches — we will call them teacher variables — were observed to have positive influence on student achievement and attitude.

Barak Rosenshine reported a list of nine teacher variables that seem to hold the most promise for positively influencing student learning:
1. Clarity of presentation
2. Variety of activities
3. Enthusiasm
4. Emphasis on learning and achievement
5. Avoidance of extreme criticism
6. Positive response to students
7. Student opportunity to learn criterion material
8. Use of structuring comments
9. Attention to various cognitive levels

Rosenshine cautions that these variables cannot, as yet, be considered absolute indicators of teacher competence, because the research is not sufficiently complete.

The teacher variables interact with teaching methods. Methods are organized instructional approaches intended to bring about certain kinds of learning. Most methods of instruction fall into five categories, depending on the kind of learning or intellectual-emotional activity they emphasize. Humanists, behaviorists, and eclectics use these various methods, although one's philosophical outlook will determine the relative emphasis that each receives. The five categories of instructional methods are as follows:

1. **Expository methods.** Expository methods are those that are used for informative and explanatory purposes. They include such specific approaches as explanation, lecture, demonstration, question and answer, and programmed materials. Their purpose is to organize, provide form and substance, fill in details, and make the material clear to the learner. The learner is directed by them and takes a subordinate rather than dominant role during instruction.

2. **Inductive methods.** Inductive methods place the learner in a dominant, active role. They include such specific approaches as discovery, inquiry, simulation, and problem solving. They emphasize problem identification, hypothesis making, information gathering, and testing of hypotheses. Their purpose is to cause the learner to practice self-directed learning and responsibility and to acquire the techniques for solving problems on their own.

3. **Interactive methods.** Interactive methods emphasize two things: (1) techniques for exchanging information, ideas, and opinions among people and (2) cooperative efforts in group enterprises. They include such specific approaches as group projects, discussions, role playing, and creative dramatics. Their purpose is to enhance communication and develop skills of cooperative work.

4. **Creativity methods.** Creativity methods are those that lay emphasis on the production of novel ideas, objects, compositions, and so forth. They include such specific activities as brainstorming, creative writing, design arts, dramatic production, and musical performances.

5. **Aesthetic methods.** Aesthetic methods require little of the teacher, and they are seldom intended to produce observable skills in learners. They provide experiences with beauty, and the

student is expected only to undergo those experiences. They include activities such as observing art objects, listening to musical compositions, and reading literary works. Enjoyment, appreciation, and occasional mystical-type feelings result from these experiences.

resume

Our tour of the behavioristic and humanistic intentions for education ends here. We have seen that behaviorists employed techniques for shaping learned behavior and that they built those techniques into precisely organized strategies such as behavior modification and mastery learning.

The humanists concentrated on purposive behavior, self-direction, and the influence of emotions on learning. They concerned themselves with establishing relations between teacher and student that would maximize psychological growth.

Both viewpoints have described important facets of human behavior, and both have contributed significantly to knowledge about desirable teacher traits and effective teaching methods.

References

Becker, W. C., Engelmann, S., and Thomas, D.: Teaching 2: Cognitive Learning and Instruction, Chicago, 1975, Science Research Associates Inc.

Block, J. H.: Mastery Learning: Theory and Practice, New York, 1971, Holt, Rinehart and Winston, Inc.

Bloom, B. S., editor: Taxonomy of Educational Objectives, the Classification of Educational Goals. Handbook I. Cognitive Domain, New York, 1956, David McKay Co., Inc.

Bruner, J. S.: Toward a Theory of Instruction, Cambridge, 1966, Harvard University Press.

Bruner, J. S.: The Process of Education, Cambridge, 1962, Harvard University Press.

Bruner, J. S.: The Act of Discovery, Harvard Educational Review **31**:21-32, 1961.

Carroll, J. B.: A Model of School Learning, Teachers College Record **64**:723-733, 1963.

Combs, A. W.: Some Basic Concepts for Teacher Education, J. Teacher Ed. **23**(3): 286-290, 1972.

Glasser, W.: Schools Without Failure, New York, 1969, Harper & Row, Publishers.

Glasser, W.: Reality Therapy: A New Approach to Psychiatry, New York, 1965, Harper & Row, Publishers.

Gordon, T.: Teacher Effectiveness Training, New York, 1974, Peter H. Wyden/Publisher.

Gordon, T.: Parent Effectiveness Training, New York, 1970, Peter H. Wyden/Publisher.

Hitt, W.: Two Models of Man, American Psycologist **24**:651-658, 1969.

Hunter, M.: Teach More—Faster! El Segundo, California, 1969, TIP Publications.

Hunter, M.: Motivation, El Segundo, California, 1967, TIP Publications.

Kohl, H.: The Open Classroom, New York, 1969, New York Review.

Mager, R. F.: Preparing Instructional Objectives, Belmont, 1962, Fearon Publishers.

Nagel, T., and Richman, P.: Competency-based Instruction: A Strategy to Eliminate Failure, Columbus, Ohio, 1972, Charles E. Merrill Publishing Company.

Neill, A. S., Summerhill: A Radical Approach to Child Rearing, New York, 1960, Hart Publishing Co., Inc.

Popham, W. J., and Baker, E.: Establishing Instructional Objectives, Englewood Cliffs, New Jersey, 1970*a*, Prentice-Hall, Inc.

Popham, W. J., and Baker, E.: Planning an Instructional Sequence, Englewood Cliffs, New Jersey, 1970*b*, Prentice-Hall, Inc.

Popham, W. J., and Baker, E.: Systematic Instruction, Englewood Cliffs, New Jersey, 1970*b*, Prentice-Hall, Inc.

Raths, L.: "Clarifying Values." In Fliming, R., editor: Curriculum for Today's Boys and Girls, Columbus, Ohio, 1963, Charles E. Merrill Publishing Company.

Raths, L., Harmin, M., and Simon, S.: Values and Teaching, Columbus, Ohio, 1966, Charles E. Merrill Publishing Company.

Rogers, C.: Forget You Are a Teacher, Instructor **81**:65-66, 1971.

Rogers, C.: Freedom to Learn, Columbus, Ohio, 1969, Charles E. Merrill Publishing Company.

Simon, S., Howe, L., and Kirschenbaum, H.: Values Clarification, New York, 1972, Hart Publishing Co., Inc.

Skinner, B. F.: Science and Human Behavior, New York, 1953, Macmillan, Inc.

Skinner, B. F.: In Rogers, C., and Skinner, B. F.: Some Issues Concerning Control of Human Behavior, Science **124**:1057-1066, 1956.

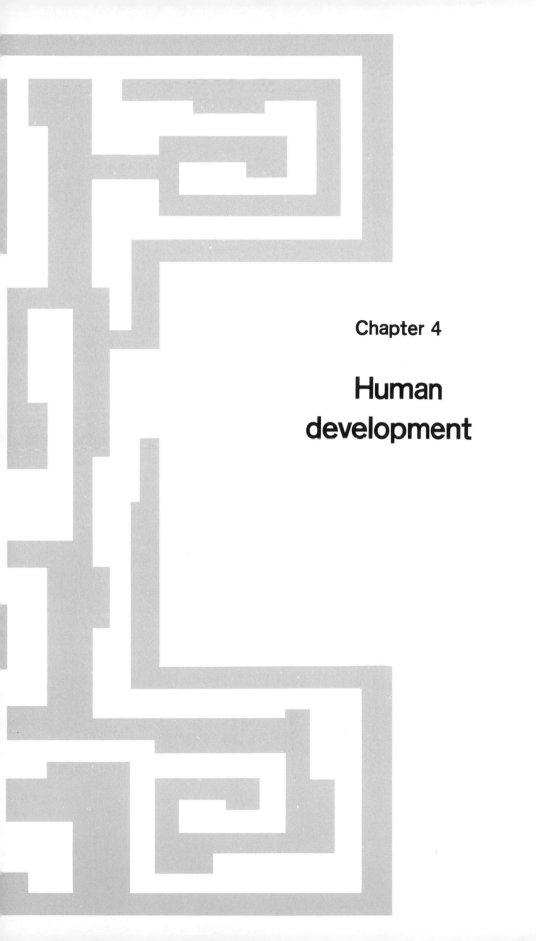

Chapter 4

Human
development

In Chapters 2 and 3 we took a scenic jaunt through the flat plains of behaviorism and the ragged uplands of humanism. The intent was to gain a conception of the nature and intensity of those two great thrusts. We saw how two other strong emphases—psychodynamics and Gestalt psychology—had blossomed and then faded into the humanistic fold.

Those four thrusts did not represent all that was happening in educational psychology. Standing aside, going about their own business, were two other movements: (1) the great objective test movement and (2) the studies of human development.

The testing movement, although not an overriding concern of today's behaviorists, has always worn the silks of behaviorism. Objective testing fit into the mold of objectivity, the scientific bent that behaviorists espoused. Moreover, the movement sprang forth from the prodigious mind of that grand behaviorist, Edward L. Thorndike. He did it all, as they say.

The objective test movement is not our feast here. Rather, it is time for us to consider that other great concern of psychology and education—human development—its nature, its progressive stages, and the characteristics of learners at each stage. This exploration will be both objective and subjective. Objectivity comes from the phenomena of physical development. Bone and muscle structure, organic development, coordination, height, and weight, are data available to all. On the other hand, intellectual and psychosocial development require interpretations and theoretical explanations. That is subjective stuff, and you can see some of the old humanistic and behavioristic arguments creeping into it. Alas. But enough of that.

human development and education

If development and learning did not affect each other, they would not concern us here. But they do affect each other, sometimes in ways that are clear, sometimes in ways that are obscure. Their effects on each other, even when obscure, are undeniably powerful.

Knowledge of human development thus provides much help to educators —teachers, administrators, curriculum developers, school psychologists, librarians, school nurses, parents, and everyone else concerned with teaching and learning. Studies of development help by providing knowledge of

Critical periods in human development
Ranges and variations from one student to another in all developmental areas
Intellectual abilities and inabilities at different stages
Interests, values, and attitudes at different stages
Social and emotional traits typical of different levels of development
Preferred interrelation and interaction patterns with adults and peers at different stages of development

To the extent that developmental behavior patterns can be identified, curriculum and instruction can be adapted to them. That adaptation is the key to making learning relevant, interesting, and profitable for students. It advances achievement, and it improves student motivation and self-image.

Such adaptation also makes teachers' lives tolerable—even exciting. What a difference it makes when you have students who are eager to learn instead of reluctant, who are warmly responsive instead of hostile, and who engage in productive activities instead of misbehavior. These happy conditions are far more likely to occur as you come to recognize and build your teaching around topics, activities, and materials that

Strongly interest your students

Lie within their capabilities to perform, understand, and use

Stress types of movement and communication favored by students at given developmental levels

Allow interaction patterns preferred by the students

Provide the kind of warm understanding guidance that your students react to best

This is not all there is to teaching. Not by a long shot. But it is the springboard from which you can bring about learning that is enjoyable, efficient, useful, long-lasting, and enhancing to the self. This is true not only for students, but for teachers as well.

In this one chapter we cannot give attention to the whole of human development. We must limit ourselves to a sampling of the tricks that our environments and genetic codes play on us. This sampling must be further restricted to a consideration of developmental characteristics that affect education, for better or worse. By that ploy we can call in the better and shoo away the worse.

Here, then, is what you will find in the remainder of the chapter:

intellectual development its nature, its course of progression, and the possibilities it affords, together with the limitations it imposes on learning. We will view this shimmering electric realm through the eyes and minds of Jean Piaget and the tandem of J. P. Guilford and Mary Meeker.

psychosocial development "What life has done to us and vice versa." Here we will note the emergence of the self and its recognition, self-concept. We will also note the great problems we all must face in our dealings with others. We will see how individuals attempt to deal with those problems and what happens when they fail. Erik Erikson and Robert Havighurst will provide the special vantage points for this examination.

intellectual development

Intellectual development has to do with the growth of the mind. "Mind" is a construct we use to explain the mechanism responsible for mental activities such as perception, imagery, cognition, thought, reason, and speech. It is evident that as individuals grow, they become progressively more able, up to a point, to perform complex mental activities. Theorists in intellectual development have attempted to map the course of such progressive improvement, along with the abilities and inabilities it affords the individual.

Jean Piaget

Jean Piaget, the eminent Swiss psychologist, is the world's foremost authority on human intellectual development. Since 1921, he has been studying the thought processes of the young. He has reported his research, along with theoretical interpretations, in more than thirty books and two hundred articles. Though now in his eighties, Piaget remains incredibly productive.

Piaget's work has made a most valuable contribution to psychology and education. It has identified significant stages in the growth of the mind. It has shown what individuals can do intellectually at those different stages. Just as importantly, it has shown what they cannot do. This knowledge guides teachers in matching instructional language materials, and activities to the functional capability of each student.

Unfortunately, Piaget's work, until recently, went largely unnoticed in the United States. American psychology was enamored with behaviorism, which did not pay attention to the intellect. Piaget called behaviorism the "empty box" theory:

This "empty box" conception of the organism, as it has been called, thus deliberately thumbs its nose at all kinds of mental life, and confines itself solely to behavior in its most material aspects. [1970, p. 76]

Piaget's name is now becoming recognized currency in the United States. Helped along by the upswelling of humanistic psychology, to say nothing of the fame of the Piagetian-based British primary school curriculum, educators and psychologists are suddenly paying very serious attention to Piaget's ideas. These ideas are being popularized in education through the efforts of a number of writers, among them Elkind (1970), Copeland (1974), Charles (1974), Furth (1970), and Ginsburg and Opper (1969).

Piaget's own writings are technical and difficult to understand. The basic ideas expressed in them, however, are easy enough to grasp. When teachers see the ideas in their clearest form, along with interpretations of their meaning for learning and teaching, their eyes gleam and their heads nod. Piaget's ideas match their experiences. Suddenly, student behavior makes sense, and teachers find hope and direction in their instructional endeavors.

To comprehend Piaget's theory of mental development, you must understand his conceptions of (1) the origins of intelligence; that is, what it grows out of, and (2) the stages through which mental development progresses, along with the characteristics typical of each stage. Once you reach that level of understanding, you will be able to organize your teaching to match the intellectual abilities of your students.

Origins of intelligence. Piaget believes that *thought grows out of action,* not vice versa. That notion runs against the grain of conventional wisdom. He says that the manipulations we perform on our environment give rise to the ability to think. The tiny infant begins to make such manipulations, but they are at first without organization. The infant begins this process by using a few mechanisms present at birth:

physical abilities these abilities include sensory processes (the five senses), gross motor processes (uncoordinated movements under control of the central nervous system), and a few reflex behaviors.

organizational ability this is an inborn ability to organize random movements into patterns, or *structures.*

adaptation ability this is an inborn ability to modify structures in accord with information received through movements. Adaptation occurs by means of two processes: (1) assimilation, the taking in of information through existing structures, and (2) accommodation, the reorganization of structures to make them consistent with the new information that was assimilated.

Although they are artificially separated here, you can see how these three inborn traits are interrelated. Physical abilities provide the raw stuff from which organized structures (movement patterns) are made. Organization occurs and reoccurs as the individual takes in new information that does not fit into existing structures. This taking-in and modifying are what Piaget calls assimilation and accommodation, which together comprise the process of adaptation.

Thus the individual has, from the time of birth, inborn abilities to receive information, make movements, organize movements, and make continuing adaptations in the organized patterns of movements.

Influences. The intellect grows out of acts performed on the environment. Aspects of the environment that play crucial roles in this process include people and physical objects. Piaget stresses that his theory does not rest solely on maturation of the central nervous system, as some critics have suggested. Physical maturation is indeed important. The brain increases its performance potential as it matures through the first fifteen years of life. But without other influences, the intellect does not develop.

Piaget credits manipulations made on the physical environment as one key factor in mental growth. The individual must act, move, observe, arrange objects, and rearrange them. That physical experience furnishes much of the data for organizing and reorganizing the mental structures that give direction and meaning to the manipulations the child makes on the environment. This organizing and reorganizing are necessary components of development.

A second key aspect in intellectual development is socialization, interaction with other people. Such interaction greatly expands the number and kinds of intellectual structures. Inanimate objects do not argue, laugh, comfort, cry, jump about, or insist on having their own way. People do. Therefore, mental schemes, structures, must be developed for guiding actions that involve other people.

Three influences thus interact with the inborn traits of sensorimotor processes and ability to organize and adapt. These three influences are maturation, physical experience, and socialization.

You can see that Piaget's theory, assuming it is correct, helps teachers by pointing out that students require two things: (1) extensive experience with physical objects and (2) a great deal of socialization with other people. In the past, schools have laid little stress on either of these two factors. Students were admonished to keep quiet and study. Keeping quiet meant no talking with other students and little physical movement. Studying meant mostly reading or writing, with little opportunity for observing and manipulating physical objects.

Piaget's ideas in this regard had profound influence on the primary school curriculum urged in the Plowden report (1967). Out of this report grew the new elementary school curriculum effected in the British primary schools. This curriculum, as you might well imagine, lays great stress on socialization and physical experience in school.

Stages. Piaget has still more to offer educators. We noted the interplay of inborn traits and influences that yielded intellectual growth. Piaget has found that intellectual growth does not occur as a linear progression. That is, it does not merely get bigger and bigger like a balloon being filled with air.

Instead, intellectual growth progresses through identifiable stages, each of which is notably different from the others. Each stage finds individuals thinking (and behaving) in ways characteristic of that particular stage. This phenomenon tells us that children's minds are not miniature versions of adult minds. Children do not think in the same *ways* that adults can think. They have their own distinct ways of considering and explaining the world. Their thought processes by no means parallel those of adults.

The stages Piaget describes indicate the *optimal* intellectual ability that typifies this stage, that is, the most advanced type of thought the individual is capable of at that particular level of development. His work shows us how to identify the stages at which individuals are functioning. Thus, we can determine their abilities, inabilities, and processes of

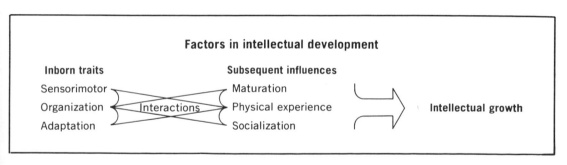

Factors in intellectual development

Inborn traits | Subsequent influences

Sensorimotor — Maturation
Organization — Interactions — Physical experience — Intellectual growth
Adaptation — Socialization

interacting with the world. Such information helps us provide optimal learning environments and experiences.

According to Piaget, children pass through the following stages of intellectual development. This progression is constant for all persons. They all go through the same stages in the same order. They differ somewhat, however, in the ages at which they enter into and exit from these stages.

Sensorimotor stage (age: birth–2 years). The name sensorimotor aptly describes the first stage in intellectual development. By means of inborn processes, the children's activity consists in large measure of sensing and moving. This stage sees the children progress through several developmental units, each one more complex than the previous.

At about 1 month of age children begin to show *primary circular reactions* in which different responses are made to different objects: the objects are differentiated and reacted to differently. At about 4 months of age children show *secondary circular reactions,* acting on objects, waiting for effects to occur, and making brief searches for objects when they are removed from sight. Symbolic meaning begins to emerge at about 8 months, with attendant active search for missing objects and imitation of other persons' behavior.

By the age of 12 months, *tertiary circular reactions* emerge. The children begin to experiment actively, use symbolic movements, and ask help from adults. By the age of 2, children can imitate behavior of humans and animals, whether they are present or absent. Rudimentary cause-effect predictions become commonplace. The children are inventive and organized in movements.

Preoperational stage (age: 2–7 years). By the beginning of this stage children have learned to differentiate themselves from other people and objects. They seek actively to manipulate objects, and try to continue experiences that are interesting or pleasant. The children are not yet able to perform *operations,* which can be thought. of as activities carried out either mentally or physically that can also be undone or returned to the original starting point. Because of this inability, Piaget selected the name preoperational for this stage.

The preoperational stage consists of two major phases. The first phase occurs between the approximate ages of 2 and 4. In this phase, children continue to see themselves as distinct from others—so much so in fact that they become very self-centered. Seldom if ever can they see another person's point of view.

The growth of language is occurring very rapidly during this phase. Symbols can now be used to represent the environment. Children's repertoires of verbal symbols amaze adults. This often causes adults to overestimate their level of intellect. In reality the children are using most of their words in an imitative way, without significant comprehension of their meaning.

The second phase of the preoperational stage has great importance for teachers. This phase, the *intuitive thought phase,* begins at about age 4 and lasts through about age 7. This age span covers typical children at kindergarten up to second grade. Since there are sizeable variations among children as regards the age of entry into and exit from stages, teachers can expect to have intuitive thought children in classes from kindergarten through third grade, though most third graders will have moved into the next stage, concrete operations.

The intuitive thought phase has great significance for teaching, curriculum, and instructional materials. This significance becomes evident when we note the intellectual traits, abilities, and inabilities of children at this level.

First, these children do not reason logically. To urge them to "be reasonable" or to "think about it" is ineffective.

Their reasoning proceeds on the basis of hunches, intuitions, not on logical reasoning. They have great difficulty recognizing the order in which more that two or three events occur. They scarcely conceptualize cause-effect and means-end relationships. They cannot remember more than three or four basic rules, and those are quickly forgotten, though not intentionally, when they conflict with self-interest. They do not understand other speakers accurately. That includes the teacher. They most certainly do not conceptualize number and number relationships, although primary grade mathematics programs have been developed on the assumption that they do.

You can readily see that children at the intuitive thought level are not capable intellectually of performing many of the learning and behavioral tasks expected of them in early primary grades. Teachers and curriculum builders, through no fault of their own, have not recognized the children's limitations. They are beginning to do so now, and as a result, the primary curriculum is being adapted more closely to children's thought processes.

Teachers will find that children in the intuitive thought phase talk a great deal, sometimes to themselves, and sometimes to others. They argue; they call each other names. They like to play games, but their play is noncompetitive and does not follow formal rules. Their judgments have absolute values — right-wrong, good-bad, and big-little. They fabricate stories that bear little resemblance to the truth. They tell them seriously, though not in a deceitful way. They are highly imitative of each other, and quite willing to accept the authority of adults.

Concrete operations stage (age: 7–11 years). Somewhere around the age of 7, children begin moving out of the intuitive thought phase and into the stage of concrete operations. By "operation" Piaget means an action that can be carried out to an end and then reversed to its

beginning. To perform an operation, children must be able to do two things: (1) *conserve,* which means that they see that objects remain the same in quantity, weight, and number regardless of how they are changed in shape or arrangement of parts, and (2) *reverse,* which means that any transformation of objects' shape, number, or arrangements can be undone, that is, returned to the original condition.

The processes of conservation and reversibility are necessary for carrying out operations, and the ability to do these things clearly sets children apart intellectually from those still functioning at the intuitive thought level. A whole new world of intellectual possibilities has opened up for the children of this stage.

Now for the first time children can do some of the things that unknowing teachers expected them to do all along. They can reason using cause-effect and means-end relationships. They no longer have to rely solely on intuitions. They can put ideas in sequence. They can divide things into component parts and put them back together again. They can make logical classifications. They can see ideas from two points of view at the same time, and by that token can see other people's points of view when disagreements occur.

Language is now used more accurately, so long as it deals with concrete objects. Abstractions, such as honesty and loyalty, are almost impossible to conceptualize. Games have become more competitive. Rules are recognized, and everyone expects others to follow rules to the letter. Losing is now hard to accept. Loud abusive arguments normally accompany competitive play.

Number and number processes are just now becoming understandable to students. Accurate one-to-one relationships and accurate measurements can be made. Grouping and regrouping are possible. The "understanding" aspect of mathematics — so stressed for the past fifteen years in our primary grades—is now accessible to the children.

While conservation and reversibility allow the performing of operations, such operations always relate to concrete objects. That's why Piaget calls this stage "concrete operations." The concrete objects need not be physically present for the operations to occur. However, children always think of real things while carrying out the mental operations. They are not yet able to do operations involving intangibles and abstractions.

Formal operations stage (age: 11–15 years). At the approximate age of 11, individuals begin moving into the stage of formal operations. While still relying primarily on concrete type thought, and even on intuitions much of the time. they can now perform mental operations that involve abstractions and intangibles. Thought can follow *formal* patterns, which involve thinking about thought. This leads into the realms of philosophy, morality, and values. It permits the formulation of varieties of hypothetical schemes, which can be tested out at the intellectual level rather than the behavioral. Students can deal with the hypothetical, the possible, and the ideal as much as with the actual.

Language, which heretofore had served for communication purposes, now provides a system of concepts and abstractions that facilitate thought. It fosters the formation of theories about everything. It allows the logical testing out of conclusions arrived at through hypothetical thought.

The student is becoming able to consider several points of view simultaneously, clarifying, weighing, evaluating, and comparing them one against the other. The purity of hypothetical conclusions leaves adolescents somewhat critical and rejecting of institutions, tainted as they are with the reality of human failings. Yet their overall behavior reflects general acceptance of prevailing conventions.

By the age of 15, on the average, the adolescent has reached the highest level of intellectual efficiency. This efficiency is not to be confused with wisdom, which grows out of experience. Yet, so far as thought processes are concerned, the end of the formal operations stage marks the level of full adult thought.

Implications for teaching. Piaget has not concerned himself greatly with education. Yet his ideas have strong implications for teaching. The following are two of those pervasive, overarching, and far-reaching implications:

1. Students must act. They must have extensive concrete experience. They must manipulate their environment and interact with other people. This action gives rise to intellectual development. Learning environments and instructional activities should maximize action and interaction.

2. Children do not think like adults. They have their own processes, different at different stages of development, for dealing with and comprehending the world. Instructional methods and materials must be adapted to children's styles of thought.

Guilford and Meeker

Piaget explained his conceptions of how the intellect grows, how it operates, and how it progresses through various stages. But he did not explain how the mind was structured. He did not attempt to identify its parts or how they worked together to process information and carry out various mental activities.

Several theorists over the years have attempted to put together a feasible explanation of how the mind is structured. The most outstanding contemporary theory is that formulated by J. P. Guilford. Guilford, to explain his conception of how the mind works, has formulated a model of the intellect. The model is metaphorical — it involves using something familiar (a cube) to help explain something that is very difficult to grasp (the intellect).

Shortly, we will examine Guilford's model of the intellect, along with Mary Meeker's suggestions about using the model in matters of schooling. First, let us briefly survey some of the work previously done in attempting to understand the nature and implications of intelligence.

Binet. Everyone has an intutitive notion about intelligence. It refers to degrees of brightness, quickness, ability to do abstract thinking, and ability to solve problems. In school it has long been evident that some students learn more quickly and easily than others. One way to account for such differences took shape out of the work of the French psychologist, Alfred Binet.

Just before the turn of the century, Binet was assigned the task of identifying slow learning children who could not profit from attendance in regular classes. No methods then existed for making such identification. After trying out several approaches, Binet and Simon, his collaborator, happened on some tests of attention, memory, and comprehension. They found that those tests could differentiate between faster and slower learners.

In 1916, Lewis Terman, an American psychologist at Stanford University, took Binet's tests and elaborated, refined, and validated them. He had them administered to hundreds of people of different ages. From those results, he established norms that showed what individuals at different age levels typically did on the tasks. That work resulted in the Stanford-Binet intelligence test, since its inception the most widely used and respected test of general intelligence.

The Stanford-Binet test was aimed at a "one-factor" notion of intelligence. That factor was ability to do abstract thinking. Other psychologists felt that there was more to intelligence than that one factor.

Charles Spearman, in 1927, proposed a "two-factor" theory of intelligence. One factor he called "g" for general intelligence. With "g" he combined "s," which stood for special intellectual abilities, such as one might see in special talents in music and art. L. L. and Thelma Thurstone (1941) used statistical techniques and identified several factors they believed to be components of intelligence. They labeled those factors "primary mental abilities."

Wechsler. The other great individual intelligence test was constructed by David Wechsler, a psychologist at Bellevue Hospital in New York City. Wechsler agreed with the multiple-factor conception of intelligence. Dissatisfied with the Stanford-Binet test, especially for measuring the intelligence of adults, he constructed, in 1944, a test for adults. He called it the Wechsler-Bellevue test.

The Wechsler-Bellevue became very popular. Yet Wechsler felt it needed further refining. He devised two new tests patterned after it. The tests were the Wechsler Intelligence Scale for Children (WISC) and the Wechsler Adult Intelligence Scale (WAIS). They replaced the Wechsler-Bellevue in mental testing.

Both the WISC and the WAIS obtained scores on ten different intellectual abilities, five included in a *verbal scale* and five included in a *performance scale*. The tests could yield scaled scores on each ability, IQ scores on both the verbal scale and the performance scale, and an overall IQ score.

The Wechsler verbal scales test areas of general information, comprehension, arithmetic, similarities, and vocabulary. The performance scales test abilities in picture completion, picture arrangement, object assembly, block design, and coding.

IQ. The Stanford-Binet and Wechsler tests popularized the concept of *intelligence quotient,* IQ, which has become a household word in this country. The concept of the IQ has fallen into disfavor in present day educational circles, because it is considered imprecise, culturally biased, and all in all useless in helping teachers provide better instruction. Still, the concept figures widely in discussions about intelligence.

The IQ is simple in concept. Suppose you are administering an intelligence test to an individual who is exactly 14 years old. You obtain the score that individual makes and convert it into a *mental age* score. That simply means that the score is equal to the average score made by a great many individuals of a given age. Suppose the score equaled the average score of individuals who were 14 years and 6 months of age. The mental age score then becomes 14.5. The individual's chronological (calendar) age is 14.0. The intelligence quotient is

$$\frac{\text{Mental age}}{\text{Chronological age}} = \frac{14.5}{14.0} = 104; \text{IQ} = 104$$

When the mental age and the chronological age are exactly the same, the IQ equals 100. Normal IQ range is considered to fall between 90 and 110.

Model of the structure of intellect. Guilford, like Wechsler and others, believed that intelligence is made up of various different factors. Unlike many intelligence theorists, Guilford did not produce a test of intelligence. Instead, he showed his theoretical conception by constructing a model, which he called the model of the structure of intellect (Guilford 1959). The model, shown below, is represented as a large cube, con-

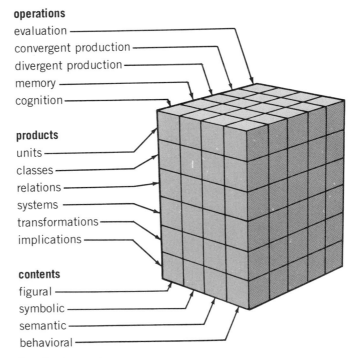

operations
evaluation
convergent production
divergent production
memory
cognition

products
units
classes
relations
systems
transformations
implications

contents
figural
symbolic
semantic
behavioral

(From The Nature of Human Intelligence by Guilford, J. P. Copyright 1967, McGraw-Hill Book Company. Used with permission of McGraw-Hill Book Company.)

70

sisting of one hundred twenty cubicles. One face of the cube represents groups of incoming data. Another face represents mental operations. And the third represents the products that result from operations performed on data.

Contents. Data that come into the mind are of various sorts. They can be figural (pictorial), symbolic (graphic/verbal), semantic (meanings), or behavioral (actions). Guilford calls these data "contents." They are the raw stuff on which the mind works.

Operations. The mind interacts with the data it receives. The interactions are of various sorts. Guilford calls them "operations." The operations include cognition, memory, convergent thinking, divergent thinking, and evaluation. You many notice that these operations parallel the cognitive functions outlined by Bloom in the *Taxonomy of Educational Objectives: Cognitive Domain.* Operations have these meanings: Cognition means becoming aware of and knowing; memory means retention in the mind of what is known. Convergent production means searching for single correct solutions to problems. Divergent production means searching for multiple plausible solutions to problems. Evaluation means making judgments of good-bad, right-wrong, useful-useless, and so forth.

Products. Out of the interplay between contents and operations, products occur. Guilford describes those products as taking the form of units (single wholes), classes (groupings), relations (interconnections among objects or ideas), systems (organized networks of interrelations), transformations (new modifications), and implications (meanings and projections).

Guilford (1959) suggested that this model of the structure of intellect could provide useful services in psychology, vocational training, and education. Psychology could benefit through using the classifications to investigate learning and the various mental operations, such as memory, problem solving, decision making, and creativity. Vocational guidance could be based on the abilities and preferences individuals showed for dealing with either the concrete or the abstract. Education could benefit by attending more than before to the processes of divergent production and evaluation, as contrasted with the more common emphases on convergent production and memory.

Meeker's contributions. Mary Meeker was associated with Guilford for some time. She has taken his ideas to the practical arena of the schools and has used them to identify special strengths and weaknesses in the intellectual functioning of school students.

Meeker points out in her book, *The Structure of Intellect: Its Interpretation and Uses* (1969), her conviction that school curricula can and should be rooted in the theory of intellectual functioning. The same holds true, she believes, for school guidance, to help in placing students, according to their intellectual strengths and weaknesses, into appropriate classes and instructional programs.

Established tests did not exist for identifying student abilities in accordance with Guilford's model. Meeker found a way to devise and use templates that could be placed over the test booklets used in the Stanford-Binet and Wechsler scales. The templates allowed one to identify strong and weak cubicles from the model of the intellect. Patterns for making those templates, together with illustrations for their use and interpretation, are presented in Meeker's book (1969, pp. 123-153).

Unlike many previous investigators who felt that intelligence was inborn and subject to little if any modification through learning, Meeker stresses use of instruction to strengthen cubicles that are diagnosed as weak (Meeker and Meeker 1973). She also advises adapting curricula to areas of identified strength.

She has found consistent patterns of strength and weakness among socioeconomic and ethnic groups. For example:

Disadvantaged boys are relatively strong in the ability to comprehend; therefore much more time should be devoted to the teaching of cognition.

Enough of the members of each group show memory weaknesses to warrant substantial time being devoted to development of specific auditory, visual, and kinesthetic memory abilities. Of all the five major operations, lack of memory skills is most predictive of failure to master academics. [Meeker and Meeker 1973, p. 349]

Meeker has provided a new and useful way of considering intelligence. She has shown how specific intellectual strengths and weaknesses can be identified. And she has strongly suggested that school curricula be arranged to capitalize on identified strengths, while remediating identified weaknesses in ability to function intellectually.

psychosocial development

Life is filled with mysteries that stir the heart with wonder, yet fill it with anguish at their unanswerability — mysteries such as: How did the whole of creation begin? How did something spring from nothing? How can the universe be so incredibly huge that it extends forever; yet if it has limits, what lies there on the other side? How does the human brain hold pictures inside itself, tens of thousands of photo-remembrances of things past and visions of things to be?

Of all such mysteries, great as they are, none is greater than this: How is it that I am I, of all the beings of all the eons? How did it happen that I came among creatures, and how is it that I am myself instead of you or that cat or that fly? This is the mystery of the self, and it has no answer. Yet, the sense of self stands colossal in human events. I am I, and thou art thou. The world turns about me, and I must become what I

must. Yet I cannot disregard you; you make me recognize myself.

the self

The sense of the self emerges during the first few months of life and grows rapidly thereafter. Long before entering school, children clearly differentiate between themselves and other people, animals, and objects. The sense of self reaches the heights of egotistical centeredness before the age of 5. By that point, individuals know they exist and know what they want. But they cannot reconcile their wants with those of others. Self-interest comes first.

Much of one's subsequent life is spent in attempting to satisfy personal needs and wants through subtle compromises with others. When desires conflict, they must be reconciled in some way.

Self-concept. Self-concept refers to what we believe to be true about ourselves, together with the importance we attach to those beliefs. What we believe about ourselves strongly influences our behavior. We tend to affirm our positive beliefs through actions. If we see ourselves as kind and generous, we tend to be kind and generous. If we see ourselves as happy, we tend to be happy, and if competent, competent.

The perceptions of ourselves that displease us often bring about counterproductive behavior. If we feel inferior, we may become reticent and self-effacing, or we may overcompensate by being unduly aggressive. If we feel ugly, we may try to act cute, or else we may fade into the woodwork.

Since self-concept affects the whole of one's behavior, teachers and psychologists have attempted to find ways to improve it. Such efforts are not idle exercise. Several studies have shown a substantial relationship between self-concept and school performance.

Gowan (1960), for example, found that the academic achievement of high school and college students was related to self-confidence, self-acceptance, and a positive feeling about the self. Shaw, Edison, and Bell (1960) found that high achievers in high school tended to see themselves as intelligent, clear thinking, reliable, and enthusiastic. Shaw and Alves (1963) found that high school underachievers had negative concepts of themselves. Similar findings were made by Brookover, Patterson, and Thomas (1964) for seventh grade students, and by Brunkan and Sheni (1966) for upper elementary students. Studies of this same type have shown conflicting results for primary grade students. Studies by Caplin (1969), Soares and Soares (1969), and Zirkel and Moses (1971) into relationships between self-concept and racial/ethnic background also yielded conflicting results.

From the studies cited, one might conclude that self-concept and academic success are related, that the relationship does not show itself clearly until children reach third or fourth grade, and that socioeconomic background has questionable relationship to self-concept.

Whether self-concept directly influences achievement, or vice versa, is not known. It is possible that either one might be causative of the other, or it is possible that they grow together out of other causes. Whatever the case might be, self-concept and success are related. Teachers attempt to increase both.

Enhancing the self. Because of the relationships that have been identified between achievement and self-concept, considerable attention has been given to identifying characteristics of positive self-concepts and to means of improving those concepts. Combs (1962) has identified traits of people who are well-adjusted:

1. They know who they are.
2. They feel they are liked and wanted.
3. They feel they are accepted and successful.
4. They feel a oneness with others.

5. They are maximally open to experience.

Anderson (1968), in listing attributes of people with good mental health, included such traits as confidence, adaptability, and self-reliance. Conversely, people with poor mental health would be insecure, fearful, and rigid. Such undesirable traits likely grow out of (1) prolonged, repeated frustration and failure or (2) sustained rejection by people significant in one's life, or both of these factors.

How does one prevent the development of such undesirable self-perceptions? And how does one counteract them after they have become established?

First, we must recognize that one's self-concept is not fixed and permanent. Self-concept is learned. It continues to be learned and relearned, and thus it changes. It lies subject to influence and manipulation.

If we accept the idea that poor self-concepts grow out of prolonged frustration, failure, and rejection by significant others, we can see that one way to improve self-concept is through correcting those conditions. We can, in school, provide success instead of failure. We can provide acceptance instead of rejection, at least by teachers, who are almost invariably considered significant by students.

Success. Academic success is potentially available to at least 90% of the students in the public schools (Block 1971). Notice the qualifier "potentially." Obviously a much smaller proportion of students actually experience success, probably no more than 25% to 30% (Glasser, 1969). Glasser concludes that students who make grades of B or above see themselves as successful. Those who make grades below B see themselves as failures.

The feeling of success depends on two things. First, we must have the satisfaction of knowing that we can perform adequately, that we are competent. Second, our performances must be recognized by others as competent and successful. These two conditions can be made *available* to all students through the following procedures:

FOR PRESPECIFIED KNOWLEDGE AND SKILLS

1. State the knowledge and skills to be learned in terms of performances— behavioral objectives, if you prefer. You tell the students exactly what you expect them to become able to *do* and under what conditions.
2. Structure the knowledge and skills so that they can be acquired in a cumulative way. Each new learning builds on past learning, with steps small enough to be handled by all students.
3. Match learning tasks to the functional capabilities of each student. The tasks must be neither too difficult nor too easy.
4. Provide constant monitoring and feedback to the students. They must always know, during knowledge and skill acquisition, how they are doing, what errors they are making, and exactly how to correct the errors.
5. Provide systematic reinforcement procedures, to speed and fix learning.

FOR EXPLORATORY AND PRODUCTIVE ACTIVITIES

6. Provide open-ended exploratory activities that are not directed toward predetermined skill or knowledge attainment. These activities should have high interest for the students. They entail exploration and creative production. They allow intellectual elbow room. Students are successful in them by dint of active involvement, letting their interests lead where they may.
7. Allow students to identify, structure, and carry out learning activities in areas important to them. This develops ability to plan and follow through, and it helps foster responsibility.

These procedures make competence available to all students. They lead the horse to the water. Now how do you entice it to drink?

William Glasser (1969), whose work was mentioned earlier, advocates a reality approach in working with students. He does not believe that ability levels, racial or ethnic background, broken homes, poverty, or any other background factors preclude the possibility of every student tasting success in school. He will not let students make excuses for their failures. He requires them to commit themselves to positive, reality-oriented courses of action, and he keeps at them to live up to their commitments. He stresses again and again that each student can make choices that lead to success or failure. The choice is up to the student, but the teacher must see that students make a commitment and live by the consequences that their behavior brings.

Other measures also help entice students along the path to success. Reinforcement can increase work output. Individualization can help match students to tasks, by allowing for student differences in ability, interest, and work pace. Opportunities to follow and develop special interests leads quickly to competence. Productive and creative activities allow students to show evidence of what they can do. All these avenues help lead toward inner recognition of success through competence.

The second essential condition for success is recognition by others. This recognition comes as a consequence of performance. You are judged successful in school by what you do. This recognition depends first on competent performance and the production of laudable work products. The means of providing recognition are myriad, ranging from casual comments and attention to critical appraisals of displays and performances. Competence and recognition are both necessary for producing a feeling of success. Neither is sufficient by itself.

Acceptance. Academic success, as we have seen, is very important to the development of self-concept. Equally important is the feeling of acceptance by people one considers significant in life. Such people typically include peers, relatives, and a few other adults, including teachers.

Teachers can do relatively little to provide parental and peer acceptance for their students. They can do much, however, to show their own acceptance. This acceptance is shown through the ways teachers talk and work with their students.

Ned Flanders and his colleagues provided much of the experimental evidence for the influence that styles of talk have on students.* He found that when teachers maximized accepting and clarifying talk, while minimizing rejecting and controlling talk, their students learned more and liked school better. His research helped develop several systems for analyzing verbal interaction. One such system, together with instructions and interpretations for using it, is the OSTRAQ, described in Chapter 9.

Thomas Gordon (1974), whose work we noted previously, has also contributed significantly to styles of teacher talk that show acceptance of students. His techniques emphasize the opening and maintenance of communication channels between teacher and student, and they help students talk out and resolve problems.

William Glasser (1969) suggests showing acceptance of students through emphasizing that they can succeed, can choose to succeed, and can and must make personal commitments to succeed. He also advocates classroom

*Much of the fundamental work in interaction analysis is included in Amidon, E., and Hough, J., editors: Interaction Analysis: Theory, Research, and Application, Reading, Mass., 1967, Addison-Wesley Publishing Co., Inc.

meetings for group solutions to problems. The teacher participates as a member of the group, but accepts students' opinions and attitudes and takes care not to influence the discussions unduly.

Carl Rogers (1969), probably more than any other, has urged a style of teaching built around acceptance and personal development of students. He sees teaching as one of the "helping professions" and believes it requires genuineness, openness and acceptance. You best help others grow toward full functioning as you show your interest in them and your willingness to aid them in their strivings however you can.

Acceptance does not mean that you must agree with what students do or say. Neither does it mean you never express your own opinions when they differ from those of your students. It does mean that you acknowledge other points of view and ways of behaving. You show yourself always willing to listen and help. You function without pretense or facade. You are genuine. But your desire to help must also be genuine.

With the emergence of self-concept, the individual begins a continuing struggle for enhancing, modifying, and protecting the self. We saw some of the ways people enhance the self, that is, make themselves seem better, wiser, and grander in their own eyes. But that self is thrown into an infinite tunnel from which there is no escape. Within that tunnel, the self is destined to be buffeted, hammered, sliced, eroded, bent, and otherwise shaped in unexpected ways. That continual modification comes as a result of the inevitable interaction with other people — people whose ideas, ideals, values, morals, and behaviors run contrary to one's own.

Although the process is continual, there are certain periods in development that, combined with the press of society, make special demands on the self. Those demands have been eloquently and convincingly described by two great social scientists of the present time, Erik Erikson and Robert Havighurst.

Erikson's psychosocial stages

Erik Erikson believes that man has an innate potential for healthy psychological growth. For that growth to lead to health instead of illness, the individual must successfully resolve key conflicts that arise at various stages in life. Those conflicts, along with their affects, are discussed in the following paragraphs.

Erikson's background is starched with Freudian psychology. He maintains an abiding interest in psychiatry, based on Freudian concepts. Yet he takes a perspective on human growth that is different from that of Freud. Freud, you will remember, worked with mentally ill people and developed theoretical explanations that accounted for their behavior. Those ideas were then used to explain the behavior of mentally healthy people, as well. That application did not sit well with many psychologists, who believed that healthy functioning could not be adequately explained on the bases suggested by Freud.

Erikson took such a position. He stressed the positive, pointing out opportunities that exist for all of us, permitting successful psychological development. Erikson is keenly aware of the great difficulty in attempting, through psychotherapy, to correct psychopathic disorders. He insists that such disorders can, in large part, be prevented. His suggestions for such preventive measures revolve about successful coping with key tasks that present themselves at various times in all our lives.

Stages. Erikson (1950) has identified eight stages in human development, each of which requires resolution of a key conflict. Those eight stages are presented here. Suggestions for their successful resolution are made, and the results of successful and unsuccessful resolutions are noted.

Trust versus mistrust (age: 0–18 months). The first of the key developmental stages for Erikson occurs during the first 18 months of life. What happens to the infant during that time, he believes, will determine in a lasting, though not irrevocable, degree whether a sense of basic trust or mistrust is developed in people and the environment.

Our tendencies to be trusting or mistrusting greatly influence our attitude toward life and our dealings with others. Erikson (1960) considers basic trust "the cornerstone of a healthy personality." He believes that trust facilitates most life encounters, whereas basic mistrust hampers them.

Trust develops during this early stage of life if the infant, helpless and dependent, has its needs met regularly and senses that others truly care. Erikson says that inordinate quantities of affection and food are not at all necessary, but what is eminently necessary is a quality relationship between adult and child. Trust grows out of the child's feeling that there is someone whose concern can be counted on at all times.

Autonomy versus shame and doubt (age: 18 months–3 years). For the first few months of life we do not recognize ourselves as separate from others. At about the age of 18 months, however, the sense of the self starts to clarify. We begin to see that what we say and do belongs to us and not to others. We show a greatly increased desire to act independently. We want to do things for ourselves instead of having others do them for us.

It is at this second stage, lasting from approximately 18 months to 3 years of age, that we either come to believe in our own abilities to behave and act, or come to doubt ourselves and feel shame. Autonomy grows out of successful behavior. The key determinant of whether children see their behavior as successful or unsuccessful is the reactions that adults make to it. Behavior that is approved and encouraged leads to a greater sense of ability and confidence in oneself. Behavior that brings on constant disapproval and punishment leads to self-doubt and shame.

You may wonder whether parents should, therefore, praise and accept all behavior. Erikson says that they should not. Limits on behavior help children recognize that there are both acceptable and unacceptable kinds of behavior. They also help provide a continuing sense of caring from adults. Therefore, inappropriate behavior should not be rewarded or encouraged. It should be humanely suppressed. Meanwhile, children should be encouraged to function on their own when they show an inclination to do so. That behavior should be accepted with approval.

Initiative versus guilt (age: 3–6 years). By the age of 3, the child's sense of autonomy, provided it has been nourished and not thwarted, has reached a high level of development. Along with this sense of autonomy comes a benign aggressiveness, an active reaching out to explore and try out the new and different. This eagerness to try one's own wings is called initiative, and the time of life in which its development is crucial falls between the ages of 3 and 6.

If the trait of initiative is to become solidly rooted, children must be encouraged in their active manipulation of the environment. Piaget stressed this activity as necessary for intellectual development. In the same degree it is necessary for psychosocial development. Initiative is a trait that serves us well throughout life. If stifled at this age, through reprimand, punishment, or reproof, it may never develop fully, or if so, only through later intensive effort.

Through encouragement of children's natural attempts to expand their realms of activity and influence, one can help them learn that they do have power, that they can direct themselves, and that they can give purpose to their own lives. They retain some of the childhood ability to seek and try. They are not so likely to sit back and wait to be directed.

When their explorations are harshly controlled and bring punishment, they begin developing a generalized sense of guilt that may plague them throughout life. Initiative aids full functioning. Guilt shackles it.

Industry versus inferiority (age: 6–12 years). By the age of 6 the child is virtually bursting with new powers. Language has advanced rapidly. The child is about to enter into a new and powerful stage of intellectual ability, that will permit operational thought and a new style of reasoning. Bones, muscles, and organs have grown in size and strength. Coordination is improving daily. New modes of interacting with peers are developing that will make possible cooperation and competition.

Here, says Erikson, is where the child must learn to channel those energies and powers in purposeful directions. Mere play, important as it may be, is not enough. The child must become productive and task oriented. The tasks need not be distinguishable from play, except that they often should lead to an end—a product, a solution, a skill, an understanding.

When energies are directed to purposeful tasks, the child develops a sense of industry. This sense of industry brings with it an increased sense of competence —of ability to do and perform. This period of life is a physically healthy one. Bodily and organic changes are occurring at a slower pace, calm before the storm of adolescence. This age then is both ideal and key for the development of a sense of industry—a sense of need for purposeful activity.

If this drive for industry is stifled

77

through adult disapproval and punishment, a debilitating sense of inferiority results. Reprimand and reproof for activities, which so often comes when the activities are noisy, cause one to feel guilty. If the products of the activities are frowned on or put down, one comes to feel inferior. Feelings of inferiority should be vigorously avoided at this stage, for it lies on the borderline of adolescence, an age fraught with self-doubt and feelings of inferiority and incompetence.

Identity versus identity confusion (age: 12–18 years). Childhood comes to an end and one begins the roller coaster trip into adulthood. No time in life is so menaced by self-doubt. Nowhere else are the feelings so sensitive. Rarely will one again experience such heights of exhilaration and such depths of despair. Never again will the heights and depths lie so close to each other or come with disquieting regularity.

One is now on the way to becoming an independent man or woman, leaving behind the dependency of childhood. But what man or woman? What sort, patterned after whom? With what uniqueness?

This stage of life, according to Erikson, is crucial in making the sort of determinations and clarifications that establish personal identity. Early in life the child became aware of selfness. But that was a self seen as distinct from others. This new independent adult self is one apart from others, yet at the same time directed by them. It is a vague amalgamation of one's unique traits, self-perceptions, goals and aspirations, and expectancies of others.

The individual now struggles with lingering questions, such as: Who am I? What will I become? What can I do? What is my relation to others? How do others see me? In this struggle, this search, adolescents mimic many different heroes and try out, mostly in talk but partly in behavior, various life styles. For adolescents, life is a supermarket filled with manikins, each exemplifying a style of human life. They are to be looked at, tried out, and accepted or rejected, one by one.

This identity shopping spree inevitably produces conflict with adults, especially parents, who have settled into comfortable life styles and who have forgotten that they, themselves, had to go through the same experiments. Yet, there is no compromising the situation. The young *must* explore. And conflict will result. As painful as this process is, for both adults and adolescents, it is natural and inevitable. Probably it is desirable, though it hardly seems so at times of conflict. Psychological weaning must occur. The young must leave the nest. Continued strong dependency of one on the other forestalls identity development and stifles independent functioning.

●　●　●

The remaining three stages in Erikson's conception of psychosocial development do not concern us as teachers. The individuals are now out of school, and the tasks and trials they face are of only passing interest to the schools. However, to complete Erikson's descriptions, we will note the remaining stages. The years between 18 and 35 are crucial in the development of a sense of *intimacy* as distinct from a sense of *isolation.* Shared lives between adults, as in marriage, is a typical way of attaining the sense of intimacy and of avoiding the trauma of isolation.

The next stage occurs between the ages of 35 and normal retirement. During this period the individual naturally strives for *generativity* as opposed to *self-absorption.* Generativity refers to one's efforts to be creatively productive and useful to other people.

Erikson's final stage spans the years between retirement and death. This can be an especially troublesome time of life. One's productive years are usually past. Children no longer remain dependent. Vitality and vigor are on the ebb. This is a time when the individual must seek a sense of *integrity* rather than succumbing to a sense of *despair*. Erikson believes that integrity—a combination of wisdom, acceptance, and inner peace—will occur naturally if the previous stages have resulted in a sense of identity, intimacy, and generativity.

the three I's

Teachers and nonteachers alike speak of the three R's, which is fine for early academic training. But for in-school development of the personality it would be well if more thought were given to the three I's—Erikson's critical stages in the development of *initiative, industry,* and *identity.*

The first I requires special attention during preschool and early primary years. Teachers should be ever conscious of the need children have for developing initiative, as opposed to feelings of guilt.

The second I requires attention throughout the elementary school years. That is the period during which students have optimal opportunity to develop a lasting sense of industry, as opposed to inferiority.

The third I absorbs students during their junior high and senior high school years. They experience a continuing struggle for clarification of their sense of identity, a sense that will profoundly influence the remainder of their lives. Teachers can help by being sympathetic and understanding of the dynamisms responsible for much of adolescent behavior that seems disorganized, frenetic, irresponsible, and at times bizarre.

Havighurst's developmental tasks

We saw how Erik Erikson identified and explained states in life that were critical in the development of key personality traits. Robert Havighurst looked at development from the same point of view. He identified many tasks that individuals must adequately accomplish at different points in life. He used and popularized the term "developmental task," which he defined as a task that "arises at or about a certain period in the life of the individual, successful achievement of which leads to his happiness and to success with later tasks, while failure leads to unhappiness in the individual, disapproval by society, and difficulty with later tasks" (1952, p. 2).

Havighurst did not consider task accomplishment crucial to adequate personality development, as did Erikson. He saw the tasks as something more akin to rungs on a ladder to be climbed. You might miss two or three of the rungs and still get to the top. But hitting most of them at the right time increases both the ease and pleasure of climbing the ladder.

Havighurst's stages within which the various tasks fell paralleled the stages that Erikson identified. Infancy to early childhood (0–6 years) made up the first stage. Middle childhood (6–12 years) made up the second. The third stage was preadolescence and adolescence (12–18 years). Except for the first, those stages coincide with Erikson's initiative versus guilt, industry versus inferiority, and identity versus role confusion. They include the tasks that have special importance for teachers.

Infancy and early childhood (age: birth–6 years). Developmental tasks that come early in this period, tasks such as learning to walk and to talk, do not concern teachers. Tasks that come toward the end of the period, however, are important in the lives of kindergarten and first grade students, and therefore important to teachers. The following are among the tasks Havighurst identified:

1. Learning sex differences and sexual modesty. This task is being accomplished during the early primary school years.

Boys and girls still have an unabashed natural tendency to explore each others' bodies. They are uninhibited in their movements and bodily positions, and they take little notice of whether dresses are down or pants are zipped. They are just beginning to notice that boys and girls at school go to different restrooms.

2. Forming simple concepts of social and physical reality. Children's conceptions of reality depend largely on their stages of intellectual development. Children at about age 6 are just beginning to move from egocentric intuitive conceptions of the world to more detached and logical conceptions. This development will provide them with more accurate concepts of reality. It puts them on an intellectual level somewhat closer to teachers, and it permits more adequate interaction with topics commonly taught in school.

3. Learning to relate oneself emotionally to parents, siblings, and other people. This relationship implies a constructive ability to give and take. Previously, the child has been very self-centered. Only now does the realization begin to grow that other people have their own points of view that must be taken into account. Children are becoming able to cooperate and help, but they are still predominantly self-centered.

4. Learning to distinguish right and wrong and developing a conscience. Again, this task requires intellectual progression into the concrete operational stage. Even then, right and wrong are seen as applying mainly (and rigidly) to other people. Development of the conscience is a slow matter.

Middle childhood (age: 6–12 years). This was the phase where Erikson saw the opportunity and necessity for developing a sense of industry. Havighurst implies much the same in the tasks he lists for the period. Among them are the following:

1. Learning physical skills necessary for ordinary games. This task has little importance for children in the primary grades. They come naturally equipped for the unorganized games they prefer. At about the age of 9, however, children become fascinated with organized, competitive games, many of which call for special skills in catching, throwing, running, and so forth. Those skills then acquire paramount importance in the children's lives.

2. Learning to get along with age mates. Piaget wrote that verbal confrontations aided intellectual development in the young. While primary teachers are not overly troubled with squabbling, teachers of middle grade children might suspect that their students were all on the way to becoming geniuses. Verbal squabbles are the bane of their existence. Fusses and fights come as surely as the day and night. Through these myriad confrontations, together with much teacher arbitration and counseling, children come slowly to the ability to get along with each other.

3. Developing fundamental skills in reading, writing, and calculating. In the main, this is what elementary school has been about. The three R's still play a dominant role in the curriculum, though far from an exclusive one. All subsequent learning is so dependent on these skills, especially on reading ability, that their importance as a developmental task can hardly be overemphasized.

4. Developing conscience, morality, and a scale of values. Toward the end of this period, the student can recognize and retain varying points of view, can make value judgments about them, and can describe many ideas about right and wrong. Conscience and morality are beginning to play important roles in life. Some of the newer instructional techniques in moral development and values clarification can help children accomplish this task more easily and fully.

5. Developing attitudes toward social groups and institutions. Awareness of

other people, places, and conditions grows rapidly toward the end of this period. That awareness, combined with developing values and senses of right and wrong, thrust students into positions of judging people and institutions. Proper attitudes toward other groups of people and toward organized ways of dealing with life problems requires accurate information, tolerance for viewpoints other than one's own, and a willingness to seek the worth inherent in others. Skillful teachers can help students avoid development of prejudice, while establishing attitudes that recognize the good and value in all people.

Preadolescence and adolescence (age: 12–18 years). Middle childhood was a time of inner calm and outward turmoil. Puberty puts an end to the inner calm. It signals the onset of what has been called the storm and strife of adolescence. Self-identity becomes the primary overlay on behavior. Doubts about the self abound. Relations with others run hot and cold. The feelings are ultra sensitive. Emotionality, rather than rationality, directs much of individuals' behavior. Havighurst's tasks for this period reflect the identity struggle that fills adolescents' lives:

1. Achieving new and more mature relations with age-mates of both sexes. Gone is unisex. Gone is the boy-girl group cleavage of childhood. Heterosexual relations step to the fore. And what a time of uncertainty and misgivings; peer relations assume gigantic proportions. Other-directedness becomes a way of life, as students search simultaneously for group and individual identity.

2. Accepting one's physique and using the body effectively. Almost all teenagers are dissatisfied with their physical appearance. They fervently regret that their nose, skin, hair, eyes, torsos, legs, and fingers do not look straighter, slimmer, brighter. They spend hours agonizing over the images in their mirrors. They want to look almost exactly like everyone else, except that they want to look better than they believe they do. Coming finally to accept one's appearance is a tedious process. Few people achieve it easily; some never do.

3. Achieving emotional independence of parents and other adults. Psychological weaning is a traumatic task to accomplish. One wants to be independent and grown up, yet one may yearn to remain a child at times. Independence is not given and accepted easily. Its achievement is marked with conflict and ill feeling. But the drive toward independence is strong. Without it one cannot move past the line that separates psychological childhood from psychological adulthood.

4. Desiring and achieving socially responsible behavior. The period of adolescence brings with it a rejection of adult authority along with rejection of many social institutions. Out of this pattern of rejection and rebellion must be pieced together a predisposition toward socially responsible behavior — behavior that, though critical, is also constructive. This outlook grows as students see that they do in fact have some control over their destiny. It grows as they are given opportunities to direct portions of their own school learning. And it continues growing with the realization that the earth is a finite space, its people and resources lying exposed, to be ravaged by the uncaring or conserved by the caring.

5. Acquiring a set of values and an ethical system as a guide to behavior. Value systems begin their growth in early childhood, but they do not become clearly definable until the later adolescent years. By that time the individuals have become more sure of themselves and of what is important, good, and right in life. Late adolescence can become a time of highest idealism, with individuals rallying around causes they consider necessary and just. Successful achievement of this developmental task gives

one a sense of direction and stability that will serve well during the coming adult years, when new life styles, occupations, and personal relationships must be entered into.

Havighurst's later periods in life continue to parallel those described by Erikson. He identifies tasks that must be accomplished in early adulthood (18–35 years), middle age (35–60 years), and later life (60 or more years). The tasks he names for early adulthood have to do with establishing new adult relationships, starting a job, starting a family, and managing a home. Tasks to be accomplished during middle age are similar to Erikson's notion of generativity. They have to do with responsible civic and social behavior, with productivity, and with being of help to others. Tasks to be accomplished during later life are mainly tasks of adjustments to declining strength and energy, loss of family members, and the economic and activity realities of retirement.

References

Anderson, C.: School Health Practice, St. Louis, 1968, The C. V. Mosby Co.

Block, J. H.: Mastery Learning: Theory and Practice, New York, 1971, Holt, Rinehart and Winston, Inc.

Brookover, W., Patterson, A., and Thomas, S.: Self-concept of Ability and School Achievement, Soc. Educ. 37:271-278, 1964.

Brunkan, R., and Sheni, F.: Personality Characteristics of Ineffective, Effective, and Efficient Readers, Personnel and Guidance J. 44:837-844, 1966.

Caplin, M.: The Relationship Between Self-concept and Academic Achievement, J. Exp. Educ. 37:13-16, 1969.

Charles, C.: Teacher's Petit Piaget, Belmont, Calif., 1974, Fearon Publishers.

Combs, A. W., Chairman ASCD Yearbook Committee: "A Perceptual View of the Adequate Personality." In Perceiving, Behaving, Becoming, Washington, D.C., 1962, National Education Association.

Copeland, R.: How Children Learn Mathematics, New York, 1974, Macmillan, Inc.

Elkind, D.: Children and Adolescents: Interpretive Essays on Jean Piaget, New York, 1970, Oxford University Press, Inc.

Erikson, E. H.: Childhood and Society, New York, 1950, W. W. Norton & Company, Inc.

Erikson, E. H.: Youth and the Life Cycle, Children 7:45, 1960.

Furth, H.: Piaget for Teachers, Englewood Cliffs, N.J., 1970, Prentice-Hall, Inc.

Ginsburg, H., and Opper, S.: Piaget's Theory of Intellectual Development, Englewood Cliffs, N.J., 1969, Prentice-Hall, Inc.

Glasser, W.: Schools Without Failure, New York, 1969, Harper & Row, Publishers.

Gordon, T.: Teacher Effectiveness Training, New York, 1974, Peter H. Wyden/Publisher.

Gowan, J.: Factors of Achievement in High School and College, J. Counseling Psychol. 7:91-95, 1960.

Guilford, J. P.: Three Faces of Intellect, Am. Psychol. 14:469-479, 1959.

Havighurst, R. J.: Developmental Tasks and Education, New York, 1952, David McKay Co., Inc.

Meeker, M.: The Structure of Intellect: Its Interpretation and Uses. Columbus, Ohio, 1969, Charles E. Merrill Publishing Company.

Meeker, M., and Meeker, R.: Strategies for Assessing Intellectual Patterns in Black, Anglo, and Mexican-American Boys—Or Any Other Children—And Implication for Education, J. School Psychol. **11**:341-350, 1973.

Piaget, J.: Science of Education and the Psychology of the Child, New York, 1970, Orion Press.

Plowden, Lady B. et al.: Children and Their Primary Schools: A Report of the Central Advisory Council for Education, London, 1967, Her Majesty's Stationery Office.

Rogers, C.: Freedom to Learn, Columbus, Ohio, 1969, Charles E. Merrill Publishing Company.

Shaw, M., and Alves, G.: The Self-concept of Bright Academic Underachievers: Continued, Personnel and Guidance J. **42**:401-403, 1963.

Shaw, M., Edson, K., and Bell, H.: The Self-concept of Bright Underachieving High School Students as Revealed by an Adjective Check-list, Personnel and Guidance J. **39**:193-196, 1960.

Soares, A., and Soares, L.: Self-perceptions of Culturally-disadvantaged Children, Am. Educ. Res. J. **6**:31-45, 1969.

Spearman, C.: The Abilities of Man, New York, 1927, Macmillan Inc.

Thurstone, L. L., and Thurstone, T.: Factorial Studies of Intelligence, Chicago, 1941, University of Chicago Press.

Zirkel, P., and Moses, E.: Self-concept and Ethnic Group Membership in Public School Students, Am. Educ. Res. J. **8**:253-265, 1971.

Part II

Planning
for instruction

explains the hows and whys of preparing instruction, beginning with relationships between **motivation** and **learning,** continuing then into means considered useful in **organizing instruction,** and finishing with the rationale and strategies for **personalizing instruction,** to be accomplished through chapters

5. Interests, needs, and learning
6. Instructional organization: intents and attempts
7. Personalized instruction: environments and strategies

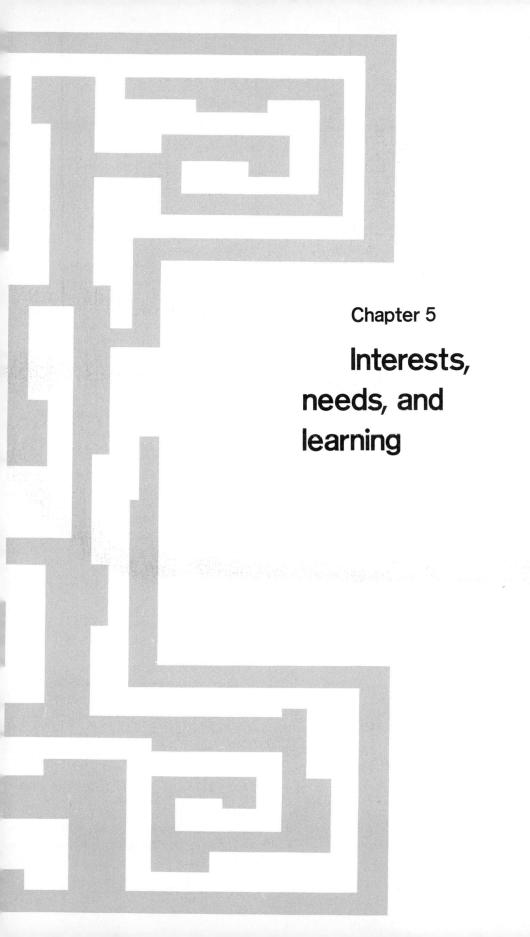

Chapter 5

Interests, needs, and learning

2 experiences

#1. An educational psychology class. Discussion topic, motivation — specifically, things teachers can do to interest learners and get them involved in lessons. Among other things I mentioned the appeal of counterintuitive events.

"What's a counterintuitive event?" someone asked.

"Anybody have an idea?"

A hand went up hesitantly. "Isn't it something that happens, but you wouldn't expect it to?"

"Uh-huh. Can you think of an example?" *(pause)*

"A needle floating on water, maybe?"

"Good. Another?"

"Well, I think people floating along in the Great Salt Lake. They can sit up in the water and won't sink."

So the ideas began coming: sailplanes (manned gliders) flying for hours without motors; the earth revolving around the sun instead of vice versa; hummingbirds flying across the Gulf of Mexico without being able to stop and rest; butterflies doing the same; a gyroscope's resistance to being tilted while it is spinning.

Anita mentioned something about boiling water in a paper cup over an open flame. Two or three students spoke up in disagreement. Pam said, "But that's really just a trick. I don't know how they do it, but I know you couldn't really boil water in a paper cup. At least not over a flame."

"Why not?"

"Well, because the paper would burn, or at least char, and let the water leak out."

"Here, I'll make you a cup out of this sheet of paper. Why don't you put some water in it and try it?"

"What are we going to use to heat it?"

"I've got some matches."

"Wait, I've got a butane lighter here. I think you can adjust it to make a pretty big flame."

I folded a sheet of ditto paper into a square cup with a flat bottom, fastening the edges together with paper clips. Mark took it to the fountain and brought it back with half an inch of water covering the bottom.

"How the heck are we going to do the rest of it?" he asked.

"We're going to have to find some way to hold the cup while we heat it."

Half the students were already out of their chairs, giving advice and trying to figure out how to boil the water. Soon all the students were up and crowded around. Someone pushed two tables close together, with a two-inch space between them, and we set the cup over the space. It sagged in the middle but stayed up.

"Put your lighter there under it."

"Hey, watch out you don't set the tables on fire."

"I'm doing it right. There."

"How long's this going to take?"

"You'll never boil the water with that lighter."

"Hey, nothing's happening!"

"Put your finger in the water and see if it's getting warm."

"Hey, yeah, it is. Is the paper burning yet?"

"No. It isn't even scorching."

"Yipes! I can smell something. It's the paper burning."

"Look under there."

"No, it's not even brown. Uh-oh. I think it's the varnish on the table getting hot."

That went on for ten more minutes, until the end of the period. We never got the water to boil, but we didn't burn the paper either.

We did have 100% active involvement. No-body took notes. There was no need to. No one was going to forget that episode.

#2. When I lived in Peru with my wife and children, we did many interesting things. We went to Chancay, a very old burial ground, and found a few artifacts and some ancient, well-preserved beans, corn, cotton, and cocoa leaves.

We went to Huancayo, Cuzco, and Machu Picchu in the high Andes and bought hats, also rugs of alpaca wool and sweaters. We went to the Amazon jungle and spent some time with Indians and with missionaries. We brought back bows and arrows, feather adornments, and fragile ceramic pottery.

Friends gave us gifts, some of copper and enamel, gold and silver. We bought some recordings, paintings, and other things. We took hundreds of photographs, mostly transparencies. When we returned, we brought these interesting things back with us.

One day Sam Jackson, a sixth-grade teacher, asked me to visit his class. The students were learning about South America, and he thought I could tell them some interesting things about Peru. I told him I would come, but I wanted to try something besides "telling about Peru." He agreed.

I arrived at his classroom at 9:00 A.M., carrying two large paper bags. Mr. Jackson introduced me to the class. He told them I had lived in Peru and that I was going to spend an hour with them that morning. I said good morning, and then:

I took from a bag a gourd, shaped like a waterfowl, with feathers, wings, etc. carved lightly on its surface. I rattled the seeds inside it. Turned it this way and that. Placed it on a table where all could see.

I took out a little tapestry that was two feet square, made by a young Indian girl. It was brown burlap, with an Andean farm scene — a hut, some people, and some chickens — sewn into it with colorful wool yarn. I held it up for everyone to see. "Made by a 12-year-old Indian girl," I said, and draped it over the edge of the table.

I took out a broken piece of pottery and held it up. "Over 2000 years old — made during the height of the Greek civilization, older than the Roman Empire. I found it." I set it on the table.

I took out a small bow and wooden-tipped arrows, colorfully decorated. "From Indians, near the Amazon River," and I placed these on the table.

"Any questions?" I asked.

For a moment no one said anything. Then one youngster asked "Is that a real bow and arrow?"

"Why don't you come up and look at it and see what you think."

For the next forty-five minutes we had one of the liveliest discussions you ever heard. The students asked dozens of questions: where had I been, what was I doing there, what did the places and people look like. We talked about rain, food, farming, headhunting, clothing, Incas and Pizarro, rivers and trees. They wanted to see on the map where the places were. They wanted to handle the objects, and I let them. They wanted to know if I had other things in the bags. I showed them a Cuzco hat and let them guess what it was. A girl modeled it. We looked at feather flowers and at an ancient cotton and bead doll.

At 10:00 A.M. I had to leave. The students seemed sorry we couldn't continue.

Classroom motivation

Teachers want students to be willing to work and enthusiastic about working at the learning activities provided for them. That's because willingness and enthusiasm go hand in hand with attention and involvement. The student who is attentive and involved will learn more, remember longer, and probably make better use of what he has learned. What's more, the student who is attentive and involved will not be a "behavior problem" in the class.

That's why teachers are so concerned about motivation. And since they recognize that they have so much influence over students' willingness and enthusiasm, they usually use the term "motivation" in a way that is different from the way psychologists use it. When psychologists speak of motivation, they usually refer to a state within the learner. Teachers refer to what they, themselves, will try to do to get their students to be willing, enthusiastic, attentive, and involved.

Some authorities point out that motivation is just an idea—a hypothetical construct—that is used to explain why organisms do what they do. From that point of view, it would not be proper to think of motivation as acts teachers do to get students interested. That is, you would not want to say you "motivated" your students.

Yet, from the teacher's point of view, using the word "motivation" to refer to acts performed to get students involved makes sense. The following paragraphs will show the logic of this point of view.

Think of motivation—a state within the individual—as an inclination to act. What things might be responsible for this inclination to act? Physiological conditions are one group of such things: hunger, thirst, and so on. Another group includes aspects of safety: we act to keep ourselves secure and to avoid threat, harm, pain, and loss. Another group includes love and belonging. Another, the earning of esteem. Another, the desire to become what we can become. Yet another, the desire to know and understand. These needs seem to be present in almost every person, and every person acts to see that they are met.

Or in thinking of what makes people inclined to act, we might consider interests and curiosity.

interests We can think of interest as a recurring inclination to be involved with a certain activity. Interest develops because involvement in that activity brings strong gratification. Thus, when we say a student is interested in books, stamp collecting, and basket-

& ball, we mean that the student has had such pleasant experiences with those things that there is a desire to continue being involved with them.

curiosity We can think of curiosity as initial puzzlement about something or attraction toward it. One might be curious about laser beams, table tennis, or a Zuni kachina doll; one might want to explore, to find out more. But there must be something that attracts the attention—something like color, movement, novelty, or incongruity.

What we should recognize is that these need, interest, and curiosity states are present in every individual. Obviously they are stronger at certain times than at others, but they are there. The teacher's job, then, is not to "pour in" motivation to fill students' tanks, as they would the gas tanks in cars, with fuel to be burned until it is used up. Teachers must begin by recognizing that the motivation—the inclination to act— is already there in students; they have to find ways of allowing students to use what they already have. The teacher has to structure lesson activities so that students, while working at them, can fulfill needs, follow existing interests, and explore new, attractive, and puzzling things.

So when teachers say they are "motivating" their learners, they mean in effect that they are performing acts that arouse students' attention and curiosity, and they are providing activities that they know students are interested in, activities that allow students to meet continuing needs.

a model

On the basis of what we have just explored, we can begin putting together a

class motivation model for teachers
In any learning activity

**capitalize on students'
needs, interests, curiosity**

**through instructional tasks involving
activities, materials, variety,
specific objectives, directly attainable goals,
friendly competition, models to imitate**

**that will allow each student to
have fun, be correct,
be first (occasionally), receive attention,
receive acceptance, receive praise,
receive privileges, receive tangibles**

Explanations follow . . .

need gratification

We can thank Abraham Maslow for his outstanding contributions in helping us to better understand motivation. In his conceptualization, Maslow saw "need gratification" as the basis for most human motivation; he thought humans had certain needs, not all of them physiological, and that most purposeful acts could be traced to attempts to fulfill those needs.

Other investigators had worked from a different basis. They thought motivation could best be explained in terms of physiological deficiencies. For instance, if an infant is hungry he is motivated to eat, and some of his acts are made in attempts to get food. Time passes, and through secondary reinforcement he comes to value certain caresses, voice tones, facial expressions, body positions, and so on that are supplied by his mother during feeding. Through this same process of association and secondary reinforcement, he acquires such socially oriented motives as the desire for belongingness, acceptance, and love.

But Maslow thought there was something more to humans — something that, while possibly present in lower animals such as rats and pigeons, was not so easily noticed and was therefore overlooked by experimenters who motivated their animals by depriving them of food or water. He didn't argue that physiological needs don't exist, for as you saw (p. 30) he included them in his hierarchy of needs, and he referred to them as deficiency or D needs. But he thought that once those needs were satisfied, there were other powerful human needs that came into play and served as prime motivators. He thought of some of these other needs as interpersonal, or social, in nature. For example, the needs he called love and esteem could be met only through feedback received from other people. He thought of other needs as intrapersonal, or private (those, for example, that he called self-actualization and the desire to know and understand).

He saw these needs as existing in every individual and as being discrete in themselves, rather than as simply outgrowths of physiological needs. Maslow believed that the desire to satisfy those higher needs was the motivation that initiated, maintained, and guided much of man's purposeful activity. These needs are discussed further in Chapter 7.

Maslow has not been alone in rejecting the idea of physiological deprivation as the prime basis of human motivation. Combs and Snygg* thought that human behavior could be attributed to one sole need — a need for adequacy. They believed that everyone constantly tries to make himself more adequate to cope with life. Robert White** postulated one basic human need that he called the "competence need." He thought of it as a need to deal with one's environment, and in it he included such factors as activity, curiosity, exploration, and manipulation.

*Combs, A. W., and Snygg, D.: Individual Behavior, New York, 1959, Harper & Row, Publishers.
White, R.: Motivation Reconsidered: the Concept of Competence, Psychol. Rev. **66:297, 1959.

Teachers also speak of needs. And though their concepts of student needs may not be precise enough to satisfy the psychological theorist, the concepts are nonetheless inferred from what students do or try to do. For example, a teacher may say that a particular student has a need for attention; the teacher reached that conclusion because the student seemed to be making unusual efforts to get others to notice him. Examples of that kind of "need" are shown in the "age × wants-interests" chart (p. 101) that follows this brief discussion of interests.

interests

We will start this consideration of interests by thinking for a moment about attention. There are two reasons for doing this. One reason is that attention is itself crucial to the larger consideration of motivation: motivation includes attention as one of its components, along with other factors such as direction and perserverence. A second reason is that an exploration of attention can help us to understand what is involved in interests, and how students develop them. To illustrate, we can show the relationships in this way:

attention ▶ involvement

involvement ▶ interest

attention ▶ involvement ▶ interest

First comes **attention.** We called it the focusing of one's senses and mental facilities on objects, interactions, and ideas. If the attraction of objects, interactions, and ideas is great enough, one experiences **involvement.** Being involved means that an individual begins trying to do such things as accept, reject, remember, emulate, interpret, manipulate, rearrange, control, predict, expand, and extrapolate. If this involvement pays off — if it brings a preponderance of pleasure — the individual will wish to continue and repeat the involvement. That desire to continue and repeat involvement in an activity or experience is what we mean by **interest.**

Granted the great importance of attention (we called it the focusing of senses and mental facilities), let's think for a moment about what it is that seems to bring about attention. We will not consider physiological and psychological states within the individual such as fatigue, emotional trauma, or mental ability levels. They do affect attention — we will recognize that. But they are conditions over which we have little control.

We will consider instead a few kinds of noises and sights and sounds and ideas that seem to attract our attention, without any effort on our part to be attentive. We must note, too, that attention can purposely be focused on almost anything — even the most bland and unstimulating object — at least for short periods of time. For example, I find while writing this paragraph that I can focus my senses on the typewriter to see it in detail and listen to its racket, and I can think (oh, joy!) about its interior mechanical workings. But I don't find that too pleasurable, so it will probably never become one of my interests.

It is the distracting stimuli—sights, sounds, and so on that divert purposeful attention—that can tell us most about what it is that captures human attention. What do you suppose might draw your attention away from this page at this moment (as if such a thing were possible!)?

sounds: laughter, bells, screams, whistles, chatter, whispers, power mowers, dogs barking, lions roaring, fingernails tapping, stomachs growling, Moog Synthesizers performing

sights: flashing lights, brilliant colors, movements, patterns, illusions

smells: hamburgers, formaldehyde, B.O., wood smoke, lemon blossoms

the unexpected: a bird loose in the room, a girl seven and a half feet tall walking by, a five-dollar bill falling from the ceiling, a motorcycle running down the corridor (that happened in an elementary school and emptied six classrooms in record-breaking time)

And so we could go on naming such things:

the familiar in unfamiliar surroundings: You meet a neighbor (with whom you've spoken only three times in two years) in Yellowstone Park and it's a time for great celebration.

the beautiful and the ugly: They are only comparisons; you can't recognize the one without the other.

the extremes of acts and thoughts

the threats and dangers of the unknown

so what...

What can we make of all this?

One thing, at least — attention is attracted by whatever stands out as different, unusual, or unique when it is seen against the background that includes it. A single rock music selection may not be attention-grabbing in an hour-long program of rock music, but it surely would stand out if it were included in a concert of chamber music. A boy jumping rope in a physical education class might not attract attention, but let him give a demonstration of rope jumping in a physics class, and he will have the attention of everyone there.

As we mentioned earlier, if that thing to which we give attention turns out to be attractive enough, if it holds our attention strongly enough, we try to do something with it: label it, visualize it, memorize it, interpret it, repeat it, perform it, rearrange it, and so on and on. Those acts all form part of what I have called becoming involved with the material that has captured our attention.

If the rewards of that involvement are sufficiently great, the individual will wish to continue the involvement or repeat it later. The desire to continue, we said, and to repeat time after time, constitutes what we called interest. Thus interest depends on repeated experiences that have pleasurable or satisfying consequences.

To speak of consequences brings us back to the matter of needs: a consequence becomes pleasurable or satisfying when it meets a human need. Maslow, as we saw (p. 30), identified six human needs, and he thought that several of those needs could be satisfied through the kinds of experiences that can be provided by schools. You doubtless realize that great numbers of different activities can yield pleasurable and satisfying consequences, and that each consequence might help meet a particular need.

For instance, take the need that Maslow called the "need to know and understand." This need, like all others, operates continually; it waxes and wanes, but it is never satisfied once and for all. And it pervades all areas into which human thought can venture: the music of the Beatles, the life of the marine iguana, mimicry as a means of pollenating orchids, effective speech, the meaning of life.

But interests, unlike needs, refer to specific topics: Mexican food, oil painting, bird watching, ceramics, automobile racing, muscle building. Few people could tell you what their needs are, at least in the sense in which psychologists and teachers talk about needs. But most people can tell you what their interests are. You, of course, are able to do both. You can say, "I have a need to belong. I have several interests that help me to meet that need—clothes, hairstyles, music—to permit me to identify with and be accepted by _____."

Experienced teachers may not know about Maslow's hierarchy of needs either, but they can tell you, based upon their work with students, what things seem to make activities pleasurable and satisfying for learners. They can tell you that students are interested in—that is, they want to repeat—activities that include:

bodily movement: playing games, running, jumping, walking, moving about, twisting, turning, dancing, manipulating, constructing

mental stimulation: solving puzzles, answering riddles, creating, brainstorming, resolving paradoxes and incongruities

adventure: in live competition, observation, exploring, and outings, but especially vicariously in books, television, movies, plays, stories, dramatic play, fantasy

the presence of other people: for psychological support, camaraderie, cooperation, competition, esprit de corps, examples and models

success: improvement, facility, skill, and mastery, substantiated either through feedback from others (such as praise) or through self-evaluation of efforts

age x wants-interests

This title should be read *age by wants-interests.* The chart on the next page shows age levels of students and the "wants" and interests that appear in general to accompany those age levels. Of course there are exceptions. Notice also that "want" in this context is almost synonymous with "need."

Age × wants-interests

age level	wants (in this case meaning things students seek and/or respond well to)	interests (here retaining the meaning that has been used previously, i.e., specific activities)
5 to 8 years	assurance, physical activity, direct sensory experience, encouragement, praise, warmth, patience, concrete learning tasks	relating experiences, stories, dramatic play, pictures, songs, poems, rhythms, animals to organized games, models, dolls, jokes, gangs and clubs, collecting, comics, books on adventure, animals, foreign lands and people
9 to 10 years	praise, physical activity, group membership, being admired	riddles, jokes, puzzles, sharing, competitive games, trips, reading, maps, letters, animals, arts and crafts boys—wrestling, sports girls—jumping rope, jacks, cooking, sewing
preadolescent	affection, warmth, greater independence, peer group acceptance	riddles, jokes, puzzles, gang and club, sports, competitive and outdoor games, hobbies, construction, pets, movies, TV, comics, reading, drama
adolescent	acceptance by and conformation to peer group, kind, unobtrusive guidance by adults, security with independence	music, dancing, cars, opposite sex, sports, trips, TV, movies, magazines, gossip, intrigue, adult roles

curiosity

For some reason I remember vividly the first time I saw an experimenter "run rats" in the laboratory. I was just becoming interested in psychology as a discipline, and I had asked for and received permission to watch one night while a research assistant put the animals through their paces.

Tiers of cages stood about the room, clean, white, and well lighted. In the cages hundreds of white rats rustled about. Most of them were adults, though a few cages contained torn paper nests, in which lay litters of hairless pink infants. Some of the adult rats were involved as subjects in an experiment: they were placed in a maze which they "ran" (actually some walked very slowly) while the experimenter—in this case a laboratory assistant—kept track of their movements, the number of times they entered blind alleys, and how long it took them to move through the maze from the starting box to the goal box.

To give the rats incentive to move about, the experimenters had placed the animals on food-deprivation schedules that presumably left them hungry and eager to find food. They could partially satisfy this hunger by finding their way successfully to the end of the maze. There food lay in the goal box, so the rats had a satisfying little snack in store for them when they got there. The hypothesis was that the rats, as a result of repeated experiences, would learn the turns in the maze that led to the food, so that they would progressively find their way from starting box to goal box more quickly.

That was the way it worked out, for the most part. The assistant ran some

naive rats—rats placed for the first time in the maze—and some experienced rats, who had been through the maze a few times before. Sure enough, the experienced rats on the average got through the maze much faster and with far fewer errors than the naive rats.

However, there were two occurrences that have stuck in my mind over the years

from the maze turned his head and bit the assistant fiercely on the index finger. The assistant, taking umbrage at this breach of etiquette, threw the rat rudely back into its cage, shouting, "All right, you bastard, no water for you!"

The second thing that sticks in my mind is really a group of occurrences. These occurrences do, I believe, pertain to our topic. I noticed that when the naive rats were put in the starting box they spent a good deal of time sniffing about, with whiskers twitching, looking casually this way and that while moving slowly around the area. Some seemed to prefer staying in the starting box, occasionally rising up on their haunches and carefully exploring the place. Once in the maze this inquisitive behavior continued. Of course they had no idea food was waiting for them at the end of the tunnel. Still, they hardly were behaving as I had thought very hungry animals would, frantically seeking food.

Even more surprising to me was that some of the experienced rats—rats who "knew" food was at the end of the maze—also exhibited bits of this exploring behavior. They seemed curious enough about their surroundings to spend a few moments looking around before dashing through the maze to the goal box.

I think those white, pink-eyed rats, presumably quite hungry yet more or less nonchalantly exploring the maze, exasperated the experimenter. The zeitgeist—the overall outlook—at that time and place was drive reduction and deficit motivation: the rats were supposed to do whatever they did in the maze because they were hungry and because through their actions they could obtain food.

since that night. One of them has nothing whatsoever to do with our topic of motivation, at least so far as I know. But I'll mention it anyway. Most of the rats seemed (my inference) to enjoy being picked out of the goal box area by the assistant, handled gently (with affection?), and returned to their cages. However, one experienced rat being lifted

Curiosity is supposed to have killed the cat. I doubt that it did. There are an awful lot of cats around, and every one I see performs many acts that I would consider to be motivated by curiosity, by a desire to look something over carefully—something different, unusual, or not clearly seen.

That inclination-to-observe phenomenon, let's call it curiosity, is very evident in many species of animals: birds, cats, dogs, porpoises, chimpanzees, and humans, to name a few. And it is evidently a very strong motive. Harlow,* for instance, found that monkeys work harder at solving puzzles just to satisfy their curiosity than they work to obtain food and water. Teachers and parents know that children often do the same. Sometimes food must wait while the newly discovered caterpillar gets a careful looking over.

No convenient theory tells us why this thing we call curiosity operates. For the present it is enough to know that it does, in all students, and that we can use curiosity to good advantage in getting students involved in lessons. In the opening portions of this chapter I related two episodes that showed how students' curiosity led to involvement in lessons. One had to do with an incongruity—boiling water, a paper container, and an open flame just didn't seem to go together. Another had to do with novel objects, things students had not seen before. Both incongruity and novelty invariably seem to draw students' attention; students are puzzled by what they perceive there, and they want to reconcile their perceptions with previous experiences.

Mysteries and puzzles that are suited to the students' ages are also unusually attractive. If you want to see students so involved in an activity that they will hardly stop work on it, give them a puzzle to solve, like one of the following:

> #1 (for upper elementary through college)
> There is a circular race track 1 mile in circumference. A racing car driver decides to drive around it twice—she will make two laps. On the first lap she averages 30 mph. What must be her average speed on the second lap so she can average 60 mph for both laps together?
>
> Hint: You may think the answer is 90 mph. It isn't. Try thinking in terms of distance traveled per units of time (minutes, in this case).

*Harlow, H. F.: Mice, Monkeys, Men, and Motives, Psychol. Rev. **60**:23, 1953.

#2 (for upper elementary through college)
To gain further insight into the solution to #1, solve this similar problem, but be sure to use time and distance, not average of average speeds.

An automobile driver sets out to drive 10 miles. For the first 5 miles he averages 60 mph. For the second 5 miles he averages 70 mph. What was his average speed for the 10 miles? (Nope, not 65 mph.)

#3 (for high school and college)
You may move one of the matches from one side of the equal sign to the other to make a mathematically correct equation. Do not touch the equal sign.

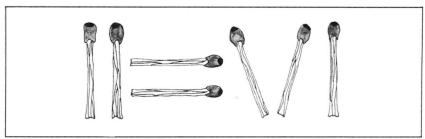

Hint: After you have racked your brain long enough, try thinking of signs.

#4 (middle elementary through college)
Without lifting your pencil from the page, draw four straight lines so that every dot is crossed.

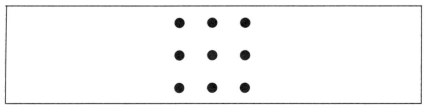

#5 (primary)
What animal am I? (Show a paper bag containing an imaginary animal.)
   The number of legs I have rhymes with door.
   My body is covered with something that rhymes with fair.
   I can make a noise that rhymes with lark.
Continue with the same for duck, squirrel, horse, etc.

To satisfy your curiosity, answers are on p. 114.

Most curriculum areas offer great opportunities to use puzzles and problems. What possibilities can you see for building them into geography (especially map skills), language, the natural sciences, and math? If you can think of some puzzles and problems, and use them, your students will be very appreciative.

Task components

If you refer back to p. 93 of this chapter, you will see our **class motivation model.** The discussions we have just completed concerned the three items listed in the top segment of the model: needs, interests, and curiosity. We now move to a consideration of the elements listed in the middle segment. Each of these elements can play a strong role in students' motivation, and though we will consider each only briefly, you will do well to try to build them into every lesson you teach to the greatest possible extent.

activities

Activity refers to physical movement, use of the senses, and such cognitive functions as perceiving, evaluating, and producing ideas. In the past, students have had overly heavy doses of the following prescription:

no physical movement,
    just sitting
limited use of only two senses,
    seeing to read and hearing to listen
heavy use of only two cognitive processes,
    perceiving and reproducing what was perceived

Yet philosophers, theorists, and practical experience have been telling us all along that students learn what they do. **Students have to be active doers, not passive receivers.** They must have physical movement involving such purposeful tasks as constructing, drawing, moving about, and manipulating objects. They must have an opportunity to use their senses in numerous ways: in general, the more senses students use in learning, the more they learn and the longer they remember. And they must have stimulating intellectual tasks—problems to solve, products to produce—that encourage the use of such higher cognitive processes as analyzing, evaluating, and synthesizing.

Activity: That's a key task element.

materials

Materials such as objects, flat pictures, models, charts, paints, saws, motion pictures, paper and scissors, animals, chemicals, and weights are indispensable task elements because activities and use of the senses require them. You have to have something to use your senses on. You have to have something to manipulate, tear apart, reconstruct.

Materials also expand the environment. How else can students "see" China except through pictures and motion pictures? Or even Navajo hogans, for that matter? How else can farm children see the inner city, or city children see the farm? How many students can hear the New York Philharmonic except through recordings? What student will see a molecule or Alpha Centauri or ultraviolet light without materials to use?

Piaget has given us even stronger evidence for the necessity of using materials with young children. His observations have indicated that students in elementary school can rarely perform "formal operations"; that is, solve problems in purely intellectual terms without the presence of concrete objects. Because they can solve problems if they have concrete objects to manipulate, Piaget selected the label "concrete operations" for this stage of mental development.

variety

. . . is the spice of life. That applies to students' lives in school just as much as to adults' lives outside school. We all—young and old alike—need periodic changes in the activities we perform, the materials we use, the people we work with, and the places (or at least the appearance of the places) where we live and work.

While such periodic changes are necessary for our students, what, how much, when, and how often the changes should be made can be determined only by carefully observing student reactions during instruction. We do need to be aware that we can provide too much change too rapidly, leaving students insecure and without a sense of direction, forcing them to spend much time learning new routines. Yet a lack of variety is far more common. Students become disinterested, lackadaisical, and disruptive. To avoid this, we watch for lagging attention, loss of enthusiasm, a tendency to daydream, nervous movement, and off-the-topic talk among students. When we note any of these, we can change the activity, the materials, the grouping, or the reward system.

As a rule of thumb, we can continue any activity so long as students respond well to it. But when they begin to lose interest, we had better be ready to give them something different to do.

specific objectives

You already know that specific objectives, stated in behavioral terms, are very helpful to you in teaching and evaluating. They have also proved themselves valuable in motivating students. Not only do they provide a definite sense of direction, but they also allow students to frequently enjoy feelings of success and accomplishment.

With a list of specific objectives, learners can be much more self-directing. Thus, when you have composed specific objectives, you should make those objectives known to your students. If you go a step further and provide a model of acceptable performance, all you have to do then is give the students a chance to practice the indicated behaviors and give them feedback about their efforts. Under these conditions, students play a strong role in directing their own learning activities, and they can also evaluate their efforts.

directly attainable goals

Nothing succeeds like success, they say. That old adage still rings true, and with regard to school learning it has been borne out by experimental evidence. The learner who encounters success seeks more of it. The learner who encounters repeated failure learns that there is little reason to try.

You can see the importance of helping learners set directly attainable goals for themselves. That doesn't necessarily mean *easily* attainable. Goals that are too easily reached present no challenge and no stimulation, and learners soon grow weary of them. Ideally, we want to help a learner set the kind of goals for himself that let him think:

> Here's something worth working for.
> By really applying myself
> I'm sure I can do it
> fairly soon.

friendly competition

"Friendly competition" is hardly an exact term. It is used here to indicate a process in which one tries to reach higher levels of performance than someone else, without at the same time doing psychological harm to the loser.

Competition is highly motivating. People constantly attempt to outdo each other; they are eager to do so. There are few games that don't include the win-lose concept, and in truth, most individuals spend much of their lives trying to better someone else.

But competition, despite its acknowledged motivating effects, can introduce some undesirable effects as well. It can be destructive when winning is everything, and humiliation is all that is left for the loser. All too often, anxiety, fear, pressure, and frustration result. So do cheating and bluffing. Moreover, some people argue that while competition may be more effective than cooperation in yielding technological and material advances, it corrodes human relations and makes harmonious coexistence more difficult—certainly a distressing condition in the face of growing congestion and increasing animosities among groups of people.

Competition, however, need not be destructive. There are ways of taking advantage of its motivating effects while avoiding its undesirable effects. The key lies in finding ways to remove the stigma from losing. One way to do this is to devise ways for an individual to compete against himself so that he is both winner and loser in his own competition. This is a very common practice in golf, for example. Most golfers find more satisfaction in playing well, regardless of the outcome, than they do in winning while playing poorly. They continually compete against their past records. In the same way, students can compete against their past records and try to do better in any curriculum or special interest area than they have done before. However, the charts showing their efforts must be kept confidential. Otherwise the process inevitably turns to the comparison of one person against another.

Another way to reduce harmful aspects of competition is to arrange activities so that each person wins part of the time and loses part of the time. Still another is to find ways for every student to be "best" in something—in neatness, punctuality, attendance, completion of assignments, special hobbies and outside interests. And yet another is to set up team activities, like athletic teams but in content areas, where each team member must cooperate and do his part to advance the team as a whole.

models to imitate

Students identify with other people, usually with those who are somewhat older than themselves, and imitate their behavior. They imitate people who are successful (by whatever criteria) and who are "with it" (usually meaning that they can cope with aspects of life in poised, sophisticated ways). Interestingly enough, students often identify with teachers, who have a decent chance of being seen as successful, with-it, wise, and even beautiful in appearance and acts. This is especially true if those teachers relate well to students, listen to them, accept them, and show willingness to help them with problems.

Quite frequently eminent people, when asked what gave them their first great push, identify a teacher who kindled their imaginations and encouraged (and prodded) them to make the most of a talent. Almost all teachers, whether or not they have taught a person recognized as "great," strongly influence the lives of at least some of their students.

Thus you have the potential for serving as a model for your students, both personally and intellectually. If you show enthusiasm for learning, your students will be more likely to follow suit. If you get excited—genuinely excited—about reading and biology and whatever else, so will many, maybe most, of your students.

You won't be the only model your students will imitate. There will be other live people, adults and students, naively exerting their influence. There will be actors and singers and athletes. There may even be heroes of the past and fictional characters. But still, of them all, you have by far the greatest opportunity to shape, by example, your students' dispositions toward learning.

Reward systems

Experimenters in behavior modification tell us we can get students to do practically anything we want them to, if we can just find pay-off systems that are attractive enough. Critics, admitting that every person has a price, would call such strategies "buy-off" systems. They scorn extrinsic rewards, considering them subversive to the aims of "true" education, one of which is learning for the enjoyment of learning.

Proponents then counter with the argument that love of learning develops from pleasurable experiences with learning. If learners first obtain pleasure only through earning stars, candy, and prizes, then those are what they must have. Later they will generalize that pleasure to the learning task itself. Success will be reward enough.

Regardless of who is philosophically "right," this fact remains: reward systems can significantly increase students' motivation to work at curricular tasks. These systems need not be elaborate. In fact, they are usually so simple it's stretching the point to call them systems (system, in this case, means nothing more than consistent method and order).

That consistency of method and order is the key to ensuring that learners experience pleasure as a result of their efforts to learn. A reward must be supplied just after the learner has responded appropriately. It should be given on both a short-term basis and a long-term basis. A short-term reward, given frequently during a lesson, guides learning and sustains effort. A long-term reward, supplied at the end of a more lengthy effort, encourages perseverance.

The term "reward" may be carrying the ring of coin and the gleam of jewel to your mind. It rarely amounts to that. Learners—all of us really—find reward in the simplest of things:

having fun	I enjoy myself, laugh, compete, cooperate, interact with friends.
being correct	Someone may tell me I am right, or I may just know it. I have the feeling of growing expertise.
being first	I am best or highest in something, at least occasionally.
receiving attention	Someone notices me—my existence and my acts make a difference somehow.
receiving acceptance	I am received with favor, I am approved, I belong.
receiving praise	Someone thinks I am special. I have done something laudable. I grow even worthier in my own eyes.
receiving privileges	What could be more fair? I work, I try, I succeed—now I don't have to take the exam. (Or I get to operate the projector or I am placed in charge of the playground equipment or . . . .)
receiving tangibles	My efforts to learn *do* pay off, not just in idle words, but in something I can see, feel, enjoy—this candy, this prize, this money.

Rare is the student who will not respond well to the first seven of these types of rewards. They are enough for the usual class. If we include the eighth, we can find something that helps motivate virtually every student we encounter. In sum, students know a reward is possible, whether it is a smile, praise, a plastic disc, or simply correct achievement. They know they can earn it, and they know how. If they want it, they will make the effort.

The model again

Now that we have considered its elements, we will close this chapter by taking another look at our **class motivation model for teachers.**

class motivation model for teachers
In any learning activity

capitalize on students'
needs, interests, curiosity

through instructional tasks involving
activities, materials, variety,
specific objectives, directly attainable goals,
friendly competition, models to imitate

that will allow each student to
have fun, be correct,
be first (occasionally), receive attention,
receive acceptance, receive praise,
receive privileges, receive tangibles

answers to the mysteries, pp. 104-105

#1 It can't be done. It has taken the driver 2 minutes to complete the first lap. Therefore she cannot possibly average 60 mph for both laps, because in order to do that she would have to complete them both in a total of 2 minutes.

#2 64.58 mph

#3 This mystery has two solutions:

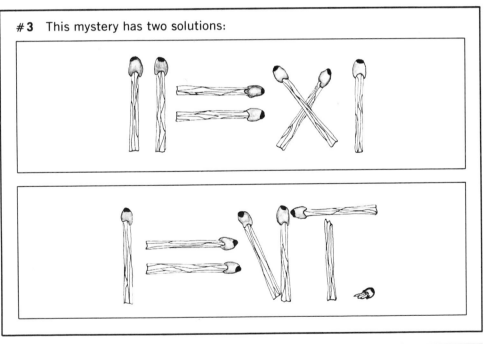

#4

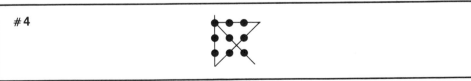

#5 If you can't handle this, ask someone else's kid brother.

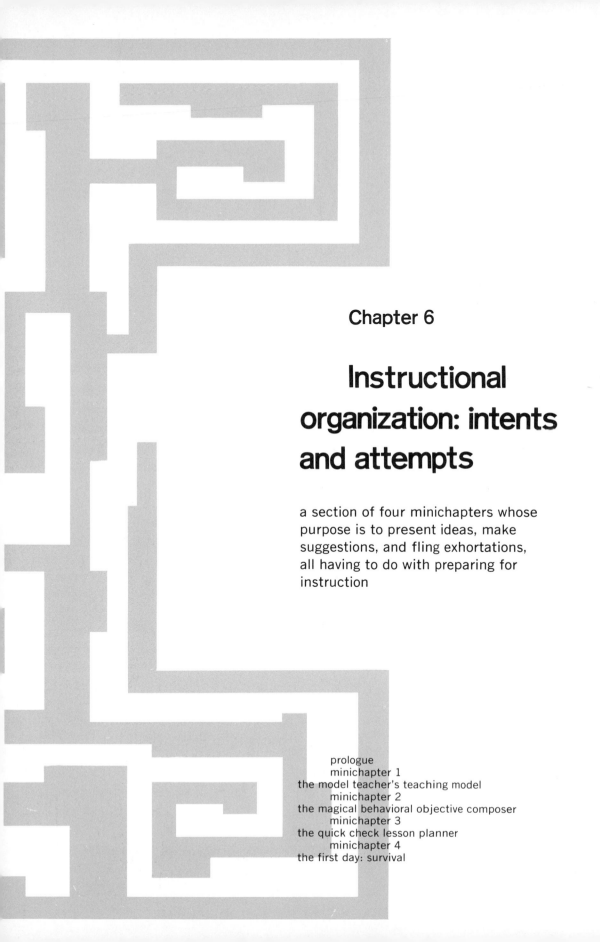

Chapter 6

Instructional organization: intents and attempts

a section of four minichapters whose
purpose is to present ideas, make
suggestions, and fling exhortations,
all having to do with preparing for
instruction

PROLOGUE

Here are your goats.
They are hungry.
You'd best take them
to the mountain to graze.

Yes, yes, I will. Of course.
But I've never been
on the mountain.
Will you give me a map?

A map?
Ah . . . well . . . . I haven't any.
But no matter.
Just sit there
and make yourself one.
But be quick, hear?
Or the goats will be
gone.

beginning with minichapter 1

the model teacher's teaching model

On the next page
you will see a
model of teaching.

On the pages that follow
you will see how that
model of teaching
was built.

a model of teaching

general objectives for learners → perceiving
relating
reproducing
analyzing
applying
evaluating
producing
with
willingness
enjoyment
commitment

that reach

and emotional climates

open
warm
nonthreatening
nonpunitive

indicate teaching functions

planning
   diagnosing
   formulating objectives
   selecting method
   arranging activities
   selecting instructional
     materials
implementing-facilitating
   motivating
   introducing
   guiding, managing
   soliciting responses
   reinforcing
   disciplining
   culminating
evaluating
   appraising
   judging
   recycling

Teaching: prismatic facets

I saw a good teacher

"I saw a real pro teach yesterday. He was marvelous."
"Yeah? What was so good about him?"
"He was . . . he . . . his . . . he was terrific!"

2 questions compared

We're out to improve our teaching ability. We want to be as good as that "real pro." Most of us, though, don't just automatically become good. Before we can become skilled we must come to grips with what teaching is all about. To do that, let's start by comparing two questions about teaching:

> question #1: What is teaching?
> question #2: What do teachers do when they teach?

Question #1 may look good and short. It is short. It is not good. If it were a road, it would be a short road to nowhere (except maybe the dictionary). If question #2 were a road, it would be longer and winding. If we traveled it, we would probably miss part of the country. But at least the road would take us to some of the places we should see. It would be a road to somewhere.

well, then, what does a good teacher...

Don't think of teaching as a single act. Think of it as a **composite** of acts—a composite like a huge and many-faceted diamond, with each facet casting a bright but elusive bit of light—a composite of so many different parts that it almost defies description. Almost, but not quite. We will be bold. We will try to catch glimpses of the different acts, pin them down, put them into groups we can take hold of. We will even be so audacious as to make ourselves a model of teaching. We will make the model so that we can get at its component parts and use them as guides for planning.

Here's how we will go about the matter.

> First, let's see what we hope learners will come to do/possess/feel in the very general cognitive, psychomotor, and affective areas.

> Second, let's see what teachers do, in general, to reach the objectives held for learners. We will call these general groups of teacher acts "teaching functions."

> Third, let's examine the emotional climate teachers try to create and maintain through their tasks and techniques.

This whole matter may sound jumbled and complex. Complex it may be. Jumbled it will not (I hope) remain.

General objectives for learners

Here you see a listing of what teachers intend, in general, that learners come to do/possess/feel. I use the labels "cognitive," "psychomotor," and "affective." Cognitive refers to **knowing.** Psychomotor refers to physical **doing.** Affective refers to emotional **feeling.**

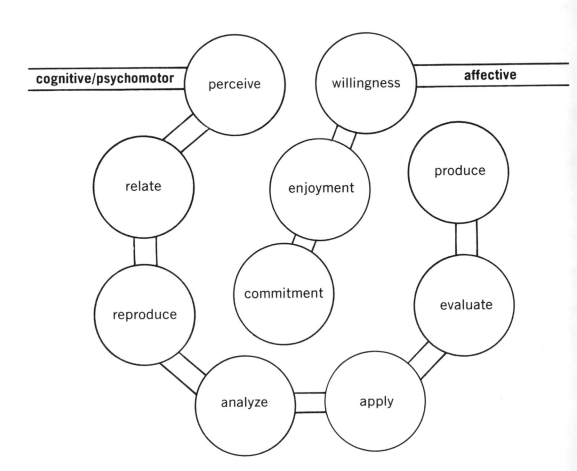

meanings & specifics

perceive

to become aware of

relate

to group; note similarities, differences, proportions, arrangements, means, causes, effects, etc.

willingness

a disposal to act without reluctance

reproduce

to repeat from memory by telling, drawing, acting out, assembling, etc.

enjoyment

a feeling of anticipation and pleasure in acting.

analyze

to break or separate into component parts

apply

to use in a new situation something learned in a previous situation

commitment

a sense of the correctness, desirability, necessity of an act

evaluate

to determine worth or quality

produce

to restructure existing parts in ways new to the learner

Teaching functions

Here we list general teaching functions. They are groupings of acts teachers perform to reach the objectives they have established for learners. Each of these general functions has several specific components, noted in the following paragraphs and examined in detail in later chapters.

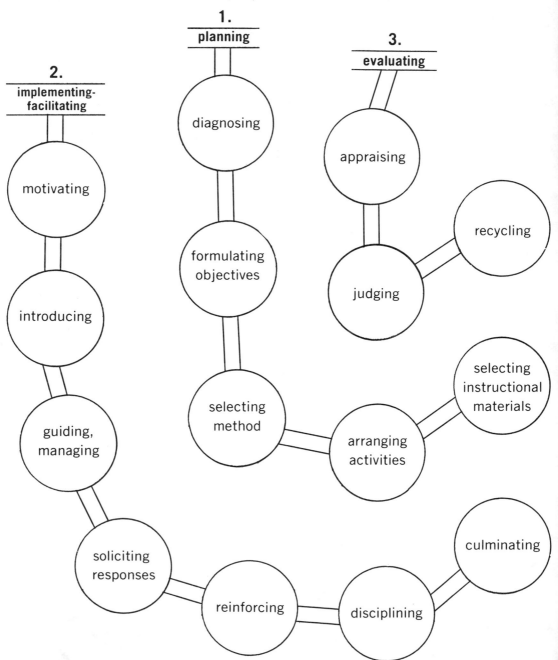

meanings & specifics

planning
preparing to teach specific topics to specific students

diagnosing
determining students' needs and weaknesses

formulating objectives
stating behaviors that students are to come to possess

selecting method
deciding whether instructional techniques will be telling, showing, questioning, or (student) doing

arranging activities
organizing instructional sessions

selecting instructional materials
choosing materials appropriate to the objectives, method, and activities you will use in the lesson

implementing-facilitating

putting activities into effect and helping students follow through

motivating

causing students to begin and sustain work — may be accomplished by building activities around psychological needs (muscle activity, achievement, esteem, affection), interests (pets, games, sports, cars, etc.), curiosity (the novel, incongruous, colorful, tangible, puzzling), variety, success, usefulness

introducing

leading into a lesson

guiding, managing

directing students' activities and handling classroom routines

soliciting responses

asking questions or giving directions that cause students to act

reinforcing

providing recognition and praise to increase the correctness of student responses

disciplining

helping students maintain self-control necessary for productive activity (primarily through preventive control — avoiding boredom, fatigue, frustration, ignorance of rules, and diversions — and corrective control — redirecting misbehavior through review of work rules, eye and hand signals, physical proximity, hurdle help, restructuring of activity, isolation, and deprivation)

culminating

bringing the lesson to a satisfactory close

evaluating

making judgments about learning and teaching (accuracy, completeness, improvement, efficiency, permanence, usefulness) and making plans for improvement

appraising

examining students' abilities to perform the acts that were the objectives of the lesson

judging

examining teaching acts and materials to determine the contribution each has made toward reaching the objectives

recycling

using insights gained through appraising and judging to modify future instruction to better meet student needs

Emotional climate: the warm and happy hours

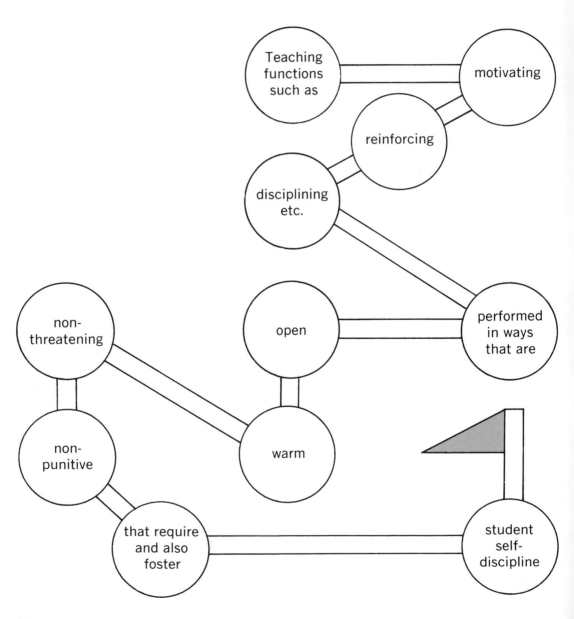

So far as we know, these elements comprise a near-ideal emotional climate for learning —near-ideal because this climate seems to yield the highest overall levels of student achievement, desire to learn, self-direction, ability to work with others, and enjoyment of school.

meanings & specifics

open

classroom climate allows diversity, freedom to explore, multiple "correct" responses, high level of student involvement in planning

warm

students have a sense of belonging; the teacher is fair, friendly, consistent, enthusiastic, with a sense of humor

nonthreatening

rules for class conduct and work procedures are carefully worked out by the entire group, so students know clearly what is expected; coercive methods for class work are not used, the threat of failure, corporal punishment, humiliation is proscribed

nonpunitive

errors are allowable and when made are turned to instructional purposes; corrective discipline involves the students' "making right" what they did wrong—no grudges held, no sarcasm or humiliation used

self-discipline

students maintain efficient work habits and effective interpersonal relations through a knowledge of rules, a sense of purpose and direction, and ample opportunity to achieve

Now, putting the described elements all back together, we again have

a model of teaching

a model of teaching

general objectives for learners

perceiving
relating
reproducing
analyzing
applying
evaluating
producing
with
willingness
enjoyment
commitment

that reach

indicate teaching functions

planning
diagnosing
formulating objectives
selecting method
arranging activities
selecting instructional
materials
implementing-facilitating
motivating
introducing
guiding, managing
soliciting responses
reinforcing
disciplining
culminating
evaluating
appraising
judging
recycling

and emotional climates

open
warm
nonthreatening
nonpunitive

herewith commences

the magical behavioral objective composer

in two parts:

- an illumination and persuasion section
(only for those who need/want it)

- the magical behavioral objective composer
itself

minichapter 2

You noticed that the model of teaching began and ended with general objectives for learners. You must convert general objectives into specific objectives to plan daily instruction.

**the magical
behavioral objective composer**
shows you how to do just that, quickly and easily, with a minimum of tears.

arguments

Critics of behavioral objectives present two strong arguments against their use:

1. That which can be stated in behavioral terms tends not to be greatly important—certainly not so important as some of the "intangibles" as, for example, patriotism, aesthetic appreciation, and genuine understanding.

2. Behaviorally stated objectives limit achievement by putting ceilings on student aspirations and by not encouraging unexpected (creative) responses.

Advocates of behavioral objectives counter those arguments with these:

1. Discussions about the "importance" of intangibles are nonproductive. Important or not, you can never know whether an intangible objective is reached, so it is far better to concentrate on the attainable.

2. Attainment of objectives does not reduce student aspirations. To the contrary, success is highly motivating. Further, the act of making divergent (creative) responses can be stated in behavioral terms. Example: the student can describe three unusual uses for a plastic comb.

rationale

Teachers must know, after their teaching efforts:
1. *whether* learning occurred
2. as precisely as possible, *what* learning occurred

If they don't know these two things, they can't assess learning and they can't improve teaching.

When you search for *evidence* of learning, you can find it only in what students *do*. Since you can't know what happens inside your students' minds, you must judge learning and teaching by what they say, write, demonstrate, act out, etc.

NOTICE

When we speak of what students do, we speak of acts. When we describe acts, we must use action verbs that represent observable acts.

verbs: examples of "goodies"		verbs: examples of "baddies"	
write		know	
tell	observable —	understand	not
sing	you can see	appreciate	observable —
jump	or hear the	enjoy	you can't see
listen	acts	internalize	or hear the acts

N.B. Nobody says "appreciate" is a bad *idea.* It just isn't observable. You still have to decide what a person *does* when he appreciates.

Now, if we use such action verbs (observable) when formulating our specific objectives for learners, we can check later to see if they are reached. If they are, the students can so indicate through what they do.

**using observable acts
for objectives
also helps students,
for it lets them know precisely
what is expected of them**

usefulness

Questions persist as to whether behavioral objectives are a real help to teachers or merely a passing fad.

Eisner* points out that despite the great attention given behavioral objectives, teachers seem not to take them seriously. He contends that if they were really helpful, teachers would use them. Popham and Baker** found that a group of secondary teachers had positive attitudes toward behavioral objectives, but still made little use of them. But Popham believes that's just because writing the objectives is too time-consuming.

When you have tried writing them as prescribed by leading proponents, you can't disagree about the time and effort involved. You not only have to state the objectives behaviorally, you also must state all the "givens," the conditions under which the behavior is to occur, and the levels of acceptable performance.

I don't believe all that is necessary. In teaching, we want to think in terms of observable student acts. We don't need to write down every word for every condition.

The **magical behavioral objective composer** will help us do the necessary and skip the unnecessary.

And with that, we launch into it. . . .

*Eisner, E. W.: Educational Objectives: Help or Hindrance? School Rev. **75**:250, 1967.
Popham, W. J., and Baker, E. L.: Measuring Teachers' Attitudes Toward Behavioral Objectives, J. Educ. Res. **60:453, 1967.

magical * behavioral objectile * composer

1. decide what you want the student to be able to do after the lesson is completed (not what the teacher will do - not what the student will do during the lesson)

2. since you need evidence for #1, you must look for a student act or product of act (meaning, you gotta think of action verbs - see the next page for a convenient, handy list)

3. plug the action verbs into the magic grid presented below, like this:

subject: _math_

objectives	action verb	object of verb	special conditions, if any
1.	add	3-digit numbers	complete 10 problems in 10 minutes - all correct
2.			
3.			

remember - these objectiles are what we want students to be able to do after an instructional episode

however, the instructional activity may sometimes be very similar to the behavioral objective

A abbreviate, abstract, accent, accept, act out, add, aid, alphabetize, analyze, apply, appraise, argue, arrange, assemble, attend, avoid

B bake, balance, beat, bisect, bat, bounce, bring, build

C calculate, carry, categorize, change, choose, circle, cite, classify, collect, color, combine, compare, complete, compose, compute, construct, contrast, count, cut

D deduce, defend, define, demonstrate, derive, describe, design, detect, develop, diagram, differentiate, discriminate, discuss, display, distinguish, divide, draw

E edit, employ, enter, entertain, estimate, evaluate, exaggerate, examine, exit, expand, explain, express, extend, extrapolate

F fill in, find, finish, fix, fold, follow, formulate

G gallop, gather, generalize, get, give, give in own words, go, graph, grasp, group

H handle, halt, hang, help, hit, hold, hop, hum, hurry, hyphenate

I identify, illustrate, include, increase, induce, indent, indicate, infer, interact, interpolate, interpret, itemize

J join, jot down, judge, juggle, jump, justify

K keep, kick, knead, kneel, knit, knock

L label, lead, lengthen, level, lighten, list, listen, loan, locate, look

M make, manage, map, march, mark, match, measure, meet, mix, modify, mold, mote, multiply

N name, negotiate, note, notice, notify, number

O obey, observe, omit, open, operate, order, organize, originate, outline

P paint, paraphrase, paste, perform, place, plan, play, point to, pour, predict, prepare, present, produce, propose, prove, pull, punctuate, push

Q question, quit, quote

R read, rearrange, recall, recite, recognize, record, relate, reorder, rephrase, report, represent, resolve, restate, restructure, revise, run

S say, select, separate, set, share, show, sing, sketch, solve, speak, specify, spell, state, stop, subtract, summarize, support, synthesize

T tabulate, take, talk, tally, tell, toss, total, trace, translate, transform, transfer, transmit, type

U underline, underscore, unite, use, utilize

V validate, vary, verify, view, voice, volunteer, vote

W wait, wash, watch, weave, work, wrap, write

X,Y,Z

some action verbs having to do with teaching-learning, alphabetically arranged, for use with the magical*behavioral*objective*composer

proceeding now to minichapter 3

the quick check lesson planner

consisting of
**the quick check
lesson planner**
and instructions
for the use of same

THE QUICK CHECK LESSON PLANNER

subject _____ time _____
date _____

OBJECTIVES

act	object	conditions	general objectives	sample action verbs
			perceive	note, point to
			relate	group, associate
			reproduce	repeat, draw
			analyze	divide, separate
			apply	use, solve
			evaluate	compare, judge
			produce	make, write

IMPLEMENTATION-FACILITATION

grouping
large
small
individual

names/responsibilities

method
telling
showing
questioning
(student) doing

sequence/names/acts

motivators
special interests
novelty
problems or puzzles
manipulable objects
competition
other:

student activities
acting out
answering
computing
constructing
discussing
drawing
listening
observing
reading
singing
taking notes
telling
writing
other:

sequence/specifics/management

materials
charts
equipment
filmstrips
games
globe
kit
lab
library books
maps
models
motion pictures
objects
pencil and paper
pictures
programs
recordings
references
supplies
textbooks
workbooks, worksheets
other:

reinforcers
fun
achievement
knowledge of results
praise, approval

marks, stars, etc.
tokens, candy, etc.
special privileges
other:

EVALUATION: MEANS OF APPRAISAL

informal observation
formal observation

student self-appraisal
oral exam

written exam
other:

Instructions for use

objectives

State behavioral objectives in as few words as necessary, using the "act-object-conditions" outline. Note the reminder of general objectives and sample action verbs provided in the right-hand column under "objectives." For refresher information see the **magical behavioral objective composer.**

---

example:

act	object	conditions
1. *identify*	*Peruvian hats (Cuzco and Huancayo)*	*teacher provides real hats*
2. *list*	*3 similarities, 3 differences between these and modern American women's hats*	

---

implementation-facilitation

Select the method(s) to be used in the lesson. Then select a student grouping for the lesson. Draw an arrow from the method through the grouping. Then identify by name the people and materials involved in carrying out the major instructional responsibilities. List these under the "names-responsibilities" heading.

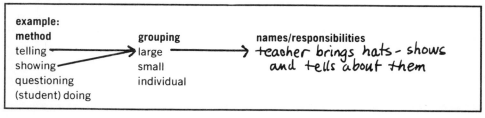

example:

method	grouping	names/responsibilities
telling	large	*teacher brings hats - shows and tells about them*
showing	small	
questioning	individual	
(student) doing		

Select the kind of motivator to be used. Sequence the motivators, including specific names and acts.

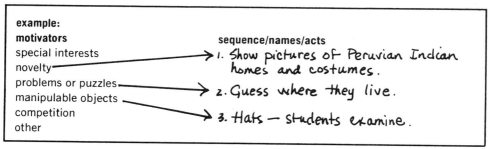

example:

motivators	sequence/names/acts
special interests	1. Show pictures of Peruvian Indian homes and costumes.
novelty	2. Guess where they live.
problems or puzzles	3. Hats — students examine.
manipulable objects	
competition	
other	

Select the type of student activity appropriate for reaching the stated objectives. Sequence the activities by drawing arrows into the "sequence/specifics/management" column. Include the names of specific activities, for example, drawing mural.

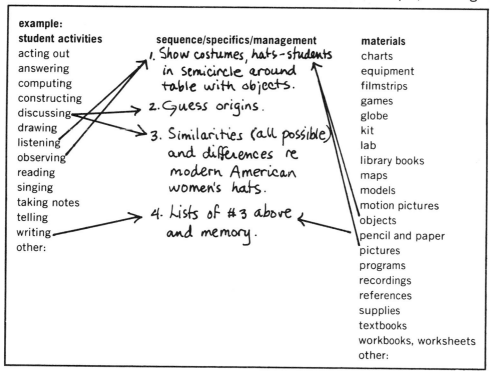

example:

student activities	sequence/specifics/management	materials
acting out	1. Show costumes, hats - students in semicircle around table with objects.	charts
answering		equipment
computing		filmstrips
constructing		games
discussing	2. Guess origins.	globe
drawing		kit
listening	3. Similarities (all possible) and differences re modern American women's hats.	lab
observing		library books
reading		maps
singing		models
taking notes		motion pictures
telling	4. Lists of #3 above and memory.	objects
writing		pencil and paper
other:		pictures
		programs
		recordings
		references
		supplies
		textbooks
		workbooks, worksheets
		other:

Select materials appropriate to the activities. Draw arrows from the material you have selected to the activity sequence. Note any special management procedures to be used with each activity-material, if necessary.

example:
see the box above

143

Select and indicate the principal reinforcers you will use. If necessary, draw an arrow and elaborate in the space at right.

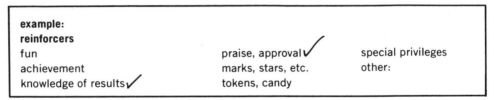

> **example:**
> **reinforcers**
> fun
> achievement
> knowledge of results ✓
>
> praise, approval ✓
> marks, stars, etc.
> tokens, candy
>
> special privileges
> other:

evaluation: means
of appraisal

Your behavioral objectives indicate what you expect your students to be able to do. Now, you must see whether students can do those things set forth in the objectives. Select and circle the means you will use to appraise student performance.

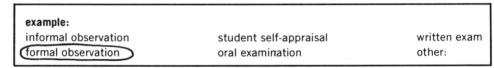

> **example:**
> informal observation
> (formal observation)
>
> student self-appraisal
> oral examination
>
> written exam
> other:

Let's take one more look at

THE

QUICK CHECK

LESSON

PLANNER

THE QUICK CHECK LESSON PLANNER

subject_____
date_____ time_____

OBJECTIVES

act	object	conditions		general objectives	sample action verbs
				perceive	note, point to
				relate	group, associate
				reproduce	repeat, draw
				analyze	divide, separate
				apply	use, solve
				evaluate	compare, judge
				produce	make, write

IMPLEMENTATION–FACILITATION

method
telling
showing
questioning
(student) doing

grouping
large
small
individual

names/responsibilities

motivators
special interests
novelty
problems or puzzles
manipulable objects
competition
other.

sequence/names/acts

student activities
acting out
answering
computing
constructing
discussing
drawing
listening
observing
reading
singing
taking notes
telling
writing
other:

sequence/specifics/management

materials
charts
equipment
filmstrips
games
globe
kit
lab
library books
maps
models
motion pictures
objects
pencil and paper
pictures
programs
recordings
references
supplies
textbooks
workbooks, worksheets
other:

reinforcers
fun
achievement
knowledge of results
praise, approval

marks, stars, etc.
tokens, candy, etc.
special privileges
other:

EVALUATION: MEANS OF APPRAISAL

informal observation
formal observation

student self-appraisal
oral exam

written exam
other:

we move on to minichapter 4

the first day: survival

to put ice water in the veins
for the first hot encounter
with cold reality—
the first day: survival

Student teachers near the end of their final semester were talking about next year, when they would be on their own in the classroom.

"I really think I can do it now," said one. "At least I hope so."

"Me, too," said another. "But I wish we'd had a little more student teaching. They ought to give us more."

"Hah! You wouldn't say that if you'd been with the class I had," said a third. "Two more weeks and I'd have been ready for the funny farm. I still have no idea about how to teach a normal group of kids."

"I imagine you'll learn that pretty quickly once you're in your own classroom."

And so the discussion continued for a while until Judith said, "I feel okay except for one thing—what do you do the very first day?"

"Yeah, I know. That worries me, too."

"Yeah."

Most beginning teachers are as worried as Judith about the first day of teaching. "If I can just get past that," they say, "I know I can handle the rest." How well you get through, and past, that first day depends a lot on the planning you do beforehand, and on the diligence with which you take care of the necessary preliminaries.

Countdown

the week before school starts

You will need to put in a good week's work before school starts. Use this checklist. It will help you make necessary preparations for either elementary or secondary teaching.

If school starts on *Monday,* have these things finished by the *previous Thursday:*

Get a copy of the school or district handbook — that should provide the following information. *If it does not, ask the principal about each item.* You must have this information firmly in mind.

- fire, earthquake, and other emergency drill procedures
- doors, staircases, halls for quick exits
- meanings of all signal bells
- procedures for students entering, leaving, and assembling in building
- regulations regarding visitors in the classroom
- provisions for covering the class when you must leave
- procedures to follow when you must be absent
- regulations regarding students leaving the room or leaving school prior to dismissal time
- means of recording attendance
- responsibilities regarding students who are truant
- provisions for students eating lunch at school
- means of securing services of the nurse, clerk, and custodian
- responsibilities for lunchroom and yard duties
- responsibilities for the plan book
- procedures for obtaining textbooks, general supplies, audiovisual materials, physical education equipment, and typing services

Introduce yourself to teachers, secretaries, custodians, nurses, and other school people who are there. Be friendly.

1 Look around your classroom. Get the approximate measurements of walls and areas. Mark midpoints. Begin deciding on themes for the first bulletin boards, pictures, and objects. Select a color scheme, using cool colors if the weather is warm. Make a list of the materials needed for bulletin boards, special work-study areas, and so on.

2 Visit the audiovisual center. Place orders for slides, motion pictures, flat pictures, filmstrips, etc. Don't wait. The good materials will be scheduled early.

3 Check the equipment already in your room. Compare what is there with what is needed. Submit an order immediately to the principal for equipment you will need.

4 Check physical education equipment, if any, to see that it is ready for use.

7 Locate textbooks and instructional materials. Ask the principal for a list of the materials with which you will be provided.

8 Locate and begin using the supply rooms and teachers' workroom.

9 Get coat hangers for the coat room, vases and flowers, dust rag, and small broom. See that the flag and alphabet are in place.

10 Visit the school library. Arrange for the use of books as necessary.

11 Locate the play area for your students.

12 Prepare charts of what games will be played on what days. Later, place the chart on the classroom window, facing out. Ask an experienced teacher for help if you need it.

13 Prepare charts for the names of class officers and for monitors who will be responsible for paper, the library, chalkboards, erasers, etc.

14 Take care of personal medical requirements.

15 If luncheons are held with parents, make a point of attending and talking with others who are there.

You can use *Friday* and *Saturday* — and *Sunday,* if necessary — to take care of the following:

1 Have bulletin boards, pictures, maps, charts, models, aquarium, etc. set up in the classroom.

2 Have reading and/or special study corners arranged and stocked with the necessary materials.

3 Learn the suggested and required time limits for instruction, recess, and other special time periods that occur during the day.

4 Have a calendar and schedules mounted so that all students can see them.

5 Print name tags for students you expect in class (primary grades).

6 Place student textbooks on the desks, or be ready to assign them quickly and efficiently.

7 Prepare a system of saving and filing the students' papers in each subject area. The papers will be useful for open house and for conferences with parents, who want to see evidence.

the first day

Come to school about an hour early. Read mail and bulletins in the office. Have coffee, if you wish. Be sure your classroom is locked.

Elementary teachers:

- Thirty minutes before school starts, go out on the grounds and locate your class. If there are new students, send them with their parents to the office to enroll. Talk with the children and parents. Be friendly.
- About ten minutes before the bell rings, have your students get a drink. Show them where to line up to go into the room. Unlock your door.
- Appoint a student to help seat any parents or visitors who may enter the room. Tell the students to put their lunches on designated shelves in back of the room.
- Have the class enter the room while you wait by the door to enter last.
- Go to the front of the room and lead the flag salute and a song. Be business-like, and do not waste time.

A general lesson plan, showing some possible activities for the first day, will follow. But first, here are some ideas you should try to keep in mind. Check yourself on them frequently.

Look your best. It will help your morale.

Be friendly, relaxed, and calm. Talk softly. Keep your voice pleasant, just loud enough to be heard in the back of the room.

Try hard to do less talking and have the students do more discussing.

Be friendly but efficient. Get to work quickly. Cut waste motion to a minimum.

About three minutes before recess, noon, or the end of school, make the assignment for the next activity. Then have students clean up, get playground equipment, lunch money, or coats. Begin and dismiss right on time.

Set standards and times for sharpening pencils. Have a supply of sharpened pencils on your desk.

Don't let students run in or out of the room. When the class walks together, teach students to walk single file, in pairs, or four abreast, an arm's-length apart. If the children are prone to hit and shove, have them walk with hands held behind them.

During the first week, practice fire drills on three different days just before physical education, then dismiss for play. Children who do not exit properly during the drills should practice again before playing.

Handle almost all the discipline yourself. Don't go to the principal until you have exhausted other avenues. Speak with parents in person or by phone. Have the parents come to school, if possible. If you think it is necessary, inform the principal of the problem and what you are doing to correct it. Ask for backing and suggestions.

Before leaving at the end of each day, put the assignments for all groups on the board. Get paper, books, and other materials ready for the next day's work.

some first day activities

elementary

first hour

opening exercise Lead the flag salute and a patriotic song, then tell the class to be seated. Discuss the theme of the bulletin boards in the room.

introductions Introduce yourself and point to your name written on the board above the attendance number. Tell something about yourself, including a recent interesting experience. Ask each pupil to come to the front of the room, introduce himself, and tell something about himself.

social studies Show students the location of special materials, books, etc. that will be used in social studies and show students how they are to be obtained and replaced. Set up the room government. Appoint monitors. If there is a text, introduce it by scanning the table of contents and some of the interesting pictures.

second hour

language It is good practice to have language follow social studies, since many good activities such as outlining, listing, story writing and story telling, and dramatic play with dialogue come naturally from social studies. Today, read the class a story or several poems related to the theme shown on the bulletin boards. You may want to leave the ending off of a story to let the class tell how they think it ended and why.

music Spend some time getting acquainted with the music book if the class has one. Sing one or two familiar songs.

recess

third hour

arithmetic Read and discuss some thought problems. Investigate the text. Try a quick review exercise in number facts. Introduce interesting new materials that will be used during the year.

noon

fourth hour

spelling and handwriting Examine the new texts. Make a cover for the speller from butcher paper you have already cut to size. Teach the first spelling lesson. Words should be on the board.

physical education During the last 20 minutes of the hour, organize teams for physical education. Take the children to the play area and introduce them to the game that will be played.

fifth hour

reading Show assignments written on the board. Introduce children to the basal readers. You may begin an informal reading survey to confirm the reading abilities shown on records from last year, if they are available. Have the students read in groups, each from a basal reader a year below grade level. Have art seatwork (coloring) ready for children at their desks.

Be sure you have planned more than can be done during the day. Have ready — should you need them — some games and seatwork. At the end of the day, spend a short time letting the children summarize what was done during the day. Instead of making assignments, talk everything over with the pupils.

secondary or departmentalized elementary

first

Introduce yourself. Give your name, background, experience, and a short account of a very interesting recent experience.

Then each student can tell about himself, or students can pair off, converse, and then each student can introduce the other member of the pair. Introductions can be varied to include such things as the student's greatest accomplishment or his most interesting experience of the summer.

second

Briefly describe the nature of the course—content and ways of working. You could begin with a discussion of what students expect.

third

Introduce textbooks, looking at the table of contents, sample illustrations, and ways in which each text will be used.

fourth

Examine samples of equipment and special materials to be used in the course.

fifth

Examine and discuss a sample lesson plan that shows behavioral objectives, activities, and materials.

sixth

Discuss possible ways of evaluating student performance. Consider student suggestions

seventh

Open with a game, thought problem, etc. that is typical of activities to be included in the course.

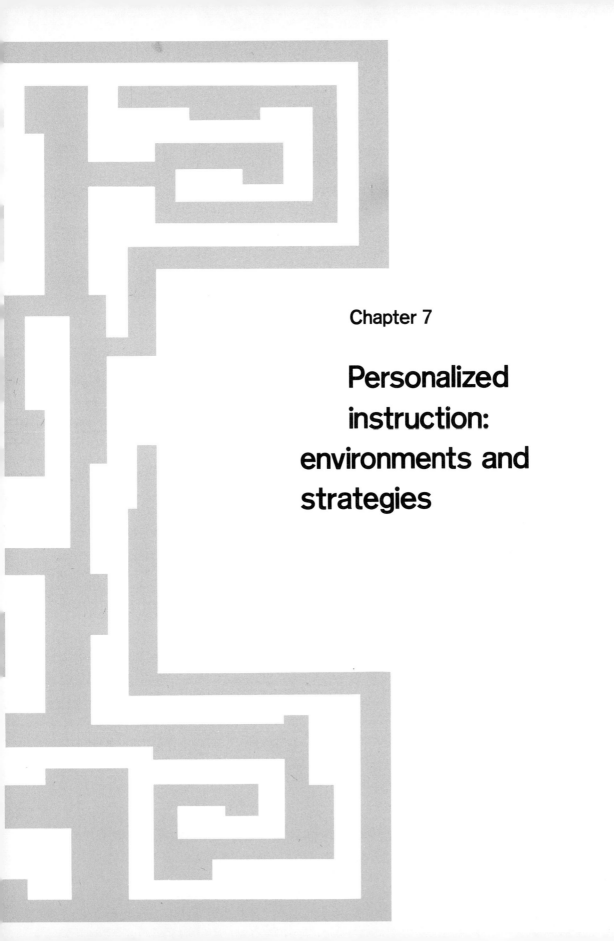

Chapter 7

Personalized instruction: environments and strategies

1.
Students differ, one from the other.

Every psychologist and every teacher can tell you that, though of course you know it already. What you may not know is that these differences have a lot of importance in teaching. They have a lot of importance because each student learns best when instruction suits his individual needs, interests, and abilities.

Personalized instruction? Right. That's what we call it when we try to teach each student in the way that is best for him—that is, when we try to match instructional experiences to his needs, interests, and abilities.

2.
The job of personalizing instruction is harder than we like.

But it is easier than we fear. In order to begin to get an idea of how it is done, take a couple of minutes to do the following exercises.

> Suppose you could have five wishes about yourself granted. What would you wish for?
>
> Again, with regard to yourself, put the following conditions in the order of importance they have in your life: health, wealth, marriage, friends, success, contentment, challenges, security.

These may seem like idle exercises to you, but your choices reflect some **psychological needs** in your life. Psychological needs may be thought of as large general goals toward which you strive. You expend much time and energy in trying to reach those goals.

Younger students, no less than you, have psychological needs they strive to fulfill. They may not know what the needs are. But by and large their basic needs are similar to yours. Soon we will look into this more deeply. For now, let's just note that every human, whether child or adult, works hard toward fulfilling his psychological needs, even when he does not know exactly what they are.

Now see what you can discover by doing the next six exercises:

> List five things you would truly like to learn more about.
>
> List the ways in which you would prefer learning about them.

List in order five things you enjoy doing most (for the purpose of this exercise, omit direct participation in breathing, eating, drinking, and sexing).

Arrange the following general topics in the order in which they interest you: love, adventure, sports, "personalities," world events, society, finance, automobiles, horses, ecology.

You have many sources of information. Depending on the topic, one source may be better than another. In general, which of the following sources suits you best? Arrange them in order: newspapers, magazines, books, radio, television, movies, illustrations, recordings, demonstrations, lectures.

Teachers have found that if students are to learn well, they must be actively involved in learning. If you are to be involved in an activity as a student, which of the following would you prefer? Arrange them in order of preference: writing, constructing, performing, telling about, singing, drawing, manipulating/ discussing.

The responses you made in these six exercises indicate some important **interests** in your life—interests in topics and activities. Students, like everyone else, work hardest at tasks that interest them.

Now a little resume of what we've done so far. First, we got a brief indication of some of your psychological needs. Second, we discovered several of your interests in topics and in activities.

3.
Now,
here's a very interesting thing.

Take a subject area that would fall very low on your interest list—say possibly medieval history or Latin grammar. If we can approach that topic through activities that interest you greatly, we can cause you to become a willing, even eager student of the subject.

Take medieval history as an example. It doesn't have to be approached through dusty volumes of dry verbiage, does it? What about the music, architecture, rituals, art, battles? How might they be reenacted, performed, compared, dramatized? How might you throw yourself into the milieu and become an active observer and reporter?

One thing we haven't done thus far is get some idea about your **ability levels.** By determining your level of ability in a given area, we can decide whether an activity is too easy or too difficult for you. If it is too easy, you will become bored. If it is too difficult, you can't perform; you will become frustrated, will not like the activity, and will not wish to continue at it. What we hope to do is arrange an activity for you at just the right level of complexity—a level that will challenge you but will allow you to successfully complete it. Under these conditions you will learn much more, and your ability level will rise.

Any given student has many different levels of ability. The student may be able to perform complicated mathematical computations but may be poor at singing. Or the student may be poor at spelling despite a large vocabulary.

Ability levels can be determined through standardized testing and through informal class surveys in which you ask students to perform very short tasks at increasing levels of complexity. Moreover, if students are given latitude in choosing materials and activities, they will usually gravitate to tasks commensurate with their ability levels. That is, they won't work at tasks that are too hard, and they will avoid repeating tasks that are too easy.

To summarize so far, then: to personalize instruction, we give each student materials and activities that meet his psychological needs, are interesting, and are appropriately challenging. Why do we personalize instruction? So that each student will make the most rapid academic gains, while developing the most positive attitudes toward learning.

4.
Is it possible
to know all students well enough
to personalize their instruction?

Look at it this way. Granted, you can never know everything about even one of your students. Granted, you will know more about some of them than you will about others. You still can start personalizing instruction in one subject area at a time with relatively little information about the students. As you learn more, you can modify each student's plan, and you can begin personalizing in other instructional areas.

Okay.
Personalized instruction
is a very important part of teaching.
But where do we go from here?

Here's how to proceed

step I: find out what the psychological needs usually are for students like yours

"Need" is a concept that helps to explain behavior.

Since small children engage in boisterous activity and look for opportunities for such play, we say they have a "need" for large-muscle activity. Since adolescents almost always rebel against parental authority, we say they have a "need" to gain independence from their parents.

Some needs seem common to all individuals. Maslow (remember that we looked briefly at some of his ideas in Chapter 5) developed what he called a "hierarchy of needs":

> 5. **self-actualization** freedom to act, to self-express, to satisfy curiosity, to achieve and produce
> 4. **esteem** feeling of worth from self and others
> 3. **love** affection from parents and friends, sense of warmth and belonging
> 2. **safety** freedom from traumatic threat
> 1. **physiological** food, water, air, elimination, etc.

Maslow judged that each successively "higher" need becomes important only when the needs that are lower on the scale have been at least partially met. For instance, the need for safety is not manifested as strongly when one is starving.

Schools exist mainly to help students fulfill their need for self-actualization. However, self-actualization can occur only if the physiological, safety, love, and esteem needs are met to some degree. Further, teachers can expect trouble when students' needs are not met, for they will seek ways to meet them in any way they can. Thus your plans for personalizing instruction must not thwart students' needs. Rather they must help fulfill them.

159

Robert Havighurst, a noted authority in the sociology of education, considered the matter from a different perspective. Reflecting on the emotional states that predominate at different points in an individual's life, he identified what he called "developmental tasks." Developmental tasks are fundamental issues with which people must deal at different points in their lives. Here are some of the tasks Havighurst identified:

early childhood
1. forming some basic concepts of reality
2. developing emotional ties to other people
3. distinguishing between right and wrong

middle childhood
1. developing physical skills for ordinary games
2. developing wholesome attitudes toward oneself
3. getting along with peers
4. learning appropriate sex roles
5. developing the fundamental skills in reading, writing, and calculating
6. developing concepts necessary for everyday living
7. developing conscience, morality, and a system of values
8. developing attitudes toward social groups and institutions

adolescence
1. accepting one's own physique
2. gaining emotional independence from parents and other adults
3. developing socially and politically responsible behavior

A student may be trying to cope with several of these developmental tasks at any age. While one or two may predominate at a given time, they do not automatically appear and disappear at certain ages. Rather, they are ongoing, unfolding processes, and some of them continue throughout life.

Now, how do you identify the needs of each of your students? Try this procedure:

1. Note the psychological needs and developmental tasks that seem to predominate for most students the age of yours. Check Maslow's hierarchy, Havighurst's developmental tasks, and the brief listings presented in the chart on p. 161. You can also check standard textbooks on human development. Two of many excellent texts are those by Jenkins, Shacter, and Bauer* and Stone and Church.**

2. Observe your students' actions in individual work, in group activities, and at play. See how they react to problems, to each other, and to you. See if they seek attention, affection, and acceptance. And see whether they do so in "acceptable" or "unacceptable" ways.

*Jenkins, G., Shacter, H., and Bauer, W.: These Are Your Children, Glenview, Ill., 1966, Scott, Foresman & Co.
**Stone, L. J., and Church, J.: Childhood and Adolescence: a Psychology of the Growing Person, New York, 1968, Random House, Inc.

3. Unacceptable behaviors often point to a student's inability to fulfill his needs. When they occur, check to see whether the student seems to be seeking attention, security, or esteem. Then try to help him through your relations with him, through appropriate class activities, and through assigned responsibilities.

step II: identify your students' predominant interests

Identifying students' interests is very important because they spend so much time thinking about them and are eager to work at activities built around them.

You can hardly help noticing many of the interests of your students. They are the topics of talk and play, and all you have to do is watch, listen, and take note. To get more information, you can encourage students to talk about their interests in group discussions, and you can ask them to tell or write about their favorite games, pastimes, sports, books, hobbies, television programs, job aspirations, and so forth.

This will help you build lessons around student interests through related reading materials and projects in areas such as social science, the natural sciences, art, and composition.

Some predominant needs and interests of students at different ages

age level	needs	interests
5 to 8 years	assurance, physical activity, direct sensory experience, encouragement, praise, warmth, patience, concrete experiences in learning	Stories, dramatic play, pictures, songs, poems, rhythms, painting, animals, organized games, models, dolls, gangs and clubs, class projects, collections, comics, books on adventure, animals, foreign lands and people
9 to 10 years	physical activity, group membership, to be admired	competitive games, team games, trips, reading, maps, letters, wrestling, sports, jumping rope, jacks, cooking and sewing
pre-adolescent	affection, warmth, greater independence, peer group acceptance	group, gang, club, sports, competitive and outdoor games, picnics, hobbies, construction, pets, movies, TV, comics, reading—science and adventure
adolescent	sense of identity, acceptance by and conformation to peer group, security with independence	opposite sex, music, dancing, gossip, sports, cars, movies

step III: identify your students' ability levels

Use the term "ability" in the sense of "able at present," not in the sense of "potentially able."

Used in that way, ability level means about the same as performance level or academic achievement level. It refers to the degree of sophistication or complexity at which a student can profitably work. We have already noted that there are great differences in ability levels among students. We have also noted that a task which is too difficult for a student produces high frustration, while a task that is too easy produces boredom. Both conditions inhibit learning.

You can take a first step in identifying ability levels for your students by noting "average" or "typical" levels for the age- or grade-level group with which you work. An "average" sixth-grade student, for example, will supposedly read profitably from a sixth-grade basal reader or from material with a similar degree of complexity. But there is a problem with the concept of "average" — a serious problem that you should recognize.

The problem with "average" is that it tells us little, instead of much, about the characteristics of most students in a class. In fact, it usually tells us what most of the students are not. Take fifth graders and reading as an example. Fewer than 20% of all fifth graders read at "fifth-grade level"; the other students stretch well above and well below that mark. The same thing is true for science and math and art and music and physical education — in short, for every other curriculum area. What's more, very few students have IQ's of 100. Only about 50% fall between 90 and 110, the so-called normal range, while the other 50% stretch below and above into the "abnormal" ranges. Such differences in ability and performance, to say nothing of specific aptitudes and interests, grow more pronounced as students get older.

So that, you see, is the problem with "average." Still, the average gives you a starting place for finding out about each of your students as individuals.

You should do two other things to determine ability levels of your students:
1. Check existing records to find scores your students have made on achievement tests.
2. Conduct informal performance surveys. This procedure requires that you ask students to perform tasks at different levels of difficulty while you note their abilities, strengths, and weaknesses. In mathematics, for example, you might ask each student individually to do a few exercises at increasing levels of difficulty in both computation and reasoning. Students verbalize the procedures they use. In reading instruction, you might ask each student to read short selections aloud to you. You would note any errors, and you

would ask the student to give the meanings of difficult words in the selections.

You can see that using such informal surveys gives you a fairly quick and accurate idea of the level at which each of your students can function with profit. Once you have this information, you can provide materials and activities that are challenging but not so difficult that they impede progress.

Now that we know something about the importance of students' psychological needs, interests, and ability levels, it is time to think about using this knowledge to build personalized instruction.

step IV: try out one or more informal personalized plans

An informal personalized plan is one you make up for your own students.

It may be simple or elegant, short or long. But it is your attempt to base instruction on your students' needs, interests, and abilities. To give you an idea of the possibilities, I include the following seven brief descriptions of informal personalized plans: math, spelling, reading, secondary math and science, secondary modern language, chemistry, and secondary English.

a general math plan

Lazerick* reported an individualized mathematics plan that produced high levels of student interest and achievement. In Lazerick's plan the teacher has two primary tasks to carry out before instruction begins:

1. A math "lab" must be set up in the classroom, consisting of materials, supplies, games, and teacher-made activities.
2. A file of assignments must be prepared. Each assignment describes the task, the materials needed, the procedures to follow, and the way in which students are to record discoveries.

According to the students' academic needs, they may either work independently through the assignment file or with the teacher in small-group skill activities.

a spelling plan

Sharknas** reported the following individualized spelling plan that produced excellent results with her students. Instead of using the common spelling books with their lists of words, the teacher keeps a list of words misspelled by students in their regular written work. Then the students are paired and follow this weekly schedule:

Monday   Students choose the words from their own lists that they want to learn to spell during the week, and they write them on a three by five inch index card.

Tuesday   Students write sentences using each of the words.

Wednesday   The teacher conducts whole-group instruction if needed.

*Lazerick, B.: We Individualized Math, Instructor **89**:64, 1970.
Sharknas, J.: I Individualized Spelling, Instructor **89:64, 1970.

Thursday Students work in pairs, learning to spell the words.
Friday Partners administer weekly spelling tests to each other.
Papers are handed in to the teacher, who checks them.

Words spelled correctly are crossed off each student's list, and the teacher continues to add new words to the lists as errors appear on students' papers. Sharknas reported that student interest and achievement far surpassed that created by the regular spelling program.

a reading plan

An individualized reading program ordinarily requires a quantity of reading materials that represent a spectrum of interest areas and levels of difficulty:

fiction and nonfiction library books
magazines and newspapers
basal and supplementary readers
encyclopedias, dictionaries, and other reference books
SRA kits
programmed materials for developing skills
games for developing skills
student-produced reading materials such as experience stories

Some teachers allow students complete discretion in choosing the materials they will use. Other teachers allow students to select from certain groups, so as to have experience with the various categories of materials on hand.

what the teacher does

Teachers have the major responsibility for planning and implementing the program. They must first obtain and make available a variety of materials. Students can help by bringing magazines, newspapers, and books from home. Teachers should have a conference with each student at least once a week. The conference concerns materials the student has read, emphasizing student comprehension and reactions. Students may be asked to read a few passages orally so the teacher can check for errors. One fourth to one fifth of the students should have conferences each day, while other students can work independently with their materials and activities.

As groups of students show the need for additional reading skills such as structural and phonetic analysis skills, the teacher conducts special small-group drill sessions with them. Teachers also keep records. Five by eight inch index cards are handy for recording the progress of each student — materials read, dates, reactions, skills needing attention, and recommendations.

what the students do

Individualized reading programs have been built around a variety of activities, including the following: free reading in library books, magazines, and newspapers;

project-oriented reading in research books and assigned reading in basal readers and workbooks.

Students also work in skill-development sessions using programmed materials or SRA kits, in small-group skill lessons taught by the teacher, and in skill development through reading games and puzzles. Students become involved in reading-related art and construction projects and in the production of experience-type readers written and illustrated by students for other students to read.

Some teachers find it easier to coordinate student activities, especially when materials are not plentiful, by dividing the students into groups. Then a master schedule is made up that indicates what each group does during a given reading period. For example, suppose Mr. Jones and his class decided they wanted to concentrate on library book reading, magazine reading, project-related reading, and systematic work in reading-skill development. They might divide the class into four groups and develop a weekly schedule that looks like this:

Sample weekly schedule for group instruction in reading

	group one	group two	group three	group four
Monday	conferences (read library books)	skill session	magazine reading	project reading
Tuesday	project reading	conferences (read library books)	skill session	magazine reading
Wednesday	magazine reading	project reading	conferences (read library books)	skill session
Thursday	skill session	magazine reading	project reading	conferences (read library books)
Friday	games, art, and construction	games, art, and construction	games, art, and construction	games, art, and construction

166

a secondary math and science plan

Marusek* reported an individualized instruction plan for slower learning high school math and science students.

A normal-sized classroom was used. The teacher sat in the middle of the room at a large table, readily available to help students. Student assignments were placed on the magazine rack. Resource materials filled the room.

When students turned in their work, the teacher looked it over at once. This provided immediate reinforcement. If the work was not acceptable, students were required to do it over. They received precise information about what was wrong and what they needed to do to make it right. Progress charts were kept for the students so they could check and have a tangible record of their progress.

a secondary modern language plan

Reimart** reported a successful arrangement for individualizing foreign language study.

A regular-size classroom was used. One area contained a tape recorder. The class members worked in small groups located in different areas of the room.

Each student received a directions sheet that detailed activities in each lesson. Students worked in groups, preparing for proficiency tests that were administered at set intervals. Quizzes were taped and used in preparation for the proficiency tests. Acceptable levels of quiz performance were set at 80%.

The teacher did not engage in any activity that could be handled by the equipment or the students themselves. That left the instructor free for remedial work, clarification, and practicing conversations.

Students moved at their own pace, but they had to reach acceptable levels of performance on the proficiency tests before being allowed to move ahead.

a chemistry plan

Denton*** reported an individualized plan for teaching chemistry in high school. Students were given guides that included the course outline, the contract grading system, course objectives, progress schedule, and criteria for evaluation. They used progress schedules that listed the number of chapters to be completed during each evaluation period. Each student had to complete the assignments before the grade card would be issued. The assignments included doing homework, lab reports, and extra projects and taking tests.

*Marusek, J.: A Program Providing Highly Individualized Instruction for Slow Learning Math and Science Students, Sci. Educ. **53**:217-219, 1969.
Reimart, H.: Practical Guide to Individualization, Modern Language J. **55:156-163, 1971.
***Denton, J.: Individualized Chem-Study, School and Community **56**:37, 1969.

The class was divided into many small groups of two to three students each. Each group progressed at its own rate. Different criteria levels were used for earning grades of A, B, and C.

a secondary English plan

Danielson and colleagues* reported an individualized English program built around the cassette recorder. It used a tape library dealing with various aspects of English study.

The tapes were used for enrichment, clarification, and application of skills. Many related to specific books or authors and served as a study guide, complete with comments and guiding questions. The tapes also included biographical information on authors, hints on good and bad writing, spelling and definitions, and word meanings and derivations.

Teachers also used taped comments to respond to student compositions. This avoided the red-ink work typically done on student papers.

The students could record some of their special project work, to be enjoyed and used by other students.

*Danielson, E., et al.: The Cassette Tape: An Aid to Individualizing High School English, English J. **62**:441-445, 1973.

step V: refine and improve your informal plans

You will learn a lot about personalizing instruction once you begin using informal plans with your students.

While we can't foresee precisely what you will learn in your own situation, we can still assume that you will acquire information that will help you to improve your attempts to personalize instruction. As you refine and improve your plans, you may also wish to add some new dimensions to them. I present three such dimensions here — readiness, learning styles, and values. I consider them important, yet I still think they are secondary to the dimensions of needs, interests, and abilities that we have already examined.

readiness

A new concept of "readiness" is emerging, one that someday may become very important in teaching. Readiness has received much attention in kindergarten and first-grade programs, especially in the areas of reading and arithmetic. But apart from such beginning programs, readiness has received little attention. Intermediate and secondary teachers rarely speak of it. But they may soon begin, because learning psychologists are beginning to think of readiness in terms of "prerequisite capabilities" for performing a new task.

In order to learn anything new — a skill, a concept, a principle — one must have existing or prerequisite learnings. According to this concept, the degree of readiness for learning equals the completeness of one's prerequisite learnings. Unlike the vague "background of experiences" fundamental to the traditional concept of readiness, these prerequisite learnings can be specifically identified.

To illustrate, note the prerequisites identified in two learning structures presented by Gagne. The first is a hierarchy of capabilities learned during reading instruction. Each is requisite to the capability that follows:

> learning language sounds
> learning simple words
> recognizing printed letters by sound
> recognizing printed words
> differentiating between similar words
> understanding the concepts of printed nouns, verbs, prepositions,
>   connectives*

*Adapted from Gagne, R. M.: The Conditions of Learning, New York, 1965, Holt, Rinehart & Winston, Inc., p. 201.

Although some reading teachers might question the hierarchy, what it indicates is this: students are not "ready" to distinguish between similar printed words until they can recognize with certainty a number of printed words. And that ability depends, at least in part, on their previous ability to associate sounds with letters.

A second example, from a more advanced level in natural science, is adapted from a learning structure in developing principles of the hydrolysis of salts:

concept of number
concept of object attributes
concept of events (electrical changes)
concept of separating and joining
concept of chemical elements
knowledge of units of measurement
use of indicators
classifying by effects
knowledge of combinations of chemical elements
inferring measurement
knowledge about hydrogen and hydroxyl ions
measurement of strength of acids and bases
knowledge of ion composition of acids and bases
knowledge of formation of salts in solutions
principles of degree of dissociation in salt solutions
principles of hydrolysis*

This adaptation of Gagne's learning structure in the hydrolysis of salts does not show his original hierarchical arrangements that indicated precisely which knowledge or skills were dependent on each other. What we want to note here is that all of the listed skills and knowledge—"prerequisite capabilities"—are necessary before a student can thoroughly understand the principles of hydrolysis of salts. That is, a student is "ready" to learn the pinciples of hydrolysis only if the listed prerequisite capabilities are present.

At present, teachers do not have repertoires of schematized learning structures such as those presented by Gagne to use in determining levels of student readiness. Neither do they have formal diagnostic testing devices to determine whether students possess certain prerequisite capabilities. Nonetheless, you will find that you can think through significant prerequisites in your own lessons with little effort and much profit. Just ask yourself what capabilities you assume each student to have, as in the following examples.

If you are a first-grade teacher having your students do worksheets in addition, what capabilities are you assuming? Probably at least the following: ability to count, recognition of number quantities, identification of number symbols, and the concept of joining groups to make a new group.

If you are a high school Spanish teacher preparing a lesson on the use of the imperfect subjunctive, what capabilities do you assume? Disregarding numerous capabilities in reading, speaking, conjugating verbs, and so on, you are assuming that students already know:

*Adapted from Gagne, R. M.: The Conditions of Learning, New York, 1965, Holt, Rinehart & Winston, Inc., p. 188.

how the subjunctive tense is used in English
how infinitive endings are changed to form tenses
the words or meanings that signal the use of the subjunctive in Spanish
how the present subjunctive is used in Spanish

Suppose you are a junior high school teacher preparing a physical geography lesson on the Rocky Mountain region. What do you assume your students already know?

1.
2.
etc.

You see that it is not difficult to identify assumed prerequisite capabilities. You will undoubtedly find that when students do in fact possess the capabilities you assume, they will be successful in the new learning activities in which they engage. When students have difficulty, make a quick check of the capabilities you have assumed. You may well find that your students don't have all the capabilities you assumed—that is, they are not yet ready for the new activities. When that happens, your personalized instruction will help each student to develop the skills and concepts he needs for doing more advanced work.

learning styles

Have you ever noticed that some people seem to learn quickly, almost impulsively, while others who are equally bright learn slowly and methodically, mulling things over? Some people seem to learn best through reading, others through observing, and yet others through talking or through working with their hands. Some people learn faster when they work under time pressure, while others seem to fall to pieces. Some learn better under continual prodding, while others do better in a very free, relaxed atmosphere. Some people prefer to work in groups, while others do better working alone.

Teachers have long recognized these differences and, through trial and error, have learned a few ways of coping with them. Test makers have also recognized these differences and have built into their test batteries both speed and power tests, with both verbal and nonverbal components.

For instance, the Wechsler Intelligence Scales consist of two parts—a verbal scale and a performance scale. The verbal scale includes subtests in general information, general comprehension, arithmetical reasoning, similarities, and vocabulary. The performance scale includes subtests in coding, picture completion, block design, picture arrangement, and object assembly. Each subtest yields its own score, and those scores can differ, sometimes markedly, for the same individual.

Similarly, aptitude tests often show large variations among the aptitudes of a single individual. The Differential Aptitude Tests, for example, include these categories: verbal, numerical, abstractions, space perception, mechanical, clerical, spelling, and sentences. A student who scores very high in the verbal category may score low in the mechanical category, although such a discrepancy is not a matter of course.

To discover the differences in learning styles that exist among your students, you can do the following things:

>   check existing records for scores on different sections of intelli-
>   gence, achievement, and aptitude tests
>   ask students about their hobbies and special interests
>   observe students at play and in art and construction activities
>   observe performance in activities with time limits and in work that
>   is highly competitive
>   observe responses to criticism, cajoling, and encouragement

Make mental or index card notes of what you observe, keeping track of which students work rapidly or slowly, individually or in groups, which react positively or negatively to pressure, to threats, and to praise, and which profit most from reading, talking, and working with their hands.

values

A value is whatever one thinks is good or right or worth having.

Most teachers have the values that have been found useful in a highly productive, democratic society—values such as hard work, punctuality, faith in education, faith in rational processes, and willingness to postpone gratification or save for a rainy day. But most teachers also have some students who do not seem to have those same values. They may consider those students irresponsible, untrustworthy, and lazy and feel they have little regard for education.

Usually such students come from what are called lower socioeconomic groups. Many belong to minority ethnic groups that traditionally hold especially different value systems. We can't do a good job of personalizing instruction unless we are fairly sure about the values our students hold. We can learn much about values from observing student behavior. We can also learn much from reading.

For instance, Davis* identified four areas where educationally important value differences existed between members of middle- and lower-class groups:

>   **time orientation** Teachers and middle-class students plan and think
>   ahead to next month, next year, to ten years ahead. Contrarily, the
>   uncertainties of poverty cause students to be preoccupied with to-
>   day, with getting by, with living for the here and now.
>
>   **person orientation** Teachers and middle-class students, while con-
>   cerned with interpersonal relations, can also assign much impor-
>   tance to career planning and working for individual advancement.
>   Lower-class students tend to be more highly oriented toward other
>   people, finding reward and security in group membership. They are
>   not well motivated through appeals to individual or career goals.
>
>   **self-image** Lower-class students have poorer opinions of their own
>   ability and worth than do middle-class students. These feelings of
>   inability to achieve reduce their drive for academic success and
>   achievement.

*Davis, A.: Social Class Influence Upon Learning, Cambridge, Mass., 1948, Harvard University Press.

physical aggressiveness While there may be no differences between the level of aggressiveness of middle- and lower-class students, the latter exhibit theirs in more physical ways, by fighting and rough-housing instead of just gossiping, backbiting, and tattling.

Personalized instruction for students exhibiting these four values implies:

establishing short-range goals, quickly attainable, with frequent rewards
     as they are attained
increasing group work and activities that allow cooperative achievement
including a preponderance of activities that allow success
providing group play and physical education activities that allow students
     to express physical aggression in "acceptable" ways

If you work with students whose cultural backgrounds are quite different from your own, you probably are already aware of how much there is to learn about differences in value systems. Consider, for example, some of the admonitions given by Polacca, a Navajo Hopi Indian, in her article "Ways of Working With the Navajos Who Have Not Learned the White Man's Ways."

1.
Avoid misunderstandings by speaking
clearly and slowly, using common words.
2.
Avoid all derogatory remarks.
3.
Don't ask personal questions.
4.
Be a good listener.
5.
Don't use the word "maybe."
6.
Expect your good deeds to be appreciated.
7.
Don't fuss over babies and very young children.
8.
Don't tease.
9.
Don't be serious; laugh and have a good time.
10.
Don't criticize Navajo religion.

Polacca, K.: Ways of Working With the Navajos Who Have Not Learned the White Man's Ways, J. Amer. Indian Educ. **2:**6, 1962.

The classroom— what it should be

"I have found that children are interested in two things— *doing* and *doing now.*"

That quotation is from a book you should read. It is called *Push Back the Desks*, by Albert Cullum.* Cullum relates fascinating experiences in organizing classrooms and activities for teaching learners in chapters with such titles as "Reading Workbooks or Reading Shakespeare?" "Flora and Fauna in the Gym," and "The Longfellow Lab."

One of Cullum's chapters has the title "Beware the Neat and Quiet Classroom." In it, he describes successful but noisy activities in a fifth-grade class. They built a Trojan horse out of chicken wire covered with pasted newspaper, hung Spanish moss from the ceiling while studying about the South, used New York newspapers for skimming practice, and made a "da Vinci" fresco with real plaster and paint that was so big the custodians had to smash it with sledge hammers before they could remove it from the room at the end of the year.

Cullum must not have read the dictum

"A cluttered room is confusing, and where confusion reigns, students act accordingly."

Or else he ignored it.
Or else he knew it wasn't true.

*Cullum, A.: Push Back the Desks, New York, 1967, Citation Press.

doing and doing now

A classroom should be a functional laboratory for learners.

It should contain space for working and quantities and varieties of materials with which to work. Don't think of such materials as nice but unnecessary extras. Piaget has shown how necessary they are for children of elementary school age, who cannot perform important mental operations without them. While most students of junior high school age and older can think about thought, they also need materials for physical manipulation to increase motivation and promote learning and retention. And, of course, learning that involves aesthetics and motor skills usually requires materials students can manipulate.

The senses are our prime avenues to knowledge, skills, and attitudes. Objects are the sources of raw data for our senses.

Each person lives a life of continual creativity. In a way, each of us makes the world he knows, and that process assures our individuality: we couldn't do otherwise if we wanted to. Our senses take in data from objects. As they do so, however, information is not just stored in the form in which it is received. Instead, we unknowingly perform mental manipulations on it—we relate it, modify it, organize it. That results in perceptions and cognitions that are unique to each of us.

The process of developing knowledge, skills, and attitudes occurs rapidly, with depth, when learners interact with objects—when they observe, manipulate, rearrange, and construct them.

This principle does not downgrade the value of learning through talking, listening, and reflecting. But even those acts must be based on and be concerned with objects (including people) and the ways in which they relate, one to the other. Unfortunately, we often think along erroneous lines when we plan our school activities. We see thought as a highly desirable cognitive act toward which we strive. But sometimes we forget that thought must be based on and validated against object reality. When we forget this, we expect students to do little besides listen and read and keep quiet. We forget that if we really want them to "think," we must see that they have continuous concrete experiences to use as the basis for thought.

Piaget has found that until children are approximately 12 years of age, they can seldom think about thought; they must think about objects. Further, it is very difficult for them to think about objects that aren't there before them in one form or another. While older students can think without the presence of objects about ideas, abstractions, generalizations, hypotheses, meaning, logic, and the like, they must continually refer back to real objects and acts if they are to test the value of the thoughts. Learners entering on new abstract territory will proceed best if they can begin with concrete experiences and move in a circular direction: from concrete experience to thought about that experience, then to thought about that thought, and finally back to checking the whole process against the initial concrete experience.

Perhaps as important as any of the foregoing considerations is the inescapable fact that concrete materials catch attention and urge manipulation.

People will gladly work for hours if they can be actively involved with material things. But without something they can move about or redo in some way, they will quickly lose interest in all but the most fascinating talk topic. But when attention is held, and learners can use their muscles and senses, they not only will learn a great deal, but they will also remember it better.

Both elementary and secondary classrooms can be made into laboratories for learners.

Materials can be kept in the classroom, finished products displayed there, and work in progress kept in the work areas. When different teachers must use a classroom during the day, problems can occur over materials. Junior and senior high school classrooms that must be shared by teachers can be equipped as laboratories, but provisions must be made to keep the work of one class separate from that of another. College classrooms, except for those constructed and used solely as laboratories, present greater difficulties, especially where one classroom must be used by six to ten different professors and classes during the course of a day. Still, portable materials kits and learning centers can be used. They store easily and can be set up and taken down in a few minutes.

learning centers

Practice has shown that most classrooms, both elementary and secondary, can be arranged to include from two to five learning centers, each complete with its own work area and materials. Centers often incorporate the following themes:

appreciation center for observing paintings, poems, sculptures, arrangements, etc.

art activity center equipped for drawing, painting, modeling, etc.

communications center equipped for listening to, viewing, and dramatizing music, stories, and guided activities

display center for showing and observing collections, projects, and hobbies

games center where students can use instructional games, puzzles, and similar aids

library and reading center containing both commercial and student-made reading materials

science center equipped for observation and project work

social science center stocked with maps, charts, documents, reference books, etc., along with materials and equipment for constructing

Where to get materials

It's one thing to talk about making laboratories in classrooms, but it is another thing to actually lay hands on the right kinds of materials to stock them. Maybe it will help if we clarify the ways in which media and materials can help learners. Then we can decide what kinds of things we want to look for. Here you see a short list of ways in which materials can be of service to learners.

catch and hold attention
encourage activity
allow tangible operations
and manipulations

allow observation
extend experiences
provide new experiences
depict and summarize

materials your school might furnish

Following is a list of instructional materials most large schools have on hand. Smaller schools usually have most of them. Check at the school where you teach or student teach to see if you can locate these things.

construction materials
drawing materials
painting materials
models and displays
collections and specimens
maps and globes
charts, diagrams, and graphs
posters
drawings and paintings
photographs and transparencies

flat pictures
motion pictures
filmstrips
recordings
duplicated materials
magazines and newspapers
professional books
encyclopedias and other references
textbooks
supplementary books

equipment your school should furnish

The following is a list of equipment your school should furnish, and for which you should not have to pay out of pocket. Check at your school to see if you can locate these items.

motion picture projectors
filmstrip projectors
slide projectors
opaque projectors
overhead projectors
projection screens
phonographs and tape players
tape recorders

duplicators
chalkboards
bulletin boards
flannelboards
paper cutter
lettering sets
microprojectors
microscopes

the audiovisual catalog

Most school districts have audiovisual centers where quantities of materials are kept and made available to teachers in the district. Such centers ordinarily stock the following materials:

flat pictures
exhibits
filmstrips

kits
motion pictures
disc and tape recordings

Many are also beginning to stock video tapes. These materials are classified according to subject matter, and notations are made about the grade levels for which they seem most appropriate. Most of them are didactic—they teach—but some are inspirational and serve mainly for motivation, appreciation, and entertainment. All are intended to provide experiences students would not otherwise have.

If you are an art teacher, you will find a number of filmstrips and motion pictures that instruct students (and teachers) in such things as finger painting, figure drawing, making collages, and modeling with clay. You will also find a number of fine art prints to use in motivation and in art appreciation. If you teach foreign languages, you will find motion pictures that depict life in typical Mexican, Spanish, French, and German families. You will also find many tapes that students can use to practice pronunciation and sentence patterns. If you teach health, you will find models and exhibits of torsos, teeth, heart, eyeballs, and so on. A well-stocked center will have materials for use in:

industrial arts
mathematics
music (the dance, instrumentation, singing, music appreciation)
physical education and recreation
reading and language arts (filmstrips, motion pictures, and recordings of fiction such as fables, myths, and fairy tales, handwriting, language usage, literature, modern stories, oral expression, written expression, poetry, spelling)
safety
science (material on air, airplanes, amphibians, animals, astronomy, birds, chemistry, electricity and magnetism, energy, fire,

fish, geology, heat, the human body, insects, light, machines, matter, oceans, plants, reptiles, rockets, rocks and minerals, the scientific method, scientists, sea life, seasons, seeds, the solar system, sound, space, trees, water, weather and climate)
social science (history, the fifty states, foreign countries, government and politics, communications, geography, Indians, transportation, the United Nations)
teacher education (general methods, subject-specific methods, guidance, and school and public relations)

Within each of the categories, you can find a number of very useful materials. It takes only a bit of preplanning and a little preliminary paper work to ensure a constant supply of materials that can help to extend your students' experiences to all the earth, to micro- and macrocosms, back into history, and even forward into the future. But remember, the best materials will be scheduled long in advance by experienced teachers.

materials from your school supply list

Many school districts make school supply lists available to teachers. These lists include many kinds of equipment and materials, where they can be obtained, and how much they cost. They usually do not include items that can be purchased locally at favorable prices such as stock ordinarily carried in food and hardware stores. To the extent allowed by their budgets, school districts will purchase such materials for teachers. Items typically included on school supply lists are the following:

brooms
chalk
chamois
charcoal
clay (modeling and ceramic)
crayons (oil and wax)
envelopes
erasers (art gum, chalkboard, pencil, rubber)
glue
ink (printing, drawing, India)
measuring tapes
mimeograph paper
mop handles and heads
needles (tapestry and yarn)
notebooks
paints (easel, finger, kalsomine, tempera, water color)
paper (art, blotting, butcher, carbon, cellophane, construction, corrugated, crepe, drawing, finger paint, newsprint, onionskin, tissue)

paper towels
paste
pencils
pens
pins
plastic bottles
protractors
reinforcements
rulers
scissors
sentence strips
soaps
sponges
squeegees
staples
tag board
tape (cellulose, magic mending, masking)
twine
wire
yarn

informal materials from house & garage

Another category of materials consists of things found in the house and the garage. It contains the simple and the ordinary — bits of cloth and old magazines, popsicle sticks and pumpkin seeds, nutcrackers and birdnests — that were never designed for instructional purposes. Yet they are the kinds of things that students left to their own devices like to mess about with. Because they cost little if anything and lie about us in such common array, we are likely to overlook them and their value. But they are there all around us for the taking.

To illustrate the possibilities, my teen-age daughter consented (for a one-dollar bill) to look around the house and garage for a few minutes and list those items that she felt might be useful in classroom activities. Having had no special instruction in what kinds of things to look for, she just used common sense. Here's what she came up with.

Check off the items that you find at home, and jot down any other good items you find.

yarn
ribbon
string
cloth scraps
rags
buttons
spools
cotton
carpet remnants
needles and thread
cellulose tape
masking tape

sponges
pipe cleaners
paper towels
toothpicks
sieves
funnels
paint brushes
old towels and wash cloths
paper cups

spices
food coloring
dried fruits
baking soda
baking powder
salt
flour
sugar
potatoes
dehydrated soups
rice
dried beans and peas
macaroni
spaghetti

tacks
nails
screws
wire
safety pins

saw
hammer

screwdriver
sandpaper
level
bolts

aluminum foil
plastic wrap
cereal boxes
tin cans
bleach bottles
jars

old magazines
old newspapers
old catalogs
cookbooks
calorie counters

paintings and prints
artifacts from other countries
pottery
phonograph records of many kinds
rock, coin, and butterfly collections
transparencies from foreign countries
old photographs

games such as Scrabble and Monopoly
old toys
old jewelry
makeup
old sunglasses

old shoes
old shirts and blouses
old neckties

barometer
thermometer
rain gauge
paint
insecticides and fertilizer
garden tools
seeds
planter mix

materials from stores & catalogs

If you live in a large community, you may have access to a store that specializes in instructional materials. If not, your school has a number of catalogs from retail companies that sell teaching materials. The variety of items available is too large to detail here, but the following list gives an idea of the kinds of things that can be obtained from these sources:

word and number trays
fraction discs
pegs and peg boards
flash cards
math bingo
toy money
flannel board cutouts
recordings
looms and yarns

oil cloth
beaded alphabets
vowel games
word family games
rhyming puzzles
sentence builders
various games
letter puzzles
activity kits

In addition to the materials listed above, there are specialty houses that deal primarily in one kind of material. For example, several companies deal mainly in science materials and equipment, and their catalogs list items appropriate to every area of the science curriculum. Others specialize in music, art, physical education and recreation, and so on.

free & inexpensive materials

Enterprising teachers can obtain quantities of professionally prepared materials that are provided free for the asking by various companies. All you have to do is write for them on your school stationery. For example, here are a few items available from the *Educators' Guide to Free Social Studies Materials:*

picture of George Washington at Valley Forge
Alexander Graham Bell booklet
Constitution of the United States
Declaration of Independence
state flag stories
American Indians (a series of leaflets)
New Mexico Indian reservations and pueblos
Lincoln and the railroads (a cartoon narrative)
bulletin board kits (automobiles and trucks)

railroad transportation (teacher's kit and manual)
historic airplanes
history of communication
man-made fibers kit
conservation activities
natural resources study guide
national parks leaflets
traffic safety posters

The *Educators' Guide to Free Science Materials* lists similar kinds of things useful in teaching science. In this catalog you can find materials having to do with flight and aviation, coal, the periodic chart of the elements, history of science, calendars, paper making, volcanoes, and water witching and hydrology.

There are also good community sources of free and inexpensive materials. You can check with:

air lines and travel bureaus for posters, itineraries, leaflets
telephone company for leaflets, dry cells, wire
lumber yards for sawdust, wood samples and scraps, plastic
hardware stores for metal, scraps of various kinds
food stores for cartons, boxes, cardboard, packing material
department, food, and drug stores for old window displays and advertising materials
Salvation Army for inexpensive children's books and games, old clothing for costumes
National Dairy Council for pictures and posters of dairy products
local newspapers for old newspapers, samples of print and type
carpet stores for carpet and drape samples and remnants
pharmacies for plastic bottles, tongue depressors
television repair shops for discarded resistors, transistors, etc.

Activities for the class-lab

By thinking of the classroom as a laboratory, we continually direct our attention to activities—to student involvement in doing. We have up to now concentrated on materials; they make a greater variety of activities possible, and they increase the likelihood that learners will become actively involved.

Now we will turn attention to the activities themselves. We will note several possibilities. However, you should remember that these suggestions are merely that—possibilities. Many valuable activities will originate somewhat spontaneously in student interests of the moment. Others may go well beyond those listed here. Nevertheless, teachers should have a number of activities ready to suggest to their students, because students by no means realize the full range of possibilities that lies open to them. A hint, a question, an allusion to things that other classes have done—that's all it takes to set students to thinking about projects, experiments, observations, and experiences they would like to try themselves.

For the sake of convenience, the activities are listed below according to subject groups, but really, they are all interrelated. Art, music, and communications, for example, might all be involved in a social science lesson.

in art

modeling and sculpting clay
making collages of various kinds
drawing, coloring, etching with crayons
illustrating talks, sayings, mottoes, stories, etc.
doing macramé
making mobiles and stabiles
making mosaics
painting with tempera, finger paints, acrylics, watercolor

doing origami (paper folding and paper sculpture)
making puppets
sculpting in soap and plaster
making silk screens and prints
making wood cuts and vegetable prints
weaving
making wire and toothpick sculpture
working in leather

in communications

setting up a creative production center for:

writing poems, stories, plays
collecting sayings, mottoes, proverbs
collecting pictures for scrapbooks and illustrations
designing scenery and costumes for plays

designing bulletin boards around current events, personal information, etc.
making flannel board stories
making puppets and giving performances
making box movies

setting up a media center for:

printing and stamping notices, announcements, mottoes
illustrating word origin booklets
illustrating creative writing booklets
illustrating stories, lessons, lectures

making personal tape recordings of poetry, letters, speeches, etc.
producing dioramas and mobiles
assembling multimedia presentations

setting up a publishing center to publish:

creative writing books
who's who books
word origin books
picture scrapbooks

class photo albums
news releases
class newspapers
class magazines

setting up a performing arts center for:

performing skits and plays
dramatizing events
giving speeches

giving book, movie, television reviews and critiques
dramatizing stories and songs

in foreign languages

preparing talks and slide presentations
making costumes
performing skits in the foreign language
acting out scenes from stories
learning typical songs and dances
interviewing and inviting to class people who speak a foreign language or who have lived in a foreign country
making collections of things from a foreign country (currency, art, music, artifacts, clothing, utensils, etc.)
subscribing to a foreign newspaper
writing a class newspaper in a foreign language, including news items, stories, poems, riddles, etc.
corresponding with foreign students
keeping a diary in the language
reading librettos of operas in the language
having in-depth study projects about the art, music, literature, politics, sports, schools, religion, costumes, industry, farming, mining, ruins, famous places, etc.
preparing a "Who's Who" of the country
preparing travel maps and itineraries
making greeting cards with foreign language inscriptions and scenes of the country

in mathematics

estimating distances, dimensions, volumes
measuring volumes, weights, dimensions of objects, rooms, etc.
planning and building a scale model house, office building, airport, city, gymnasium, football or baseball field
studying and preparing architectural plans
computing interest rates, commissions, profits, discounts, income tax, property tax
constructing measuring wheels, balances, quadrants, other similar devices
constructing geometrical shapes and forms boards

making and using number games, counting devices, charts, graphs, posters, flash cards, meters, speedometer, abacus, fractions
setting up and using an "arithmetic discovery table" with objects and directions
keeping cost records for feeding pets, family budgets, etc.
making scales for barometers, thermometers, rain gauges
making graphs for daily temperature, rainfall, etc.
keeping statistical records for the class

keeping football, basketball, baseball statistics

making time and distance lines and models

making lists of personal uses for arithmetic

making illustrated reports on the history of numbers

using adding machines and calculators

computing costs for various kinds of historical and present-day trips

practicing making exchanges between United States and foreign currencies

in music

identifying the musical resources of the school (instruments available, musical groups, performers, talented students, teachers)

setting up musical groups in the class (singers and instrumentalists)

identifying music typical of festival days (Christmas, Hannukah, Chinese New Year, Easter, Cinco de Mayo, etc.)

studying the music of a foreign country, learning typical songs and dances, performing them for other classes

making a list of musical programs on AM and FM radio, television, community concerts, etc.

making a study of folk music of any time or place, learning to perform it and presenting performances to other classes

identifying and learning typical songs of Italy, France, Spain, England, Scotland, Ireland, Germany, Switzerland, Russia, Hungary, Greece

learning typical folk songs of ethnic groups in the United States

dramatizing ballads and folk songs such as "Aunt Rhody," "Cockle Shells," "Dublin City," "Ballad of Barberry Ellen"

making appropriate costumes and performing the minuet, gavotte, rondo, jig, modern dances

setting short poems to music

composing and presenting a class opera that dramatizes a contemporary or historical event

in science

setting up and maintaining a "discovery table" with many kinds of objects for observing and experimenting

setting up an electricity lab with cells, wires, bulbs, buzzers, switches, fuses and making electromagnets and telegraphs

setting up an optical lab with lenses, prisms, light sources, colors

setting up an acoustical lab with sound-producing objects, transmission media, amplifiers, insulators

setting up a machine lab with simple machines, weights, spring scales

setting up an air and water pressure lab to check pressures, densities, weights

setting up a power-harnessing lab for using solar, wind, water, steam, muscle power to drive small pieces of equipment

setting up a weather station and keeping daily records

making and using telescopes, microscopes, thermometers, barometers, sundials, compasses

setting up, maintaining, observing aquaria, terraria, ant colonies, etc.

growing and observing cultures of microscopic plants and animals

raising butterflies, silkworms, tadpoles and observing and recording their development

conducting nutrition experiments with plants

developing and using systems for classifying plants, animals, minerals

making collections of insects, rocks, fossils, leaves, seeds

making models of atoms, molecules, solar system, galaxies, watersheds, geological formations, volcanoes, parts of the body, etc.

in social science

maintaining a current events bulletin board

making a time line for students' own lives

making a time line for the school, street, community, country, mankind, etc.

writing a history of the school, street, community with interviews, checks of city documents, etc.

describing the sources of common foods

selecting one food and making lists of all the people who help process it

doing studies of different cultures and comparing them to our own

describing schools in other societies

contrasting primitive and modern means of travel and communication

diagramming latitudes and longitudes and reading these positions on the globe

determining the date and time of day in various parts of the world

making relief, outline, salt and flour, jigsaw puzzle, topographical, product, pictorial, population maps, etc.

drawing political cartoons

interpreting political cartoons

utilizing role-playing to enact such situations as "Meet the Press," "You are There," interviews with historical figures, dramatizations of such historical events as the Scopes Monkey Trial, Constitutional Convention, signing of the Mayflower Compact, court trials, sessions of Congress, a New England town meeting, etc.

keeping actual or imaginary diaries of events, travels, etc.

interviewing students and parents on any issue

interviewing policemen, pilots, farmers, etc.

conducting debates on issues of current interest

comparing authors and newspapers for accuracy and objectivity

keeping track of the stock market during the year and trying to explain its advances and declines

choosing the five greatest ideas, men, women, world events, books, etc. and then defending the choices

doing and doing now

Now that you have read through these many lists of materials and activities, stop for just a minute.

Let your own ideas float to the top of your head, then jot them down. You may want to start an "idea file." You may also want to begin a collection of materials — odds and ends that catch *your* eye and hold *your* interest — materials we have mentioned and others you may come across on your own.

Remember "doing and doing now"? That applies to teachers as well as students. And if you begin to gather ideas and materials now, you'll be better prepared to proceed to . . .

Classroom/ class-lab reality

All the activities and materials we have considered could be accommodated in a typical classroom only with considerable difficulty. Most classrooms are too small, have too little open space, and have too little work and storage space.

Nevertheless, additional counter space and work areas can be made from hollow doors, and much additional storage space can be managed with cardboard cartons and wooden packing crates that are shelved and nicely painted.

What kind of classroom arrangement would you like to have? On the next page is a diagram of a desirable classroom made by a student teacher who was working in a second grade.

Whether you teach at elementary or secondary level, you can arrange your classroom to facilitate laboratory experiences. Take a few minutes to sketch out various classroom arrangements. Give attention to different uses for different areas of the room. Show where activities will take place and where quiet work can be done. Mark storage areas for materials. Use your imagination with tables, bookcases, and foldable screens that can be used as room dividers.

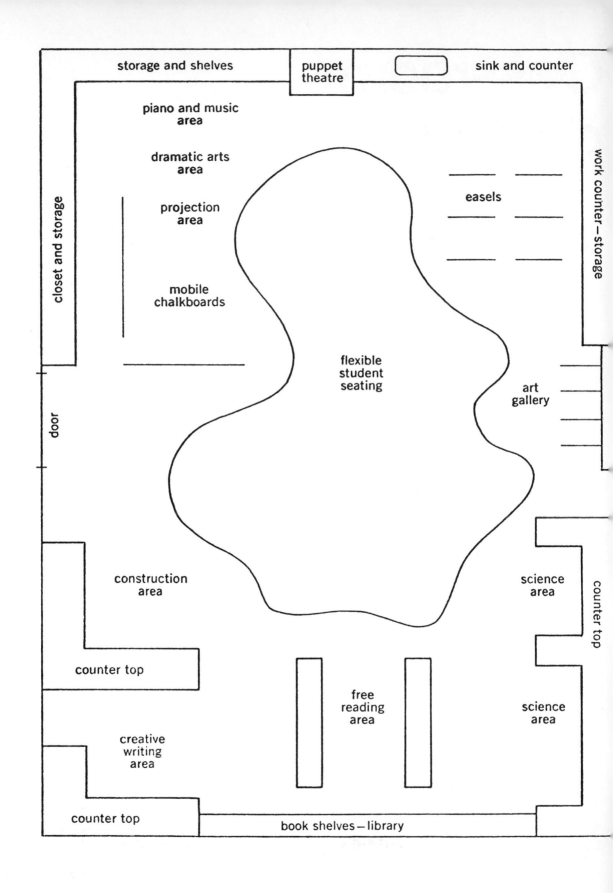

3 formal plans for personalizing instruction

I used the term "informal plans" in reference to those developed by one or two teachers for their own use within their own classrooms. Here I use the term "formal plans" to mean those developed for wide-scale use. They are usually developed by a school, a school district, or a team of educators and psychologists. Many people cooperate in producing such plans.

While we have used the term "personalizing instruction," the plans described in the paragraphs that follow are more commonly referred to as plans for "individualizing instruction." They attempt to provide work that students can select and do individually, work that is suited to their ability levels and that allows each student to move at a separate pace.

Here we will briefly consider three formal plans: the Duluth Plan, Individually Prescribed Instruction (IPI), and Program for Learning in Accordance with Needs (PLAN).

the Duluth Plan

general description

This plan was developed in the Duluth, Minnesota, Public Schools for students in kindergarten through sixth grade. At the heart of the plan are "contracts" that teachers prepare in advance for later selection by students. Each contract consists of the following parts:

> name of the curriculum area—for example, math
> a stated criterion of acceptable student performance
> a description of the activities that will enable the student to reach
> > the performance criterion

a list of available resources students can use in the activities
sample test items for students to use

These contracts and lists of activities and resources are prepared by teachers in in-service workshops. They are not commercially available.

what the students do

Students go first each day to a homeroom, in groups of about thirty. There, with the help of the teacher, they select contracts and plan their schedules for the day.

From the homeroom, students go to a lab of their choice. There is a lab for each subject area—language arts, social studies, mathematics, and science. Labs are for students of all ages; they are not organized for students of single grade levels. Students may move from one lab to another during the day; however, they must spend at least twenty-five minutes in every lab they enter. In the labs, students work toward completion of the contracts they have selected, choosing from the materials and activities available there.

what the teachers do

In workshops, teachers prepare contracts, plan appropriate activities for students within each contract, and acquire materials for students to use in the activities.

During a normal teaching day they may administer pretests and posttests, help students to select contracts, supervise lab work, and conduct small-group tutorial sessions.

Individually Prescribed Instruction (IPI)

general description

Individually Prescribed Instruction, developed by the Learning Research and Development Center of the University of Pittsburgh, is a fairly elaborate, commercially available program for kindergarten through sixth grade. The program includes the curriculum areas of mathematics, reading, science, spelling, social studies, and handwriting.

Each curriculum area is divided into a number of "levels" that do not correspond to grade levels. In mathematics, for example, there are 7 levels that contain almost 400 behaviorally stated objectives. The reading program consists of 11 levels, with just under 300 behavioral objectives.

Within each curriculum area, the general instructional strategy is the same:

> The teacher gives a pretest.
> The teacher prescribes work for the student based on the results of the pretest.
> The student goes to a teacher aide for help in obtaining materials.
> The student does the prescribed work.
> The student takes a posttest to determine whether the objectives have been met.

Many materials are available with each program. They include:

> tests—placement tests, pretests, posttests, Curriculum Embedded Tests
> teacher materials—study guides, Skillsheets, profile sheets, IPI storybooks, discs, Discbooks

A wide variety of other materials are also needed in the programs. They are not provided by IPI but are commercially available from other sources.

what the students do

As previously outlined, students' activities include:

> taking a pretest
> obtaining prescriptions from the teacher
> asking a teacher aide if necessary for help in obtaining materials
> completing the prescribed activities
> taking a posttest to determine the degree of their mastery of the stated objective

what the teachers do

The teachers perform the following functions:

> administering pretests and posttests
> preparing prescriptions for each student (usually this entails selecting a Standard Teaching Sequence and certain workbook pages for the student to complete)
> conducting small-group sessions as necessary
> administering CET (Curriculum Embedded Tests) to determine the level of student achievement

Program for Learning in Accordance with Needs (PLAN)

general description & what the students do

Program for Learning in Accordance with Needs was developed by the American Institute for Research in the Behavioral Sciences. It covers the curriculum areas of math, language arts, social studies, and science, and it uses a computer for scoring, record keeping, matching student with learning materials, scheduling, and making other recommendations.

The program consists of a number of "modules," each containing four to six behaviorally stated objectives. Accompanying the modules are TLU's (Teaching Learning Units), of which several relate to each module. Students select the TLU that is most interesting to them. Each TLU contains:

> a statement of objective
> examples of the types of questions that students should be able to answer after attaining the stated objective
> a list of instructional materials that can be used in the unit (these materials are all commercially available but are not produced by PLAN)
> a list of activities appropriate to the TLU

what the teachers do

Teachers have the following duties:

> organize and regulate the classroom so that students can work on their own initiative
> help students select their programs of study
> tutor and serve as resource persons
> assign module tests

What was that again?

When we personalize instruction, we try to teach in accordance with each student's interests, needs, abilities, and experiences. We teach students individually when necessary and in groups when necessary. But always the focus is on what is best for each individual student.

Almost every teacher would like to teach that way. Almost every teacher *would* teach that way if he could manage it. Unfortunately (well, let's be honest), it *is* a bit difficult to tailor instruction for every one of a teacher's 30 elementary or 125 secondary students.

Yet the picture grows brighter every day. New techniques and new materials are appearing in volume. Interest is on the upsurge. We see an increasing use of informal or "teacher-made" personalized schemes in reading, math, science, spelling, art, and so on. Programmed materials are available in practically every curriculum area, and they allow students to work and pace themselves independently. And now we have elaborate commercial packages, often expensive, for personalized instruction. Some use large computers to select materials, score tests, and keep records.

Every teacher can personalize instruction to some extent. Plans can be small at first, then expanded as experience brings new insights and skills. The students will appreciate it.

Materials, activities, objectives for learners

Will you indulge me for a few more lines and return your attention to the model of teaching in Chapter 6? That model showed some general objectives for learners, separated into two groups: cognitive/psychomotor and affective.

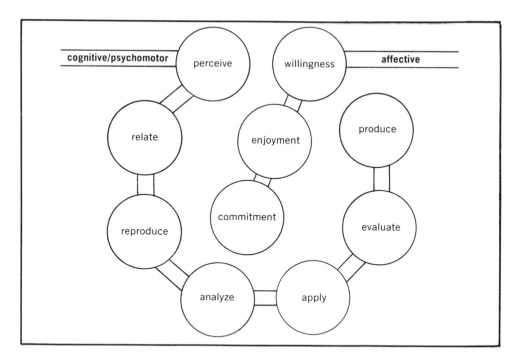

Your last job in this chapter: think about those objectives, and think about the contributions that materials and activities (such as the ones we have just considered) make toward attaining them. Try to match objectives, materials, and activities to each of your students. That's what it means to personalize instruction.

Part III

Working
with learners

deals with means of encouraging students to increase their amounts of **purposeful behavior,** with the rationale and techniques for **analyzing verbal interaction,** and with numerous strategies for increasing and improving **classroom interaction and communication,** done through chapters

8. Facilitating purposeful behavior
9. Analyzing verbal interaction
10. Enhancing classroom communication

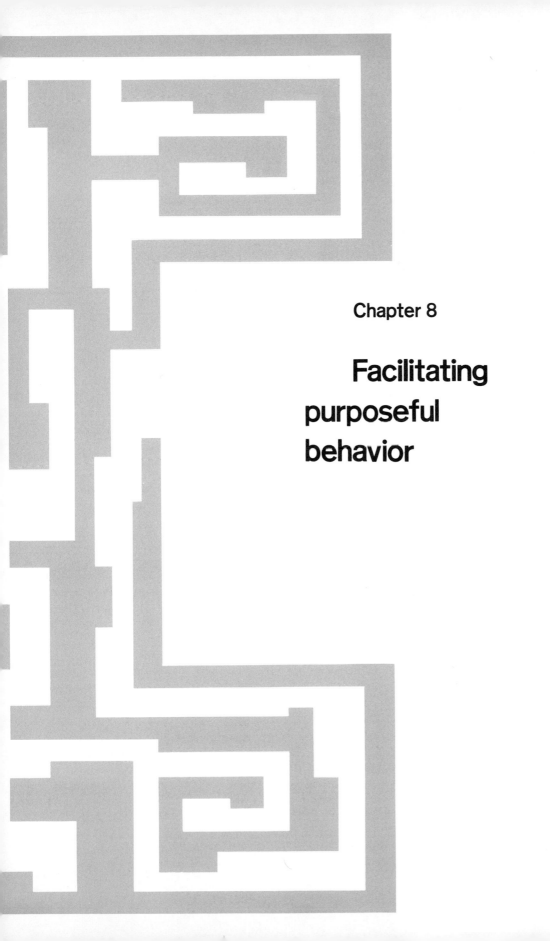

Chapter 8

Facilitating purposeful behavior

1. Behavior modification

how Tim & I trained Willie

Willie is a small brown dog, half cocker spaniel and half dachshund. When Willie was 3 months old, Tim decided that he should be trained. How, or for what reason, he didn't know. But that didn't matter; all dogs should be trained, and Willie was to be no exception.

We discussed the matter to decide what we should teach Willie to do. Tim thought we should train him to go to his dog house. Tim had told him to go there several times, but Willie hadn't even looked in the right direction. He had just chewed at Tim's shoe laces. We agreed it would be a good idea to train Willie to go into his house when we told him to.

First we had to decide what command to use. Tim thought we should say "Willie, go get in your house!" When we remembered that Willie was only 3 months old, we were afraid that "Willie, go get in your house!" might be too many words for a puppy to remember. Tim suggested that we just point to the house. I thought we should say "house." We decided to do both—to point and say "house" at the same time.

We tried the command a couple of times, but Willie didn't pay any attention. He jumped and tried to bite our fingers when we pointed.

"Tim," I said, "we're going to have to find a way to get Willie to do what we want him to. Maybe he will be interested in something he really likes. What does he like better than anything else?"

"I think he likes cat food best."

"That's in a can, isn't it?"

"Yeah."

"Well, that's too messy for us to use. What else does he like?"

"He likes dog biscuits."

"Okay, let's get a few."

We got a couple of dog biscuits, and I broke one up into little pieces. When Willie smelled them, he became very excited and started jumping toward my hand.

"Okay," I said, "let's see if we can get him to go close to his house."

Willie stuck right with me, trying to get at the dog biscuits. When I moved over to his house and put my hand on the flap door, he bumped his nose against my hand, so I gave him a tiny piece of dog biscuit.

He downed it at once and jumped against my hand again. I gave him another piece. He gobbled it and was back instantly. I put the goodies in my left hand and tapped the flap door with my right hand. Willie didn't realize I'd changed hands. He jumped and sniffed around my right hand. He bumped his nose on the flap door, and I immediately tossed him another reward. We repeated that three or four times.

Willie was working eagerly, so I crumbled another biscuit. Now I tapped the flap door with my finger and said "House! House!" Again when he touched the flap I rewarded him. I moved my hand a foot away from the door, pointed, and said "House." He looked at my finger, then turned and bumped the door. Reward. Now we had him going to the door on command. He would go eagerly, touch the flap, and then wheel around for his morsel.

I don't know how much further we might have gone then, for Tim wanted in on the act, so I reluctantly gave him the remaining dog biscuit and he took over. Oddly enough, Willie saw it as a different game. Tim pointed and said "House!" but Willie just tried to get the food from him.

"Tim," I said, "you'd better start like I did." So Tim touched the flap and said "House!" Willie nipped at his hand but did touch the flap. He got a crumb. After a bit Willie tired of the game — or had enough biscuit. We decided to stop for a while.

That evening after dinner, Tim and I decided to show Mom what Willie could do. I took the dog biscuit out, pointed to the dog house, and commanded "House!" Willie ran directly to Mom, who usually fed him. We had to have Mom go back inside the house and watch from behind the window curtain.

I pointed and commanded again, and good old Willie went right to his door, bumped it, and whizzed back for his reward.

Willie was playful again. I began to reward him only if he pushed the door, then only if he put his head inside. Tim took over and put Willie through his routine. So far so good, but we still didn't have him inside the house. The puppy was tired, so we stopped.

The next afternoon we took up the lessons again. Tim warmed up Willie, who remembered all his duties well. We had some trouble getting him to go completely inside his house. Finally, I had to push him inside and pitch in a piece of biscuit to get him to stay for an instant. After a couple of trials he got the idea, and then suddenly old Willie had it. Tim or I — it made no difference — could point and say "House!" and he would trot to his house, go completely inside, and then come galloping back.

Later, we trained him to remain inside when we said "Stay."

how Ruth trained Terry

Terry is a boy, a first grader with normal intelligence. He was a behavior problem. Was, but isn't. Ruth trained him to control himself and relate to others in acceptable ways.

You may have blanched at the use of the word "trained." Educators have scorned that word. *Train,* they say, is for dogs, seals, and horses; *educate* is for people. The implication is that training is a process that doesn't allow learners to make decisions about what they will do. Educators say that education is different because it is a process of helping learners to perceive a number of alternatives so that they may then intelligently choose the best alternative.

That reasoning is hard to support, at least in the light of what really occurs in schooling. Certainly the fundamental skills of reading, writing, and computing aren't taught as groups of alternatives.

But let's not spend time on that controversy. While "education" sounds better to me too, I have used the word "train" for Terry to make this anecdote tie in more closely with the story of Willie's training.

Okay. I could have used the term "behavior modification." It carries good credentials.

Terry was a behavior problem in Ruth Baker's first-grade class because so often he disrupted the class with shouts, refused to do his work, and badgered other children.

Ruth tried patience, understanding, and kindness, but Terry continued to misbehave. (See how effective her positive reinforcement was?)

Then she tried scolding, isolating, and sending Terry to the principal's office. Terry still continued to misbehave.

At her wit's end, Ruth asked her principal to call in the school psychologist, who talked with Terry and gave him some tests. Nothing unusual showed up in the test results.

The psychologist, however, did have a plan. Truth was, his plan sounded theoretical and textbookish. Ruth couldn't help wondering to herself, "Has this guy ever worked in a real classroom?" She was also worried that one part of the plan would be the ruination of her class—the part that required her to ignore Terry's bad behavior.

But the psychologist was very persuasive—friendly, relaxed, sure of himself—and he claimed that the scheme had proved itself in many similar situations. Besides, Ruth realized that nothing else had worked; she was miserable and ready to grasp at any straw, so she agreed to try.

This was the plan, simple and sweet:

1. Ruth and the students were to make rules about behavior in the classroom. These rules were to be few in number, and they were to be emphasized and reemphasized to the students.

2. The class—and Ruth—were to agree to *ignore*—to pay no attention at all—to students who failed to abide by the class rules. But if violation of the rules became disruptive, Ruth was to stop the classwork, state that rules were being broken (no names), and review the rules with the class.

3. Meanwhile, she was to praise students and groups (especially Terry) when the rules were being observed.

The strategy, then, in a nutshell:

rules   ignore   praise

Now, what do you suppose happened? Did this situation have a happy ending? The answer to that question depends on how high you set your expectations. After several weeks:

1. Terry still misbehaved more than any other student in the class.
2. But his misbehaviors had become less frequent, milder, and shorter in duration.
3. The behavior of the rest of the class had also improved.

Ruth was happy again, most of the time. Since Terry no longer kept it in turmoil, her class could almost always do its work. Ruth also noticed that her students showed a greater sense of responsibility. And they seemed to enjoy school just as much as ever—and the fact is, they enjoyed it quite a bit, because Ruth took pains to see that the class activities were always interesting.

I won't describe specific instances where Ruth reinforced Terry's appropriate behavior. Yet I think you can see some striking similarities between the training of Willie and the training of Terry. Let's look at them in capsulized form on the following page.

Willie's training program Terry's behavior modification

plan

Elicit appropriate behavior and reinforce it. Ignore instances of inappropriate behavior.

Same as for Willie

eliciting appropriate behavior

You can't tell Willie what to do; he won't mimic descriptions or demonstrations. So you have to work through "successive approximations," rewarding him each time he comes closer to the desired behavior.

Terry can understand descriptions; he can mimic demonstrations and examples, so he knows from the outset what is expected of him. He will show the appropriate behavior if the payoff is attractive enough. He can be expected to behave properly for increasing periods of time as the weeks go by.

reinforcement (reward system)

Willie works fastest for what he likes best—food when he is hungry. But you give him the food only when he has behaved in an appropriate manner. From time to time you have to expect more; he has to come closer to the most desirable behavior to get his reward. Otherwise he will not improve.

Terry would probably work like crazy for food, especially if he were hungry. But food is awkward to use in the classroom (although M & M's have proved to be effective reinforcers). We know that people will work to gain recognition, approval, and affection, so teacher praise serves as a good reinforcer for Terry. Like Willie, Terry should gradually be expected to do better, so that his reward will be given after increasingly longer periods of appropriate behavior.

maintenance

Learned behavior that is not reinforced tends to die out—to become extinguished. This means that we must continue to reinforce Willie's performance from time to time if we want it to remain strong and reliable.

Terry may stop behaving well if Ruth stops reinforcing his good behavior and if he again finds rewards in misbehavior. We hope he will find internal rewards for good behavior, rewards such as the realization that his proper behavior allows the best compromise between his own interests and those of the group. However, Ruth had better continue to praise him so long as he behaves well.

how Mr. Felton
trained Steve

Steve was a sophomore in high school. Mr. Felton was his physical education teacher.

Steve had a very outgoing personality. But it was not exactly a pleasant one. Steve saw himself as a young Don Rickles. Unfortunately, he lacked Rickles' redeeming qualities. He made disparaging remarks about everyone around him. The remarks weren't funny to anyone except Steve. Still, he made them right and left, and he did so to get attention. Steve didn't see that the attention he was getting made everyone dislike him.

The high school counselor determined that Steve had a poor self-image and did not consider himself masculine enough. He recognized that Steve's behavior traced back to that self-image. He enlisted a sympathetic teacher, Mr. Felton, to help work with Steve. Steve reluctantly agreed to the arrangement.

Mr. Felton began by discussing Steve's attitude with him, and the two agreed to work on eliminating Steve's negative, degrading verbal attacks on others. They informed Steve's parents about what they were doing, and the parents supported the idea. Everyone was aware of what behavior was to be changed, what kinds of punishment would be used (it was isolation from the group), and what kinds of reinforcers would be used to increase Steve's appropriate behavior.

Mr. Felton and Steve also agreed that Steve should complete certain activities in a "self-discovery unit." Those activities included Steve's drawing a picture of himself, writing a brief description of himself, writing a brief description of how he would like to be and have others see him, and completing a checklist that rated his personal traits. Steve also wrote paragraphs about what he believed five other people thought of him. Those five people were a best friend, an enemy, a teacher, a sibling, and a parent. Then Mr. Felton got those people to write paragraphs about what they thought of Steve. Mr. Felton and Steve matched the paragraphs to compare Steve's perceptions with those of the other people.

For eight weeks Mr. Felton made special efforts to work with Steve. He used a combination of behavior modification strategies and self-discovery exercises. At the end of that time Steve's disparaging remarks about others were greatly reduced, though they had not completely disappeared. He grew to accept and enjoy his relationship with Mr. Felton. He freely commented that he knew Mr. Felton was trying to help him and that he appreciated that help. Other students began to become more friendly toward Steve, as well.

reinforcement & learning

Learning is a change in behavior resulting from experience. That definition is not very precise: it must imply that the behavior change lasts for at least a short time beyond the experience during which it occurs. Further, the experience has to exclude certain things such as the process of growing older and the use of drugs that produce temporary or sometimes permanent changes in behavior. Still, the definition can serve us well enough, if we remember to emphasize **experience** and **behavior change.**

As we saw in the cases of Willie, Terry, and Steve, changes in their behavior were brought about and maintained by systems of reinforcement. The main reinforcers were food for Willie, praise for Terry, and personal relationship for Steve.

Reinforcement is not necessary for learning, especially not for human learning. You can go to Mount Rushmore, see the huge carvings of the Presidents, and be able to tell something about the experience for as long as you live.

But there can be no doubt that reinforcement is a powerful factor in most learning. It is doubtful that people past early childhood set out to acquire new learnings unless they see a payoff in store for them; and if they don't get some payoff or reward, they won't make the effort that is necessary to learn. Notice that I am referring to conscious attempts to learn. Most people can't live without learning new things regularly; experience forces the learning. But when someone sets out purposely to learn, knowing it will require an expenditure of time and effort, he expects and must receive something in return.

What is that "something in return"? For humans, it can be one of a great number of things that seem to fall roughly into categories paralleling Maslow's concept of human needs:

> food, water, sex
> safety, shelter
> love, affection, belonging
> recognition, praise
> knowledge, understanding

We can think of these categories as consisting of "primary reinforcers." These primary reinforcers have intrinsic value for human beings.

But the list of effective reinforcers for humans is very long because so many things become "secondary reinforcers." That is, an object or an act that becomes associated with a primary reinforcer takes on value to an individual. That's why a baby thinks so much of its bottle (even when there is no milk in it), why a ten-dollar bill is so nice to have (even in a piggy bank), why a smile from the teacher makes a student feel so good (even when no words are spoken).

reinforcement—some specifics

reinforcer a stimulus whose provision or removal, after an organism performs an act, increases the likelihood of the organism's repeating that act.

reinforcement the process of providing reinforcers.

  positive reinforcement the provision of reinforcing stimuli.

  negative reinforcement the removal of aversive stimuli.

  punishment the supplying of aversive stimuli following performance of an act. Punishment is often confused with negative reinforcement. The two are not the same.

shaping the progressive step-by-step changing of behavior through reinforcement.

contingency management the systematic use of reinforcement to shape behavior in desired directions.

behavior modification the process of shaping the behavior of school students through use of contingency management.

We have learned to put smiles and praise and plastic discs and M & M's to work in the classroom because of the contributions of the eminent psychologist B. F. Skinner. You have read about him in earlier sections, and you know about his pigeons, his "Skinner boxes," and his concepts of positive and negative reinforcement.

His work, first with rats and pigeons, later with humans, laid the groundwork for putting "contingency management systems" to use in educating learners. Contingency management refers to reward systems and the ways in which they are used.

Skinner's work has shown us many important things:

1. When certain stimuli are supplied or removed after an individual performs a given act, the individual becomes more likely to repeat that act. Such stimuli are called "reinforcers." The act of supplying or removing them is called "reinforcement."

2. Reinforcement can speed up and give direction to the learning process. It can be used to "shape" behavior. It can also be used to maintain desired behavior.

3. When learned behavior is not reinforced over a period of time, it tends to disappear. The procedure used to effect the disappearance of such behavior is called "extinction."

4. Behavior that has been maintained with "intermittent reinforcement" (reinforcement supplied at irregular intervals) is comparatively hard to extinguish. But behavior maintained with regular and frequent reinforcement is comparatively easy to extinguish.

5. Punishment can help extinguish behavior, but it often has undesired side effects in human learning.

How did Skinner make these discoveries? We can get an idea if we mentally conduct an experiment similar to many of those conducted by Skinner.

1. We select an organism whose behavior we want to shape—that is, we will try to teach it to do something. Let us select a pigeon, since that animal played such an important role in Skinner's experiments, and let us try to teach it to turn in a full circle to its right.

2. We place the pigeon in a specially designed environment. It is a small enclosure, just large enough to allow the pigeon to move around. It has glass walls so that we can see what the bird is doing. It has been fitted with a mechanism that can dispense reinforcers at the will of the experimenter; in this case, it contains a food box into which a pellet of food can be dropped whenever we wish.

3. We begin the procedure. The pigeon is placed in the environment, which is popularly called a "Skinner box." The bird is hungry, and it is curious about its environment. It looks this way and that, moving around, exploring. We watch and wait. Since we want the pigeon to turn in a circle to its right, we look for the first movement in that direction. Soon it happens. The pigeon makes a slight turning movement to its right. We activate the mechanism that drops a pellet of food, with a slight noise, into the food box. The hungry pigeon hears the noise and investigates, sees the pellet, and eats it. But the pellet was only enough for an appetizer, and the bird is as hungry as ever. Again we wait. Before long the bird makes another random move to its right. Again we drop in food. We repeat the procedure a few times.

4. Now the bird has begun to get the idea. He has learned that by making a short movement to his right he can get food. True, he has made a lot of false moves in the meantime, pecking at the empty food box and so forth, but now he makes the proper move every time. Only that little move is no longer good enough. He must turn farther to the right before we will reward him. He makes a slight turn and reaches to the food box. No food appears. He makes another slight turn. Again, nothing. Then he makes a bigger turn. Reward. And so the process continues until soon, surprisingly soon, the bird makes a complete circle to his right. That was the desired behavior, and we shaped it through successive approximations—that is, by rewarding the bird each time he made a small improvement over his previous performance.

5. Just as we taught the bird to turn in a circle, we can unteach him by extinguishing (or causing him to lose) the behavior. We do that in a different way; we simply stop giving the bird food after he turns in his circle. He will turn and turn, but after a period of appropriate behavior with no payoff, he will stop and will no longer perform his act.

In this same manner, Skinner taught his birds to do an amazing number of complex acts. They learned to peck out tunes on toy pianos, to chain long series of complex acts together, and even to play vigorously competitive games of ping-pong, in which each tried to drive the ball with its beak past the other.

It is to Skinner's credit that he didn't stop there. He crossed the chasm between experimentation with animals under very controlled conditions and the application of those results to human learning under much less controlled conditions. His writings about teaching machines and his experiments in using programmed materials with students have had a heavy impact on teaching methods. In fact, several "teaching machine" companies sprang up in the early 1960s, producing materials that learners could use to teach themselves.

reinforcement—
applications

If you think back to the training episodes for Willie and Terry, you will recognize that they were patterned along lines suggested by Skinner's experimentation. Appropriate behavior was shaped through the reinforcement of acts that came increasingly closer to the desired behavior. Those cases represented an application of reinforcement theory to the modification of behavior. We will come back to this point later.

programmed materials

I mentioned the emergence in the 1960s of companies that produced teaching machines and "programmed materials." The term "teaching machine" was initially popularized by Skinner himself in an article he wrote entitled "Teaching Machines." In reality, though, the heart of the teaching machine, the only really important part of it, was the programmed material that went inside. Soon the machine part—the metal box, the mechanism, the keys to punch—faded from the scene, and what we had left were the printed programmed materials. Programmed means that the content to be learned is broken into small sequential steps. Completion of all the small steps, accompanied by reinforcement in the form of "being right," leads students through successive approximations to the overall desired behavior.

Although few of the teaching machine companies turned out to be economically successful, programmed materials continue in vogue because they can be used effectively and efficiently to transmit factual information and build certain kinds of skills.

Most of the programmed materials differ from Skinner's original conception, that of the "linear program." In that kind of program, every learner went through every step. Many students found this to be very boring and pedantic. Since linear programs require a virtual 100% mastery, each step is often so small, so simple, and so plodding that the students who were more adept soon lost interest.

The nonlinear or "branching" program was devised as an alternative. It allows more knowledgeable learners to follow a track or sequence that skips many of the smaller steps, while less knowledgeable learners follow a track appropriate for them. The idea is to allow learners to skip work that they are already capable of doing.

A further change in some recent programs requires learners to respond with interpretations rather than miniscule bits of information. Lengthy feedback is provided to let learners know why they responded appropriately, or it indicates the errors they made and the part of the program to which they can return in order to correct their misinterpretations.

general classroom use

Reinforcement theory is proving to be of great value not only in programmed learning materials but in general classroom practice as well. Terry's case, which we described earlier, is a good illustration of this point.

Terry's misbehavior had to be changed. Otherwise neither Terry nor the other class members could profit adequately from their experiences in class. Unlike Willie or one of Skinner's pigeons, Terry could understand what was expected of him. He could hear verbal descriptions and see demonstrations of appropriate behavior. The problem to be solved in Terry's case was twofold. Ruth first had to identify something that Terry considered attractive and desirable. She then had to find a way in which Terry could earn that "something" through appropriate behavior.

That strategy is central in any scheme of behavior modification. What does the learner want (that can be supplied in the classroom) so much that he will be willing to earn it by doing what we want him to do?

For most learners, adequate payoff is readily at hand. It takes the form of:

> being right
> being first
> receiving attention
> receiving praise
> receiving privileges*
> receiving stars or marks
> receiving discs
> receiving trinkets
> receiving toys
> receiving edibles
> receiving money

Usually, classroom reinforcement doesn't have to involve more than the first four items on the list. Only in very difficult cases—with exceptional or extremely uncooperative learners—is it necessary to use toys, edibles, and money. But they serve when necessary and serve well.

Once suitable reinforcers are chosen, you have only to decide when to reinforce. Usually, reinforcement should come within a few seconds after an appropriate act. This is almost always the case with laboratory animal conditioning. Humans have the capacity to understand delayed gratification; that is, to relate reinforcement given some time after an appropriate act to the proper performance of the act itself. As a rule, however, reinforcement or at least acknowledgment that an act has been appropriate should come as soon after the act as possible.

At first, reinforcement should be given frequently and for even the slightest improvements. Later, more advanced or more complete behavior should become a prerequisite for reinforcement. As the behavior becomes well established, it is necessary to provide only occasional reinforcement.

*The use of more preferred activities to reinforce less preferred activities is called the "Premack Principle" after David Premack, who described and suggested it. Lloyd Homme has called it "Grandma's Rule"—first you do what I want you to do, then you can do what you want to do.

extinction

Experiments in contingency management have repeatedly shown that the way to extinguish undesirable behavior is simply to see that it does not get reinforced. That is why a teacher must ignore misbehavior that is to be extinguished, and that is why the class must also participate in ignoring the behavior: attention from classmates is just as reinforcing, if not more so, as attention from the teacher.

Yet ignoring inappropriate behavior when it has to do with attitudes and relations with others (that is, when it does not involve merely errors made in learning the subject matter) is for most teachers possibly the most difficult part of contingency management. You can understand this point fully if you have been in charge of a class that has some very disruptive students in it.

For this reason, teachers should not feel that they have to ignore *all* disruptive behavior. There are times when they must say "No, we cannot do that in this room." And there are times when they must isolate students who continue to be disruptive. But they must realize that isolation by itself does little to help misbehaving students improve their behavior. But it will stop the misbehavior for a time. And that, in itself, may be a blessing to the teacher and to the class.

But let's continue on a positive note: ignore inappropriate behavior when you can. The student will continue to use it only if some sort of payoff results.

punishment

We noted that punishment can serve to extinguish behavior. It can also serve to teach learners that there are times and places where a given kind of behavior will not be accepted. This can indisputably have a very desirable effect at times. Yet punishment, if it is used at all, should be used only as a last resort because along with its beneficial effects it creates numbers of undesirable effects that teachers hope to avoid.

> 1. It produces anxiety, together with escape and avoidance behaviors. Lying, stealing, and cheating are common behavior patterns that students develop in order to avoid punishment.
>
> 2. Hostility, aggression, and hangdog submission can result from severe punishment, especially if it is continually applied.
>
> 3. Punishment administered by adults sets up models of aggressive behavior for the young. Children of punitive parents tend to be

punitive toward other children, and when they reach adulthood, they tend to be punitive toward their own children. It has been reported that most cases of severe child abuse involve parents who were themselves abused as children.

4. Punishment may prevent the development of a loving relationship between adult and learner, although this is not necessarily the case if the learner feels that the punishment is deserved and just. However, there is potential danger here, for the youngster who maintains a loving relationship with a punitive adult (teacher or parent) may decide that any punishment is just and desirable. Such a child therefore becomes punitive.

Before they resort to punishment, teachers should try to provide the misbehaving student with an alternative behavior that is suitable and acceptable. If the student is pestering other students, for example, assign the misbehaving student a special lesson or cleanup job in the back of the room or outside, away from the other students. But be sure that this alternative isn't so attractive that it reinforces the pestering. Tasks that remove a misbehaving student from the other members of the class are usually quite effective. Students would usually rather stay with their classmates and work than be by themselves and play.

Like any other effective technique, contingency management used for behavior modification has its hazards. Just as we can shape behavior in desirable ways, we can shape it in undesirable ways as well. That is, we can encourage students to develop "bad" character traits as easily as "good" traits, and we can use reinforcement to keep students at work on the most useless and boring of tasks, tasks that are in no way valuable to the learners except for the immediate reward they receive for persisting.

Educational systems are very visible. And they have numerous watchdogs: parents, boards of education, accrediting agencies, state departments of education, special interest groups, and of course the professional educators themselves. Thus any inappropriate uses of behavior modification, even by one individual teacher, will almost surely be noted and stopped.

---

reinforcement— tangible systems

Most classroom reinforcement occurs through such intangibles as verbal and nonverbal acceptance, recognition, and praise. Tangible reinforcers such as candy and toys are also effective, sometimes far more effective than the intangibles. Let us end this discussion by noting five ways in which tangibles have been used as reinforcers in effective programs of behavior modification.

point system Students can earn points for good behavior, work accomplished, progress, improvement, initiative, or whatever. Points can be accumulated, kept track of on a master chart, and cashed in for such things as privileges, candy, or prizes.

token system This system uses tokens instead of points. Tokens, plastic discs, fake coins, and so on are given as reinforcers for desired behavior. These objects can be assigned different values. For example, five green discs can be exchanged for one red disc. Ultimately, the discs should be exchangeable for something like toys or prizes. However, the discs often become sufficient in themselves; students will work to earn them without a thought of cashing them in.

toy money system Toy money such as the bills that come with Monopoly games can be used to "pay" students for making desired responses. The different values are shown on the money, and the bills can be accumulated, traded, and used to buy candy, materials, and so on.

candy system M & M's make handy reinforcers because they are small, relatively neat, and popular with students. They work very well in behavior-shaping episodes where frequent reinforcement is supplied for very small steps. This system has been used experimentally in various ways: for teaching young children to tie their shoe laces and for teaching lisping students to pronounce "s's" correctly. Hard candy and gum also serve well. (One teacher of mentally retarded children bought a used glass globe dispenser such as those used to sell penny gum balls. He filled it with M & M's, and let his students earn pennies that they could then use in the dispenser to get candy.)

real money system An interesting idea now being tried in some places involves paying students real money for adequate school performance. The basic idea is that schooling is a student's job, just as selling insurance might be an adult's job. Therefore students ought to be paid for it. However, most teachers couldn't afford to pay their students very much—buying M & M's is costly enough. The real money systems have to depend at present on special funding that comes from outside the school's regular budget.

2. Classroom control

YOUNG MAN!
EITHER YOU BEHAVE
YOURSELF OR I'M
GOING TO KNOW
THE REASON WHY
!!!

Hey, that's great!
The first half of the battle in helping
students establish self-control is knowing the reasons
why students misbehave. In this discussion we will learn some of
the "reasons why."
The other half of the battle is figuring out what to do once
you know the reasons for misbehavior. We will also learn some strategies
for preventing and correcting student misbehavior.

Understand first that class control, or "discipline" as it is commonly called,
is *not* an end in itself. It is not a scheme to make learners behave themselves just because that's what learners should do. Class control
is necessary in classrooms for two reasons: to reduce dis-
ruptions so that students may work actively at their
learning tasks and to help students become
responsible and self-directing.

DOTTY & SAM

Dotty was a peach of a gal. Motherly, chubby, smart, and outgoing, she seemed a sure bet for success as a primary teacher. As it turned out, she wasn't.

Her first class of second graders almost drove her over the brink. She couldn't control them. They talked, laughed, yelled, and punched. They ran about the room. They did as they pleased, and what they did hardly pleased Dotty. At first she scolded, but they happily ignored all her directions and warnings. Soon she was just closing her eyes and ears and going through the motions of teaching.

After six weeks the principal had to intervene. He taught some lessons for Dotty, demonstrated control techniques, and talked with the children about proper behavior at school. He also talked with some of the parents, and he saved the class for Dotty.

Today Dotty is a successful teacher. She is lucky. Many like her don't survive the first three months.

In the shade near a big sprinkler that swept water across a thousand square feet of lawn, George Mobile leveled with me about Sam, a student teacher in his school.

"Going strictly on his knowledge, planning, resourcefulness, and personality, we would hire Sam in a minute. But we have doubts about his ability to control the students. We've decided not to take a chance on him."

My thoughts flashed back to a history teacher I had known years before. He hadn't finished the second week of school—his sophomores had literally driven him from the room. But I told George Mobile about Dotty, who had learned, with help, to manage her class.

"I know," he said. "Maybe it could be done in this case, too. But we have enough good applicants to choose from, and we're not going to risk trouble. Most teachers either have it or they don't."

YOU HAVE IT
OR YOU DON'T?

School administrators like George Mobile will tell you this: the most common failure of student and beginning teachers is an inability to control a class.

That's why, when they consider hiring a teacher, one of the first points they look at on the applicant's record is what it shows about classroom control. Despite that fact, most teacher education programs provide little systematic instruction in techniques of classroom control. Moreover, experience in student teaching seems to help only slightly. Some people even believe that the ability to control students is not learned. As Mr. Mobile would say, you either have it or you don't.

There is no doubt that some beginning teachers are skillful at controlling misbehavior while others aren't. Nonetheless, I have seen student teachers achieve marked improvement in control during a few weeks' time. This makes me sure that almost anyone, experienced or not, can increase the amount of purposeful learning activity in the classroom, reducing at the same time the amount of disruptive behavior. That's what we strive for through class control.

BEGINNING TEACHERS CAN IMPROVE THEIR CONTROL SKILLS THROUGH PRACTICE IN:

1. **identifying specific misbehaviors likely to occur in the class**

2. **determining the reasons for those misbehaviors**

3. **learning to remove or minimize causes of misbehavior (preventive control)**

4. **learning to stop misbehavior that does occur (corrective control)**

The remainder of this chapter presents information and suggests activities to help you develop these four skills.

BECAUSE IF YOU DON'T HAVE IT YOU CAN LEARN IT. STARTING NOW.

misbehavior

When you get right down to it, misbehavior simply means student behavior that the teacher doesn't like. Teachers have different likes, dislikes, values, and tolerances. Therefore, they won't always agree on whether a given action constitutes a misbehavior.

In addition, some behaviors that are considered serious by teachers are judged harmless by mental hygienists, and vice versa. For example, Sophie Ritholz did a study and found that teachers and mental hygienists often assigned very different "degrees of seriousness" to the same kind of misbehavior. The results of her study are shown below:

"seriousness" rank on a list of 50 items of student behavior*

student behavior	ranking by teachers	ranking by mental hygienists
heterosexual activity	1	26
stealing	2	13.5
truancy	3	23
cruelty	4	6
impertinence	5	37.5
disobedience	6	41
withdrawing	30	1
suspiciousness	41	2
depression	19	3
resentfulness	26	4

*Adapted from Ritholz, S.: Children's Behavior, New York, 1959, Bookman Associates, Inc.

Despite some differences of opinion, teachers find far greater agreement than disagreement regarding misbehavior.

Teachers see misbehavior mainly as:

1. unwillingness to work at assigned activities
2. disruptive acts that reduce learning efficiency during a lesson

The misbehaviors most often mentioned by teachers can be placed in seven main categories. Here you see those categories, with examples of specific acts:

student misbehaviors

categories	examples of specific acts
inattention	daydreaming, staring out window, squirming, reading something else, doodling, playing with object on desk
talking	whispering, interrupting, reading out loud, talking to neighbor or across room, mumbling and humming to self
unruliness	shoving, stomping feet, moving chairs, moving around room, laughing, calling out, making faces, jumping out of seats
aggression	fighting, kicking, calling names, throwing things, sassing, bullying
attention-seeking	showing off, clowning, teasing, aggravating others, tattling
defiance	refusal to obey, refusal to talk or move, talking back, doing the opposite of directions, writing hate notes
dishonesty	cheating on assignments, tests, and games, lying with intent to deceive, stealing

some misbehavior causes

Misbehaviors can have many causes. Some of these causes can be discovered only by highly trained diagnosticians, but most of them can be fairly easily identified by teachers. When a cause of misbehavior is eliminated, the misbehavior usually stops.

Let's break the causes of misbehavior down into four major groups and look at their component parts before we bring our information back together again in a **misbehavior-cause grid.**

group 1: learning tasks

Three important causes of misbehavior are related to the tasks, or activities, of a lesson. These causes are:

fatigue The students become tired and seek rest or change of activity.

boredom The activity fails to hold the students' interest, and they seek other things to do.

frustration The activity is too difficult, resulting either in excess nervous energy that takes the form of hostility or aggression or in withdrawal, apathy, and regression to behavior such as crying.

These three causes are easy to correct. Careful attention to them will prevent most behavior problems.

group 2: the teacher

Four important causes of misbehavior are related to the teacher. They are:

lack of clarity Students do not understand what is expected and therefore sit idly or do inappropriate things.

poor voice characteristics The teacher's voice is monotonous, grating, or whining. It conveys no sense of excitement. Some students can't hear distinctly. Others may be made nervous by the quality of the voice.

inconsistency The teacher is lax one day and strict the next or does not treat all students fairly. The students become unsure about the limits of acceptable behavior and resentful about unfair treatment.

poor classroom climate Serious misbehaviors often occur in classrooms that are psychologically cold, that allow little activity, that do not involve students in planning, and that do not reinforce desirable behavior.

These causes of misbehavior can all be corrected by the teacher.

group 3: the student

Four important causes of misbehavior reside within the student. They are:

ignorance Students don't know what is acceptable behavior and what is unacceptable behavior.

mimicry Students imitate each other. Misbehavior, especially by a class leader, can be very contagious.

habit Students often misbehave because of habits developed in other classrooms or outside of school.

displacement Some of the more serious misbehaviors such as aggression, defiance, and withdrawal result from emotional pressures. Unloved children, children of tyrannical parents, and children of broken marriages often find undesirable ways of seeking attention or venting hostilities.

Teachers can do much to correct ignorance, mimicry, and habit as causes of misbehavior. But they can do very little to correct unfortunate conditions outside the school. At best they can hope to help students find suitable means for getting needed attention or releasing pent-up emotions.

group 4: other causes

Two other causes of misbehavior are especially noteworthy. They are:

special events Holidays, athletic contests, special assemblies, and so on often make students more excited and boisterous than usual.

the unexpected Weather changes, fire drills, visitors, accidents, startling news, and so on often unsettle students and make them unable to work at previously planned activities.

These causes of misbehavior can be effectively neutralized and even used profitably through adequate advance planning.

misbehavior-cause grid

The misbehaviors and causes identified in the preceding section can be summarized and shown in the following model. When you look through the **misbehavior-cause grid,** you will notice that some categories overlap. The **x's** indicate causes and misbehaviors likely to go together.

	learning tasks			the teacher				the student				other causes	
	fatigue	boredom	frustration	poor voice characteristics	inconsistency	lack of clarity	poor classroom climate	ignorance	mimicry	habit	displacement	special events	the unexpected
inattention	x	x	x	x			x		x	x	x	x	x
talking		x				x	x	x	x	x		x	x
unruliness	x	x	x	x	x		x	x	x	x	x	x	x
aggression			x				x		x		x		
attention-seeking											x		
defiance			x				x				x		
dishonesty			x						x	x	x		

222

preventive control

From our listing of misbehaviors and their causes, we can see that many disruptive acts result from causes that can be easily controlled by the teacher. Good planning and preparation will cut misbehavior to a minimum and let you control the class by preventing undesirable student acts.

On the following pages we will briefly examine some ways in which you can become more adept at preventive control by avoiding some of the causes of misbehavior we have just examined.

learning tasks

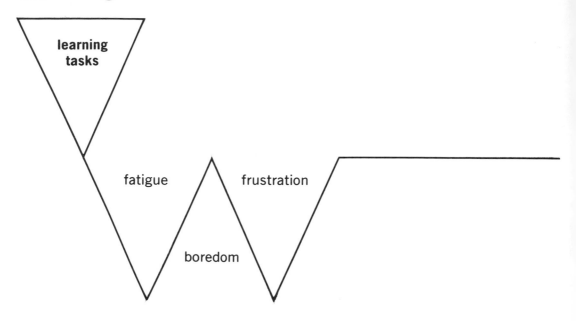

fatigue

As it occurs in school, **fatigue** is more often mental than physical. We know that there is a limit to the amount of time students of any age can spend attending closely to any activity. First-grade children grow tired of most activities quickly. We say they have short attention spans—no more than about twenty minutes for most school activities. High school students may work several times that long at highly interesting tasks. But everyone needs periodic changes of activity to avoid fatigue. A high school history lesson may last an hour; however, for best results it should be broken up into three or four different kinds of activity—reading, discussing, role-playing, and graphic work, for example—to keep students alert and actively engaged.

boredom

It is also easy to minimize **boredom** through advance planning. We know that learners seldom enjoy hearing lectures or reading textbooks, while they do enjoy such things as discussions, physical movement, novelty, concrete objects, puzzle situations, competition, and dramatic reenactment. To avoid boredom as a cause of misbehavior, you may build into your lessons objects, activities, and ideas that you know are interesting to your students.

Be ready to change pace or activities when you see students beginning to lose interest.

frustration

When you keep trying hard to do something you can't do, **frustration** occurs. This condition, with its undesirable side effects, often occurs in school, especially in reading and mathematics. Somehow we gladly accept large differences in physical and artistic abilities of students. But we don't want to accept the fact that not all students read or do math "up to standard."

We have long known that students progress fastest when they are given work that is challenging but is within their capabilities. We must be sure that every learning task, reading and math included, is suited to the ability of each of our students. When they have difficulties with parts of the tasks, we must give them "hurdle help." If the activities still prove too difficult, they should be made easier or set aside until later.

also...

At this point I want to add a few more observations about learning tasks. Several times during each day there are some awkward moments—moments of a few minutes' length when some students have finished their work but don't have time to begin a new activity before the period ends. Among these awkward times are the minutes just before recess or change of class, just before the lunch break, and just before dismissal for the day. If students don't have something to occupy their time for those short periods, they will often misbehave. To prepare for such times of the day, you can plan high-interest activities that can be used on a moment's notice. If students are working independently, they will be finishing their work at different times.

Tiedt and Tiedt* suggest two independent activities for such occasions. They call one of these activities a "box of challenges." In the box are crossword puzzles, magic squares, synonym studies, word quizzes, anagrams, antonyms, and so on. Different boxes of challenges can be prepared for different curriculum areas. They also suggest an "exploring time" that allows students, when there is sufficient time, to work on individual research projects.

Such activities, along with the traditional free reading and artwork, provide a variety of worthwhile tasks for students at awkward times of the day.

When students finish group work early, they can enjoy different kinds of activities together: mental math, favorite class songs, or various kinds of word games. These short times also provide good opportunities to practice creativity exercises such as brainstorming and composing captions for cartoons.

Awkward moments often occur during the distribution of materials. To avoid behavior problems, you will want to streamline such procedures for maximum efficiency. Place materials on students' desks for the beginning activity. For activities

*Tiedt, S., and Tiedt, I.: Elementary Teachers' Complete Ideas Handbook, Englewood Cliffs, N. J., 1969, Prentice-Hall, Inc.

that follow, have books, papers, pencils, and other materials stacked at your desk or ready in storage cabinets. Assign students to help distribute the materials. Have cleanup procedures well organized.

the teacher

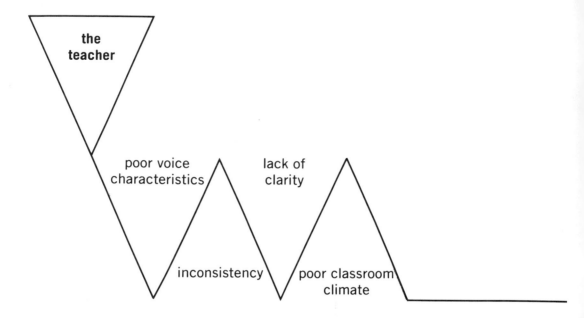

Characteristics of the teacher that cause discipline problems can be corrected, too, but not so easily as the learning tasks. Teachers, like everyone else, do not see themselves as others do.

poor voice characteristics

That's why a teacher who may hear her own voice perfectly because she is near it, or who finds her voice pleasant because she is accustomed to it, may go for years without ever realizing that she speaks too softly or that her voice characteristics irritate others. The **voice** can be checked in two ways. One way is to record your classroom talk and then listen to it. That will tell you something about how your voice sounds to your students. You may also notice a tendency to overuse words and sounds such as "um," "ah," "okay," "good," "yeah," and "well." Another way to check your voice is to ask your principal or a fellow teacher to visit and tell you how your voice sounds and carries in the classroom.

inconsistency

It will be hard for you to recognize **inconsistency,** even though your students will be sensitive to it. You will have to double check yourself to decide whether you seem to be enforcing the rules of conduct in about the same way each day, within moderate limits, and whether you treat all your students about the same. Here you will find it necessary to walk a narrow line. You may recognize the necessity of giving Tom, whose home life makes him demand attention, what he so sorely needs. Your students may see your conduct as favoritism toward Tom.

lack of clarity

Though it is often a significant problem, **lack of clarity** can be corrected easily. First, require attention from your students. Give directions only once, as clearly as you can. Then ask whether the directions have been understood. Occasionally call on a student to repeat what you have said. You may want to discourage students from asking questions about procedures after the lesson has begun. Or you may want to alternate "talk" activities with "silent" activities. During silent activities no one should talk, including the teacher. You can use symbols or signs to give necessary directions during the silent periods.

poor classroom climate

If you are unfortunate enough to have a **poor classroom climate,** it will be the hardest of your characteristics to correct. Poor climate was previously described as cold, with little activity, where students were not involved in planning. We should add to that the use of such punishing verbal behaviors as sarcasm and negative criticism.

As the teacher, you are the one who sets the classroom tone. To improve that tone, you may want to begin maximizing verbal interaction and begin practicing the "accepting" behaviors of questioning, active listening, constructive criticism, and rewarding. Try to relate to each student as an individual. Involve the class in as much cooperative planning as possible. Let them help decide on activities, procedures, and rules. The main objective is to involve students as much as you can without abdicating your responsibility of functioning as the leader of the class.

also...

Let's add a few words about physical position and nonverbal signals. Students must feel that their teacher is there to help them learn. They must recognize the teacher as the classroom leader.

Teachers who move about the room project an image of helpfulness and leadership. By standing near students who are inclined to misbehave, they help maintain students' self-control. Signals also help. Practice making eye contact, facial expressions such as lifted or knitted eyebrows, smiles, frowns, and grimaces, head nods and shakes, and hand signals such as the palm-out caution signal.

These signals help your students feel you are interested in them and want to help. They will help keep you out of a predicament such as the one in which Martin, a beginning student teacher, once found himself. His college supervisor told me how surprised she was at Martin and how hard she had to work with him during the semester. Martin planned beautifully. The objectives, activities, and materials components of his lesson plans were outstanding. But in the classroom, Martin was wooden. His expression never changed. He saw only the back of the room over his students' heads. He seemed frozen in position at the chalkboard. His supervisor finally had to require that he practice moving about the room, looking each student in the eye, and changing facial expression every few moments.

the student

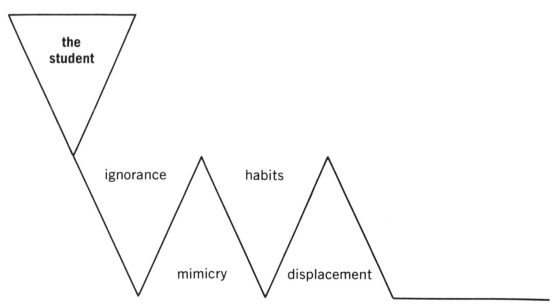

You can't remove all the causes of misbehavior that reside in the student. You can, however, affect some of them.

ignorance

When the cause of a student's misbehavior seems to be **ignorance**—a simple lack of information about the rules—you merely have to review such rules with the class. You will need to review them from time to time in any case, to help students keep them in mind.

Regarding rules, you and your students should compose a list that is short, to the point, educationally relevant, understandable, and positive. I remember hearing a first-grade class discussing its rules of conduct. Not all the rules were positively stated. However, they were short, to the point, and understandable:

1. We raise our hands before talking.
2. We don't interrupt.
3. We don't disturb others.

That was their list. The children (with the help of the teacher) decided on them, understood them, and for the most part practiced them.

mimicry

There is little you can do in advance to inhibit **mimicry** other than discuss with the class the possibility of its occurring, what might cause it to occur, and what its detrimental effects can be. We can urge students not to imitate bad examples, though with older students that has to be done tactfully. And we can urge them individually to conduct themselves in ways that bring credit, rather than discredit.

habits

Poor conduct **habits** carry over from class to class and year to year. Habits are actions that do not require conscious thought. Out of habit, Sammy may shove other boys in line or Mary may speak disrespectfully to the high school librarian.

Habits can sometimes be erased through calling them to the student's conscious attention. When they persist, this two-step remedy can be the answer. First, use negative practice — that is, assuming your students are willing to change their behavior, have them consciously practice the misbehavior they want to change. That helps them become fully aware of it. Second, help them practice a suitable alternative. That allows them to make a habit of the desirable act. Be careful, though, to use negative practice only when you are sure students want to change misbehavior. Otherwise you will only add fuel to the fire.

displacement

You can do practically nothing about removing **displacement** as a cause of misbehavior. Ann may continue to bully smaller children so long as she is bullied at home. Bill will continue to daydream so long as he finds fantasy less painful than reality. At best you can forewarn and forearm yourself by knowing as much as possible about each student's background. Then the outbursts will not take you by surprise, and you will be better prepared to cope with them.

other causes

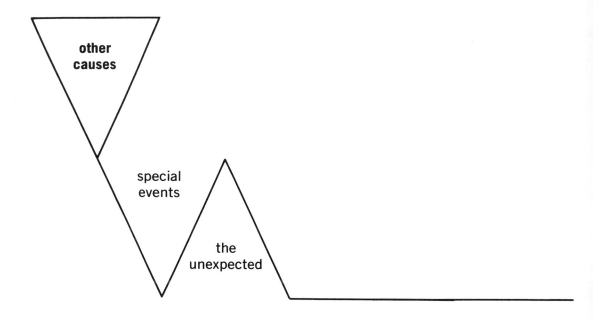

In this category we have included two kinds of occurrences that often cause misbehavior. Those occurrences are **special events** and **the unexpected.**

special events

Teachers often comment on the rowdiness their students exhibit near holidays, important athletic contests, school celebrations, and so forth.

Experienced teachers learn to adjust their lessons to take advantage of such events. At Halloween, elementary teachers introduce stories, games, art projects, and music activities—in short, almost everything in the curriculum—with a Halloween motif. Secondary teachers have some of their best discussions and group activities in planning school proms, carnivals, science fairs, and so on. When you capitalize on student interests at such special times instead of struggling against them, you can turn potential misbehavior into an educational advantage.

the unexpected

In this category we can lump all occurrences that you don't anticipate, such as accidents, animals in the classroom, severe weather changes, and your having to leave the classroom.

You should expect the unexpected and intend to make the best of the situation. When a class becomes upset because a student gets injured, the regularly planned lesson will seldom succeed. That's a good time for games or special activities you have held for just such times. When a child brings an animal such as a snake into the room (and don't flinch—it may well happen), first have him put it into a screen cage you have on hand in the cupboard. There all students can look at it without danger of being injured or, what is more likely, injuring the animal. Then you have a good opportunity for a lesson on observation and description or for a discussion or creative writing lesson. Once the students' curiosity is satisfied you return to the regular lesson.

Severe weather changes, wind, snow, and rain often make students especially restless. There, too, you can bring out materials you have prepared and kept aside—crossword puzzles, riddles, songs, poems to read aloud, choral verse activities, creative writing assignments.

Always have in mind two or three of your class's favorite group activities to be used in case an emergency requires that you leave the room. Ask the principal or another teacher to watch your class for you. Students can play their favorite games, sing songs, or work on group projects. Or they can work on individual projects, do artwork, or read library books.

corrective control

We will use the term "corrective control" to refer to what the teacher can do to stop misbehavior that does occur despite best efforts at preventive control. Through foresight we can keep misbehavior to a minimum. But when it does occur, especially if it disrupts the class, we must see that it stops at once.

In this section we will examine various corrective control techniques recommended for use by teachers. The following outline material has been adapted from selected writings.*

influence techniques

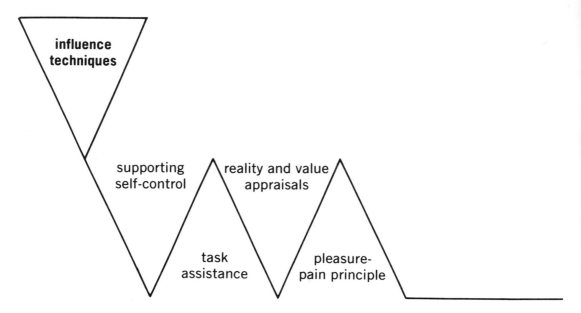

Redl and Wattenberg summarize four categories of what they call "influence techniques" commonly used by teachers. The categories are supporting self-control, task assistance, reality and value appraisals, and invoking the pleasure-pain principle. Brief descriptions follow.

supporting self-control

In this category, Redl and Wattenberg include teacher techniques that help students to control misbehavior that is just beginning. Among the techniques discussed are:

> **signals** head movements, eye contact, facial expression, hand movements, silence, bells, symbols on the chalkboard

*Cuffs, N. A., and Moseley, N.: Teaching the Disorderly Pupil in Elementary and Secondary School, New York, 1957, Longmans, Green & Co.; Kounin, J.; et al.: Explorations in Classroom Management, J. Teacher Educ. **12**:235, 1961.; Redl, F., and Wattenberg, W. W.: Mental Hygiene in Teaching, New York, 1959, Harcourt, Brace & Co.; Redl, F., and Wineman, D.: The Aggressive Child, Chicago, 1957, The Free Press of Glencoe, Inc.

proximity physical nearness to students showing an inclination to misbehave

humor

interest boosting interjecting at appropriate points in a lesson words, actions, or objects to increase students' interest

task assistance

Here Redl and Wattenberg suggest actions that help remove frustration at difficult places in a lesson:

hurdle help providing helpful hints and clues at difficult parts of an activity

restructuring making corrections or changes in the middle of a lesson

reality & value appraisals

The teacher points out realities and consequences of student behavior: "It is dangerous, it is destructive, it harms others." Or he may turn to the student's superego: "You are capable of much more, you don't want to be like that, is this something you will be ashamed of?"

In this category, Redl and Wattenberg also include positive, constructive criticism and the interpretation and reflection of behavior: "I know you are tired . . . ."

invoking the pleasure-pain principle

Since this category, as constructed by Redl and Wattenberg, emphasizes pain far more than pleasure, let's begin with the positive.

promises and rewards Most of the experimental work in shaping behavior through operant conditioning has involved positive reinforcement. That is, when an animal—pigeon or human—does what we want it to do, we give it something it wants. Hungry pigeons want food. Students want praise. Think back. Remember the rewards you got in school for good behavior? Praise, gold stars, special privileges? Let's try always to remember the value of positive reinforcement. Hopefully we won't often have to resort to punitive acts such as those mentioned in the remainder of this section.

threats You probably remember the threats, too. Maybe some were even carried out. Often, though, threats are idle. Students soon learn if you don't mean what you say. Then they will disregard you.

deprivation When your students misbehave, you take away a privilege they otherwise had. They are not allowed to work with other members of their group, they can't participate in games, they are not considered for special duties or awards, and so forth.

restitution When students destroy something, you require them to pay for it or replace it. When they do something wrong, they make restitution through good deeds.

corporal punishment This is the spanking, the cuff on the head, the hair pull, the pinch. It is whatever causes physical pain, even when it comes in such forms as standing on knees in the corner and the too-firm grasp on a small shoulder. Corporal punishment is a last-resort control technique. It is legal in most places, it seldom causes more than passing discomfort, and it is often very effective in stopping misbehavior. But it is highly **undesirable** for two reasons:

> 1. It teaches students that might makes right and that it is all right for them, in turn, to use it on weaker classmates.

> 2. Once the corrective control is done, the slate should be clean. Bygones should be bygones. Good relations should be maintained between teacher and student. But the lasting mental sting of corporal punishment is very hard for most students to forget.

review

At one time or another you will have students exhibit the full range of misbehaviors listed in this chapter. They will be inattentive, they will talk when directed to be quiet, they will be unruly, aggressive, and defiant, they will seek attention, and they will be dishonest.

When any of these misbehaviors occur, you will be able to select an appropriate control technique if you can quickly answer these questions:

1. Why is the student behaving this way?

2. How has the student reacted, or how will the student react, to available control techniques?

3. How will a given control technique affect this student's relationship with me and the class?

Now you must stop the misbehavior so it won't spread. But you don't want to wound the students or disgrace a particular student before the class.

At this point let's draw together what we have considered so far. We have examined:

common classroom misbehaviors

some of their causes

preventive control techniques — ideas for warding off misbehavior

corrective control techniques — ideas for correcting misbehavior

Now we will put them together into a **classroom control model.**

a classroom control model

misbehavior cause:

learning tasks
fatigue
boredom
frustration

preventive control tactics:

plan short work periods with frequent changes of activity; capitalize on students' special interests; use objects, novelty, color, movement, competition, puzzles, challenges; assign work within capabilities of students; help with difficulties

corrective control tactics:

make mid-lesson corrections when fatigue, boredom, or frustration become evident; add interest, help with difficulties, change activities if necessary

misbehavior cause:

the teacher
voice
inconsistency
lack of clarity
poor climate

preventive control tactics:

check for proper volume, pitch, and quality of voice through recordings or requested observations; determine whether students understand directions; treat them fairly, as individuals, with warmth and humor; use much questioning, listening, constructive criticism, and rewarding; involve students in planning and evaluating

corrective control tactics:

alternate talk periods with periods of quiet when no one talks; ask misbehaving students if they understand directions; increase and improve verbal interaction; ask students to make suggestions for desirable changes in lessons

misbehavior cause:

the student
ignorance
mimicry
habit
displacement

preventive control tactics:

cooperatively formulate and periodically review class conduct rules; discourage imitation of misbehavior; reward appropriate behavior; know students' backgrounds

corrective control tactics:

review class conduct rules; support students' self-control through signals, proximity, and humor; use incentives and praise to establish good behavior habits; isolate chronically disruptive students; punish when necessary with deprivation and restitution

misbehavior cause:

other causes
special events
the unexpected

preventive control tactics:

anticipate and use to advantage students' interests in holidays, contests, etc.; have high-interest or class-favorite activities preplanned for use in emergencies

corrective control tactics:

when misbehavior occurs in these circumstances, have students diagnose "what went wrong"; plan procedures to eliminate future misbehaviors

misbehavior causes · preventive and corrective control tactics

cases

 # 1 Harold told me the following story as we were on the way to a meeting. "There were these two girls," he said, "who whispered together in class every day. I wanted them to stop, but I didn't want to call attention to them. I threw them questions, fixed them with glares, and often paused in exasperation, hoping they'd get the point. Nothing worked. This went on for weeks and it really bothered me. Finally, in desperation I asked them to stay after class, and I told them how much their whispering bothered me. Now, get this! They both got tears in their eyes and told me how sorry they were they had let me down!"

 # 2 Mr. Layton's sixth graders ordinarily worked very well when given assignments to do at their seats. In February, however, he let Washington's birthday slip his mind when he planned the week's work. Back from the holiday, he hoped to make up lost time. He passed out worksheets on prefixes and suffixes and extended the study session so it ran through a thirty-minute period usually intended for art.

Mr. Layton soon noticed that the noise level in the room began to rise. Feet shuffled, and books fell from desks. He reprimanded the class for not keeping their minds on their work. Three students broke their pencil points and walked to the front for replacements. John tipped his chair and fell out of it. The class laughed. Mr. Layton scolded them again and wrote John's name on the board. John stared hard at his dictionary but didn't finish his work. Neither did several other students who would ordinarily have done the work easily.

If this scene could be erased and played again, what changes would you suggest for the benefit of the students and Mr. Layton?

 # 3 Miss Silva's Spanish II class was composed of top students from the previous year's Spanish I classes. The students were very accomplished. They liked Miss Silva and she liked them.

At the beginning of each week, Miss Silva made assignments for the entire week so that her students could work ahead when they had time. An interesting pattern began developing. One week, for example, the students were assigned to read two chapters in a Mexican novel, with a first class discussion due on Wednesday and a second on Friday. They were also assigned a dialogue skit to be practiced and memorized during the week and to be played from memory on Thursday.

On Wednesday, Miss Silva found that the class had not read enough of the novel chapters to discuss them. The students laughingly made some excuses about too much other work. Miss Silva laughed with them and said they'd better expect a double dose on Friday. Then she spoke in Spanish about some experiences she had had in South America and asked questions to check the students' comprehension.

On Thursday, the students were not prepared to perform the skit. They ad libbed, making several errors in language usage. Miss Silva held her nose each time she heard an error, and the period passed quickly with everyone laughing.

On Friday, two students and Miss Silva discussed the chapters assigned. The others glanced sideways at each other with little smiles.

That pattern became established. The students and Miss Silva usually passed the time agreeably. But no one really liked the class, and everyone knew something was wrong.

How do you think the situation could have been improved?

#4 Mr. Johnson, in his first year at a small junior high school, dreaded the 9:00 A.M. period. His assignment for that hour was supervising a study hall of fifty eighth graders that met in the school library. Mr. Johnson urged the students to use the hour to prepare for their day's classes. He told them that if they didn't need to study they could always get a book or magazine to read.

In no time the students stopped thinking of the hour as a study time. Sitting six to a table, they spent the time talking, laughing, and passing notes. They constantly asked for passes to go to the restrooms.

At first Mr. Johnson expected that he could use the hour to make plans and check work for his general math classes, but he found that he had to spend the time glaring fiercely at the students and calling authoritatively for quiet every few minutes. He tried sending some of the offenders to the principal's office. But that didn't help, and he was embarrassed to have the principal think he couldn't control 13- and 14-year-old youngsters. At last Mr. Johnson had to admit the situation was out of control. Swallowing his pride, he asked the principal for suggestions.

Put yourself in the principal's place. What might you plan to help Mr. Johnson?

#5 Alex was the worm in Miss Christensen's apple, the despair in her joy, the failure in her success, the puncture in her ego. Alex: 7 years of age, IQ measured at 86, repeating first grade.

He was the one misbehavior problem among twenty-nine delightful children. Unable to stay in his seat, he constantly jumped up and walked about the room. He thumped well-behaved children on the head, pulled their hair, and called out to them at any time across the room. On the playground he bullied the others, hit and pinched them for no apparent reason, and continually annoyed them by kicking balls away from them and disrupting play.

Miss Christensen usually used no more than three corrective control tactics: a reminder of how good citizens behave (keep hands to themselves, keep lips closed, raise hands before talking); an appeal to the superego ("Do we think that's the way we want to behave now that we're almost seven?"); an authoritative verbot ("We must not pull hair in this room."). None of these tactics worked with Alex.

Miss Christensen continued her search for a means to end Alex's disruptive behavior. She talked with the boy's mother and found out that Alex's father had deserted the family when Alex was 2 years of age. His mother had tried to work but couldn't hold a steady job; she had remarried when Alex was 6. Alex's stepfather was abusive and domineering, and he often gave Alex severe spankings with a belt.

With this information, what might you try if you were in Miss Christensen's shoes? Her continuing attempts at working with Alex are described in the following paragraphs.

After her informative visit with Alex's mother, Miss Christensen asked the school psychologist to talk with Alex.

Meanwhile she made a point of speaking alone with Alex whenever possible, reasoning with him and praising every indication of proper behavior. She gave him clay to pound with his fists whenever he felt the urge to hit, and he pounded it often. She gave him all sorts of jobs to do—dusting erasers, arranging chairs, opening blinds, passing out paper, passing the wastebasket. The other children in the class, evidently sensing her motives, did not seem to resent the attention Alex received.

She did, however, continue keeping him isolated from the other children, sitting apart in his chair at a small table. He was pleasant and cooperative when working and talking alone with Miss Christensen, but he still could not interact properly with the other children. Under these conditions his disruptive behavior diminished, but it was still much worse than that of the others.

The school psychologist did talk at length with Alex, and he told Miss Christensen he was trying to arrange a talk with the boy's parents.

Think about these cases, and then review the **misbehavior-cause grid** and the **classroom control model** before moving on to the next page.

performance
criteria

College students have found these performance criteria helpful in developing their skills in classroom control. Maybe you'd like to try your hand at them.

1. Identify seven categories of misbehaviors likely to occur in the classroom.
2. Name four specific acts of misbehavior included in each of the seven categories.
3. Identify thirteen possible causes of classroom misbehavior.
4. Indicate twelve causes of misbehavior that can be controlled by the teacher.
5. Select two specific misbehaviors from each of the seven categories. Describe a method of *preventing* the occurrence of each of those misbehaviors.
6. List Redl and Wattenberg's four categories of teacher influence (corrective control).
7. Name one advantage and one disadvantage of each of the following punishments: threat, deprivation, restitution, corporal punishment.
8. Using the **misbehavior-cause grid,** analyze a hypothetical misbehavior problem. Name the misbehavior(s). Indicate probable causes. Describe means of preventing the misbehavior. Describe desirable means of correcting the misbehavior. Make a list of alternative corrective tactics, and indicate the order in which you would use them if each, in turn, did not succeed.
9. In an actual classroom where you are teaching or observing, identify a group or individual misbehavior situation. Describe how you would/did correct tne misbehavior and describe or predict the results.
10. In your college classroom, demonstrate through role-playing your ability to correct misbehaviors in each of the seven categories. Show how you would use punishment if necessary, and how you would try to maintain good relations with the students who have been punished.

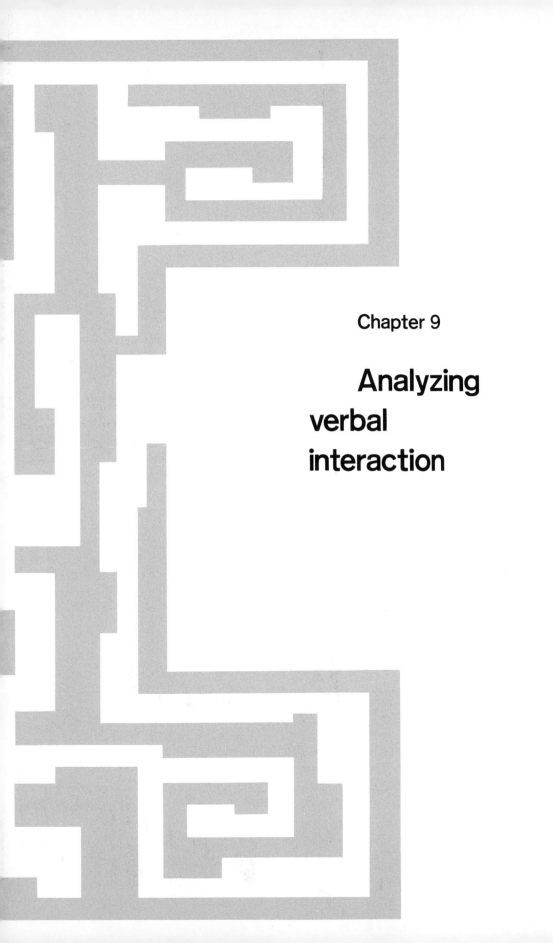

Chapter 9

Analyzing verbal interaction

3 short stories

1.

Long ago Frank told me he was taking a high school government class in which the teacher did almost no talking. The class was terrific, Frank said, the very best he had ever had. I couldn't believe him, not until ten years later.

It was no secret that Frank liked to talk just as much as he hated to work, so the class format sounded as though it would suit him well. But I just couldn't fathom any decent teacher turning a class over to the students. A teacher was supposed to know and tell. If he didn't, it meant (to me) that either he didn't know his subject or he didn't care about his students.

But for some reason, Frank's story stuck with me. Maybe because it was different. Maybe because I really did know, deep down, that there was something to what he had said.

2.

Jim says that, of his elementary school years, he remembers only the fourth grade. During that year, he was Miles Standish cut loose when Priscilla encouraged John Alden to speak for himself, a cowboy pony, a pilot, a spinning wheel operator, a public speaker, a lost little boy, a talking dog, and so on and on. He was all of these in the classroom, understand, not on the playground or after school. He spoke the words and played the roles. He talked a lot, and in order to do it right, he learned a bit about the minds and circumstances of all of these characters, and to help things further, he often made and wore the proper hat or mask.

3.

When Mrs. Simpson asked me to tell her kindergarten class about Mexico, I gathered a few slides, a jungle bow and arrow, a pillow cover made by a child, a Saltillo sarape, and a Chihuahua hat to share with the children. I went in prepared to tell them exciting anecdotes that would tickle their fancies.

Those kids greeted me with a barrage of questions that they rattled off while trying on the hat, pulling the bow, and examining the arrows. They talked excitedly (though not too boisterously), each telling of his own marvelous experiences (or fantasies—they're much the same at age 5). For twenty minutes they asked questions, talked, shared, and handled the objects. Most of my stories never got told.

With that episode in mind, I planned a great strategy for the first meeting of my college class. The topic was to be motivation. When I brought in those same objects, spread them out on display, and handed them to the students, their eyes opened and glowed and smiles spread across every face. I braced to field the questions. (I would categorize comments, abstract salient points, pinpoint emerging insights, and move on to powerful generalizations about motivating students to learn.) The students did not speak a word.

That was early in the semester. Afterward, they changed, but at that time, unlike the kindergarteners, my students waited for me to talk, to tell. They showed their training and manners; they had note pads ready and pencils poised. We were twenty minutes into the period before students began talking.

1.

2.

3.

Perhaps it wasn't evident, but those three little stories were all about classroom talk—what we will now begin calling "verbal interaction." Verbal interaction means exchanges of talk among people.

The kinds of verbal interaction hinted at in the stories are varied. The first story, for example, implied that students talked a lot in class, enjoyed it, and learned a lot. The third story showed what one group of college students expected in the way of classroom talk.

Our purpose in this chapter is to learn how to pay attention to verbal interaction, learn how to analyze it, and begin learning how to improve it. We will learn to be sensitive to how much the teacher talks and how much the students talk. We will learn to recognize kinds of talk, such as "telling," "asking," "accepting," and "rejecting." We will learn what effects different kinds of teacher talk have on students. And we will learn several techniques for improving the effectiveness of talk that occurs in the classroom.

3.

2.

1.

The Flanders system

Ned A. Flanders, an American university professor, gets much of the credit for what has been done in interaction analysis. Many others have contributed, of course, but Flanders developed the most widely known classification categories, and he and his students have done much of the research that supports the effectiveness of analyzing verbal interaction.

If you are interested in reading the research, you will find a large number of important reports compiled by Amidon and Hough.* Several of those reports show essentially the same thing: teachers who are more "indirect" (and you can become indirect through working in interaction analysis) have students who learn more and like school better.

In 1957, Ned Flanders was working in Wellington, New Zealand. He had tabulated some interaction codings made in an elementary classroom there. He discussed the codings with a statistician and became convinced that they could be placed into categories that were distinct one from the other.

Those tabulations led to Flanders' conceptualizing a matrix that would show shifts in classroom conversation. The shifts would indicate what talk led into what. From the matrix pattern, it slowly became evident that some kinds of teacher talk could suppress student responses. Whereas other kinds could cause them to respond energetically and ask questions of their own.

He concluded that suppressive talk could fit into several different categories that combined to form a "dominative pattern." Flanders later called such styles of talk "direct influence." They included such talk as lecturing, criticizing, and giving orders and directions.

He also concluded that encouraging talk could fit into several different categories that combined to form an "integrative pattern." Flanders later called such styles of talk "indirect influence." They increased the amount of student participation and included such talk as questioning, accepting, and encouraging.

Flanders concluded that patterns of classroom talk could be laid open to scrutiny by using an analytical system consisting of ten categories. Those categories could be coded, and trained observers could use them to identify and summarize the patterns of verbal communication occurring during instruction.

*Amidon, E., and Hough, J.: Interaction Analysis: Theory, Research, and Application, Reading, Mass., 1967, Addison-Wesley Publishing Co., Inc.

Categories based on the Flanders system

teacher talk	indirect influence	1. accepts feelings 2. praises or encourages 3. accepts ideas 4. asks questions
	direct influence	5. lectures 6. gives directions 7. criticizes or justifies authority
student talk		8. student response 9. student-initiated talk
		10. silence or confusion

Here's how you use the Flanders system to analyze verbal interaction.

First, you memorize the ten categories in the system. You will have to code by number, so you must learn to associate the category of talk with its corresponding numeral.

Second, you listen to episodes of classroom verbal interaction and then code that interaction, using the numerals of the categories you have memorized. Every three seconds during a given episode, you write down the numeral that represents the kind of talk occurring at that instant. If the teacher is asking a question, you jot down a **4**; if a student is responding to the teacher, you jot down an **8**. It is crucial that you learn to code at consistent intervals.

Third, at the end of an episode you interpret your findings. You have been coding at the rate of twenty marks per minute. Those marks can give you a detailed picture of the verbal interaction that occurred, for when you tally your code marks, you can determine what percent of the time the teacher talked and what percent of the time the students talked; how much of the teacher talk was lecture or criticism or praise or questioning; and how much the teacher used "direct" influence and how much he used "indirect" influence.

This analysis and interpretation can be carried to even higher levels of sophistication, but we have gone far enough at this point for most neophytes. If you should wish to read further, check the book mentioned earlier: Amidon and Hough's *Interaction Analysis: Theory, Research, and Application.*

Kirk and Amidon* did make a disturbing finding about interaction analysis training. They found in one study that a group of student teachers who had had several hours of training in interaction analysis did not become more indirect in their own teaching. The authors concluded that a minimum of twelve hours of training seemed necessary to produce a noticeable improvement.

If you have tried using the Flanders system, you understand why it can't be learned in a few minutes' time. There are ten categories of classroom talk to learn to recognize and code. Those categories are coded with numerals that do not suggest the nature of the categories to which they correspond. For example, although the numeral **2** stands for "teacher praises or encourages," there is nothing about the **2** itself that helps you remember the kind of talk it stands for.

Those two hinderances—the number of categories and the difficulty of associating numeral with category—can be substantially reduced by small modifications of the Flanders system.

*Kirk, J., and Amidon, E.: When Student Teachers Study Interaction, Elem. School J. **68**:97, 1967.

The OSTRAQ system

The OSTRAQ system is a compact group of categories, patterned after those developed by Flanders. The categories are associated with letters instead of numerals, and they are arranged so that their corresponding letters form a pronounceable word, in order to make the coding system easy to learn. Although it is compact, this system allows teachers to obtain all the basic information necessary for analyzing verbal interaction in their classrooms.

Here's how the OSTRAQ system is used.

Categories of the OSTRAQ system

	O	**silence or confusion**
	S	**student talk**
teacher talk	**T**	**telling** (lecturing, telling about, giving directions)
	R	**rejecting** (sarcasm, reproof, criticism)
	A	**accepting** (praise, encouragement, positive redirection
	Q	**questioning** (Q_1 — **narrow question** for short answer)
		(Q_2 — **broad question** for longer answer)

To remember the code letters, pronounce aloud the mnemonic **OSTRAQ**. You will find it sticks with you: OSTRAQ — ostrich track with six toes? (Okay then, let's hear *your* system.) Each code letter suggests the category it represents, except possibly for the letter **O**. Even then you can think of the **O** as a zero, representing nothing — no talk.

Now you can use these category symbols for coding verbal episodes, just as described for the Flanders system. Again, you can find all of the following:

> the amount of teacher talk
>
> the amount of student talk
>
> the amount of teacher telling
>
> the amount of teacher questioning
>
> the amount of teacher accepting
>
> the amount of teacher rejecting
>
> the kinds of questions — broad or
> narrow — that the teacher asks

In the OSTRAQ system the **A, Q$_1$**, and **Q$_2$** represent "indirect" teacher behavior. The **T** and **R** represent "direct" teacher behavior. In order to determine the i/d ratio (amount of indirect teacher behavior as compared to the amount of direct teacher behavior—to be described in sections that follow), you divide the total number of indirect tallies by the total number of direct tallies.

---

example:
i/d ratio = ratio of indirectness to directness in teaching
$$\text{i/d} = \frac{\text{A's} + \text{Q}_1\text{'s} + \text{Q}_2\text{'s}}{\text{T's} + \text{R's}}$$

Though you can learn the OSTRAQ coding system in a few minutes, you must practice to become adept at using it.

coding practice

Whether you use the OSTRAQ or the Flanders or yet another coding system, you must practice before you can code accurately. You will find all of the following coding activities helpful. They are arranged in increasing order of difficulty (though none is really hard), and the conditions become increasingly similar to real classroom situations.

discussion typescripts

You can find typescripts of discussions that have been copied verbatim from the classroom. Among the more valuable are discussions especially selected and prepared for interaction analysis training. The following is such a script. The numerals in parentheses indicate three-second intervals that occurred in the original discussion. Numerals standing outside the dialogue represent intervals that occurred during silence. Use the OSTRAQ system to code the typescript.

typescript for coding practice

Teacher: Okay, this morning we're going to do some (1) arithmetic. We will talk about numbers (2). Actually, we will talk about just one number. Take (3) a look at our group. Who can (4) tell me how many are in it?

Student: (whispering) One, two, three, four, (5) five, six, seven, eight.

Teacher: Let's count and be sure. One two, three, (6) four, five, six, seven, eight. All right, I only (7) have circles, I don't have children (8) to put up on the flannel board, but (9) let's pretend that these circles are the students (10) in our reading group. So let's count (11) eight of them out. One, two, three (12), four, five, six, seven, eight. This is all (13) one reading group. If I wanted to (14) make two separate reading groups, one here (15) and one here, how could (16) I do it? (17) (18)

Student: Four each. (19)

Student: Take it out of there and have four. (20)

Teacher: Take it out of where? (21)

Student: Take it. . .(22)

Student: You take four out of (23) there and have two groups and you have another (24) left.

Teacher: All right, you want me to take and put four in each (25) group. All right. Let's try (26) that and see if it works. How many do I have there? (27)

Students: (in unison) Four. (28)

Teacher: Four. All right, four is how (29) much of our reading group?

Student: Eight.

Teacher: Susan, you are not paying (30) attention.

Student: Half.

Teacher: Good (31). Yes, it's half, isn't it James. We just took our group (32) and cut it in half, didn't we? (33) And we put four on one side and four on the other side (34). Well, today we are just going to work with the one (35) number four. With just the one (36) number. All right, I've got some pencils here (37). What do you suppose I am going to do (38) with them?

Student: Divide them.

Teacher: Yes (39). How?

Student: Into fourths (40).

Teacher: No. Listen, have we divided into fourths? (41)

Student: I mean into fours (42).

Teacher: That's better. Keith, see if you can (43) take four.

Student: One, two, three (44) four.

Teacher: Did he do it right, (45) Jane?

Student: Yeah.

Teacher: He certainly did. He knows his (46) number four, doesn't he? Now we're going to try something (47) with the circles. And let's see if I can get you (48) a little bit mixed up. Let's leave all the circles (49) pink this morning, and then we can try (50) something with them.

Typescripts have some advantages over live discussions. You can practice individually, at your own pace, and whenever you like without special equipment. You can stop, go back, or reflect. Difficult interpretations can be noted and discussed later.

audio tapes

Taped discussions can be realistic. As in live discussions, you have to judge the speaker's tone of voice as well as his words in order to determine his meaning. Still, the tape can be stopped or replayed as desired. Specially prepared tapes are available for coding practice.* The quality of some of these prepared tapes is often better than what you can get by taping classroom discussions. Nonetheless, you can tape class discussions, and you will benefit from analyzing them, especially if you led the discussion. Ask students to keep very still during the taping to cut down background noise.

video tapes

Video tapes are easy to prepare, and they are more interesting than audio tapes. Nevertheless, they offer few advantages for practicing interaction coding. Watching the monitor may even be disconcerting and may make coding more difficult at first.

While video tapes offer no special advantages for coding practice, they do help you to see yourself as your class sees you, showing all your warts, postures, movements, facial expressions, and other means of nonverbal communication you might like to change.

role-playing

Amidon believes role-playing is the best way to learn the behavior categories of an interaction analysis system. You should try the technique; you will find it interesting and helpful.

Four of the OSTRAQ system's six categories refer to teacher behaviors. The quickest way to recognize these four behaviors is to practice performing them in groups of three or four people. One person acts as teacher and practices "telling," "rejecting," "accepting," and asking broad and narrow questions. The other people act as students. Everyone gets a turn as teacher, leads a short discussion, and performs different kinds of teacher behavior.

practice with students

If you possibly can, you should practice leading and coding discussions with small groups of school-age students. But first you should sharpen your skills through

---

*Paul S. Amidon and Associates, Inc., 1035 Plymouth Building, Minneapolis, Minn. 55402.

practice with tapes and role-playing so that you won't have to stop the discussions because you have forgotten what to do.

Elementary teachers should lead and code discussions with both primary and intermediate grade children. Secondary teachers should lead and code discussions in two different subject areas. A good time to practice is during student teaching, when you can pair with a fellow student: one can code while the other teaches the class.

what you should be able to do now

After you spend three or four hours learning and practicing the OSTRAQ system, you should be able to perform the following acts:

1. Name the categories of the OSTRAQ system quickly and without error.
2. Identify the categories that refer to direct teacher influence and the categories that refer to indirect teacher influence.
3. Describe in a few words the relationship that has been found between indirect teacher influence and students' achievement and attitudes toward school.
4. Using the OSTRAQ system, accurately code short discussion sessions from at least two of the following: typescripts, audio tapes, video tapes, role-playing, small group discussions.
5. Analyze the codings obtained in # 4 to show:
   percent of time the teacher talked
   percent of time the students talked
   percent of time the teacher used direct influence
   percent of time the teacher used indirect influence
   the kinds of questions (broad or narrow) the teacher asked

If you can do these things, so far so good. But even more important to you as a teacher is a second phase that has two distinct parts:

1. The ability to plan lessons that increase teacher "indirectness" and allow more student talk.
2. The ability to use "indirect" behaviors in real teaching situations.
   We will now set our sights on those two goals.

Becoming a more indirect teacher

Doing interaction analysis has one main purpose: to help teachers become more "indirect"—to ask more questions, encourage more student talk, and become more accepting of student talk.

We can prejudge teachers in general as talkative in their classrooms and as inclined to guide more through telling than through questioning.

Hughes, in her study of teachers, found that "Over 80 per cent of the teachers were dominative in more than half of the acts they performed. The most often used function was control, while memory-recall was the mental activity most often used."*

Flanders'** findings led to his expression of a "two-thirds rule":

> two thirds of the time in an ordinary classroom someone is talking
> two thirds of that time it is the teacher talking
> two thirds of that time the teacher is using direct influence

So we can begin with the recognition that most of us teach in ways that encourage too little student talk. We know, however, that some teachers do encourage student participation and talk. One of Flanders'*** most important studies involved a group of mathematics teachers and a group of social studies teachers. He found great differences in teaching behavior among the members of those groups. He also found differences in achievement for students of those teachers. The following points summarize his comparisons of teachers with the highest achieving classes to teachers with the lowest achieving classes. Teachers in the former group used five to six times more acceptance and encouragement of students' ideas, used five to six times less direction and criticism of student behavior, talked 10% less, encouraged two to three times more student talk.

By this point, you may have begun to ask yourself some perplexing questions:
1. Should you never tell, criticize, or direct students?
2. Must you accept everything they do and say?
3. How much is too much teacher talk? How little is too little student talk?
4. Can teachers get anywhere if all they do is ask questions?
5. Should all lessons be the same? Aren't some best done mainly through teacher talk, while others are best done through student talk?

*Hughes, M. M.: Utah Study of the Assessment of Teaching. In Bellack, A., editor: Research and Theory of Teaching, New York, 1963, Teachers College Press.

Flanders, N. A.: Using Interaction Analysis in the Inservice Training of Teachers, J. Exper. Educ. **30:313, 1962.

***Flanders, N. A.: Teacher Influence, Pupil Attitudes, and Achievement, Washington, D.C., 1965, United States Government Printing Office.

Flanders doesn't give definitive answers to these questions, but he does give us some figures we can use as general guides.

These figures come from observations and analyses of two weeks of classes taught by thirty-two teachers uninstructed in interaction analysis. Of the sixteen teachers in each group, Flanders selected the four most *direct* and the six most *indirect*. The findings are shown in the chart below.

Some i/d ratios for direct and indirect teachers

social studies	4 most direct	i/d ratios ranged from 0.01 to 2.0, with majority below 0.4
	6 most indirect	i/d ratios ranged from 0.01 to 18.0, with majority over 1.0
mathematics	4 most direct	i/d ratios ranged from 0.01 to 2.0, with majority below 0.4
	6 most indirect	i/d ratios ranged from 0.01 to 11.0, with majority over 1.0

The chart does not show the fact that i/d ratios for any one teacher vary from lesson to lesson; sometimes they are high, sometimes low. In other words, sometimes a teacher will "tell" a lot. Other times he will ask questions and encourage student talk. Indeed, experience seems to show that there are times when good teaching is direct and times when good teaching is indirect. The important question is when should a teacher try to be more direct, and when more indirect?

Again, Flanders* gives us a glimpse of some i/d ratios, and their changes, at different points in the development of a lesson or series of lessons:

*Flanders, N. A.: Teacher Influence, Pupil Attitudes, and Achievement, Washington, D. C., United States Government Printing Office.

Mean i/d ratios for direct and indirect teachers

		planning	new material	discussion	work	evaluation	routine
social studies	indirect teachers	5.14*	3.25	1.72	0.84	0.93	0.30
	direct teachers	1.30	0.23	0.51	0.03	0.20	0.17
mathematics	indirect teachers	not given	3.64	6.83	2.24	2.24	0.59
	direct teachers	not given	0.72	0.21	0.15	0.25	0.14

*Interpretation: teachers used about five times as much indirect influence as they did direct influence.

256

Take special note of the i/d ratios at various points in a lesson. You can see indirect teachers have high i/d ratios during planning, introduction of new materials, and discussion. The ratios then drop off noticeably for the work, evaluation, and routines. Direct teachers, on the other hand, maintain comparatively low i/d ratios throughout the lesson.

Flanders generalized his findings as follows:

1. Restricting student participation early in the cycle of learning activities makes students more dependent on the teacher, and they learn less.

2. Restricing student participation later in the cycle of learning activities does not increase dependence on the teacher.

3. Increasing participation early in the cycle of activities decreases dependence and increases achievement.

In a nutshell, Flanders judged that i/d ratios should be kept high during the introductory parts of a lesson (planning, presentation of new materials, and discussion). He judged the i/d ratios should be kept comparatively low during the later parts of a lesson (work, evaluation, and routine).

Practicing & applying what you know

With what you know at this point, you should be able to plan lessons that increase indirect teacher behavior and that vary the i/d ratios according to the stage in the sequence of lesson activities.

What remains now is for you to put into practice what you know. You will find these activities helpful:

1. Here are a number of comments that are considered to be "accepting" when they are used earnestly and not sarcastically. Select those that seem compatible with your personality. Practice using them in role-playing and in working with groups of school-age students.

okay	brilliant	fantastic
yes	fine	exactly
keep going	un-huh	splendid
excellent	perfect	fabulous
good	true	of course
all right	terrific	well put

you've worked hard
that's well thought out
you're on the right track
you're doing fine
keep up the good work
you're improving every day

2. Compose and ask a number of broad questions. They should require rather lengthy replies from students. Concentrate on:

explanations "Can you tell us how to bathe a dog?"

applications "Now use what you know about triangles to measure the height of that tree."

production "Think of all the ways you can improve agricultural practices in Latin America."

evaluation "Why is a two-semester program of student teaching better/worse than a one-semester program?"

3. Compose plans for a series of lessons so that i/d ratios will be high in early portions and lower in later portions.

4. In role-playing or actual teaching situations, demonstrate indirect teaching skills you have identified beforehand.

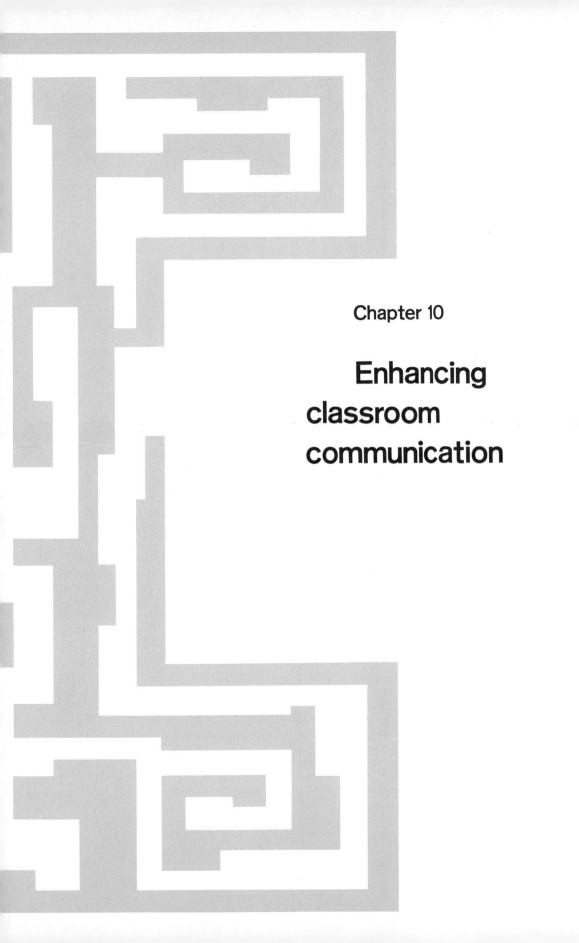

Chapter 10

Enhancing classroom communication

STORY HOUR

I was in the fifth grade in 1941 when the United States went to war with Japan. Only incidentally do I remember that the two events coincided. Though I remember both powerfully, it's about that fifth-grade class that I want to reminisce now.

Here is something that perplexes me— while I remember the fifth grade so well, I remember very little about my fourth-grade year in school, except that my brother and I rode together to school on the same bicycle, that I went from class to class (we were departmentalized like a high school), and that in art class I made a soap carving of an elephant that looked remarkably like a pig.

The same is true for my sixth-grade year, except that my memory is even more vacant. Even when I really put my mind to it I can recall only one thing about classwork that year. We had those old-fashioned desks, attached to the floor in straight rows, with little ink wells in the right-hand corners. Once, as I checked my weekly spelling test, I methodically placed a little ink dot over the top of each letter in each word. I had spelled all the words correctly, so I gave myself 100 and passed in the paper. The next day my teacher (whom I remember neither by name nor by image—have I repressed her?) returned the paper. But it now bore a grade of 0 instead of 100. I had missed all the words because I had dotted not only the i's but all the other letters as well. Probably it served

me right. But I wonder now what else we did during our nine months in that room?

I point out the dullness of those two years merely to highlight that remarkable fifth year. I can write pages, chapters, reams, volumes (I'm getting carried away) about it. But as I stop and reflect, I realize that except for the fascinating stories read to us by Miss Osborne (that was her name, a lissome redhead with freckles who seemed as old as any other adult, except for very old people), every episode I remember is one of "doing" activities, involving other students. What I'm saying is, I remember the plays we performed in class, wearing paper costumes we had made (who cared if they didn't look real?). I remember parching corn, smashing it up into cornmeal, and having a Mom bake it. We ate the stuff with butter and gusto. I remember when the whole class went to Miss Osborne's house to look at a spinning wheel, a real one, and she let us turn it. Later, we caught bees in glass jars in the lawn clover, and one stung me on the toe. I guess she let us run barefoot in the grass.

Enough of that.

It was the talk with others, you see? It was the work in group activities, right there in school, interacting, exchanging real talk and ideas and emotions and experiences. Now, as a teacher, I see many lessons from 1941. One of them concerns us here—classroom interaction.

The remainder of the chapter will turn on three important questions about classroom interaction.

1. How can we facilitate classroom talk?

> That is, what can we do
> to make it easier for students
> to exchange ideas, opinions, and
> feelings?

2. How can we improve classroom talk?

> Or, what can we do to improve
> the quality of talk that occurs in
> the classroom — our own talk
> and that of the students.

We will consider some answers to those two questions. Regarding the first — facilitating classroom talk — we will explore the value of

> **psychological support**
> **seating arrangements**
> **interaction exercises**

Regarding the second — improving classroom talk — we will explore some aspects of

> **body talk**
> **telling about**
> **talking with**

3. How can we improve questioning skills? How can we cause students to compose longer reponses and use different cognitive abilities?

We will consider a rationale for questioning, we will see how to compose good questions, and we will note suggested techniques for asking the questions.

1. Facilitating classroom talk

psychological support

Psychological support refers to acts that show students they may speak their minds without fear of punishment, sarcasm, or being put down. It depends on the teacher, and it depends on every other member of the group, too. Here are some of the things teachers and students must do to provide psychological support.

teachers

Research in classroom climates and interaction analysis has shown us several things about teachers. It has shown that traditional teachers tend to be quite dominating in class activities, using about two thirds of the "talk time" and deciding on and directing most of the students' learning activities. It has shown that teachers can accept students and reject them with powerful effects. It has shown that students of indirect teachers (those who ask many questions, accept students' responses, and involve students in planning activities) usually learn more and like school better.

These findings help us to see what teachers should do, in teaching, to establish and maintain the psychological support necessary for full student involvement.

---

teachers must
ask many questions to encourage student response
accept students' responses and avoid damaging rejection
involve students in planning, interpreting, and evaluating their class-
     related experiences

---

students

The burden of psychological support by no means falls entirely on the teacher's shoulders. Students, while freed to participate actively, incur responsibilities that they must meet.

262

students must learn
through practice

to listen actively to other students
to be tolerant of others' opinions—that is, even while disagreeing they must not make hostile, aggressive, and sarcastic responses, for those only produce defensive reactions and shut off communication

Participants in the group must come to trust each other and be concerned about each other's feelings, so that every participant feels secure; they know they will not be laughed at, rebuffed, or ignored. They know they will be listened to and accepted as they are.

This feeling of security cannot be reached until group members are freed from concern about

other group members—whether they will be hostile, aggressive, and competitive or friendly, cooperative, and supportive
themselves—whether they see their contributions valued and whether they see themselves accepted or rejected by others in the group

procedures

The teacher must serve as a model. His acts must show warmth, concern, and a desire to help. Humor serves well; students identify it as one of the traits most desired in teachers.

Together, students and teacher must establish ground rules that assure psychological support. The ground rules should be as simple and short as possible. One class, for example, agreed on the following rules:

1. Listen when others are speaking.
2. Use first name when speaking to another person.
3. Avoid sarcasm and derogatory terms.

These ground rules must not be teacher-made. They must be group-made. Further, establishing them doesn't guarantee that everyone will automatically follow them. They are goals. They can be reached through practice. In discussions the group can name a member to note violations of ground rules, not for the purpose of punishing offenders but to help participants remain aware that violations damage the emotional climate that the group must maintain to protect and support each individual member.

seating arrangements

A ninth-grade general science class:

Tchr: Now let's review some of the things we have learned about dinosaurs. One thing we learned was the meaning of the word "dinosaur." Who remembers what that was? Mary?

Mary: It comes from two Greek words that mean terrible lizard.

Tchr: Yes. But were dinosaurs really lizards? Tom?

Tom: No.

Tchr: No. And were they all terrible, Tom?

Tom: No.

Tchr: No. Some were small and harmless, weren't they? Who can give us an example of one of the small dinosaurs? Felix?

Felix: There was this one that was three feet long and always stole eggs.

Tchr: Yes. What was its name?

Felix: Uh . . . I can't remember it.

Tchr: John?

John: Oviptor, or something like that.

Tchr: That's close. Oviraptor.

Don't think of this teacher as a model you want to copy, because he unknowingly did a few undesirable things in leading the discussion.

One of the undesirable things was maintaining a **communications bottleneck.** That is, every bit of talk was channeled through the teacher, as shown in this diagram:

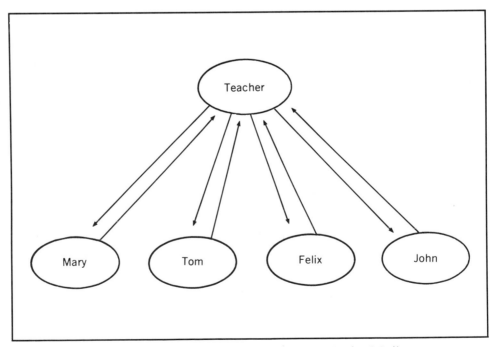

You can see there was no student-to-student talk.

Okay, so what does that have to do with seating? **Seating alone does not break the communications bottleneck.** The teacher must see that it is broken, and some helpful activities are suggested later in the chapter. **But seating can help to facilitate verbal interaction — student-to-student talk.** It can allow students to face each other, to make it easier for them to talk to each other. It can reduce group size so that everyone gets a chance to participate more. Visualize the traditional classroom seating arrangement, which looks something like this.

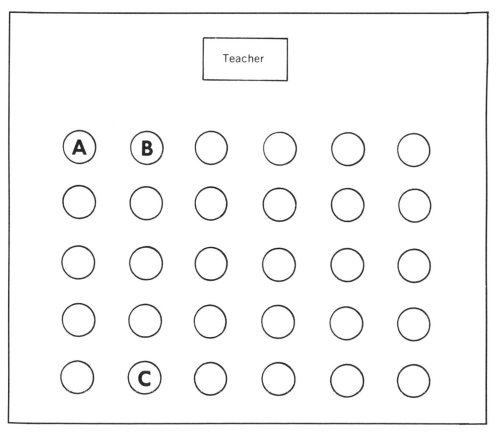

This traditional seating arrangement is fine for listening to the teacher. But it makes classroom talk among all students difficult. Students A and B can talk to each other easily. But it is very hard for either A or B to talk to C.

Let's look at some other seating arrangements that make it much easier for students to talk one with the other. We will keep in mind that there are times when we would want a large group—perhaps the entire class—for discussions and viewing, and times when we would want small groups for discussions and work activities. And we would want seating arrangements that allow students to move from large to small groups, and back again, with a minimum of confusion.

Here are three possibilities to consider—the **basic oval, semicircle clusters,** and **modular clusters.** Each arrangement facilitates student-to-student talk, and each allows easy regrouping into smaller and larger units.

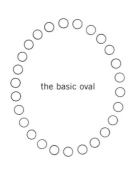

the basic oval

basic oval
advantages
excellent face-to-face positioning of all class members
easy to regroup into smaller units by forming circles of 4 to 6 students
disadvantages
requires considerable space
opposite ends of oval far apart
some students have to look at windows

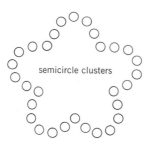

semicircle clusters

semicircle clusters
advantages
very good face-to-face positioning of students
very easy to regroup, forming small groups from each semicircle
disadvantages
essentially the same for the basic oval

modular clusters

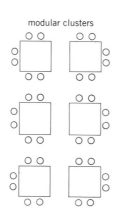

modular clusters
advantages
better face-to-face positioning than with traditional seating
very easy to regroup into 2's, 4's, 6's, 12's
compact, requiring little floor space
disadvantages
some students must turn to see the teacher
somewhat awkward to re-form into total group with good face-to-face positioning

interaction exercises

In this section we will examine briefly some exercises that can help improve both quantity and quality of interaction. These exercises emphasize student-to-student talk, and they help teachers relinquish much of their traditional dominance over class discussions.

The exercises are not well-defined techniques. Rather, they are general kinds of activities that help students learn to talk together more easily in class settings. Most of them can be conducted in either large or small groups, but of course the small groups—four to eight members—offer the greatest opportunity for all members to participate.

As you arrange to practice the interaction activities, remind yourself of the following points:

seating The size of the group and the ability of participants to see each others' faces influence the amount of verbal interaction that occurs.

topic The topic to be discussed should be one that every participant knows a good deal about. It should also be one about which participants have different ideas, viewpoints, and opinions.

teacher role The teacher may choose to participate as a regular member of the group. To help students talk more freely at first, however, the teacher should assume the role of reflector and clarifier of student expression. She should neither guide the discussion nor make evaluative statements about student contributions.

protocol exercise

We noted earlier that any group that is to function effectively must establish and maintain an atmosphere that is psychologically supportive. The protocol exercise helps students get off to a good start in that direction. They take turns telling something about themselves — hobbies, background, special interests, unique experiences. When each has finished, the person next in order asks one question about something that was mentioned.

Meanwhile, the other members of the group memorize the speaker's name and associate it with experiences, interests, and so on. After three participants tell about themselves, members test themselves on their ability to recall names and something special about each person.

Often, students find it easier to interview and introduce an adjacent student than to tell about themselves. Let the group members decide which procedure they prefer.

active listening exercise

This exercise helps participants learn to listen more attentively to what other participants say. They take turns expressing opinions about controversial topics (such as the extent to which students should participate in hiring the people who are to be their teachers) or in describing detailed procedures (such as how to take care of a baby goat).

Each speaker is allowed to talk for about one minute. Then the speaker points to another participant who does two things.

1. Paraphrases as accurately as possible what the speaker said.

2. Indicates points that have not been understood or points that the speaker should tell more about.

agree-disagree exercise

The agree-disagree exercise can be very helpful in stimulating active participation in group discussions. Here's the way it is used. The instructor prepares a list of statements about a topic of concern to the students. He purposely selects statements about which he thinks students have different opinions. For a college class in teacher education the following list of statements would serve well.

1. Teachers have the same political rights as any other citizens. Therefore they should have no restraints placed on their freedom of speech before the class, provided they point out that the opinions they express are their own.

2. If we want to show that individuality ought to be valued, we should allow students to dress and style their hair in whatever ways they think best.

3. We know that behavior can be extinguished if it is not reinforced. When a student misbehaves in class, therefore, it is best to ignore the behavior, for giving attention may in fact serve to reinforce the misbehavior.

4. Students should help plan lessons occasionally so they will feel they have a part in making decisions. Most of the time, however, lesson planning should be left entirely to the teacher, who after all is the trained educational expert in the classroom.

5. Flanders' work in interaction analysis showed that teachers often reject students. The remedy for that would be to have teachers practice acts that are known to show acceptance so they could accept all student behavior.

The instructor distributes the lists of statements to students, either in large or small groups. Students check each statement to see whether they agree or disagree with it. They then exchange reactions to and ideas about the statements.

student-conducted discussion exercise

This exercise helps break the communications bottleneck by requiring the instructor to assume a new role. He neither directs the discussion nor expresses his own opinions. When a question or comment is directed to him, he replies only with items of factual data, or he restates the comment. Occasionally he may attempt to summarize what students have said up to that point in the discussion.

The student-conducted discussion can be practiced easily in large groups following an agree-disagree exercise.

brainstorming exercise

Brainstorming has proved to be remarkably effective in producing new ideas. It is best done in groups small enough to allow full participation, yet large enough to yield a high divergence of ideas. About eight to twelve persons make an ideal group, although any number up to a full class can participate.

step 1. The group leader introduces a specific question or problem. For example:

1. What can we do to make the school grounds more beautiful?

2. How can we make an imitation Navajo hogan large enough for us to get inside?

3. What can we do to make foundations courses more relevant to actual teaching?

Participants are asked to start tossing out possible solutions to the problem. All responses are encouraged, the "wild" just as much as the "reasonable," and they are recorded on a chalkboard or chart as fast as they are given. No evaluation is made at this time. Piggybacking, or building on someone else's idea, is encouraged.

Brainstorming groups often reach a dry spell fairly quickly; ideas seem almost exhausted. When this occurs, keep the group at work a bit longer. Some of the best ideas often come after this brief dry spell.

step 2. At the end of a specified period of time, or when the ideas stop coming, the group goes back over the notations made during the session. At this point the group judges the ideas. Judgments should not be made in terms of good-bad, right-wrong; rather, they should be made in terms of usefulness, practicability, novelty, and probable results.

step 3. An optional third step is to select a promising solution and brainstorm it again. The purpose here is to spell out the details necessary to make the plan work.

case analysis exercise

The case analysis exercise begins with a written account of a problem, and it is best practiced in buzz groups of four to six participants.

The written account provides background data. It includes the circumstances, the problem, and the acts taken up to the point where a decision has to be made. Now the buzz group participants apply their knowledge, skills, and insights to the solution of the problem.

sample case for teacher education students. James, a first-grade student, is an enigma. At times he is docile, affectionate, cooperative, and eager to work. At other times he has fits of rage, destroying other students' work, attacking them physically, and even kicking and hitting the teacher.

Miss Johnson, the teacher, noted that James's rages usually occurred during work periods. She reported James's behavior to the principal, and she visited James's mother and discussed the problem with her.

His mother defended James strongly, maintaining that he had always been a loving and happy child and implying that the fault must lie with Miss Johnson or with other children in the room.

Put yourself in Miss Johnson's place.

What do you do try to solve the problem?

sample case for high school students. Michael attends a high school whose modular system requires that he be responsible for preparing his own class and study schedule. Michael is taking algebra and American literature. They are both hard for him, and he can see little value in either. He enjoys only one class—a class in automotive mechanics—and would spend the entire day working on cars if he could.

Recently, Michael skipped algebra and American literature classes several times. The vice-principal contacted his parents, who felt that Michael was letting them, and himself, down. The vice-principal, after talking with Michael's parents, agreed to let him continue at the school, provided he attended class faithfully and made up the work he had missed. But Michael was now hopelessly behind in algebra. He dreaded the class and knew he could never pass it.

Put yourself in Michael's place.

What do you do to solve the problem?

sample case for elementary students. Mary was in the third grade. She liked Sarah, who was a fifth grader, and wanted to be friends with her more than anything in the world, but Sarah didn't want to be friends with a third grader. The two girls walked along the same street to and from school.

One day Mary had an idea. She decided to skip lunch and use her lunch money to buy candy to share with Sarah on the way home from school. Sure enough, Sarah decided to be friends with Mary, although all she *really* liked was the candy.

The next day, Mary decided to skip lunch again. This time her teacher noticed it and asked why she hadn't gone to the cafeteria. Mary said her mother had forgotten to send money. The teacher gave Mary money for lunch but wrote a note to Mary's mother, asking her to repay the money the next day. She gave the note to Mary to take home.

Pretend you are Mary.

What do you do now?

role-playing exercise

Role-playing is similar to case analysis in that it encourages active participation in a realistic situation. It differs in that the participants assume the roles of identified people in the problem situation and behave as they think those people would behave.

The instructor's responsibility in role-playing activities consists of describing the situation and indicating the beliefs and personalities of the people whose roles are to be played. Benefits to students lie in the reality of the situation, in the opportunity to practice skills vis-à-vis live people.

sample role-playing situation. A custodian was pushing a cart for transporting folding chairs along a concrete walk just as the junior high dismissed for the afternoon. Dalton ran and jumped on the cart for a ride. Rick ran after him and jumped on, too, pushing Dalton off at the same time. Dalton leapt back on and shoved Rick painfully against the end railing of the cart. The custodian admonished Dalton, who in turn unleashed a torrent of profanity at the custodian.

Mr. Brown, the principal, overheard Dalton. He had already talked with him on two occasions about swearing at school. This time he resolved to call a conference to see what could be done. He decided to include Dalton, Dalton's parents, Dalton's teacher, the custodian, and himself.

The conference is set for 3:30 P.M. the next day. Dalton's father will have to leave work early to attend, and he will be disgruntled about that and will be anxious to get the conference over with.

Dalton's mother will be very supportive of him and will maintain that he is a very good boy in every way. She sees nothing wrong with healthy self-expression and does not consider profanity anything to get upset about.

Dalton, recognizing his mother's support, will blame Rick for the trouble and will claim he did not use very bad language.

The custodian feels that profanity is "disgraceful and despicable." He was incensed that Dalton spoke to him that way, and he is still upset.

Dalton's teacher has heard him use profanity several times. She has overlooked it because Dalton is energetic and bright and is usually, though not always, a good student.

Assign the roles and play out the conference in the principal's office. Try to be faithful to each person's traits, but try to work out a solution that is suitable to all involved.

■   ■   ■   ■   ■   ■

2. Improving classroom talk

teacher talk

Let's spend a few moments considering teacher talk. First we will examine nonverbal communication that teachers use — body talk. Then we will see how teachers can improve two important kinds of word talk. We will call those kinds of talk **telling about** and **talking with.**

And now, on to

I.
body talk

Mr. Hotchkiss' office.

Carpet. Green. Oaken desk. Hotchkiss seated behind it. No, in it . . . part of it . . . a man-desk centaur . . . an intellectual Pizarro.

I sit down, blotting my palms on the sides of my trousers.

"Yes?" he barks.

"Mr. Hotchkiss, I'm Frank Jones. I called earlier."

He looks at me. Face expressionless. Lips puckered like disgruntled cupid. Myopic eyeglasses. Early-age jowls over tight collar.

My left eye itches uncontrollably. My God! He isn't going to answer me. His face. Coldly angry? Did he hear me? Testing me, my poise? (I have none.) My tunnel vision sees only his brass nameplate: W. Hotchkiss.

He will throw me out. Won't even listen.

Is he daydreaming? Heart attack? Indigestion?

Is he a mannequin?

Ugh. That's a true story. Sort of, anyhow. Do you recognize it? Put yourself in my quivering place. Mr. Hotchkiss held his pose for an interminable five seconds.

what might he have meant by it?
1.
2.
etc.

what would you have done?
1.
2.
etc.

What do you think your interpretations and reactions might have been if Hotchkiss had:

act	**interpretation**	**reaction**
1. laughed		
2. scowled		
3. stood		
4. reached out his hand		
5. looked out the window		
6. motioned to a chair		
7. nodded but kept reading papers on his desk		
8. winked		
9. moved around beside you		
10. tapped repeatedly on his desk		

■ ■ ■ ■ ■

body talk
the body talks
sometimes it talks by itself
sometimes it accents word talk
sometimes it guides
sometimes it accepts
sometimes it rejects

Yes, by gar, it does those things. Usually unconsciously. But we can teach it to do those things consciously. We can learn to **recognize** body talk, by gar. We can learn to **use** it

by GAR

G body talk that **guides**
A body talk that **accepts**
R body talk that **rejects**

You remember what Flanders and others found—that teachers categorized as more "accepting" and less "rejecting" usually have students who learn more and like school better. Of course, Flanders' work dealt with verbal interaction—word talk.

But man does not talk by word alone. No. A nonword act, or body talk, often sends messages more powerfully than words. If you have time to stop and reflect a moment, you will think of cases in which this happened in your own experience:

> a hand lightly cupped on the shoulder
> a 6-year-old's smile through tearful eyes
> faces drifting away while you are talking
> a sigh
> an expressionless stare
> a sarcastic laugh
> a grin of uncontained joy

You may be a good body talker already. But if you want to learn to be even better, there are some things you must take into account:

> 1. You use body talk all the time, though you may not be aware of much of it.
>
> 2. You probably do most of your rejecting (of others) non-verbally, through acts instead of words.
>
> 3. You can become fully aware of the kinds of body talk that accept and reject. It helps to practice both kinds, knowing what you are doing.
>
> 4. You can learn to be a very effective teacher, and very accepting too, by shaping up your repertoire of nonverbal talk acts. But you must practice.

Do it. Yes, practice the acts—both the good and the bad. Use the summary on the next page entitled **some body talk, by GAR**

■ ■ ■ ■ ■ ■ ■ ■ ■ ■ ■ ■ ■ ■ ■ ■ ■ ■ ■

Some body talk, by GAR

GAR behavior categories	examples of sounds	examples of facial expressions	examples of gestures	examples of body movements, acts, positions
guide focus demonstrate direct	shhh un-huh (encouraging)		beckon cup hand to ear put finger to lips motion with hand	act out flick lights on and off help do something lead by hand open to right page point a direction point to place set example show how show where walk with
accept show interest encourage praise	giggle laugh with whistle mmm (tasty)	grin lift eyebrows smile wink	applaud give OK sign give "v" sign nod affirmation nod agreement thumbs up	hug look attentively open arms pat on back or shoulder shake hands
reject ignore suppress punish	clear throat expell breath in exasperation groan moan laugh at laugh sarcastically sigh sniff	bite lips clench jaws close eyes slowly give dirty look furrow forehead frown glare grimace look bored look disgusted lower eyebrows press lips together smirk sneer squint stare down	cover ears point, to blame shake head no shake finger thumbs down	fold arms, waiting grab hands on hips, waiting pinch pull hair push student aside shake student slam book down swat student rap ruler tap foot impatiently turn away look away while student is talking

2.
telling about

Sarita is now a woman. But when I first saw her she was in the seventh grade, and I remember her because of a spelling lesson. One of the words on her list was "honest." She knew how to spell it, and she knew how to say it. When the class was asked to compose sentences using their spelling words, she wrote this: "The bird build a honest."

At that time Sarita was still learning English, and her mistaken use of "honest" was easily cleared up. She only needed a translation of the word into her native language. But we might still wonder how well students whose native language is English conceptualize "honest." To find out, we would have to ask them to tell what honest means to them and to give some examples of what honest people do.

Of course, we do get a lot of laughs out of kids saying the darndest things—a household expression thanks to Mr. Linkletter. Like an adjective being a word that hangs down from a noun, or like the circulatory system is where blood goes down one leg and up the other. And yet, how often we adults use words attached to the vaguest of concepts—words such as clap-trap, adamant, supercilious, nuclear fusion. We use other words that have very different meanings for different people, especially words such as patriot, deadbeat, rugged individualist, private enterprise, socialism, supply and demand, free school, professor.

But if we would help ourselves by giving examples of what we mean by such words when we use them in conversation, we could help others to receive the exact message we intended to send.

Take the word "patriotism." My meaning for the word may be very different from yours. So if we discuss the concept, I had better tell you, with examples, what I mean by the word, for I may be using it to mean

>   saluting the flag, or
>   going to war for one's country, or
>   struggling to keep one's country out of senseless wars, or
>   abiding by the laws of the land, or
>   practicing civil disobedience of immoral laws, or
>   fighting out against treasonable dissenters, or
>   fighting to guarantee free speech for dissenters

Talk is a very important part of teaching. While we want to emphasize student talk, there are times when teachers must tell about or explain things to their students.

When they do, they must be sure that students recognize the words used, and they must be sure that students conceptualize accurately what it is they are telling about. Toward that end, teachers should be sure to:

1. Identify words that students might not hear correctly. Clear, slow pronunciation helps. So does writing the word on the chalkboard. This helps prevent such instances as that in which a teen-ager discovered by accident that the expression was "It didn't dawn on me," instead of "It didn't *dom* on me." Or that in which another wondered about *four-stair heat* until he read "forced-air heat."

2. Use "picture words"—nouns that stand for real objects and verbs that stand for observable acts—to help students visualize what you are talking about.

3. Give word definitions if you think some of your words might not be understood:

A **lemur** is a small animal that looks much like a monkey. It lives in trees and hides during the day. It has a muzzle (mouth and nose) similar to a fox, large eyes, and soft fur.

4. Show real objects whenever possible. If not, show a model. Or show a picture, which usually is worth more than a thousand words:

Here you see a picture of a **gauntlet.** Notice how it is made to protect the fingers, hand, and wrist from wounds.

5. Give as many examples as necessary. For instance, first graders who are to practice being good citizens must know what good citizens do:

They don't hit or push others at the water fountain.
They don't tear other children's papers.
They take turns at the slide.

6. Describe and demonstrate processes.

I brought this potter's wheel to show you how to turn clay.

7. Check students' comprehension by asking them to paraphrase, demonstrate, or act out what you have explained.

■　■　■　■　■

3.
talking with

Remember the old story? Two psychologists meet in the hall . . .

psychologist #1: Hi. Nice day, isn't it?
psychologist #2: (I wonder what he means by that?) Yeah, it sure is.
psychologist #1: (I wonder what he means by that?)

Talking with people can become very difficult if we assume there is a veiled meaning in everything they say. Still, when teachers talk *with* students—when they cast themselves in a psychologically helping role—they must try to identify the important meanings that lie partly obscured in what students say.

For instance, what do you think your students might mean if they were to say
Oh, boy! Only five more days until Easter vacation.
I can't stand English.
When we went to the zoo, everybody misbehaved except me.
Roger got all his algebra problems right again. Smart guy. Oh, yes.
I wish Mr. Samuels (sixth-grade teacher) was my father.

receiving

The first thing we must do when we talk with students is try to receive their messages accurately. That's not always easy to do, as experience shows us every day. Nevertheless, there are things we can do to make students' messages come through clearer. We can do all of the following.

1. Really listen to their words, not just fake it while thinking of what we are going to say next.
2. Paraphrase and reflect back what students say. This helps them to say what they mean to say or show what's on their minds.

student: Those seventh graders think they're so smart. Man, I can't stand those big rats.
teacher: Mad at 'em about something, are you?
student: Yeah. They think they're so big and tough.
teacher: You know somebody in particular who acts that way?
student: Yeah, I do. George Smith and Allen.
teacher: Allen, your brother? He's acting mean to you?
student: Know what they said? They said if I ever tried walking home with them again they were going to shove me off into the street.

281

3. Help students to give more information, examples, and illustrations.

student: Avocado trees aren't hard to grow, but there are some things you have to do, like water and fertilize them and take out the dead wood.

teacher: What do you mean about "taking out the dead wood?"

student: Well, lots of small branches die every year. If you don't take them out, they can rub against the avocados and make black marks on them.

teacher: You break them out?

student: No. You use those little curved saws on long poles. You reach up in the tree and saw them out. You can just knock the real small ones out.

teacher: You like working with avocados.

student: Yes. Anyway, it's better than some things. You can be in the grove where it's cool, by yourself sometimes.

teacher: You think there are times when it's good just to be alone.

student: Sure. I mean, don't you? Where you can think and it's quiet, without all your brothers and sisters around?

responding: accepting & rejecting

A second thing we should do when talking with students is reply in ways that are accepting and helpful. Accepting does not mean automatic agreement; in fact, agreement helps only when a student needs reassurance or ego-boosting. We must also distinguish between *acceptance of acts* and *acceptance of individuals.*

For instance, you may not be able to accept the *act* of Johnny bullying other children on the playground; you won't nod or smile when you see him do it. But you can accept Johnny as a person—a person like any other who has needs he is trying to fulfill. You accept *him,* while rejecting (as nonpunitively as possible) his bullying acts. You show him you care about him. You "help" him get the attention he needs. You help him improve his self-image by giving him tasks to perform—lessons, jobs, and so on—that allow him to earn legitimate praise and approval.

We think of acceptance as a willingness to listen, to tolerate, and to help. Acceptance keeps communications open. Rejection, on the other hand, closes communication channels.

We have already noted many of the ways in which teachers can show acceptance and rejection of their students. Most of the ways we noted consisted of gestures, facial expressions, and short verbal expressions such as "good" or "get quiet." Those ways of accepting and rejecting have to do with teacher responses to student talk concerning lessons and classwork.

Much of the talking we do with students occurs at another level. That level has to do not with the subject matter of a lesson but rather with students' feelings, attitudes, values, and behaviors related to personal concerns — group norms, relations with others, search for identity, power, war, politics, and so on.

Teachers are often ineffective, or worse, when interacting with students about such matters. That is, they cannot adequately carry out their helping function, because what they say often causes students to

> stop talking
>
> feel inferior
>
> feel guilty
>
> lie, hide feelings
>
> become defensive
>
> become frustrated
>
> become angry
>
> counterattack

Obviously these student reactions do not help in coming to grips with problems or in finding ways to solve them.

Yet you would be hard pressed to find teachers who do not believe that their job is essentially to help students. This paradox—that teachers want and try to help students, but often don't—has a simple explanation. Their years of experience, first as children and students themselves and later as parents and teachers, have emphasized and reemphasized ways of talking with young people that hinder rather than help.

Thomas Gordon,* a clinical psychologist, has provided a great service to teachers by identifying twelve talk styles that produce the undesired reactions noted previously. He calls them the "typical twelve." They are:

1. ordering, directing, commanding
2. warning, admonishing, threatening
3. exhorting, moralizing, preaching
4. advising, giving solutions or suggestions
5. lecturing, teaching, giving logical arguments
6. judging, criticizing, disagreeing, blaming
7. praising, agreeing
8. name-calling, ridiculing, shaming
9. interpreting, diagnosing, analyzing
10. reassuring, sympathizing, consoling, supporting
11. probing, questioning, interrogating
12. withdrawing, distracting, humoring, diverting

*Gordon, T.: Teacher Effectiveness Training, New York, 1974, Peter H. Wyden, Inc., pp. 47-49. (You may feel that #7, #9, and #10 are helpful talk styles, but Gordon disagrees. He feels that students who are trying to talk out problems are hindered rather than helped by adults who use them. Talk styles #7 and #10 produce frustration because they don't help to clarify; #9 produces feelings of inferiority. If you're intrigued, see Gordon's explanations of these paradoxical components of the "typical twelve.")

Granted we want to avoid using the "typical twelve" when we talk with students. But what do we do instead? What styles of talk should we use when we talk with students?

Gordon has written a great deal about what we *should* do. We can summarize his positive approach in this way:

1. Listen actively to what students have to say.

2. Reflect back to them the feelings they are expressing. But do so only if it is evident that there is need to help them talk out a problem.

3. Use *I-messages* instead of *you-messages.* When confrontation with a student occurs, it is effective to tell him how the behavior, situation, or whatever makes you feel:

"I'm discouraged about the slow progress we are making in our group work."

"The noise is making it very difficult for me to work with Cindy."

At the same time we want to avoid using *you-messages* that almost always fall in the typical twelve:

"You are just not working as hard as you should."

"Sam, you are making so much noise I can't work with Cindy."

4. Use the no-lose approach in resolving conflicts. Most people think of conflicts as win-or-lose situations and, of course, everyone wants to win. The problem is that there has to be a loser every time there is a winner, and the losers do indeed lose. Gordon strongly urges a no-lose approach. Put simply, the no-lose approach means this: the crucial points of conflict are identified, and a solution to them is sought. The solution must be satisfactory to both parties, and so they are thrown together as partners working together to find a solution; they are no longer combatants.

3. Improving questioning

Here are five questions for you:

1. What was the name of that Greek guy who taught by asking a lot of questions?

2. Let's see now—how was it he did his questioning?

3. How could he have used questions to teach about marriage practices in Greece?

4. All in all, how do you compare questioning with lecturing as a method of instruction?

5. How many advantages can you think of for teaching by questioning?

May your joy at answering them all not be squelched. But our purpose here is not so much to answer them correctly as it is to look at the nature of the questions.

We must begin by agreeing on one point. That point has to do with the way "question" is used in this chapter.

A question is intended to elicit a response. It need not be followed by a question mark.

If you will agree to that, you will agree that our five questions would still be questions if we wrote them like this:

1. I bet somebody can tell us the name of the famous Greek who taught by asking questions.

2. Tell us in your own words how he did this questioning.

3. Describe how he might have used questioning to . . . .

But the following would *not* be questions, according to our agreement, because they are not really intended to elicit responses:

1. Will you please shut up?

2. When will you learn to act your age?

The first thing to remember, then, is that when you see the word "question" you know it means **a statement intended to elicit a response.**

Beyond that, this chapter will help you learn three other important things about questions and questioning. Those three things have to do with:

what can be gained by good questioning

how you should compose questions

how you should ask the questions you have composed

what can be gained by good questioning

Socrates has been greatly celebrated for his style of teaching. He taught by asking questions, with the idea that people already had in their heads most of what there was to know. He believed that through asking the right kinds of questions he could help people become aware of what they already knew but didn't know they knew.

If Socrates could see the way in which his ideas have been used, he would probably look for some more hemlock. That's because of the way teachers have dealt with the "Socratic method." They said it was good, but they didn't act as though they believed it. Their acts showed what they really thought — that teaching meant a smart person (teacher) telling something to an ignorant person (student). If you have heard a lecture on the Socratic method, for example, you probably know from boring experience how well that particular idea about the smart enlightening the dumb sticks with us.

Still, we have reliable evidence of the value of questioning, and we are beginning to make progress in learning to carry out the technique effectively. We know it can motivate learners, cause them to think, cause them to talk more, cause them to use various mental processes, and guide them into the practice of inquiry. There is strong belief that it can even help in mental development. If you will look back to the five questions at the beginning of the chapter, you will see that each one encouraged you to use a different mental process.

The first question asked you to reproduce a name.

The second question asked you to analyze a procedure.

The third question asked you to apply what you knew.

The fourth question asked you to evaluate procedures.

The fifth question asked you to produce ideas.

Insights into what questioning can do for learners are turning the spotlight more strongly on the processes of composing and asking questions. Where once we questioned students only to test whether they remembered what they had been taught, we are now beginning (forgive us, Dr. McLuhan) to

use the questioning medium as the mental massage

mental massage?

Right. That gives you some idea of what can be gained through good questioning. Specifically, we will consider ways to accomplish the following four large objectives:

decrease the amount of teacher talk

Teachers have a compulsion to "tell." That's understandable. After all, that's what their teachers did. Studies show that in typical classrooms (remember Flanders?):

> someone is talking two thirds of the time

> of that time, the teacher is doing two thirds of the talking

You can see the students get only one third of the talk time in those classrooms, and if there are thirty students, each one gets a fair share of only twenty-six seconds per hour to talk. That adds up to a good two and one-sixth minutes per day.

increase the amount of student talk

Evidence indicates that when students get a chance to talk more than their twenty-six seconds per hour, they learn more and like school better.

improve the quality of student talk

We can help students go far beyond the one-word contribution. We can help them explore, expand, explain, justify, generalize, avoid logical fallacies, and so on.

cause students to use higher cognitive/psychomotor processes

Cognitive processes are mental acts, and psychomotor processes are physical acts. Both are involved in learning. Usually teachers' questions cause students to reproduce material they have learned. Less frequently they cause students to employ the higher processes of analyzing, applying, evaluating, and producing.

mental massage!

We take an important step in the direction of accomplishing these four objectives by proceeding to the next page to learn . . .

how to compose good questions

For present purposes, we will call a question "good" if it does one or more of these three things:

elicits a quantity of student talk

encourages a high quality of student talk

causes the student to use higher cognitive/psychomotor processes

To help increase the quantity of student talk,

we can do the following five things.

1. Compose questions that are worth answering.

If a topic clearly does not merit attentive discussion, students won't respond, and you will come to an immediate dead end. Be sure your questions have some evident interest for students.

example: "What kind of project shall we do for Parents' Night next Monday?"

2. Compose questions that are open-ended.

Open-ended questions invite personal reactions. Every student can contribute. There are no right or wrong answers.

example: "What do you see in this cubist painting by Picasso?"

3. Compose questions that focus on process description.

Process questions could be called "how to" questions. The responses can be judged correct or incorrect, useful or not useful. Responses will be lengthy and varied.

example: "How do you bathe your cat?"

4. Compose questions that focus on explanations.

Explanations are clarifications of "why's." They can be judged correct or incorrect, useful or not useful, and they will be lengthy and varied.

example: "Tell us why the sun disappears during a solar eclipse."

5. Compose questions that focus on evaluations.

Evaluation is a process of making judgments about worth, correctness, desirability, and the like. When short responses occur, ask "why?"

examples: "Tell us what you thought of the play *Cyrano de Bergerac*."

"Which game provides better overall exercise, tennis or volleyball? Why?"

Now we turn our attention to the quality of student responses to questions.

We can help students to make higher quality

responses by asking questions that encourage more complex thought than that to which they are accustomed. This kind of question can follow a response that is shallow or too brief. Here are three specific things we can do to help improve quality.

1. Ask questions that help students clarify and illustrate.

Ask students to enlarge on their remarks by using examples, similes, metaphors, and analogies; or ask them to restate their remarks or use actions and tangible objects.

examples: "You mentioned honesty on the playground. Can you give some examples of what you mean?"

"Show us how you make your papier mâché."

2. Ask questions that help students expand their horizons.

Ask for examples and applications in other realms of activity.

example: "Marsha has remembered that we want to keep the classroom neat and clean. What are some other places where we want to practice neatness?"

3. Ask questions that help students avoid logical fallacies.

Such questions can draw attention to issues, assumptions, motives, persuasion devices, overgeneralizations, non sequiturs, cause-effect confusions, and so forth.

examples: "Do *all* fish lay eggs?"

"Who can tell us what our legal system says about guilt before a trial is held?"

"What do you think the author meant when she used the word 'deadbeat'?"

In a series of three steps, **we will see how questioning can help students use higher cognitive/psycho-motor processes.**

1. We can identify cognitive/psycho-motor acts that seem to be important in learning and mental development.

Here are seven of them:

7. producing
6. evaluating
5. applying
4. analyzing
3. reproducing
2. relating
1. perceiving

They are listed in this way to emphasize "higher" and "lower." Evaluation, for example, is considered to be a more complex process than application; analysis is considered to be more complex than perception. Usually, however, when people speak of "higher processes" they mean those indicated by numbers four through seven on this list. Traditional instruction has placed greater emphasis upon the "lower processes" that are indicated by numbers one through three.

2. We can identify five categories of information* available to students.

Each of these categories can be processed through the seven cognitive/psychomotor acts. The five categories are:

1. objects
2. symbols
3. meanings
4. behaviors
5. compositions

3. We can see how the cognitive/psychomotor acts and information categories interact, and how question composition is suggested by that interaction. We will proceed with that effort on the pages that follow.

*These categories are patterned after the Contents Facet of Guilford's Model of the Intellect (see Guilford, J. P.: The Structure of the Intellect, Psychol. Bull. **52**:267, 1956), which consists of the following categories: figural, symbolic, semantic, and behavioral.

In this section we will again note the seven cognitive/psychomotor acts, and we will see how questions can bring them into play. The key words should be considered as general ideas to be stated as the situation indicates. For example, "notice" might be changed to "where do you see" or "point to." "Similarities" might be changed to likes, similes, metaphors, analogues, and so on.

acts	question purposes
perceiving	guide learners to awareness **key words:** notice, point out, distinguish, identify, recognize, which, where
relating	help learners process information for comprehension and retention **key words:** associate, separate, visualize, similarities, differences, opposites, cause-effect, means-end
reproducing	direct learners to repeat information from memory **key words:** repeat, draw, show, tell, write, play, reconstruct, paraphrase
analyzing	help learners break information or products down into component parts **key words:** abstract, outline, dissect, divide, take out, summarize, break down, show where
applying	help learners make use of information and skills **key words:** use, compute, draw, decide, figure out, determine, generalize, relate, develop, organize, employ
evaluating	require learners to make judgments about information or products—their adequacy, correctness, usefulness, desirability **key words:** decide, compare, contrast, appraise, value, judge, assess, select
producing	stimulate and guide learners in generating new information and products **key words:** make, compose, tell, write, sing, act out, build, design, show, describe, deduce, induce, infer, extend, expand, reduce, summarize, specify, project, foresee, substitute, modify

section 2 ???????????

In this section we move to an examination of information categories and the question content they suggest.

categories	possible content
objects sensory data from tangible objects and their representations	form, shape, color, odor, sound, strength, texture, likenesses-differences, relations, quality, figure completion, physical analogies, spatial relations, missing parts, groupings, classifications
symbols sounds and marks that stand for things (numerals, letters, codes, graphics, musical notes, tones, vocal utterances)	identification, association with referents, naming and labeling, classification, shape, form, sound, sequence, relationships with each other
meanings cognitive and affective associates of words, acts, symbols, etc.	verbal and operational definitions, classifications, analogies, idioms, metaphors, myths, similes, synonyms, antonyms, similarities, differences, facts, concepts, generalizations, interpolations, extrapolations, interpretations, implications, alternatives, trends, rules, logic, analysis
behaviors actions, movements, events, changes (of both living and nonliving things)	acts, performances, movements, positions, gestures, changes, classifications, comparisons, controls, cause-effect, means-end, analysis, interpretation, extrapolation, alternatives, social interactions, physical interactions
compositions coherent conglomerates of meanings, often for vicarious experiencing	phrases, sentences, paragraphs, articles, stories, poems, novels, music, films, plays, paintings, drawings

We will now place the cognitive/psychomotor acts and the information categories side by side and look again at how they can be used together.

cognitive/psychomotor acts

We want learners to practice all these acts often. Not necessarily all of them must be present in a single lesson, and it is not necessary to include only one of them at a time.

1. perceiving (noticing)
2. relating (associating)
3. reproducing (repeating)
4. analyzing (breaking into parts)
5. applying (using)
6. evaluating (judging)
7. producing (creating)

information categories

Students have these categories of informational inputs available through observations, materials, talk, acts, etc.

A. objects
B. symbols
C. meanings
D. behaviors
E. compositions

interactions of acts and categories

Each cognitive/psychomotor act interacts with each information category. Those interactions give us systematic guidance in composing questions. To illustrate, suppose we are teaching primary reading. One thing we want learners to do is **perceive important symbols,** an interaction of **1** with **B.** From this interaction we compose the questions:

"Can you point to the letter that makes the first sound in 'acrobat'?"

"What other word do you know that begins with that same sound?"

Similarly, if we want college students in a questioning skills lesson to practice **evaluating their own behavior,** we compose the question:

"How well do you think your questions helped the students apply their map-reading skills?"

In this same manner you will find you can systematically and easily compose an array of good questions. Just consider:

the cognitive/psychomotor acts you want students to perform

the information available to students

the key words provided with the descriptions (presented earlier) of the cognitive/psychomotor acts

section 4 ? ? ? ? ? ?? ? ? ? ?

35 sample questions

The seven cognitive/psychomotor acts and the five information categories can be combined in thirty-five different ways. Below you will see a sample question provided for each of these combinations.

perceiving

1. **perceiving objects**
"Point to the largest red block."
2. **perceiving symbols**
"Which symbol stands for sodium?"
3. **perceiving meanings**
"Raise your hand when you hear the colloquialism that expresses surprise."
4. **perceiving behavior**
"Who noticed what Jack did in the pet shop?"
5. **perceiving compositions**
"Does the nursery rhyme 'Little Bo Peep' come first, second, or third on the record?"

relating

6. **relating objects**
"In what ways are a lemon and a grapefruit alike?"
7. **relating symbols**
"What do you think the following abbreviations stand for?"
8. **relating meanings**
"How are these sayings alike? How are they different? 'Look before you leap' and 'Strike while the iron is hot'?"
9. **relating behaviors**
"How does rapid walking affect the heartbeat?"
10. **relating compositions**
"Which of these paintings fall in the American Primitive group?"

reproducing

11. **reproducing objects**
"Construct a model of the hydrogen atom."

12. **reproducing symbols**
"Draw whole, half, quarter, and sixteenth notes."
13. **reproducing meanings**
"Can you tell the fable of the fox and the grapes in your own words?"
14. **reproducing behaviors**
"See if you can serve the tennis ball the way I showed you."
15. **reproducing compositions**
"Who thinks he can recite the Gettysburg Address?"

analyzing

16. **analyzing objects**
"Where does the spark plug fit in this Wankel engine?"
17. **analyzing symbols**
"Can you circle the letters in the Spanish alphabet that don't occur in the English alphabet?"
18. **analyzing meanings**
"What are the word origins from which our word 'neology' is derived?"
19. **analyzing behaviors**
"Summarize the main things an artist does as he prepares his canvas."
20. **analyzing compositions**
"In which part of his poem did Frost hint at a possibility of suicide?"

applying

21. **applying objects**
"How are you supposed to use the grafting compound to seal wounds on the tree?"
22. **applying symbols**
"See if you can use these pictographs to write a message to a friend."

23. **applying meanings**
   "What trend is the food-population ratio likely to follow in Bolivia?"
24. **applying behaviors**
   "Now see if you can use the scale to play this simple tune."
25. **applying compositions**
   "Use these articles to illustrate Marcuse's point of view."

evaluating

26. **evaluating objects**
   "Is this cake sweet enough?"
27. **evaluating symbols**
   "Which of these drawings best represents the spirit of ecology? Why?"
28. **evaluating meanings**
   "Why do you think the statement 'All change must come in the hearts and minds of men' is valueless for change?"
29. **evaluating behaviors**
   "Overall, who has had a greater influence on their respective sports—Bill Russell or Arnold Palmer? Why?"
30. **evaluating compositions**
   "Compare Marlowe's and Goethe's delineations of Faust, with emphasis upon his believability as a human being."

producing

31. **producing objects**
   "Can you cut a Christmas scene on this linoleum block?"
32. **producing symbols**
   "What do you think would be a good code mark to represent happiness? Show us."
33. **producing meanings**
   "How could we go about writing our own mottoes?"
34. **producing behavior**
   "Show us how you'd react to a surprise birthday party."
35. **producing compositions**
   "What melody can you compose to go with this verse?"

how to ask
the questions

Observe any teacher, even a highly skilled one, and you will probably hear her do several unnecessary things when asking questions. We will call those unnecessary things "common mistakes in questioning." Four of those common mistakes are:

> changing the question
>
> repeating the question
>
> answering one's own question
>
> repeating students' responses

Most of us do these things unconsciously, not realizing we are losing a good deal of efficiency. We can correct these mistakes easily. First, we need to conceptualize the behavior that occurs in each of them. The following examples illustrate this teacher behavior.

error: changing the question

error example: questions are asked in a series without allowing a student response

"What have we learned about water conservation on the Nile River? What part does the Aswan Dam play? First, how can we remember where the Aswan Dam is?"

This kind of error occurs when the teacher asks a question, realizes she has not asked what she intended, and changes it at once, often several times. The error can be corrected by practicing model questions. Formulate a few good questions, using appropriate cognitive/psychomotor acts and available information. Then practice asking the questions until they come naturally. Take a look at the following practice hints.

> cognitive/psychomotor acts to be emphasized:
>> perceiving, relating, producing, evaluating
>
> available information:
>> map of the Nile River Valley showing agricultural areas,
>> cities, river features, archaeological sites

model questions:

(relating) "Do you see any way we could draw imaginary lines on the map to help us remember the location of the Aswan Dam and the ruins that had to be moved?"

(perceiving and producing) "Notice the agricultural valleys and river features. Why do you think the Aswan Dam site was selected, even though it would cause water to cover some very important ruins?"

(evaluating) "Everything considered, do you think the Aswan Dam was placed in the best possible location? Why?"

error: repeating the question

error example: the teacher repeats the question in various forms without allowing time for student response.

"How do we conjugate the verb *ser* in the present indicative tense? How do we do it? Who knows how we do it? Who can conjugate *ser*?"

This repetition is unnecessary, of course, and it increases the amount of teacher talk. It occurs either because the class is not paying attention when the question is first asked, or because the teacher feels uneasy when students don't respond immediately and just keeps talking.

Of course, it is fruitless to ask questions if the class is unable to attend to the exercise. Otherwise it is a good idea to practice pausing after asking a question, for several seconds if necessary. Just be sure you have asked the kind of question you wanted to ask. If none of the students can respond after several seconds, give a hint or ask an alternate question.

error: answering one's own question

error example:

"Okay, Mike, now how're you going to toss up the ball to serve it? You have to toss it without spin, right? So your best bet is to pitch it from the palm of your hand, am I right?"

Two of the reasons we ask questions are to elicit responses and improve the quality of responses. We don't accomplish either of those ends when we answer our own questions. Again, we should pause after asking a question until students can respond. If they have difficulty, we can either give hints or ask questions that are similar but easier.

error: repeating students' responses

error example:

Teacher: "Now you see water boiling in the top of the test tube while there is ice still in the bottom. Why doesn't the ice melt before the water boils?"

Mary: "It's because . . . let's see . . . the hot water rises . . . well, the hot water stays in the top of the test tube. The cold water is heavier so it stays in the bottom, and the boiling water stays in the top."

Teacher: "Yes, the boiling water stays in the top of the test tube while the cold water, which is heavier, stays in the bottom."

Almost all teachers repeat their students' answers. The practice does, in truth, serve two useful purposes: it emphasizes correct responses, and it assures that all students hear the responses.

On the other hand, the practice also has two undesirable effects. It increases the amount of teacher talk, and students learn to believe that their responses are poor unless repeated by the teacher. To avoid these two effects, you can do two things. You can reinforce students' responses nonverbally, with a nod, smile, or other sign of approval. When other students do not hear or understand the response, you can ask the student to repeat it or ask another student to tell what he thinks the response meant.

Those, then, are four common mistakes teachers make in asking questions. You can easily correct or avoid those mistakes by doing the following things:

1. Observe yourself making the mistakes. Tape recordings are very helpful for this purpose. Consciously perform the errors to fix them clearly in your mind.

2. Practice composing and asking prototype (or model) questions.

3. Pause after asking each question, until you are sure the students have had an opportunity to answer.

4. Give hints, clues, or alternate questions if students have difficulty responding.

5. Accept responses nonverbally, with nods, smiles, gestures, and so on.

in a capsule

Properly used, questions can be very helpful in decreasing the amount of teacher talk, in increasing the amount of student talk, in improving the quality of student talk, and in causing students to use higher cognitive/psychomotor processes.

To increase the quantity of student talk, we can use questions that are open-ended and that focus on process description, explanation, and evaluation. To improve the quality of student responses, we can use questions that help students clarify and illustrate, expand their horizons, and avoid fallacious logic.

To cause students to use higher cognitive/psychomotor processes, we can ask questions that emphasize analysis, application, evaluation, and production. We can also identify categories of information to be processed through cognitive/psychomotor acts: objects, symbols, meanings, behaviors, and compositions. The interactions between these acts and information categories suggest specific formats for composing good questions.

Once the questions are composed, we can practice asking them so as to avoid four common mistakes: changing the question, repeating the question, answering one's own question, and repeating students' responses.

If we do make mistakes in asking questions, we can correct them by observing ourselves make the mistakes, by composing and practicing model questions, by pausing after asking each question, by giving hints or alternate questions when students can't answer, and by accepting students' responses nonverbally.

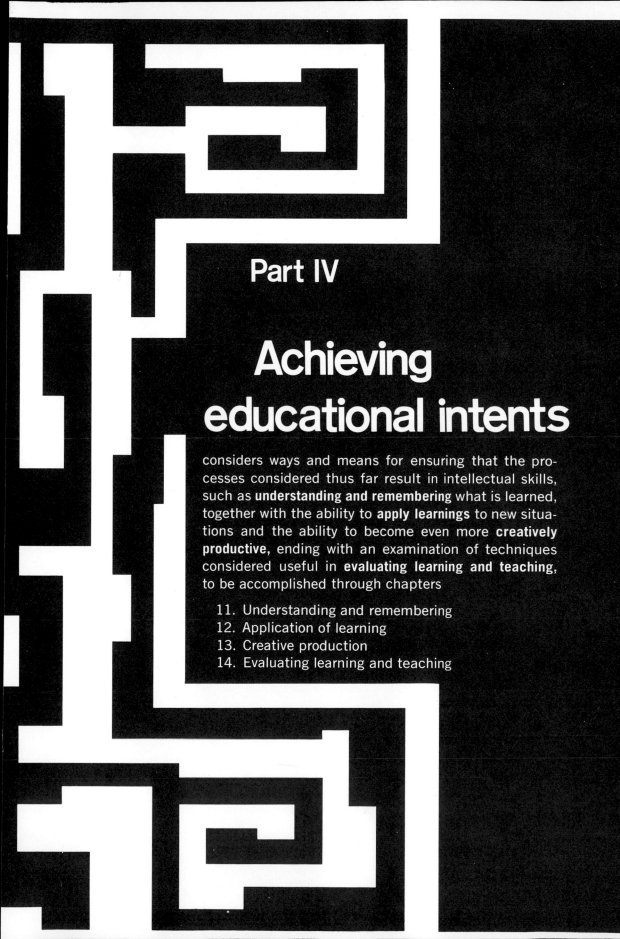

Part IV

Achieving educational intents

considers ways and means for ensuring that the processes considered thus far result in intellectual skills, such as **understanding and remembering** what is learned, together with the ability to **apply learnings** to new situations and the ability to become even more **creatively productive**, ending with an examination of techniques considered useful in **evaluating learning and teaching**, to be accomplished through chapters

11. Understanding and remembering
12. Application of learning
13. Creative production
14. Evaluating learning and teaching

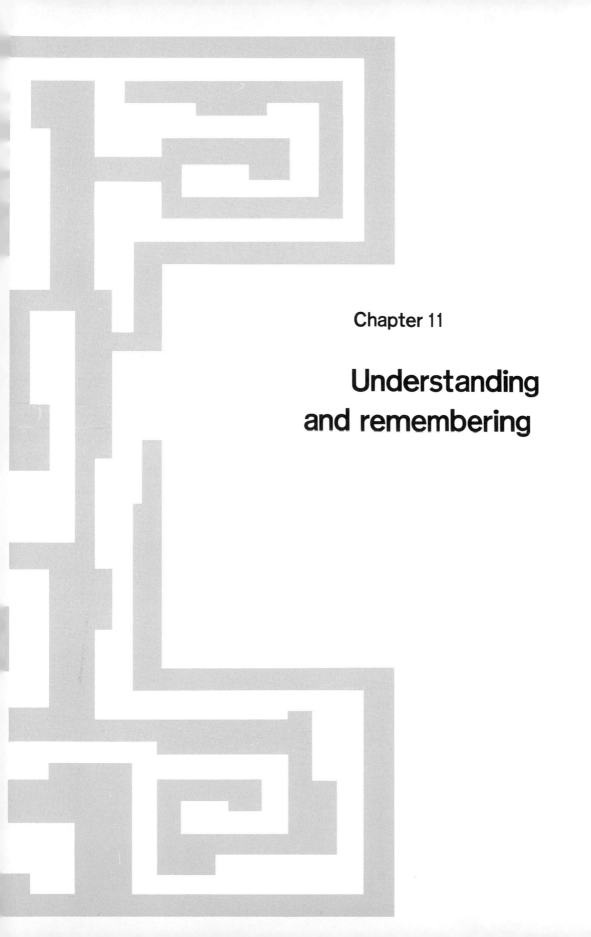

Chapter 11

Understanding
and remembering

Understand
Johnny,
try to understand

Teacher: Johnny, how much is three plus four?

Johnny: Seven.

Teacher: Good. Now tell me: what does it mean when we say three plus four? What are we doing?

Johnny: Adding.

Teacher: Yes, we are adding, aren't we? What else can you tell me?

Johnny: I don't know.

Teacher: Sure you do. What does it *mean* when we say three plus four? Are we putting something together?

Johnny: Yeah.

Teacher: What are we putting together?

Johnny: Umm . . . I don't know. Three minus four?

Later, to Johnny's mother: "Johnny is progressing nicely in his number facts. He can add well. Now we have to work on his understanding."

Well,
what does it mean
to understand?

1. understand

"To understand," says *Webster's New Collegiate Dictionary,* is "to apprehend the purport or meaning of." That's only one of several definitions given. But it is the one that comes closest to describing what teachers have in mind when they say they want their students to understand.

The trouble with dictionaries, wonderful as they are, is that they use words to define words. They are closed systems that can send you in circles. For example, our word "understand" was defined as *gaining meaning.* But one definition of "meaning" from the same dictionary is "the sense in which a statement is *understood*" (italics mine). So what do we have? To understand is to gain meaning, to gain meaning is to understand. That still leaves us with only intuitive notions about what people do, or can do, when they understand.

We will try to see how students can give us evidence that they understand, but first we will take a moment to see why understanding is important enough to deserve attention from teachers.

In much of this chapter we will give attention to *evidence* of understanding—to what learners can *do* that convinces us that they understand what they are learning. But for the moment, in answering the question "Why understand?" we will look at the matter from the learner's point of view.

In every human there seems to be present a drive to know and understand—a drive to find out new things and make sense of them. Have you ever noticed how frustrating it is to be unable to make sense of what you see? To be unable to resolve an optical illusion, where your senses tell you a ball is rolling uphill, contrary to all you know. Or to lie outside on a warm night, gazing at a black sky brilliant with stars, and find no way to comprehend the beginnings, organizations, and destinies of those giants so incredibly far away? Or to wonder about the "you" inside your body and try to decide whether there would still be a you if there had been a different mother or father?

We recognize, then, that there exists in all of us the powerful urge to know and understand. Helping learners to satisfy that urge would in itself be reason enough for giving attention to meaning and understanding in every part of the curriculum.

There are other reasons, too. If learners feel that what they are learning makes sense, they can learn it faster, remember it longer, and use it to better advantage. You struggle with trying to comprehend the process of meiosis. You try to find out how cells reduce their chromosomes by half. Then you see it shown in diagrams, and suddenly it's clear. You grasp the process almost at once, and you remember it easily.

But that process of seeing the parts fit, of grasping the significance, or satisfying the urge to make sense of things learned—that process is a private one. It occurs within the individual and is undetectable to others. Often learners who feel that they understand do not. We say they misunderstand; they haven't fitted the parts together just right.

These observations point to two questions that remain for teachers to answer:

1. How can we help learners understand, instead of not understanding or misunderstanding?

2. What can learners show us as evidence that they understand?

That's what the rest of this chapter is about.

Understanding—
5 approaches

This section describes five means students can use to gain a greater understanding of the material they are learning. The five approaches are:

reporting

symbol defining

territory mapping

observing and imitating

doing the thing

reporting

The reporting approach to understanding emphasizes identification of **who, what, when, where,** and **why** in the material being learned. These elements are often, though not always, present in verbal material and live experiences.

The following sketch is an example of one kind of material in which the cub reporting approach can be used profitably.

Amazon Naturalist

One of the first great explorers of the regions along the Amazon was a young Englishman named Henry Bates.

Bates was no ordinary adventurer, longing for gold and riches. He was quite the opposite. Early in life he developed a keen interest in the natural sciences and built large collections of butterflies and beetles. When he was only 18, he wrote an article about them, and it was published in one of the leading zoological journals of the day. This interest in nature greatly influenced Bates' entire life.

Bates and a friend named Wallace heard tales of unknown creatures that inhabited the vast, unexplored river jungles of South America, and they resolved to carry out an expedition to that continent. May 28, 1848, found them at the mouth of the Amazon River, a strange and beautiful place of perpetual summer and brown-skinned people. Bates, then only 23 years of age, could hardly have imagined that he would spend the next eleven years on the river.

Despite poverty, poor health, and isolation (Wallace returned to England after two years), Bates methodically observed and collected quantities of creatures, especially insects, in the regions along the Amazon. When at last he decided to return home, he had collected and categorized 14,712 species of animals. An amazing 8,000 of them were new to science.

Though Bates gained eminence in scientific circles, he never returned to the Amazon. Before his death he was decorated by the Emperor of Brazil in recognition of his work, which still stands as one of the greatest contributions ever made by a naturalist.

Now go back over the "Amazon Naturalist" and be sure to identify the who's, what's, where's, when's, and why's. On the next page you will see one way to do it.

who	what	where	when	why
Bates	collected beetles and butterflies	England	in his teens	interest
Bates	published an article on beetles and butterflies	scientific journal	at age 18	interest
Bates	went on an expedition	Amazon	at age 23	to observe and collect animals
Bates	etc.	etc.	etc.	etc.
Wallace	accompanied Bates	Amazon	1848	to observe and collect animals
Wallace	returned to England		1850	?
Emperor of Brazil	decorated Bates	?	before Bates' death	in recognition of his work

symbol defining

Another approach to understanding is symbol defining, or determining what a given symbol stands for. Symbols don't have meanings inherent in themselves. They stand for meanings that people have agreed on, more or less—more or less because symbols sometimes represent different things for different people. For instance, you may have seen the following symbol associated with two very different meanings:

meaning #1 Peace, the hope of mankind

meaning #2 The great American chicken track

symbols are super shorthand

They let us manipulate vast arrays of meanings in very condensed form. Prominent kinds of symbols (with obvious overlapping) include:

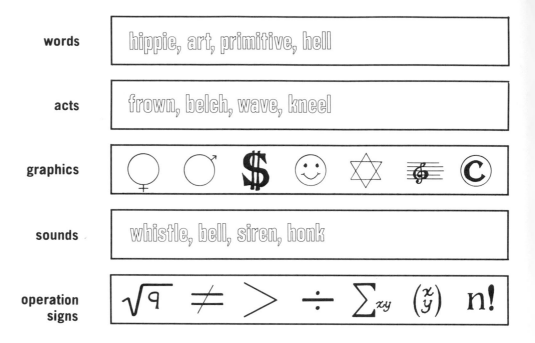

words	hippie, art, primitive, hell
acts	frown, belch, wave, kneel
graphics	♀ ♂ $ ☺ ✡ 𝄞 ©
sounds	whistle, bell, siren, honk
operation signs	$\sqrt{9}$ $\neq$ $>$ $\div$ $\sum_{xy}$ $\left(\frac{x}{y}\right)$ $n!$

words

Word symbols have two authentic kinds of definitions. One kind, found in dictionaries, is the standard usage and indicates the meaning(s) that the word represents over a period of time. In living languages, however, word usage changes. A word may, in a short span of time, take on a different meaning. The words "queer," "gay," and "fairy," for example, have dropped from genteel conversation in the past few years because they have been used as slang to mean something that is not included in standard dictionary definitions. In a like manner, different groups use certain words to represent very different meanings: welfare, conservatism, hippies, and free enterprise are examples. Look at the italicized words in the following letter and see if you can tell what the writer intended them to symbolize.

> Editor:
> Our *clabber-headed* leaders are *playing into the hands* of the *duped* and *misled sheep* in this country. I shudder at the *ominous unreasoning roar* of the mob, *spawned and driven* by *treasonably twisted minds.*

acts

A great variety of acts—body motions and positions—are used to symbolize meanings. The Navajo may point direction with his lips; the Mexican may show pleasure by tugging at an imaginary beard. We continually use frowns, smiles, smirks, gestures, bows, handshakes, and so on to send messages. Many acts symbolize meanings differently according to the situation in which they occur. For example, a smile can symbolize pleasure and it can symbolize derision. See if you can think of two quite different meanings that are often associated with:

> a frown
> a wink
> a pinch
> a yawn
> looking at one's watch
> being fifteen minutes late
> leaving food on the plate
> disobeying a teacher

graphics

Maps, charts, and graphs symbolize quantities of information in pictorial form. In order to read them, however, you have to be able to identify the meanings symbolized by all those markings. The same thing is true for musical notation and markings, for chemical abbreviations, for schematic drawings of electrical circuits and components, for highway signs, logos that represent company names, and so on.

Acts and words may symbolize varieties of meanings, but graphics of the sort mentioned here have precise definitions. Unless you understand what each mark stands for, you can't read the representation accurately. For this reason, you should be sure your students can correctly identify the meanings represented in graphic material.

sounds

Our environment is filled with sounds, and we can divide them into three categories to make it easier to examine them. One category consists of sounds we all hear incidentally and normally in the course of an ordinary day—airplanes, clocks, cars, running water, footsteps, birds, rustling papers. These sounds usually are not thought of as symbols. They are, rather, manifestations of the objects that produce them.

The other two kinds of sounds fall into the realm of the symbolic. One of them is the category of signals. "Less precise" signals might include shouts, honks, and whistles—they are less precise because they can have a variety of meanings. "More precise" signals might include clock chimes, doorbells, and fire sirens. They are more precise because they stand for fewer meanings—in most cases only one.

A third category consists of aesthetic compositions—music, verse choir, and so on, where the sounds are designed to produce or evoke an emotional rather than a literal response in the listener.

operation signs

Like the graphics mentioned earlier, the symbols used to indicate operations have very precise meanings, and they play important roles, especially in mathematics and the sciences. To function mathematically, for example, you must unfailingly interpret the symbols that indicate combining, regrouping, and so on. Varieties of interpretations are not permissible, and a commonality of meaning is essential. Therefore teachers must take care to see that students can:

> identify operational symbols accurately
> describe the process indicated by each symbol
> invariably perform the processes indicated by the symbols

territory mapping

The name for this road to understanding doesn't involve real mapmaking of real geographic territory. Rather, it is a concept that general semanticists have used to remind us of the difference between objects or processes or ideas on the one hand and the words used to symbolize them on the other hand. There is a real difference, for example, between the word "cow" and the four-legged, milk-producing animal. There is a real difference between the word "milking" and the actual process used to obtain milk from the cow.

Semanticists would refer to the process of milking as the **territory.** They would refer to the word description of the process as the **map.** They make a big thing (and rightly so) of reminding us that **the map is not the territory.**

That idea helps people remember that words are useful tools, but they are not object or process reality in themselves. Humans must continually use words to map territories, just as I am doing here. Obviously, we could not continue our civilization without it. What we want to do, however, is learn to make better maps of the territories we want to describe. One reason for that is to help readers or listeners to "see" the territory more accurately—to visualize more exactly the process of milking, for example. We also want to help *ourselves* comprehend the territory more accurately.

If you want to learn something well, they say, teach it to others.

If you want to *understand* something well, we might say, explain it (map it) to others.

How do you go about making a good map of a territory? Here's a three-point mini-mini course in territory mapping.

First, you must have some conceptualization or visualization of the territory. We will take that for granted.

Second, you must use words or other symbols that are commonly used and that have only a small range of meanings and interpretations.

Third, you must try to emphasize three important kinds of relationships; we will call them the **what's, how's,** and **why's.**

what's Think of the what's as labels—names for objects, processes, ideas. Take the word "tapir" as an example. Suppose we have to explain what a tapir is. We could do this most easily by pointing to a live tapir. Or we could use a model or a picture. If we don't have those things handy, and we must use words, we can proceed best by telling what the tapir is *like:*

He looks something like a small horse in size and shape.

With that established, we can go on to relate other what's— what he does, what his nose is like, what his feet are like, what he eats. In each case, we try to relate the aspect we are describing to something our readers or listeners already know about. That is, **we try to use likeness relationships to explain the what's.**

how's How's refer to procedures—to actions that lead to an identifiable end. How does the tapir get his food? How does he cross swollen rivers? How does he escape his predators?

The word "how" directs attention to means-end relationships. The end (food, safety, comfort, whatever) is something desired. The means are procedures used to attain the end.

why's Why's describe or seek relationships between causes and effects. They focus on reasons for occurrences—on conditions that seem to produce certain consequences. Why is the tapir so seldom seen in the wild? Is it because he is shy, camouflaged, nocturnal? Why is the tapir considered one of the closest relatives of the rhinocerous? Is it because of his habits, his habitat, his shape, his internal structure? **Notice that why's are answered with (be)causes.**

observing & imitating

This road to understanding is related to the how (or means-end) relationship discussed in the previous section. It differs in that it focuses not on describing (or mapping territory) but on recognizing and performing processes — on *doing* acts instead of describing them.

Observation means taking in information through the senses. Imitation means trying to perform an act like someone else (a model) does. This road to understanding, then, involves first observing a model perform an act, and later trying to copy the procedure that the model used.

Most skills cannot be conceptualized adequately through reading or listening to descriptions. You have to see and hear a model perform the acts. Take an act as simple as the serve in table tennis. You have probably seen and played table tennis, but try explaining to youngsters, through words alone, how to serve. Tell them (do not show them) how to grip the paddle, how to pitch the ball out of the palm, how to strike it so it bounces first on the near side of the net and then on the far side.

Now contrast that procedure with a demonstration, where you show the learners rather than tell them. A few words can help greatly in pointing out certain things you are doing. But the essence of the instruction lies in the acts you perform: you *show* the learners how to grip the paddle, how to toss the ball, how to strike it. Now they have a greater degree of understanding than they could ever achieve through words alone. And as they begin to imitate your performance, their understanding grows greater yet.

Of course, it helps if the model performance has standard accuracy. A lady from New Delhi once told me about her first experiences in learning English in school. In unison, she said, students and teacher would chant English sentences such as "The calf is a young cow." But they pronounced it "The ca-leef is a yoon-je cow."

We laugh at that, though it is reminiscent of some attempts to teach foreign languages, in which teachers give faulty models for many words. For example, in Spanish, teachers often model "grah-shus" for *gracias,* "buh-ree-toe" for *burrito,* "pin-yadda" for *piñata,* and "bway-nus dee-us" for *buenos días.* We could continue with a great many such examples. The point, though, should be clear: students should have accurate skill and process models to imitate; their levels of understanding increase through observing and imitating the models.

Of course, teachers can't demonstrate everything, and other live models aren't easy to obtain for instructional use. Still, there are other good sources of models. Motion pictures and video tapes (especially with slow motion and stop action segments), transparencies and flat pictures, and simple diagrams are all valuable in helping learners conceptualize processes.

316

doing the thing

As we noted, imitation of a model yields a level of understanding not otherwise attainable. You may be thoroughly versed in every phase of the game of basketball that is open to spectator observation. But yet there are things you can never understand well until you have observed them as a participant—the physical sensations of sweaty bodies and sharp elbows smashing each other underneath the basket, the in-game as distinct from the in-crowd sounds, the blurriness of frantic movement in the periphery of vision.

The "doing the thing" road to understanding stresses such activities as **gaming, messing about,** and **creating,** all of which inevitably bring higher levels of understanding.

Gaming is a word used here to refer to participation in games of any sort—loosely or highly organized, competitive or cooperative, group or individual, instructional or for fun only. What sets gaming apart into a category of its own is that every activity we call a game has at least some rules to follow. Even an informal game of tag has its acceptable and nonacceptable acts. So do solitaire, tic-tac-toe, and spelling baseball.

Gaming is highly attractive to students. They seek competition and interaction with others. Almost any instructional activity can be made attractive if it is cast in the form of a game. That idea has been put to use in simulations—instructional games that are proving themselves valuable in classroom use.

Messing about refers to a general kind of activity—individual or small group—where there are no rules to follow, no assignments to complete, no winners and losers, and no ends in mind except the pleasure of the activity itself. A learner may mess about with tempera paints, with toy cars in the dirt, with wires and electric cells, or with a guitar. Such activities are serendipitous; they often yield useful understandings that were not expected; they almost always foster new skills, concepts, insights, and refinements; they almost always help learners perceive relationships they hadn't recognized before.

Creating refers to the act of producing objects, ideas, processes, or compositions. Production of a painting brings increased understanding of many things—line, color, composition, perspective, technique. Production of a poem can bring increased understanding of imagery, semantics, word sounds, and the private experience. Building dirt roads, whistling tunes, narrating experiences or fantasies, decorating automobiles—these activities and thousands more like them are creative acts in which individuals fuse observations with personal "inner visions" to produce new and different things. Along with that production come ever higher degrees of understanding. One understands better many things about guitars for having played them, about car building for having built them, about pie baking for having baked them.

Evidence of understanding

We have discussed several ways to increase levels of student understanding. Now we must decide what we will accept as evidence for understanding—what we can observe our students do that convinces us understanding has occurred. On the following pages you will see notations of several student acts that can provide such evidence.

translation

To translate means, among other things, to change from one condition to another. There are several activities that help learners to translate what they have learned in one form into another. When students can do this successfully, we see evidence of understanding. Such activities include:

1. Translating into a second language what was learned in a first.

example How would you say "Où sont les neiges d'autrefois?" in English?

2. Expressing in words that which was written in other symbols and vice versa.

example Express the following equation in words:
$$6CO_2 + 6H_2O \xrightarrow{\text{Light}} C_6H_{12}O_6 + 6O_2$$

3. Expressing in one's own words what has been learned.

example Tell us in your own words what Sam had to do in order to get his driver's license.

4. Drawing, diagramming, charting, or graphing what has been expressed in words and vice versa.

example Draw a picture of firemen to show what they wear and carry while fighting a fire.

5. Building a model of what has been learned.

example Build a model of the Taos Indian Pueblo.

6. Demonstrating a procedure.

example Show us how you divide the word "indefatigably" into syllables.

7. Dramatizing an occurrence.

example Role-play a visit to the doctor's office for a checkup.

interpretation & explanation

We shall use the words "interpretation" and "explanation" in slightly different ways. **Interpretation refers to an individual's perception of meaning. Explanation refers to an individual's attempts to make that meaning clear to someone else.**

Interpretation serves as evidence for understanding when we ask learners to tell us what something means to them—a word, a political cartoon, a graph showing population increase, a pun such as "no noose is good noose," an expression such as "the straw that broke the camel's back."

You can see that these activities are very similar to translations. Translations, though, are fairly literal restatements, while statements of interpretation often differ markedly from the original. An example is the saying "pulled himself up by his own bootstraps." A translation of that saying might be "he caught hold of his boots and yanked himself up." But an accurate interpretation would be something quite different.

Explanation serves as evidence of understanding when one person tries to make a thing clear to another person. Here our what's, how's, and why's show their usefulness. For example, suppose you want to explain the technique of pruning grapevines. You want to make the process clear to your listeners, so you tell what pruning means, why pruning is necessary, how you prune the vines, and what tools you use when pruning. As we noted in the section on territory mapping, if you want to understand something well, prepare yourself to explain it to others.

extrapolation

Extrapolation is educated fortune telling; it entails making predictions based on past trends. Through extrapolation students can show understanding of trends and the future consequences that will result if those trends continue. Weather forecasting is just such an activity. It is based on conditions of humidity, temperature, pressure, wind, and what has been happening elsewhere. And it shows an understanding of the interplay among those weather components.

In a similar way, students can extrapolate numbers of trends: population—(how many inhabitants will different countries have twenty years from now?), food (with present rates of population increase and agricultural production, what will the food supply be like worldwide in the year 2000?). The same can be done with standard of living, use of automobiles, women's fashions, air pollution, human life expectancy, censorship, freedom and oppression, and so forth.

application

A crucial test of understanding is the ability to apply or use what one has learned. Experiments have shown us that, as a general rule, the better you understand a thing the better able you are to use it in other circumstances. The students who can say $2 + 2 = 4$ but don't understand the process involved can't use their knowledge to solve problems.

Unfortunately, students have few opportunities to apply outside of school much of what they learn inside school. That can mean one of two things: either the curriculum is philosophically wrong (it ought to be "learning for living and living for learning") or the curriculum is structurally wrong (it ought to provide students with an opportunity to apply everything they learn in lifelike, in-school situations).

Individual teachers can do something about the second of these possibilities. They can find many good ways of helping students to apply learnings. Chapter 12 deals with just that, so we will wait until then to explore the ways in which students can make immediate use of what they have learned.

Teacher-judges

So far we have examined three things. The first was why we consider it important that students understand. The second was kinds of activities that can help students to understand. The third was student acts that give us evidence of understanding. That brings us to a fourth and final consideration: teachers must judge how well their students understand the material being learned. How do they go about it?

match-ups

Remember our discussion of territory mapping—how learners make thought and word pictures (maps) of the material they learn about (territory)? We noted that semanticists stress the point that the map is not the territory—that the words are not the same as the reality. Yet the concern of semanticists and teachers alike is to help people learn to make maps that more accurately represent the territory. We used the concept of territory mapping as an analogue of understanding.

That raises the point of teacher maps. While students make their cognitive maps, so do teachers. Now the teacher will judge the student's map, its accuracy and completeness, in terms of his own map. In other words, he will make judgments about student understanding. To get a picture of how this occurs, let's use our imaginations a bit. Let's suppose a first-grade teacher has asked a child to explain how frogs grow from egg to adult. Let's suppose further that the teacher has a large and detailed word picture of that egg-to-adult frog process lodged in a corner of her memory. The child says:

> "First the mother frog lays some eggs in the water. Then they
> hatch into baby tadpoles. Then the tadpoles grow legs and
> lose their tails. And then they are frogs."

The teacher checks each statement against her own word map to see whether there are disagreements (she would call them student errors). She also decides, using her knowledge of first-graders' thought processes and language ability, whether the description is complete enough. If the two pictures match up—if there are no areas of disagreement between them—the teacher judges that the student understands.

In a similar way, a college English teacher reacts to a student's paper.

excerpts from student paper	instructor's marginal notes
Thomas More recognized that differences exist among people, and he tried to provide for those differences. Restless people could change occupations from time to time; individuality could be expressed through styles of gardening; a person could worship any god he chose.	"yes" (meaning: your map coincides with mine)
Utopians could worship any god they wanted to, so long as they worshipped some form of supreme being—atheism was not tolerated.	"overstatement—atheism could not be preached, but could be privately accepted" (meaning: your map doesn't quite agree with mine—you have a slight misunderstanding)

What we take for granted in such match-ups is that the teacher's map is an accurate one. Of course, we know it isn't perfect; at best it can depict only sketchily the territory (or reality) it represents. That's all the more reason why teachers who will judge student understanding must be sure they have thought through material students are learning. They need the best maps they can have. Yet, since they can't know all about everything, they should not hesitate to encourage students to turn to expert references—books, models, films, and so on—for help in checking understanding.

understanding misunderstanding not understanding

When teachers examine match-ups, they decide whether students understand, misunderstand, or do not understand. Among these three conditions there exist some differences that we should take into account.

Understand means that the student expresses a concept—through explanation, demonstration, and so on—that satisfies the teacher. That is, the student's expression seems sufficiently accurate and complete. You recognize the subjectivity that prevails when teachers make such judgments. What might seem good to one might seem poor to another. Still, the process of judging understanding appears to be much the same from one teacher to another.

Misunderstand falls very close to understand. Even though students misunderstand, they have still conceptualized a phenomenon or idea, and they can express their conceptualizations. They are judged to misunderstand, though, if there is some fault in the accuracy of their expressions, when compared to the teacher's. For example, a student may show understanding of ocean tides by explaining that two high tides and two low tides occur every day because of the pull of the earth's gravity. The teacher would judge that the student misunderstands the cause: the student didn't include (and evidently didn't conceptualize) the role played by the action of the moon's gravitational attraction on the earth. The student did include the concept of high and low tides related to gravity. Part of the explanation was simply inaccurate.

Not understand means that students do not conceptualize an idea or phenomenon, or that they cannot express their conceptualization. One does not understand the metamorphosis of insects if one has no concept that some insects pass through different physical forms in their development. Students do not understand the international monetary system if they do not conceptualize the gold standard. They do not understand the game of rugby if they do not conceptualize the scoring system and basic game strategies.

In summary, teachers judge that students do not understand a thing if they cannot express its fundamental concepts. They judge that students understand if they can express those concepts at a satisfactory level of accuracy and completeness. They judge that students misunderstand if they can express fundamental concepts but make errors in accuracy or do not make the expression complete enough.

questions:

What do you do when you see that your students misunderstand?

What do you do when you see that your students do not understand?

**understanding increases retention
and the ability to apply learnings**

five roads to understanding:

reporting

symbol defining

territory mapping   **learning activities for
students**

observing and imitating

doing the thing

evidence for understanding:

translation

interpretation and explanation   **student abilities
teachers should look
for**

extrapolation

application

teachers as judges:

making match-ups

understanding, misunderstanding,   **the process of judging
the judgments**

and not understanding

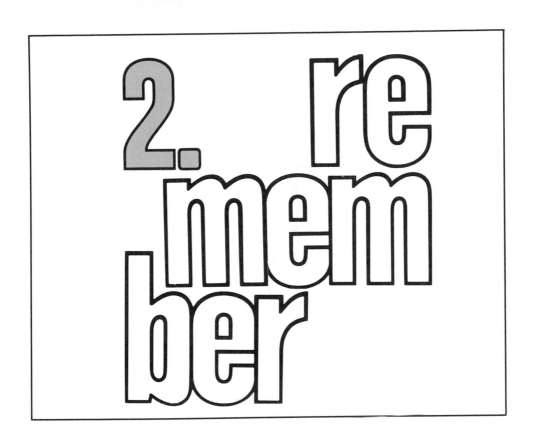

2. remember

"I suppose you wouldn't . . . . Naw, I know you wouldn't really want to . . . to have, you know, a real good memory. . . a . . . that is, be able to remember all sorts of stuff? I mean, things you really need to remember? Like this guy I know. Fantastic the way he remembers. Names, poems, telephone numbers, addresses, facts, stories, places, everything. But like he has a system, see? A way of doing it, you know what I mean?"

"What in the world are you talking about?"

"Oh. Well, I knew you wouldn't . . . well, I . . . aw, forget it."

WAIT!

DON'T FORGET IT!

Don't forget it. That's step #1 to having a good memory. Decide you're going to remember. You—with your terrible memory for names, dates, facts, and so on—can remember. You will remember. You will teach your students to remember. But before we begin in earnest, let's take time out for . . .

a trick

Think you can remember four words? If you can, you will be able to perform a trick that will astound your friends and make your enemies green with envy. Here are the words you have to remember, in order:

atlas

goose

linen

thigh

To be sure you remember them, make vivid mental images of each. Then chain, or relate, each to the other. For instance, you might visualize *Atlas*, muscles bulging, holding up the world, honking like a silly *goose*, and straining and splitting the *linen* that covers his *thigh*. But don't just read the words—**visualize** them as vividly as possible. *Please* be impressed with this advice. (Notice, too, that the four words are in alphabetical order. That will keep you from getting them mixed up.)

Now. Take twenty cards and deal them face down in ten separate pairs.

Ask three or four people each to look at one of the pairs, remember the cards, then replace them face down on the table. You do not look while they do this.

Now you pick up the cards in a group, *taking care that each pair remains together.*

Visualize your code words on the table like this:

atlas

goose

linen

thigh

Now deal the cards out face up in this fashion:

1. Note that in your code words there are ten pairs of letters —one pair of letters for each pair of cards you hold.

2. Begin with **atlas**. Place a card face up in the spot you visualize for the first **a** in **atlas**.

3. The second card (which forms a pair with the first) is placed on the second **a,** which is also in the word **atlas.**

4. Place the next card on the **t** in **atlas.** And the next (the second of that pair) on the **t** in **thigh.**

5. Continue in that fashion until all the cards have been placed on the table.

Now ask one of the participants to point to the row or rows that contain her pair of cards. After a moment's reflection (in which you visualize the letters common to the rows indicated) you pick up the two cards that form the pair she observed. Use the same procedure for the remaining participants.

There's something you can do that most people can't. At least, not until they learn how. Better guard your secret.

a tricklike skill

Here's another very interesting activity you and your students can perform. You can get the hang of it in a few minutes. When you do, your performance will amaze people, and they will want to know how you do your trick. (Really this is not a trick at all. It's merely a display of memory skill. Remember, we said the important thing is how you *use* your ability to remember.)

This activity is a game called "Detective." I first saw it described by Young and Gibson,* who believe that the key to remembering is associating one thing with another. The stronger and more vividly you make the association, the better you remember, they say.

Here's how you play "Detective":

1. Get forty blank index cards and divide them into two groups of twenty each.

*Young, M., and Gibson, W.: How to Develop an Exceptional Memory, Philadelphia, 1962, Chilton Book Co.

330

2. On one group write the following list of "places," one to a card, in red ink:

freezer	hayloft
lake	bowling alley
station wagon	pine tree
tunnel	zoo
tollbooth	ball park
steeple	dressing room
elevator	television studio
red barn	airliner
furnace	post office
nightclub	barber shop

3. On the other group of cards, write the following "articles" in blue ink:

diamonds	door knob
culprit	fingerprints
victim	poison
knife	bullet
will	butler
bowling ball	race horse
bloodstains	teeth
revolver	missing heir
treasure	key
map	wig

4. Thoroughly mix the cards in each group and place them in an "articles" stack and a "places" stack, face down. Then draw a card from each stack, turn the pair over, and quickly link them by simple association. Return each face down to the bottom of its respective stack. After you have associated a few pairs—you will probably be able to associate all twenty pairs fairly easily—ask a participant to call off the names of the "articles." As he does so, you tell the "place" where each article was located.

5. The key to playing "Detective" lies in the associations you make between articles and places. The associations must be very vivid, striking, or ludicrous. For example, if you are associating "bowling ball" with "airliner," it probably won't be enough simply to think of a bowling ball riding comfortably in a bag on the plane. Rather, it should be sitting in an airplane seat like a passenger, hat on head and smile on face, trying to take photographs out the window. And don't just think it. Make yourself see it clearly.

6. As a teacher, you may want to mystify your students a couple of times before you let them in on the secret. They will enjoy playing this game, and it will help them learn to make strong associations that are very easy to recall. They may like to make up their own lists of things to associate.

Memory

We won't get into neural or chemical theories about how we remember. We will just begin with these two simple ideas:

1. we all *have* an ability to remember

2. what's important is how we *use* that ability

The sad fact is that most of us use our ability to remember in haphazard ways. We quickly forget almost everything we read, hear, see, and think each day. (So do students in school, eh? How little they remember of all those tremendously important things we teach them!)

Certainly not everything is worth remembering. But we all encounter principles, facts, dates, names, and other information that we would like to remember. Nonetheless, they soon escape our every effort at recall. So what we want to do is use our ability to remember in a special way. First, we select those very important things we truly want to remember. Second, we use a technique to, shall we say, "put a handle" on the information, so that we can retrieve it when we want to.

the importance of memory

Memory, as a matter of school concern, has suffered a bad reputation for the past three decades or so. That's unfortunate. Here's how it happened.

Educators noted that students could commit to memory many things they didn't understand. For example, young children could memorize the multiplication tables without understanding the process of multiplication. Or they could memorize the *Pledge of Allegiance* without understanding what any of the big words meant.

The main problem of memorizing without understanding was that students couldn't apply what they had memorized to the solution of problems. In other words, they couldn't really use what they knew.

So teachers began trying to ensure that students understood everything they learned. Rote memory (memorizing through drill, usually without understanding) became a bad word, and teachers started soundly rejecting it. The trouble was that the "memorizing" got thrown out along with the "rote." Teachers seemed to assume that students, once they understood what they were learning, would automatically retain the information thenceforth and forever.

332

It didn't work out that way. True, when you understand what you learn, the chances are that you'll remember it better. But you, we, all of us constantly forget most of what we learn, even when we understand it. At least we seem to forget. We can't seem to recall it when we would like.

But still and all, is memory or memorizing all that important? If you need more convincing, consider these points:

1. Everyone agrees that the ability to think has paramount importance. Yet, no one can just think about nothing. When you think, it has to be about something. And that something is whatever you remember.

2. The statistical technique called factor analysis has shown memory to be basically important in mental functioning. Guilford,* a noted psychologist who has attempted to describe the makeup of the intellect, includes memory as one of five mental operations in his model of the structure of the intellect.

3. Curriculum planning is based on the implicit belief that students will remember at least a large portion of what they learn in school. (Nevertheless, numerous studies have shown that students are able to recall only a small portion of what they learn in school, even after a lapse of only a few days.)

memorizing: a strange lack of emphasis

Educators and learning psychologists assume that remembering is very important. Nonetheless, what they have done gives little evidence of their conviction. Educators seldom try to improve their students' ability to remember, and psychologists have not tried to obtain much scientific evidence regarding the improvement of remembering ability. Still, there is a certain amount of reasonable conjecture and a modicum of experimental evidence that we should consider.

Hunter** reports experiments that give us the following information about memory span:

*Guilford, J. P.: The Structure of the Intellect, Psychol. Bull. **52**:267, 1956.
**Hunter, I. M.: Memory, Baltimore, 1964, Penguin Books, Inc.

1. It is decreased by fatigue, distractions, and the consumption of alcohol.

2. The span (that is, the number of items that can be remembered) varies according to the type of material memorized. The following are given as immediate recall spans for British university students: digits, 8.5; consonants, 7.5; common nouns, 6; simple geometrical figures, 6; pairs of common words, 3; nonsense syllables and short simple sentences, 3.

3. The span varies with age: the average digit span reaches 5 items by age 7 years; 6 by age 10 years; 7 by adulthood; and by the middle fifties has shrunk again to 6 items.

bits & chunks

Miller* has cleverly used the words "bits" and "chunks" in discussing memorizing. He says the human mind seems capable of retaining only about seven items of information, give or take a couple, without *reorganizing* them in some way.

Miller called the separate items of information "bits." A group of around seven bits makes up a "chunk." To remember more than about seven items of information the mind must reprocess that information into more than one chunk. To remember more, you simply learn to combine chunks with each other to form still larger chunks.

short- & long-term memory

Most psychologists agree that information is stored in at least two different forms and that those two forms have different capacities, storage periods, and retrieval periods.

One form is long-term memory, and it is considered *unlimited* in size and thus not fillable. The other form is short-term memory. It has a very small capacity that seems to correspond to Miller's seven bits, give or take two. Anything new that is being learned must be held in short-term memory while it is being fixated and transferred to long-term memory.

*Miller, G. A.: The Magical Number Seven, Plus or Minus Two: Some Limits on Our Capacity for Processing Information. Psychol. Rev. **63**:81, 1956.

Can we learn to remember?

Psychologists seem to agree overwhelmingly: yes, we can learn to remember. What you and I want to know is — how do we do it?

Norman* says yes, it's true experimental evidence is scarce. Yet, well-defined techniques for improving recall have been known for centuries. He points out that although the techniques make easy work of the memorizing task, they tend to be associated with trickery and fakery, and thus do not receive the deserved attention today. Nonetheless, he says, there is no denying that they work. Some of the techniques to which Norman refers are presented in the following paragraphs.

directing attention

Have you ever noticed how you can direct your attention at will? Strange, isn't it, that we can look directly at something without actually "seeing" it at all. We can be surrounded by sounds and yet not "hear" them. Or when several people are talking in a group, we can listen to whomever we want, tuning out the other voices.

As we learn consciously to focus our full attention, we become better able to perceive, distinguish, conceptualize, and remember.

sensing

In general, the more we involve our five senses in learning, the better we remember what we learn. Have you noticed that whenever possible we remember a person, thing, or event in terms of appearances, sounds, smells, feels, or tastes? True, we can remember both the word "mango" and its dictionary definition without ever having any direct experience with the real thing. Yet, how much more vivid and permanent the memory will be if we taste and smell the fruit and observe its color and texture (and perhaps break out with an allergic reaction to it).

*Norman, D. A.: Memory and Attention, New York, 1969, John Wiley & Sons, Inc.

imaging

When you can't see (or sense) what you want to remember, well, see it anyway. Force yourself to see an image of the thing in your mind's eye. This is a way of doing make-believe sensing. It's not as good as the real thing, but it is definitely better than nothing at all.

associating

To associate is to link one thing mentally to another. Our minds automatically associate everything we learn that is new with something we already know. So all that we do here is consciously help and improve the process. We group items of information (we associate them) in terms of similarities, uses, functions, and so on. We can improve the process by making the associations as intense, interesting, and striking as possible. If we can't find logical associations, we can make artificial ones.

organizing & understanding

Understanding means perceiving valid relationships among concepts. We understand a cotton gin, for example, to the extent that we perceive relationships among its working parts and between those parts and the acts of seeding, cleaning, and baling cotton.

Many experiments have shown that we remember best what we understand. Typical of those experiments is the following, in which people are checked on their ability to remember the following lists of words:

list 1	list 2
girl	every
roof	day
boulder	this
between	little
therefore	bird
wishful	sings
consequence	merrily
into	from
trying	my
upstart	rooftop

Obviously you can remember the second list far more easily and for a longer time. That's because each word relates to the next in a very common way. (It would be another matter, however, if the list were presented in reverse order.) Thus, you see that you "understand" the second list far better than you understand the first, even though you probably conceptualize the separate words in the lists about equally. And, of course, you remember the second list far more easily.

Now we get to the point of *organizing*. When relationships among concepts are not so apparent, we can usually organize them into patterns that do yield clearer relationships. Let's take our first list again as an example. If the task is simply to remember all the words, regardless of order, we could rearrange them like this:

upstart
girl
between
roof
into
boulder
therefore
trying
wishful
consequence

On the other hand, if the task is to remember the words in the order presented, we can make an artificial organization into which we fit the words. We can use a little story here:

A **girl** sat on the **roof,** with only a **boulder between** her and the ground. Not knowing how to get down, she **therefore** engaged in **wishful** thinking. As a **consequence,** she fell **into** despair, **trying** to understand why she had been such an **upstart.**

Make up your own story with the words. *Visualize* the scenes and key word concepts as vividly as possible. You'll be surprised how easily you can remember. Again, the point here is that you should try to *understand* as clearly as possible what you are trying to remember. *Organizing* the material into meaningful patterns makes remembering easier. *Mnemonic devices* provide an excellent means for organizing unrelated material. More about them later.

using

If you want to remember knowledge and skills, use them. It's as simple as that.

Were you (un)lucky enough to study a foreign language in high school using the old traditional grammatical approach? If so, you probably remember precious little of it. That's because you never *used* what you knew, later on. On the other hand, given the proper conditions, you can learn to speak a foreign language in a few months' (or even weeks') time. And you will never forget how to speak it, so long as you do speak it fairly often.

in short...

The question was, can we learn to remember?
The answer was, yes.
How?
By directing attention, sensing, imagining, associating and organizing, and using, using, using what we know.

Mnemonics— those wonderful little aids

Mnemonics (don't pronounce the first "m") are specialized plans for remembering. You already know and use several of them:

Thirty days hath September . . . .

Every good boy does fine.

Spring forward; fall backward.

But you think they're just gimmicks, don't you? Just tricks. Let's change that idea and give mnemonics respectability. Let's recognize and use them for the fine help they give us in remembering. They have proved to be effective through thousands of years' use. Those aren't bad credentials, eh?

Mnemonics operate this way:

1. Take a scheme, pattern, rhyme, whatever, that's easy to remember.

2. Take new information that's difficult to remember, and associate it (vividly, remember?) with your easy-to-remember scheme.

3. Recall your scheme, and each part of it brings forth the hard-to-remember information you've associated with it.

The key process in using mnemonics is the associating of unknowns with knowns. There has been some theorizing about how the mind does that associating, and I'm going to mention some of it briefly on the following pages. Read it if you like; if not, skip ahead to descriptions of useful mnemonics.

on associating

We have already noted that to associate is to mentally link one thing with another. We also noted that our minds continually associate items of information, though they ordinarily get little cooperation from us. (Now, how's that for separating our minds from our selves? You have to recognize that I'm using artificial structures in an attempt to improve understanding.)

Gestalt psychologists, just after the turn of the century, began noting that the human mind formed perceptual groups among discrete items of sensory data. They established four "laws" to summarize those grouping tendencies:

the law of similarity	Data similar to each other in some way tend to be placed together.
the law of proximity	Data perceived as near each other tend to be placed in groups.
the law of good continuation	Data are extrapolated (that is, projected into the future) in ways consistent with past perceptions. In other words, if Sam has been a good boy for fourteen days running, we see him as being a good boy tomorrow.
the law of closure	The mind tends to complete patterns that are incomplete when first perceived.

The Gestalt psychologists also noticed that when individuals were shown a pattern, then asked to reproduce it from memory, they tended to make certain consistent changes in the pattern. Those changes included:

sharpening   an accentuation of the most noticeable features in the pattern

leveling   a tendency to make nonsymmetrical patterns more symmetrical

normalizing   a tendency to make unfamiliar patterns resemble familiar objects

---

While that work by Gestalt psychologists tells us something about how the mind automatically associates items of information, it doesn't give us the complete answer about associating for improved recall. To find further help, we need to identify the kinds of experiences that the mind ordinarily seems to retain best. That idea has been approached experimentally through studies of the retention of words. A typical experiment might require that you first examine a list of words such as the following:

walk
tirade
countryside
marvelous
withall
greenery
belly-pelican
interior
homosexual
sprinkler
geranium

Given a few minutes to memorize the words, you are then asked to repeat any that you can remember. Such experiments usually show that people remember best those words and experiences that are

"sinful"	startling
frightening	humorous
disgusting	ludicrous

What does that tell us for remembering? This: when we want to be sure to remember something, we should associate it with something we *know* we will remember, in a way that has a heavy emotional impact. That is, the association should be ludicrous or shocking.

That is the general technique recommended by writers of popular materials on improving the memory. They say, make vivid, shocking, ludicrous associations among:

matching pairs	things of the same species
whole and part	means to ends
cause and effect	opposites and analogues

And they remind us to group and regroup items so we do not exceed seven items in any one "chunk."

By the way, have you ever wondered about the following? Miller has.

wonders of the world	levels of hell
seas	notes of the
deadly sins	musical scale
daughters of Atlas (Pleiades)	days of the week
ages of man	point rating scale

Some mnemonics you & your students can use

topical systems

The ancient Greeks made a big thing of rhetoric. In rhetoric, memory played a very important role, so the Greeks used mnemonic devices to remember all the major points in a speech. They could then speak at great length without notes and without forgetting what they were going to say.

One of their favorite mnemonics was one called *loci,* or places. You will find it very easy to use. Here's how you do it.

> Envision the interior of a building with which you are very familiar. Your own house will serve well. Now suppose you have a group of twenty things you want to remember. Begin with a first room, say the living room. See clearly in your mind five outstanding parts of the room—perhaps a sofa, television set, fireplace, drapes, and lamp. With those five parts, vividly associate the first five items on your list to be remembered. (Remember to "see" the associations clearly and strikingly.) Now go to the next room, perhaps the dining room. There again visualize five outstanding parts—the buffet, the wallpaper, the shuttered windows, the serving cart, the chandelier. Associate the next five items on your list with those parts of the dining room.
>
> When you have done this for all the items you want to remember, you will discover several interesting things. You can "stroll" through your house and remember all the items in order. You can also call off the items just as well in reverse order. You can recall any numbered item at will—take number sixteen, for example—it's the first item in the fourth room, right?

You will find these associations very lasting. Fortunately, you can erase them much as you erase recording tape. Simply record over the same objects in your house with new information you want to remember. If you don't want to erase the associations, just pick another house or building. Or use items in a car. Or objects on the four walls, floor, and ceiling of a single room. Or . . . or . . . .

342

one is a bun...

How about a neat little ten-item mnemonic—one that rhymes, that permits very vivid visualizations, and that even young children easily learn? Well, here it is:

one is a bun	six are sticks
two is a shoe	seven is heaven
three is a tree	eight is a gate
four is a door	nine is a line
five is a hive	ten is a hen

And you use it (can you guess?) like this. You have your short list—ten items or fewer—of steps, points, objects to remember. You associate the first very vividly with a bun, the second very vividly with a shoe, the third very vividly with a tree, and so on.

Early primary-grade children can learn the rhyme and remember it. However, children on the average can't visualize associations well enough to use it to remember until about the second or third grade.

picture peg

Here's another neat little ten-item mnemonic. Only instead of rhyming, this one has numbers that look like objects. Can you believe that? Here is how it works:

1 = a candle	6 = a snake
2 = a swan	7 = a semaphor
3 = a pitchfork	8 = an hourglass
4 = a pennant	9 = a rural mailbox
5 = a hand	0 = a saucer

To use this mnemonic, first visualize each of the numbers. That is, you see a candle, which you associate vividly with the first item you want to remember. You associate a swan with the second item, a pitchfork with the third, a pennant with the fourth, and so on. But, of course, this mnemonic has its limitations numberwise. Such is not the case for the mighty . . . .

von Wenussheim mnemonic

Sometime around 1648, a smart gentleman named von Wenussheim invented a system of substituting letters for numbers. That may not seem so great at first glance. But what it did was this: it provided a way of making up easily visualized nouns that correspond to numbers running into the hundreds. You may not want to play around with the system. But if you do, here it is:

1 = t (th, d)	6 = sh (j, ch, soft g)
2 = n	7 = k (hard g, hard c, q, ng)
3 = m	8 = f (v)
4 = r	9 = b (p)
5 = l	0 = z (s, soft c)

Now make a noun for each numeral 1 through 9. For these first numerals we will select nouns that *end* with appropriate consonant sounds. Here is a list you may want to use:

hat	hash
hen	hack
ham	half
hare	hope
hall	

At 10 and beyond, we add consonants, that correspond to numerals, to the beginnings of the nouns we select:

toes (the noun begins with a "t" and ends with a "z" sound: therefore 10)	tale (ends with consonant sound)
	tissue (well, they don't all come out perfect)
tot	tack
tan	taffy
tam	tap
tar	

And on to 20 and beyond: nose, note, noon, and so on. Carry it as far as you like. Who knows the limits?

We had better stop here with mnemonics. They are so interesting you may begin to remember only them. We don't want to forget the other aids to remembering.

Other memory aids

So you want your students to remember better? They can. They just have to do some of the things we discussed. And you have to help them. Let's look at some of those things again.

students should

1. use conscious plans for remembering
2. make vivid mental images of the things to be remembered (this requires careful observation and the use of as many senses as possible)
3. associate and chain unknowns with knowns
4. review, repeat, and use information memorized

teachers should

1. maintain student interest
2. maximize meaning
3. maximize the use of students' senses
4. organize material into patterns
5. teach memory devices (mnemonics)
6. see that students use the information they have memorized

still more on what teachers should do

Learners seldom do what they are merely exhorted to do. They often do what they have practiced doing, however. Since we don't want to waste our time and theirs, we must see they have a lot of practice *doing* the activities that improve ability to remember.

Attention depends on curiosity, interest, pacing, and environment.

Curiosity means initial puzzlement or wondering about something. It is often produced by novel situations. It is also produced by seeming incongruities, such as the boiling of water in a paper cup over an open flame without the cup's burning.

Interest comes from repeated pleasant experiences with an object, a game, or what have you. It also comes from physical activity and the use of the senses.

Pacing refers to the timing of activities—to starting, stopping, and changing them to take advantage of curiosity and interest and to avoid student fatigue.

Environment refers to physical space, lighting, ventilation, furniture, and the other elements that make up the surroundings within which students must work. The environment must be comfortable and nondistracting.

Meaning is what students encounter when they understand, or when they see valid relationships among concepts. We can help students see relationships by providing practice in noting similarities, analogues, causes and effects, means to ends, parts of wholes, and so forth.

Sensing just means using the senses. In general, material can be better remembered if learners use several of their senses in dealing with it. We should help students learn to use their senses in many ways. Sight can be used to determine colors, shades, shapes, movements, textures, spatial contiguity, and so on. Hearing can determine tones, pitches, and qualities. Touch can determine texture, hardness, resiliency, shape, and temperature. Smell can determine sharpness, pungency, and acridity as well as an immense variety of "likes"—like bananas, like fish, like grass. Taste can determine salty, sweet, sour, and bitter, plus a great variety of "likes."

When senses cannot be used directly, they can be used in the imagination. While few of us will ever see Iguazu Falls, we can read about them and in our imaginations hear their thunder, feel their spray, and see their mountainous waters slide for incredible distances before bursting into foam. We do that by imaging—by sensing it all in our imaginations.

Organizing material into patterns is necessary for remembering. Remember when as a student you had to memorize long lists of presidents, states and capitals, Latin American countries, imports and exports, national boundaries, and on and on? Can you remember now some of the systems you used to organize the material—systems you probably had to learn by trial and error?

We now know that school students usually can't remember nonorganized items in groups larger than five or six. When we want students to remember larger amounts of information, we should help them by:

> making up "chunks" of information no larger than four or five items
>
> finding self-evident, logical patterns for relating the various chunks to each other
>
> directing attention to similarities, means-end relationships, and cause-effect relationships

Using mnemonics is a legitimate, valuable way of associating unknown information with knowns so the new material can be recalled more easily. It is not a tricky form of cheating. If we really expect students to remember, we should help them in every way. That includes direct teaching of mnemonic techniques of associating, chaining, and organizing information.

Application or use of what has been learned greatly aids remembering. That fact should constantly remind us to provide frequent opportunities for learners to review, apply, and otherwise use what they have learned. The variety of activities in this category includes drawing, dramatic play, creative writing, classroom contests, production of newspapers, keeping diaries, solving practical problems, and teaching other students.

on observing

One last word on observing. I return to that topic because I want to leave it last, and lingering, in your mind. Most students need much more practice in observing than they usually get. Memory depends largely on the ability to look very carefully and to form vivid images. Students can practice examining an object in the classroom for a few minutes. Then after about an hour they should try to draw it from memory as accurately as possible. Look again at the object. Correct errors in the original drawing. This exercise can use pictures, diagrams, maps, books, magazines, objects of all kinds, or parts of the classroom. Instead of drawing, students may list as many details as possible, either orally or in writing.

Students should also practice observing with their ears. They can identify various noises, human voices, instruments. With the sense of touch, students can learn and remember much about objects that ordinarily goes unnoticed. An excellent exercise requires the student to insert one hand into a bag containing several objects of different sizes, textures, and shapes. The student describes as accurately as possible the feel of the object being examined. Other students can participate by guessing the identity of the object from the descriptions the observer provides.

And so it is that we end this little excursion into the realms of memory with one final gadget—a checklist for you, to help you remember to help students remember.

directing attention
  curiosity: novelty, incongruity
  interest: pleasant experiences, color, movement
  pacing: opportune beginnings, changes, endings
  environment: physical space, lighting, ventilation

using the senses
  seeing
  hearing
  touching
  smelling
  tasting

emphasizing visualization
  seeing or sensing in the mind: making mental pictures (when direct
    sensing is not possible)
  practicing association
  grouping: similarities, proximity, extrapolation
  imaging: vivid, humorous, ludicrous

maximizing understanding
  material organized: patterns, "bits and chunks"
  relationships noted: similarities, analogues, means-end, cause-effect,
    part-whole, opposites
  artificial structure: applied where existing structure not evident

teaching mnemonics
  imaging
  associating
  systems: e.g., topical, "one is a bun," picture peg

using information
  extension of lessons: drawings, dramatic play, construction, creative
    writing, debates, etc.
  problem solving
  contests

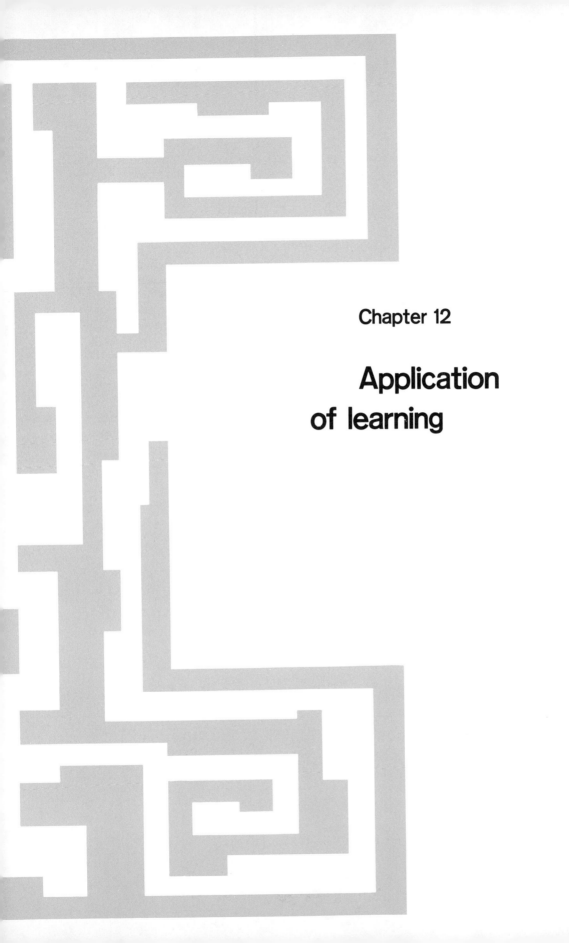

Chapter 12

Application
of learning

The Paper Grocery

Caroline was in her second semester of student teaching when she happened upon the newspaper grocery gambit. Nothing unusual was involved—just the grocery ads from a plain, ordinary newspaper. They helped her more than she ever dreamed, and she says she would take them over the arithmetic textbook if she had to make a choice.

It started, she said, because her sixth-grade students had become so tired of arithmetic. They moaned, groaned, and sighed over every drill, every assignment, every mention of the subject. Even the "supposes" had lost their appeal (the "suppose you had twelve candy bars you wanted to divide among sixteen people" routine). Then out of the blue (or did someone mention it—a classmate, a teacher?) came the idea of using grocery ads for a more true-to-life application of arithmetic skills.

The grocery stores in the community printed their weekly specials in the newspaper every Thursday. Caroline noticed that different stores often advertised the same items, but not at the same prices. Each store would have a few items at prices well below the other stores. So she hit on the idea of letting students do some intelligent shopping—imaginary but realistic, to be sure—by buying hypothetical lists of groceries from the advertisements.

The first activity she used was this: she examined the ads from three grocery stores and identified the following list of items and prices that she duplicated for the class:

items	store A	store B	store C
chuck roast	$1.03 lb.	$1.09 lb.	$1.09 lb.
orange juice	.46 can	.41 can	.43 can
flour	.80 5 lb.	.73 5 lb.	.92 5 lb.
bananas	.13 lb.	.13 lb.	.17 lb.
wieners	1.19 lb.	.89 lb.	.79 lb.
chicken	1.05 lb.	1.30 lb.	1.15 lb.
bread	.49 loaf	.63 loaf	.45 loaf
potatoes	1.70 10 lb.	1.20 10 lb.	1.25 10 lb.

Then she gave the class this list of groceries to buy:

3 lb. of chuck roast
6 cans of orange juice
5 lb. of flour
3 lb. of bananas
2 lb. of wieners
3 lb. of chicken
4 loaves of bread
10 lb. of potatoes

And this list of questions:

1. At which store could you buy all the items on the list for the least amount of money?
2. What would you have to buy at each store to get all the items for the least amount of money?
3. It costs 15¢ per mile to drive your car. Using the following map, decide where you should shop in order to spend the least amount of money, including the cost of car mileage.

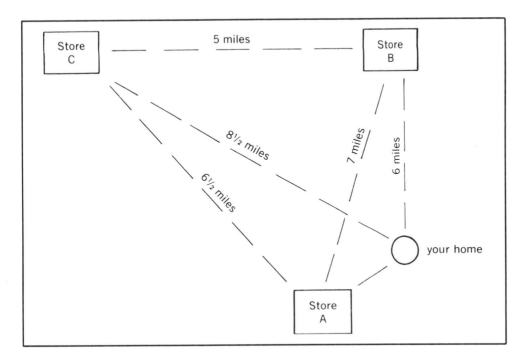

The students went at the exercise (not called arithmetic) with a good deal of enthusiasm, and they had a lively discussion afterward about the best routes for buying the groceries most economically.

Caroline had brought the newspaper ads to class to introduce the activity. She noticed that some of the students went to look at the ads, which were lying on her desk, later in the morning. That gave her another idea. She asked the students to bring grocery advertisements from their newspapers at home. Most of the students brought several of them. Caroline then gave one ad to each student, with these directions:

You have forty-eight dollars. Use your ad to buy groceries for a family of three—a man, woman, and 11-year-old child—for one week. Each person must have at least one full serving of meat, green vegetables, bread, and fruit each day. Each person should also have something for a small tasty snack each day. Otherwise buy whatever food you wish, but try to get the best combination of quality, variety, and quantity.

The students worked at that exercise eagerly, too, and they had good discussions about food value and cost of items selected. In fact, they enjoyed using the grocery ads so much that Caroline developed some language and reading exercises around them. Later, she collected quantities of advertising papers from drugstores, furniture stores, discount stores, and so forth and planned money-spending exercises involving addition, subtraction, multiplication, division, fractions, percentages, and interest around them all.

There were probably many reasons why the advertisement activities proved so successful. Important among them was the chance students had to use—to apply—skills they had acquired in math. They were using those skills to handle, in an enlightened way, realistic concerns that every family must meet in managing a household.

Transfer— proof & promise

Schooling for the young has only one justification. That justification is **not** to keep kids out of their mothers' hair, to keep kids off the streets, or to keep kids out of the labor force. That justification is the conviction that what youngsters can learn in school helps them to live more satisfactorily, now and in the future.

Living more satisfactorily means youngsters have the ability to solve problems better, enjoy life more, interact more effectively with others, and realize more of the potential they are born with than do similar people without schooling. Put another way, we provide formal education because we believe that what students can learn in school will serve them outside of school as well.

Few people disagree with that notion, at least when the basic skills of communication and mathematics are considered. Who can doubt their evident usefulness in life? Doubt does arise, however, regarding the value, to most people, of such courses as trigonometry, elementary foreign language, chemistry, and English literature, to name a few. The reason doubt arises is because most people have so few necessities— or even opportunities—to apply what they learn in those courses to problems outside of school.

Think of your own situation. How often do you use advanced algebra? How often (and how well?) do you speak with a Spaniard, equipped as you are with your one year of high school Spanish? You just don't have a chance to use what you know, and when you don't use it, you lose it. You do use reading and arithmetic skills, and there is never a doubt about their value.

Such questioning of the relative value of courses is certainly nothing new. No doubt it has been going on since men first decided they should establish schoollike institutions for fitting out the young for adult life. If you want some unusually interesting reading about school curricula, find a copy of Pediwell's *The Saber-Tooth Curriculum.** It is a classic—short, humorous, and insightful. And it will help you understand why fish-grabbing and horse-clubbing survived as courses long after the fish and horses were gone.

Lest you misunderstand, these paragraphs make no plea for the inclusion of certain courses to the exclusion of others. The point is this: schoolwork must have value apparent to learners. It must be enjoyable, entertaining, or of obvious practicality. Further, teachers of courses should make those values evident to learners, through myriad opportunities to apply knowledge and skills in lifelike situations. If none of these things is possible—if the course work is neither enjoyable nor practical—then the only justification left is embodied in an idea called *formal discipline,* which we will note again in a moment.

Psychologists use the label "transfer" to refer to the concept of one activity having an effect on a later activity. When one learning helps another, the transfer is called "positive." It is called "negative" when one learning hinders another.

transfer

Until the turn of the century, the prevailing theory of transfer (though the word "transfer" wasn't in use) was one called "formal discipline." Formal discipline involved a concept of the mind as divided into "faculties"—the faculties of attention, judgment, memory, and reasoning are examples. It was believed that hard study could toughen those faculties, just as hard physical labor toughened the muscles. That's why the curriculum consisted of "hard" subjects. Mathematics could strengthen the faculties of judgment and reasoning, and Greek could strengthen the faculty of memory. You were never expected to talk to a Greek; studying Greek was simply good for you.

Experimenters in the first quarter of the twentieth century, most notably the psychologists Thorndike, Woodward, and Judd, cast grave doubt on the validity of the theory of formal discipline. They showed that the "hard" subjects didn't seem to strengthen the mind any more than "easy" subjects such as modern language, spelling, and reading. They further implied that "practical" subjects—things like carpentry, typing, and cooking—should be included in the curriculum, since they had the advantage of being directly useful to the students.

*Pediwell, J. A.: The Saber-Tooth Curriculum, New York, 1939, McGraw-Hill Book Co.

Thorndike proposed a major break from the theory of formal discipline in his theory of "identical elements." This theory held that positive transfer occurred to the extent that the new task contained elements identical to those in the original learning task. Soon afterward, Judd formulated a "generalization" hypothesis, which held that it was not identical elements that transferred, but rather generalized ideas about how to solve problems. That is, knowledge about driving a bicycle would help in learning to drive a car (if at all) because of general ideas about steering, starting, stopping, and keeping on the right side of the road—not because there were identical elements in bicycle and car driving.

Today, we have no widely accepted theory of transfer as a total, rigorous system. Rather, we have knowledge about the conditions that seem to maximize positive transfer, and we are content to work toward establishing those conditions in school learning. The following list summarizes, in the main, the conditions we should seek to maintain for a higher degree of transfer. The items are all closely interrelated, and are not at all discrete as their presentation here might lead you to believe.

1. The curriculum should contain a high percentage of activities that are very lifelike, not phoney nor unconvincingly contrived.

2. Students should understand the meaning and operation of what they are asked to learn.

3. The learning activities should provide practice in a variety of contexts. For example, multiplication learning should allow students to practice with real objects of various kinds, with abaci, with paper and pencil, mentally with eyes closed, as a rapid means of addition, and so on.

4. Students should comprehend the purpose of everything they are asked to learn—the possible uses, newer learnings made possible, and so forth.

5. Students should have numerous opportunities to directly apply what they have learned to realistic concerns.

6. Teachers should endeavor to relate or correlate each discipline with the other—music and art with history, for example—so that transfer from one area to another can be enhanced.

Activities for applying skills & knowledge

Up to this point you have read a case for the use of realistic activities that allow students to apply what they have learned. The case stressed the desirability—the necessity—of activities that require immediate use of skills and knowledge. Such activities do two things: they enliven and make relevant the learning sessions conducted in school, and they maximize the possibilities for positive transfer of learning.

If the arguments have convinced you that teachers must seek out and arrange these application activities, you may be wondering where you can find ideas for your own activities. Here are a few places: you can look in methods texts, curriculum guides, enrichment guides, and journals for teachers. You can ask experienced teachers about the activities that have worked best for them. You can attend college and in-service workshops dealing with new materials and activities. Best of all (easiest, anyhow), you can read through the suggestions presented in the sections that follow. Almost all of the suggestions can be modified to suit students of different age levels. And though they are listed within subject categories, the majority can be used in two or more different areas. You will see the possibilities.

And for still more suggestions, turn back to Chapter 7, *Personalized instruction: environments and strategies.*

but now, application activities ———⟶

The English language curricula in schools emphasize the art and skills of listening. Instructional activities in listening are intended to help individuals become more attentive, to help them hear correctly, to help them anticipate what's to come, and to help them interpret what it is they have heard.

As those skills develop, students need to continue with activities that encourage use of the skills. The following activities suggest a few realistic ways in which the skills can be put to use.

1. Take turns summarizing points made in class discussions.
2. Make lists of school and community lectures, concerts, etc. Attend some of the events and report major points to the class.
3. Listen to a television newscaster for one week, then to a different newscaster for a second week. Note similarities and differences in reporting style. Also note the powerful, unusual, descriptive words used.
4. Listen to television commercials. Make note of provocative words used and unfounded claims made. Compare with other commercials for similar products.
5. Interview adults and fellow students to determine their views on controversial issues.
6. Record students' voices during a presentation or discussion to identify speech traits that could be improved.
7. Make a creative recording of various sounds around school, in a shopping center, and in other similar places where people gather.

reading

One thing you can be sure of — students will use their reading skills. They will read comics, magazines, signs, menus, labels, advertisements, recipes, directions, and so on. But even in adulthood, a great number of individuals never go beyond about a fourth-grade level of reading skills — a level that will let you get by in the modern world. That distresses teachers, of course. Teachers would like to see their students develop an abiding interest in book reading, in higher quality magazine reading, and in intelligent newspaper reading. They would like to see them interpret and use varieties of words in sophisticated ways and know something of recognized writers and their lives.

The application activities listed here help students develop habits and attitudes about reading that can enrich their lives. They allow students to use, over extended periods of time, some of the skills teachers have helped them develop.

1. Keep personal charts for speed and comprehension levels.
2. Keep an annotated bibliography of books, articles, and stories read.
3. Learn as much as possible about the life of a favorite author.
4. Note and analyze biased words and terminology. For good sources, read editorials and letters to editors.
5. Make studies of the origins and derivations of words and names.
6. Create and play word games, using homonyms, antonyms, synonyms, and words with multiple meanings.
7. Play word discovery games, using the dictionary and *Roget's Thesaurus.*
8. Devise and play matching games, using *Bartlett's Book of Familiar Quotations.*
9. Read literary supplements of the *New York Times* and *Saturday Review.*
10. Compare reviews of movies, books, etc. in different publications.
11. Maintain a small class bulletin board for "picture words," "emotion-packed words," "clichés," etc. Change the topic every couple of weeks.
12. Have "pot-luck" reading assignments in class, selecting a page at random from an encyclopedia, a dictionary, a thesaurus, a book of antonyms and synonyms, a book of quotations, an almanac, or any such reference book and reporting its contents to the class.

speaking & dramatizing

Ever notice how many people who are avid talkers in ordinary conversation lose their voices completely before a tape recorder or audience? It's a strange thing. Talking has become almost as natural as breathing for most of us. We do it without giving it a thought. Then, sooner or later we find ourselves in a situation—before an audience or even in a conversation—where we become tongue-tied, disorganized, and unable to find the right words or expression.

The reason we find ourselves in such situations probably has a lot to do with the naturalness of speaking: we don't give it a second thought and therefore never think about practicing to improve our poise and skill in saying the right thing. What a great favor we can do for students by finding numerous, nonthreatening situations in which they can talk before audiences, so that it becomes almost as natural as normal conversation, without the fears, chills, trembling of knees, and shortness of breath that have afflicted almost all of us at one time or another before an audience.

The application activities listed here help students develop the poise and skills for more effective and enjoyable presentations before audiences.

1. Plan clever ways to tell familiar stories and fables, using pantomime, masks, large drawings, flannelboard characterizations, choral speech, puppets, and costumed dolls.
2. Tell the stories to the class and to other classes of students.
3. Produce commentaries and use them with slide and musical presentations.
4. Make tape recordings of oral presentations for analysis by the speaker.
5. Make collections of colloquialisms and regional expressions, and practice using them in talks, discussions, and conversations.
6. Make collections of interesting words and expressions—similes, metaphors, hyperboles, highly descriptive terms, the latest slang—and use them in talks, discussions, and conversations.
7. Make collections of sayings, mottoes, proverbs, fables, and weave them into your conversations and talks.
8. Set up a tape exchange with a class in another school. Send recordings of poems, mottoes, advertisements, short plays, news items, individual experiences, etc.
9. Role-play short episodes from reading materials, social studies units, current and historical events, etc.
10. Select topics for plays, skits, monologues, and puppet shows. Write the play, produce costumes and scenery if desired, and present it in class.
11. Practice performing various phases of dramatic productions—acting, directing, lighting, sound effects, scenery arranging, etc.
12. Plan and write very short plays for young children, and then help them present the plays.
13. Create and produce a comic opera built around some funny incident at the school. Use lavish makeup and costumes, and sing the parts.

writing

As ineptly as most of us speak, we write more poorly yet. Most people never write more than an occasional letter outside of school, and the majority of those letters are deathly boring. Few people enjoy writing. How many do you know who write for the fun of it, like they might read or talk? This lack of interest in writing has several causes. One is that, aside from letter writing, there are few reasons for writing any kind of composition that isn't part of some school activity. Another is that writing is a different kind of activity than talking, almost a different language. The youngster who got the insight that "reading is just talk wrote down" probably lost it when he tried writing down some of his own talk, because when we talk we don't have to use correct grammar, complete sentences, spell words correctly, and use proper capitalization and punctuation.

Yet there is no denying that writing can help us with language use in several ways. It can help us to organize our thoughts, let us work on wording until we say exactly what we intend, and give us an avenue for the creative use of words and expressions. It can certainly help us to do better work in school, because so many school assignments require written presentations. And for at least a few of us, it can offer stimulating vocations and avocations: somebody, after all, writes down all of the stuff that there is to read.

The activities listed here provide realistic situations and assignments for practicing writing skills that have been stressed during instruction.

1. Write dramatizations of historical and contemporary events that may possibly be acted out by members of the class.
2. Write scripts for mock television shows, interviews, etc.
3. Write short columns—television, movie, book, and record reviews, for example—for a class newspaper or bulletin. Also write advertisements, slogans, editorials, and letters to the editor for publication.
4. Write letters of all sorts—to request materials, to obtain information, to inform politicians, to exchange ideas with students in other schools, cities, and countries. Also write letters to imaginary friends about imaginary travels, sights, and people.
5. Write and illustrate stories. Bind them and circulate them to other classes.
6. Establish a creative writing club. Write stories, poems, sketches, and reviews. Duplicate and distribute.
7. Write unfinished stories, to be finished by classmates or students in lower grades.
8. Keep personal diaries or diaries for a real or imaginary person during a unit of study.
9. Write obituary notices for people like Bach, Mendel, and Shakespeare that might have appeared the day after their deaths. Contrast them with notices that might appear about them today.
10. Collect large photographs from magazines. Write a poetic line or short verse to accompany each picture. Use verse forms—haiku, cinquain, etc.—that have been learned in class.
11. Write brief descriptive passages that show character traits such as shyness, hostility, egoism, etc. without actually naming the traits. Have other students read the passages and try to identify the traits.
12. Read such publications as *The Writer's Digest, The Writer's Market,* and directories of small presses for hints on writing material for sale.
13. Invite poets, novelists, or journalists living in the community to visit the class. Ask them to describe their work, read samples, and review some of the students' work.

Math suffers from the same application anemia that afflicts writing and public speaking. People just don't use it very much in their daily lives. They do count, make change, and figure out how many days are left before the weekend. But few do much more, despite the fact that most adults pay interest (without knowing how much), keep bank balances (often unbalanced), read newspaper charts and graphs (with less than 100% comprehension), and are always on the lookout for bargains (that often aren't).

The truth is, however, that there are a lot of very interesting and important things one does in life with mathematics. Applying skills in the following activities helps prepare for them.

1. Develop and use different systems for estimating numbers, measurements, weights, and answers to problems.
2. Have a regular time reserved for practicing mental arithmetic. Have contests.
3. Conduct contests in estimating dimensions and answers to problems.
4. Search out, from magazines and books, quantities of number games and problems in logic. Set aside class time to play and solve them.
5. Compose number games and teach other class members how to play them.
6. Keep graphs of changes in temperature, the stock market, cost of an item of food, population, etc.
7. Make scale drawings and models of airports, school grounds, houses, local buildings, city streets, etc.
8. Compose time-distance problems for space travel, submarines, airplanes, river boats in currents, etc.
9. Compute the cost of building an average house. Secure plans and lists of building materials. Interview contractors.
10. Compute present-day travel times by land, water, and air. Compare them with travel times of the 1700s.
11. Obtain air, bus, and railroad timetables. Plan imaginary itineraries and compute time in transit and layover time.
12. Determine ways to increase purchasing power — through specials, discounts, paying by cash, etc. Illustrate with specific examples.
13. Establish and maintain a personal budget.
14. Keep a record of a parent's auto expenses for a month.
15. Keep records of expenses for food, lodging, transportation, and recreation on a family trip.
16. Become expert on some aspect of the history of mathematics such as Boolean algebra, non-Euclidian geometry, and the work of Pythagoras, Euclid, and Newton.
17. Become expert on the laws of probability, especially as related to gambling.
18. Construct a probability board and use it to illustrate binomial expansion, the gaussian curve, individual cases, and so on.
10. Learn the theory and operation of computers, including computer programming.
20. Publish a class or school mathematics journal. Include problems and puzzles, mathematics news items, individual student projects, scale drawings, etc.

Instruction in natural science helps learners to do three things: it helps them explain, predict, and control natural phenomena. That order also represents the order of success a person is likely to have. Learners can explain better than they can predict, but they can predict better than they can control.

The skills one acquires in explaining, predicting, and controlling comes from experiences in doing those things. They come from the "process" side of science, the methodology of doing science—observing and determining consistent relationships among objects and events observed. True, those acts involve the "content" side of science, too—the facts, hypotheses, and theories that competent scientists have established. But it is the "doing" aspect of science that lets us begin to cope more satisfactorily with our physical world.

Numerous excellent activities are available to us. Those listed in this section are merely a sampling of the possibilities. Most of them involve the doing of science, as scientists themselves might work. All require the active application of facts, principles, and skills of science that students learn in school.

1. Plan ways of conserving local resources.
2. Identify sources of pollution and determine their effects on ecological systems.
3. Determine ways in which students can help reduce various kinds of pollution.
4. Interview or correspond with forest rangers, conservation workers, agricultural experts, game-management officials.
5. Identify harmful pests such as rats, gypsy moths, and boll weevils. Find out how they can be controlled.
6. Identify local migratory birds and prepare maps that show their travels during the year.
7. Learn how to compute distances to the moon, sun, planets, and stars.
8. Use stick shadows to plot positions of the sun at a given hour over an extended period of days.
9. Learn about the uses of radio telescopes and spectrographs in astronomy.
10. Use binoculars and telescopes to look at the moon and stars.
11. Learn how to build a telescope like the one Galileo used.
12. Learn to use various kinds of tests to identify types of rocks and minerals.
13. Learn how to test soils for alkalinity-acidity, mineral content, and compactness.
14. Grow plants such as beans and grass indoors under varied conditions of soil, water, light, and colors of light (use cellophane). Compare growth rates of these plants with the rates of control plants.
15. Learn to grow plants such as radishes and tomatoes indoors without soil (on sponges, in sawdust, etc.).
16. Make models of the human heart and eyeball, dinosaurs, the molecular structures of elements and compounds, solar systems, etc.
17. Set up, care for, and record observations of inhabitants of aquaria, terraria, and ant colonies.

18. Set up and maintain a class weather station. Make and record systematic observations. See how accurately you can forecast the weather. Make daily predictions. Have contests.
19. Make working models of windmills, Egyptian water lifters, and water and steam turbines.
20. Make telegraph sets, electric motors, and crystal radios.
21. Make regular observations of local vegetation. If weather permits, plant a class flower or vegetable garden. Consult nurseries for proper watering, fertilizing, tilling, etc.
22. Use calorie counters and vitamin and mineral charts to compose menus of balanced meals. See what unusual but nutritionally balanced meals can be planned.
23. Make systematic collections of insects, butterflies, rocks, fossils, leaves, seeds, etc.
24. Learn to start, control, and systematically observe cultures of microscopic animals.
25. Plan a class science fair for the exhibition of individual projects. Invite parents and other classes.
26. Learn the mechanics of rockets, automobile engines, and jet engines. Illustrate and describe them to younger students.
27. Interview a doctor or nurse to find out what various tests — basal metabolism, albumin, blood pressure, blood sugar, electrocardiogram, and electroencephalogram — are used for and how they work.
28. Identify and describe some of the major procedures used to determine the ages of fossils.
29. Prepare an almanac for Laplanders living at a selected spot on the globe, showing the hours of sunlight and the height of the noon sun for the first day of each month of the year.
30. Learn to graft plants, and see what kinds of grafts you can get to "take."
31. Take special note of science sections of magazines and newspapers. Report and discuss new advances.
32. Keep a log of personal science projects with descriptions and explanations of successes and failures.

Like natural science, social science has its two distinct sides — process and content. The process is the general methodology used by social scientists to establish facts and to develop principles, hypotheses, and theories. The content is that resulting body of facts, principles, hypotheses, and theories.

Students learn both these aspects of social science. They learn to perform the processes of social inquiry, and they try to remember important content material. Unless the content is used in some meaningful way, however, it is soon forgotten. The exercises suggested in this section allow students to apply what they have learned in their studies to the resolution of realistic and interesting concerns.

1. Role-play "you are there" sessions depicting historical events, but have the characters use contemporary language.
2. Role-play interviews with citizens during historical events such as the 1929 stock market crash, the San Francisco earthquake, the surrender of General Lee, etc.
3. Develop multimedia reports of visits to various states, cities, and foreign countries. Include sound effects.
4. Develop illustrated presentations, using the flannelboard, on such topics as clothing, community workers, and local resources.
5. Select an imported food such as coffee, tea, or bananas, and make a box movie or mural showing how it is grown, processed, and transported to local markets.
6. Plan an imaginary trip to Europe or the Orient. Use airline schedules and travel folders to plan the itinerary.
7. Locate old textbooks such as *McGuffey's Reader.* Conduct lessons with them, using procedures from the "one-room school" era.
8. Conduct a survey of the neighborhood to note where houses, apartments, and stores are located. Interview adults about zoning restrictions and their effects.
9. Trace and reenact, if possible, the historical origins of present holidays. Decide what thing(s) have happened during the last ten years that could be commemorated by holidays.
10. Identify ten things that give foreigners false impressions of typical Americans and ten things that give accurate impressions.
11. Select several city streets and find out how they were named. Check city records and interview long-term residents.
12. Identify local recreational areas, visit them, and make an illustrated brochure describing them.
13. Write a history of the school, featuring interviews with long-term teachers and adults who were former students.
14. Invite parents to visit the school and interview them to find out how it compares and contrasts with the school they attended.
15. Make collections of artifacts, stamps, postcards, etc. from other states and foreign countries.
16. Make travel posters for countries being studied.
17. Visit local stores that sell building materials. Arrange interviews with the managers to get samples of materials and descriptions of where they originated.
18. Watch the construction of a house or building. Keep notes on daily

progress, and interview some of the workers, if possible, to get their impressions on the building trades as professions.

19. Produce neighborhood maps for new students. Point out interesting places and show how to get to them safely.
20. Keep a map of the United States (and world) to show where the students lived previously. Have those students describe the schools and areas where they lived.
21. Keep a world news map, pinpointing areas important in the news and showing their physical relationship to other countries.
22. Make doll clothing that is copied from the traditional costumes of people living in various areas of the world.
23. Develop guidelines for use in detecting propaganda and persuasion devices.
24. Analyze opinions expressed in editorials, letters to the editor, advertisements, etc.
25. Try to disprove statements whose accuracy appears in doubt.
26. Allot a quantity of credit to individual class members. Use that credit to buy and sell stocks on the stock market, using the daily quotations and various analyses of market trends. See who gains the largest amount of money during the year.
27. Make an analysis of major advances and declines in the stock market and see if they can be associated with events of national and international importance.
28. Invite a stockbroker to class to tell how stocks are bought and sold and to report on the possibilities and dangers of investing in the stock market.
29. Keep an imaginary personal diary for a historically important period of time.
30. Draw political cartoons that express students' points of view.
31. Attend community events such as school board and city council meetings. Report procedures to the class.
32. Plan a model community for the year 2000. Try to foresee present problems that will have been solved and new problems that will have arisen.
33. Make comparative historical time lines for Asia, Europe, and North America.

One more time

Students should be given frequent and varied feasts of realistic activities — activities that allow them to use what they have learned. Such a diet accomplishes several important things. Two of those things are high student interest level and increased likelihood of positive transfer of learning.

Every curriculum area, without exception, can be filled with such activities. Teachers will be relieved to find (those who haven't done so already) that only moderate enterprise is required to turn up valuable application exercises. Some such exercises were mentioned in this chapter. Many more await discovery, most of them for the nth time.

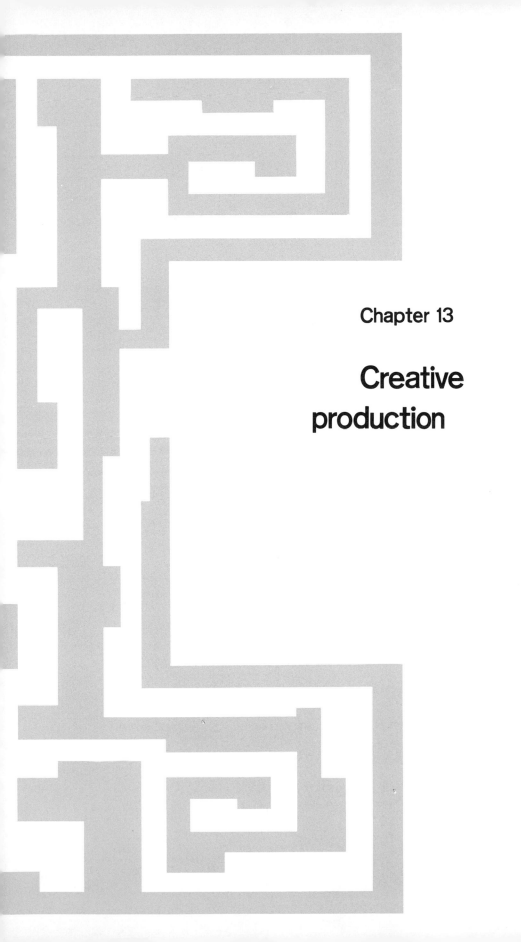

Chapter 13

Creative
production

a

collection

of

? bits of wisdom

&

44 exercises

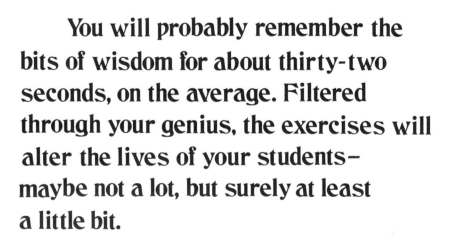

You will probably remember the bits of wisdom for about thirty-two seconds, on the average. Filtered through your genius, the exercises will alter the lives of your students– maybe not a lot, but surely at least a little bit.

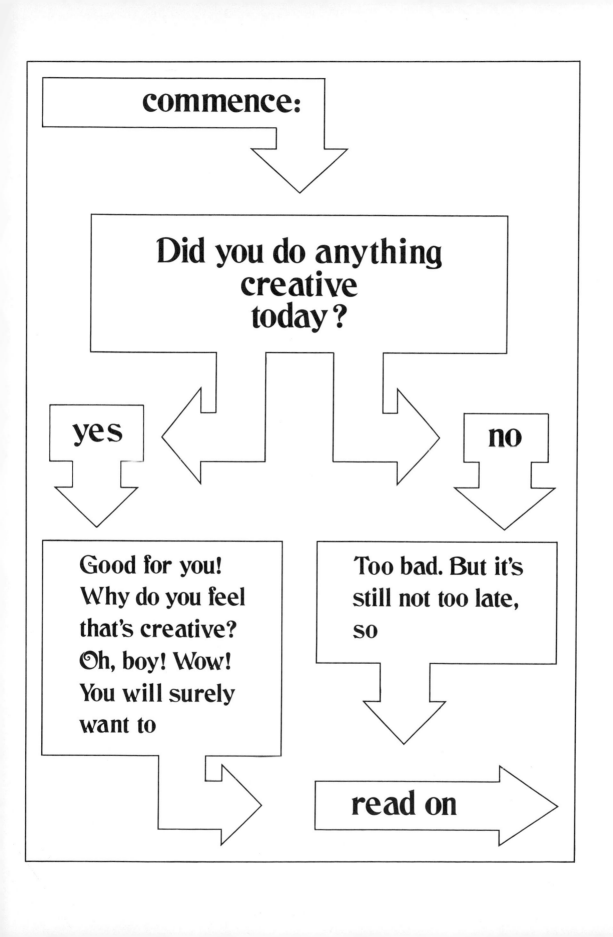

Now you have a (near) perfect chance to be creative. The following exercise comes from our Department of Famous Scenes Revisited.

Pocahontas: *(Enters, sees Captain John Smith about to be slain. Flings self over his body, shielding him. Cries)*

No! You must not kill this man! Spare him— spare him and I will take him for my husband!

(Aside to Captain Smith)

How about it, Johnny? You game?

exercise: You supply Captain Smith's reply. While you're at it, why not five different replies, and why not make each reply as clever as you can.

Got that, did you? All right, now try your hand at this.

exercise: Think of the five cleverest possible titles for the story. Can you beat such gems as:

> Life is Just a Bowl of Cherokees
>
> Soldier of Bad Fortune
>
> Poca Comes to Haunt Us

Okay...

Here's your second chance to be creative. This one is drawn from our Department of Famous Lost Words—fill 'em in.

You & Me

me: What did you think of that exercise?

you: I liked it pretty well. But surely you don't mean *that's* creative.

me: Yes.

you: Ah . . . how come?

me: You ever see that dialogue before?

you: No, I guess not exactly.

me: There you are.

you: Where?

me: I mean, there's the point. Sure you've seen the words before. But you've never seen them put together like that, in that situation, have you?

you: Do I see a wise definition coming?

me: Right—here it is. **Creativity means putting old ideas together in new ways.**

you: That's all? Just putting old ideas together any old way?

me: Any new way. Any way that's new to you, that is.

you: I don't see anything very hard about that. Do you mean to say every one of us are creative?

me: "Is." Yep.

you: Well, then I don't see anything unusual about "creativity."

me: Nope. Every one of us are like that.

you: You mean to say "is."

me: Yeah. What we want to do is make every one of us even *more* creative than we already are.

you: Okay, I see the point. But shouldn't you say "than he already is"?

You want (you want your students) to be more creative?

yes → Fine! That's the spirit! You should be very proud of your- self. Please

no → Well, by gum, you owe it to your students. So if you know what's good for you,

don't stop—read along →

In his *Journal* for October 1872, Emerson wrote that creative thoughts "come unlooked for, like a new bird seen on your trees . . . ."

He wrote sweet and poetic. But for most of us the birds don't come often enough. What we have to do is learn to call them. We can. And we can teach students to call them.

call #1: ideas & associations

Creative people seem able to produce quantities of **ideas.** They also seem easily able to make **associations between ideas.** Can you and your students learn to produce more ideas and make more associations?

Yes sir/ma'am. How? Here's.

Ideas — ideational fluency Please take note that here I am using the word "idea" in this way: **idea** = a thought that occurs to you about something.

How to get ideas about objects:

visualize the object imagine all the parts, their looks, feels, movements, sounds, smells, tastes

visualize the object's origins raw materials, manufacturing processes, who does the work, costs, supply sources

visualize the object in use movements, sounds it makes, purposes, end products, value, impact on life

How to get small ideas about big ideas (such as patriotism, inflation, and so on):

seek definitions
seek connotations
list uses of the idea — who uses it? what people use it differently?
who's strongly for, and who's strongly against it?
list its impacts on life
visualize *behavioral* manifestations — what does an "honest" man *do*?

Skill-building exercises:

1. List all your ideas about a cotton gin.
2. In thirty seconds, see how many ideas you can mention about a robin.
3. List the definitions and connotations of the word "socialism."
4. List all the things a patriotic person does that make you consider him patriotic.

Associations — associational fluency To associate is to link, or group, one thing with another. You can see that associating is a crucial aspect of putting old ideas together in new ways.

associating words bases: sounds, meanings, analogues, opposites, idioms, colloquialisms

associating objects bases: shape, color, texture, taste, smell, use, origin, etc.

associating ideas bases: similarities, origins, destinies, cause-effect, means-end, part-whole, opposites, contrasts

Skill-building exercises:

1. List all the words you can think of that rhyme with "noose."

2. Can you make any puns with "noose"? ("For a hangman, no noose is bad noose.")
3. List definitions and connotations of "welfare."
4. Salmon: list nonfish objects that are similar or analogous to the salmon in shape, behavior, and origin.
5. List all the ideas you associate with Thomas Edison.

call #2: flexibility

Most creative people seem to be very **flexible** in the way they look at things. They see the unusual, the out-of-the-ordinary possibility.

To illustrate:
Question: what is a clothespin used for?
Noncreative answer: to hang clothes.
Creative answers: to hold unpaid bills, to clamp for glueing, to make tents out of blankets, to pinch your big sister.

You already practiced flexibility at the beginning of this chapter. Know where it was? In the exercise where you thought up titles for the Pocahontas and Captain Smith episode.

In one part of the exercise you were asked to compose five titles for the episode. In another part of the exercise you were asked to make those five titles as clever as you could.

Researchers in creativity have discovered that this flexibility factor plays an important role in the creative act. You can help your students become more flexible by having them practice exercises similar to the samples included in the following skill-building section.

Skill-building exercises:

1. Think of all the uses you can for a nail.
2. Think of five unusual uses for a book.
3. Think of two things that would make television watching much more enjoyable. Make them very unusual.

call #3: elaboration

Researchers have found that creative people are usually very good at **elaborating** ideas. If you give them the outline of a plan, they can spell out the details that will make the plan work.

To fill in details of a plan, you need to be able to visualize elements or components involved in the plan. For example, there will most likely be

people Who? What are their duties? What activities, interests, rewards, comforts?

animals, plants, objects What, where, where obtained, how arranged, doing what, how used.

If we ask students to list all such elements that they can think of, they can more easily figure out the role of each element.

Skill-building exercises:

1. Plan a class picnic.
2. Describe how to build a log cabin.
3. The class wants to have an archaeological dig. What plans should the class members make?

call #4: open-ended questions

Questions that have no "right or wrong" answers help students produce a greater quantity and diversity of ideas. The "what do you think would happen if" question is a good example. What do you think would happen if:

> dinosaurs still existed
> the earth moved closer to the sun
> the automobile were outlawed
> girls were eligible for the draft

call #5: manipulation

Virtually all creative invention entails nothing more than changing one or more characteristics of already existing products or ideas.

What could be more useful, then, than learning to list characteristics, qualities, uses, and so forth for an idea or object? Listing makes it easier to see attributes that could be changed to improve the object or idea. Ordinarily, characteristics that can be changed fall into two broad categories:

uses
appearance and arrangement of parts

Students can practice listing uses and aspects of appearance and arrangement; then, for changing an object or idea, they can use a checklist such as the one described in **call # 6.**

call #6: checklists

Since creativity often means the modifying of a characteristic of an already existing object or idea, it stands to reason that the more possibilities we can find for modification, the better our chances for doing something creative.

Osborn* followed that line of reasoning. To make the task easier, he developed a checklist for use in asking questions about objects and ideas, to help you pile up many possibilities for change. The following is a modified form of Osborn's checklist:

Regarding an object or idea:

1. Can it be put to other uses? In what ways, with what modifications?
2. Can it be adapted to existing situations?
3. Can it be modified? What would result from a change in wording, meaning, color, motion, sound, odor, shape?
4. Can it be expanded? What could be added, made stronger, made bigger?
5. Can it be reduced? What could be subtracted, made smaller, condensed, lowered, shortened, lightened, softened?
6. Where can substitutions be made? With what other processes, materials, ingredients?

*Osborn, A. F.: Applied Imagination, New York, 1963, Charles Scribner's Sons.

7. Can it be rearranged? Could there be an interchange of components, other patterns, layouts, sequences?
8. Can it be reversed—made opposite, backward, upside down?
9. Can it be combined or blended with, attached to or made part of something else?

Skill-building exercises:

1. List attributes of a school textbook. Use Osborn's checklist to decide which attributes could be changed to improve it.
2. Have students list attributes of a play area, a map, the classroom, the school, etc., and use an Osborn-type list to suggest improvements.
3. Have students select an idea such as ecology, modern transportation, or poverty. List characteristics and suggest possible changes.
4. Show students a large painting. Let them list characteristics of form, color, contrast, mood, etc. Ask them to suggest changes that would make the painting more enjoyable for them.
5. Play a selected recording. Ask students to list characteristics of rhythm, melody, beat, counterpoint, instrumentation, mood, etc. Ask them to suggest changes that would make the composition more enjoyable for them.
6. Select a written composition such as a poem or narrative description. Follow procedures mentioned in exercises #4 and #5 above, concentrating on word selection, sentence structure, dialogue, mood.

call #7: brainstorming

Osborn, that ultracreative man, also invented the technique called brainstorming, now used so widely that it is part of our everyday vocabulary.

Brainstorming is successfully used in a number of endeavors to produce new ideas. It provides a free and uninhibited group outpouring of ideas in response to a problem. To get that free outpouring, no one makes any evaluation of the ideas until later. To brainstorm, follow this procedure:

1. Identify the problem. (Example: Millions of starlings have descended upon a small community in an agricultural area. They roost in the town trees at night and constitute an awful nuisance. By day they take a heavy toll on the crops of surrounding farms. Problem: what to do about the starlings.)
2. Rapid-fire suggestions to solve the problem. Every contribution is encouraged and accepted. No evaluation is made at this time; the recorder simply jots the ideas down on chalkboard. Suggestions such as the following would be accepted: bring in cats, electrify the trees, use noisemakers, get a huge birdcage, use bright lights at night. In short, every answer is acceptable here.
3. Once the production of ideas ceases, recorded ideas are examined and evaluated. Evaluation is made in terms of what is useful, possible, practical—not in terms of what is right/wrong, good/bad.

Skill-building exercises:

1. Prepare for teaching students to brainstorm by practicing in your college class. Select a topic that everyone is especially interested in. Decide what size groups you will use, how you will begin, how you will record responses, and what you might do with the responses that have been recorded—that is, how you will evaluate them in terms of effectiveness.
2. Think of an imaginary class of school students. Decide on a problem topic

they could brainstorm. Write out verbatim what you would say to help them to begin learning the procedure.
3. Conduct brainstorming sessions with small groups of elementary or secondary students. Help them select a topic of concern, and teach them how to do the exercise.

call #8: forcing relationships

We noted earlier that creative people seem able to make unusual, unexpected associations between one thing and another.

The practice of forcing relationships seems to improve one's ability to make unusual associations. What you do is this: arbitrarily select two objects or ideas. Then identify all the relationships you can between the two, as shown in the following examples:

Young students might determine relationships between a *chair* and a *table*. To help them begin, you could ask, "How do you think a chair and a table are alike? How do you think they are different?" If necessary, you can help students expand possibilities by asking further questions about uses, materials, origins, and locations.

Older students can begin with easy activities and work into more difficult levels involving idea relationships such as *courtesy* and *self-image*, or *philosophy* and *science*.

Ultimately, it is possible to examine relationships between seemingly unrelated objects and ideas such as *malaria* and *garden hose* or *overpopulation* and *palm trees.* As students become adept at this practice, they learn that everything can be related, usually in several different ways. And we hope that this insight helps them put old ideas together in new ways—our beginning definition of creativity.

Skill-building exercises:

1. Compose a list of pairs of objects or ideas to use in forcing relationships. Take into account the age of the students who would use them. Very young students can relate objects such as *dog* and *cat* or *car* and *bus.* Older students can relate objects such as *bacteria* and *elephant* or *rocket* and *pigeon.*
2. Conduct practice sessions in forcing relationships with students. Report and discuss the results.

We've gone pretty heavy on creativity exercises that chiefly involve the use of words. How about moving away from the words for a moment and looking at a couple of exercises involving graphics.

call #9: pattern & figure awareness

Here are two useful exercises:

1. Take a spirit master (Ditto) and fill it with randomly spaced dots, leaving a margin around the edge. Run off copies for your students. Ask them to connect the dots with lines in any way they wish to produce patterns or figures that are either realistic or abstract. Allow them to shade or color the work if they wish. Have the class vote to select the most beautiful, most unusual, most bizarre, etc.

2. Fill a spirit master with a long continuous line that crosses and recrosses itself until it forms a big tangle. (An alternative is to let each student build his own tangle.) Now with shading or coloring, students produce patterns, figures, etc.

call #10: form expansion

Prepare a spirit master that contains three each of three different geometric forms, and distribute it to students. They can add lines or shadings to the forms to expand them either into familiar objects or into abstractions. Useful forms include ovals, circles, triangles, trapezoids, hexagons, squares, pyramids, cylinders, cubes, etc.

Skill-building exercises:

1. Pattern and form building.
2. Form expansion.
3. For individual projects, allow the students to make toothpick sculptures by glueing toothpicks together in any way they like.

So far we have looked mainly at exercises that give students practice in performing creative acts. So that those exercises can be effective, we must think about two other major points, the **physical** and **psychological classroom environments.** These must remain at optimal levels so that students (and teachers) can exercise their creativity.

point A: physical conditions

The room should be well lighted, well ventilated, and attractive. Teachers and students together can work to keep it stocked with varieties of materials that encourage exploring, manipulating, problem-solving, and discovering. If possible, the room should be divided into separate work-study areas— materials depository, reference section, work-construction area. Elementary classrooms should have self-contained areas for social studies, science, language, math, references, art, music, and construction.

Furniture, physical arrangements, and materials should encourage student movement and activity.

Skill-building exercises:

1. Make a diagram of the interior of an imaginary elementary or secondary classroom. Show locations of equip-

ment, materials, and special work areas in the room. Make the room any size and shape you wish to accommodate what you include. Justify the inclusion and location of the various features.

2. Visit a classroom. Quickly diagram its shape and approximate dimensions, showing locations of equipment, materials, special corners. Compare it to the classroom you created above.

3. Take the real classroom you have diagrammed. Show how you could include in it a maximum of desirable equipment, materials, and work areas. Compare it to the classroom you created in #1.

4. Identify as many manipulable items as possible to include in either a single-subject classroom or a self-contained classroom. Concentrate on free and inexpensive materials, and take into account the ages of students involved. Select items that will supply the greatest variety of colors, shapes, textures. Check teachers' guides, instructional aids catalogs, free and inexpensive materials catalogs, and audiovisual centers or their catalogs.

point B: psychological conditions

I am using the term "psychological conditions" to refer to the social and emotional climate that prevails in the classroom.

Teachers are responsible for establishing the social and emotional climates of their classrooms. Conditions beyond their control may prevent them from establishing the sort of climate they want, but in the end it remains their responsibility to enlist their students' help in developing the psychological conditions that foster creative activity.

How do they work toward establishing the best climate? They can begin by becoming very sensitive to their students—to their likes, dislikes, aspirations, frustrations. They can try to relate to each student personally, warmly, openly. They can learn to be more accepting of students and less rejecting. They can learn some of the roadblocks that prevent effective communication, and learn to surmount them by listening actively to students, avoiding moralizing, and avoiding the "judge" role in every student act.

More specific to creativity, teachers can greatly encourage the production of creative ideas by:

teasing out the ideas showing appreciation in the new, sustaining students' delight in novelty, constantly probing with questions like "What would happen if . . .?"
accepting and rewarding creative behavior
showing respect for and acceptance of *unusual* questions or answers or ideas, showing students that their ideas have value by seeking to apply them, tying evaluative comments with reasons—"I like this *because* . . ." or "You used _____ in a very clever way."

Skill-building exercises:

1. In your college class write down all the ways you can think of for getting a kitten down from a tall tree. Exchange papers and write evaluative comments on the paper you receive. Practice using comments that are accepting, that reward imaginative ideas, that tell why you like certain ideas, and that indicate in a positive way other avenues that might be explored. Discuss selected compositions and accompanying evaluative comments.

2. Role-play classroom discussions to practice encouraging and rewarding creative behavior. One good activity is to tell a very short story, leaving off the ending. Let the class finish the story in unusual and clever ways. You (the teacher) respond to their comments in appropriate ways.

3. Try #2 above with a group of learners. Report and discuss the results.

perspective

Man's cultural advances come from his ability to think creatively. Until recently, the advances came slowly. Most societies abhorred change, thought the tried the true, and guided themselves by imitation and ritual.

Today, what we call "advanced societies" increasingly recognize the desirability of creative thought. They find it leads to creature comforts, conveniences, and group security. They are becoming more apt to reward creative people, less apt to punish them. They are adopting creativity as a major cultural value.

In recent years, as educators and psychologists have become more concerned with the nature of the creative processes, there has been disagreement about creativity and whether it could be taught and learned. We can now put that argument aside. Ample evidence exists to show that people can learn to perform acts and produce objects that are considered to be creative. The act of being creative may still be mysterious, but it is no longer completely unknown territory.

The activities people can practice to make themselves more creative usually involve a process called **divergent production.** Divergent production calls for many and different "correct" solutions to problems. So instead of a question such as "What (one thing) is a nail for?" we pose a question such as "What are the many, clever, unusual things we can do with a nail? In fact, with what kind of a nail?"

We can contrast this divergent production with the more familiar process of **convergent production.** Convergent production means the act of producing the single correct answer to a question or the single correct solution to a problem. It is the act we have emphasized so strongly in education over the years. Thus what we want to teach ourselves to do now is to help learners become adept at divergent production. We want to do that not because we have seen some folly in convergent production and want to eliminate it as a process. We do it because creativity and divergent production are closely tied together, and one of our educational aims today is to help learners become more creative.

Skill-building exercises (your last):

1. List school curriculum areas where convergent thought receives especially strong emphasis; e.g., spelling and arithmetic.
2. Within the areas you have listed, think of instances when divergent thought could be emphasized. (Example: using these five discs, make as many different groups as you can.)
3. List curriculum areas where divergent thought usually receives strong emphasis.
4. Change the following questions so they call for divergent instead of convergent thought.

   What was the cause of the Civil War?
   Who discovered America?
   What are Boston's three main imports?
   What is a suburb?

Are your changes clever and unusual? If so, please accept your responses and reward yourself.

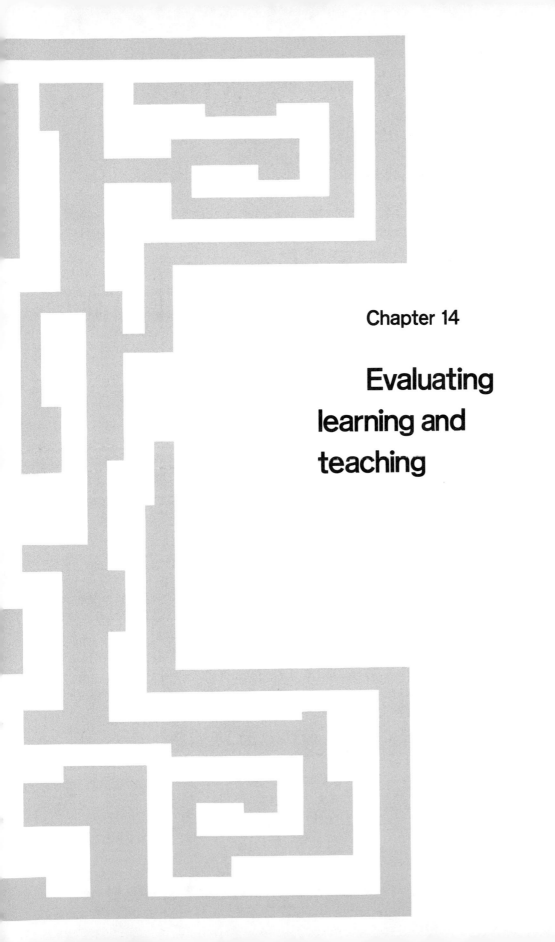

Chapter 14

Evaluating learning and teaching

good old Mr. Bennett

Mr. Bennett taught first grade. Early in the year he became convinced that performance criteria could help him in teaching his students and also in conferring more adequately with parents and fellow professionals. So with the help of a curriculum consultant, he wrote several dozen behavioral objectives—statements of hoped-for student performance—that covered most of the subject areas he taught. As best he could tell, the objectives were appropriate to the ability levels of his students.

Reading received the greatest emphasis in Mr. Bennett's first-grade curriculum, so naturally he composed a good many behavioral objectives for reading. He included eighteen of them for "word analysis" alone. To illustrate, five of them were:

what the students can do	percent accuracy required*
pronounce the diphthong sounds of *ou, ow, oi,* and *oy* when encountered in different words	80
say the names of the individual letters that make up the following three-letter consonant blends when heard in familiar words: *spl, spr, str, scr*	90
pronounce the consonants *c* and *g* correctly when encountered in words beginning with *ca, co, cu, ga, go, gu* and *ce, ci, cy, ge, gi, gy*	90
indicate the number of syllables in carefully pronounced words of one, two, and three syllables	80
substitute consonants at the beginnings of the words "back," "log," "night," "pick," and "tame" so as to make new words	100

*For example, if 80% accuracy is required, the student must get four out of five correct.

At the end of the year Mr. Bennett found that sixteen of his students could perform the acts indicated in those five objectives without error. Of the remaining fourteen students, six could perform four of the objectives, but eight could perform three or fewer. Two students didn't reach acceptable levels on any one of the five objectives.

Now what does that mean?

Did the class do well or poorly?

Did Mr. Bennett do an adequate job of teaching?

Was something wrong with the objectives?

Was something wrong with the activities or materials?

What makes you think so?

What difference does all this make anyway?

If you can give satisfactory answers to these questions, you may be a whiz at the evaluation of teaching and learning. On the other hand, maybe not — it depends on the definition of satisfactory answers. Or, on the third hand (?), maybe you can, after all, give better answers to the questions than anyone else, even though they aren't very insightful.

Impressed by the ambiguity? Good. That means you have reached entry level for this chapter, which has to do with procedures you can use in trying to figure out the meanings and implications of all those complicated results of instruction.

You start with objectives

Some people believe that an act or object can only be evaluated by comparing it to a specified set of standards. That is, you might say, "Man, this is a good tape recorder," and you would be basing your judgment that it is "good" upon a comparison with qualities found in other tape recorders about which you know.

That belief is not entirely correct. You can have good or bad, pleasant or unpleasant reactions to any number of things you've never so much as thought of before. When you are attracted by an optical illusion, you aren't comparing it to others you have known. When you taste a new food, hear a new sound, or play a new game, you may be either attracted or repelled, irrespective of comparisons.

Yet if precise judgments are to be made about acts and objects—if you are to be able to say, "This is good Bahianna sauce, but it needs a little more pepper to be like the real stuff"—you do have to have fairly explicit standards in mind. You use those standards not only to judge overall quality but also to identify and judge specific elements that make up the whole.

That kind of evaluation is what we try to get at in the evaluation of learning and teaching.

We want to know generally

how well our learners have learned

and how well we have taught.

We also want to know specifically

whether Mary can identify consonant blends

and whether we used instructional techniques that were appropriate for her.

That brings us back to the role played by behavioral objectives—or performance criteria, if you prefer—in helping us to guide and evaluate learning and teaching.

To note again the **general objectives** we hold for learners, here is the list as you saw it presented with the **model of teaching** in Chapter 6.

386

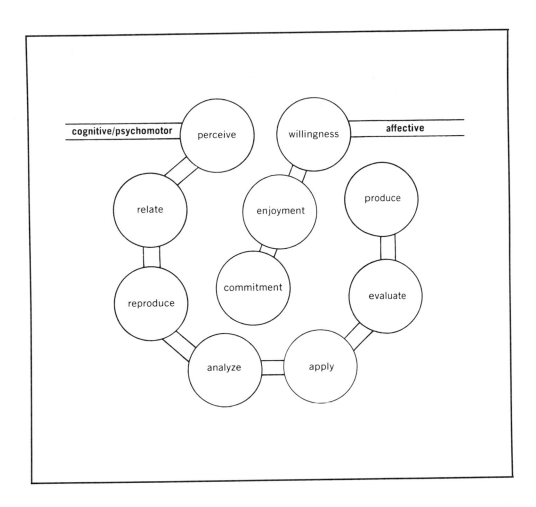

Remember what we mean by **general objectives.** They are *kinds* of mental and physical acts, accompanied by emotional reactions to those acts. But of course the acts and emotions have to be related to something specific. We might call them "subject-specific" to indicate that they are related to specific subject matter. For instance, in science you might *perceive* the sounds made by a cricket when it rubs its legs together. You don't just perceive, you perceive something specific.

You realize too that the cognitive/psychomotor and affective behaviors arch over all subject areas. Thus those general objectives hold for every curriculum area in school as well as for the activities conducted in those areas.

Therefore, whether you teach art or music or physical education or home-making, you want your students to **perceive** specific points, **relate** those points to each other and to other points, **reproduce** them from memory, **analyze** them, **apply** them, **evaluate** them, and **produce** new ones. Further, you want students to do all of this willingly, with enjoyment, and with a sense of commitment.

When a teacher composes his behavioral objectives, he makes statements of acts he hopes his students will become able to perform. He tries his best to help students learn to perform them. All the while he checks to see whether, to what extent, and how well his students can perform the acts. The objectives tell him what to look for when he appraises and evaluates.

Behavioral objectives may be tiresome to write, and you may wonder whether you are hitting everything that counts with them. But once they are done, they do help instruction and evaluation. Mr. Bennett, for example, can check to see whether his first graders can substitute initial consonants and make new words out of "back," "log," "night," "pick," and "tame."

You ascertain behavior

The word "ascertain" means to find out about—to get to know with a degree of certainty. Commonly you see the word "measurement" used in this context, as in "measurement and evaluation." However, measurement has come to be associated with formal testing, and for that reason it is not used here. Testing does have its place in overall evaluation procedures, but its value has been greatly exaggerated in the past.

Observation of students during instructional episodes and project work offers a far better avenue for ascertaining performance levels than does a teacher-devised testing regimen, where we think of tests as those knuckle-whitening pencil and paper adventures that, for some students, could more accurately be called torture sessions or nightmares.

You can adequately ascertain what students can do simply by devising schemes for observing the students at work. Some of the schemes should be formal, specific, and detailed: they should involve observation guides and check sheets that you use while observing students during guided activities. Other schemes should be informal yet systematic: you decide one day to take special note of the work habits of each student; on another day you note specific strengths and specific difficulties that students encounter.

You will do well to begin with a list of behavioral objectives. If you want students to learn to reduce fractions to lowest terms, you watch for that performance during instructional and practice sessions. If you want them to identify obtuse triangles, you watch to see whether they can pick out the obtuse triangles from a page filled with many different kinds of triangles. But you must keep track, through checks or notes, of what you observe for each student. Otherwise you won't be able to remember exactly what you saw, and you will have lost a useful piece of evidence for conferences with students, other professionals, and parents.

observation guides

The job of using guide sheets for observing students is not at all a hard one. The sheets are easy to prepare. What goes on them for guides depends, of course, on your classroom situation—the students' abilities and interests, the curriculum area, your own predilections. The sample sheets presented here give an idea of some of the possibilities. Make them up for yourself, write them on spirit (Ditto) masters, and run off several dozen copies. As you use them, you will give yourself a fairly objective picture of different students' performances, interests, strengths, weaknesses, skills, and so forth. You will also have a compilation of specific evidence that will be quite useful in conferences with students, parents, and professionals.

You will see six illustrative guide sheets presented in this section. The first is a student personal log. Most students in third grade and above can keep logs, and they are quite valuable to teachers, parents, and the students themselves.

The second is an observation guide that can be marked with checks to show whether (or how nearly) students have attained specific objectives.

The third sheet helps you note students' specific strengths and weaknesses in any curriculum area.

The fourth sheet provides a quick check and record of students' work habits and social behavior.

The fifth suggests questions you can ask or ideas you can explore when conferring individually with students—a practice that you will find very helpful and well worth the effort.

The sixth guide sheet is one you can use to make a quick check and record of your own lessons, with specific reference to methods, grouping, materials, and reinforcers.

A reminder: using these guide sheets as models, you can make masters of all six in about one and a half hours. Then you can run enough copies from the masters to last all year.

student personal log

There is no need to prepare this sheet as an outline for the students; each person can keep his own log in whatever manner he prefers. The log should have entries made in it once or twice a week during class time especially set aside. You can keep the logs in your possession during the week so they won't get lost. They provide an excellent record of the student's view of his achievements, and they are helpful to everyone concerned during personal conferences.

You may wish to decide with the class what the general content of the log should be, or you may prefer to let each individual include whatever he wishes. Some possibilities you might suggest for starters are:

attendance-absence
books and articles read
extra assignments undertaken and completed
individual projects begun
individual projects completed or not completed, with reasons why
hobbies pursued
awards, citations, honors, grades
trips and outings
attendance at movies, concerts, plays, ball games, etc.
new skills acquired (baking, painting, etc.)

attainment of student objectives

date _____ topic(s) _____

objective(s) _____

students observed*	degree to which objective reached		degree of willingness		degree of enjoyment	
	high	low	high	low	high	low
Amy _____						
Bill _____						
Carl _____						
Darlene _____						
Elsie _____						
Frank _____						
Gerry _____						

*List all the students' names but circle only the names of those observed.

students' strengths & weaknesses

date _____ topic(s) _____

students observed	specific strengths	specific weaknesses
Amy		
Bill		
Carl		
Darlene		
Elsie		
Frank		
Gerry		

students' work habits & social behavior

date _____

activity (circle one): constructing, discussing, drawing, listening, observing, playing, project work, reading, speaking, taking notes, other _____.

students	work habits		social behavior		misbehavior causes	assignments completed/ not completed
	good	poor	good	poor		
Amy						
Bill						
Carl						
Darlene						
Elsie						
Frank						
Gerry						

interview guide

student _____ date _____

1. What have we done during the past week that you especially enjoyed?

2. How many things can you name that you have learned in the past few days?

3. What do you seem to be having the most trouble with in school? What do we need to do to help?

4. What things do you dislike most in school? Why?

5. Let's look at your personal log. What have you included since our last talk that you are proudest of?

6. I notice that you have read (written, drawn, figured out, etc.) _____.
   Tell me something about that.

7. Do you have any special plans for next week in reading (social studies, special projects, etc.)?

suggestions or notes:

teacher self-rating sheet: instruction

date(s) _____ topics(s) _____

	effectiveness		
	high	medium	low
method of presentation lecturing demonstrating questioning student activity other _____			
grouping large small individual			
materials books charts equipment filmstrips games globes kits maps models motion pictures three-dimensional objects pictures recordings workbooks, worksheets other _____			
reinforcers fun success praise marks, stars, tokens, candy privileges other _____			

You use teacher-made tests

I strongly believe that most of the time, under most conditions, systematic observation gives teachers a better overall grasp of their students' successes, problems, and failures than does formal testing. Despite that belief, I do recognize that there are times when testing can serve useful purposes—when a school or district wants to see how it compares with other schools and districts in terms of student achievement, for example. That is a time for standardized testing, which we will consider later. Another of those times occurs when a teacher needs to do the following in a minimal amount of time:

> determine existing student abilities related to specific behavioral objectives (for example, Mr. Bennett may need to know which of his students can identify initial consonants and their sounds before he attempts to teach initial consonant blends)

> diagnose specific strengths and weaknesses in a content/skill area for all members of the class (this step is often necessary before appropriate objectives can be formulated for class members)

> determine whether class members have met stated behavioral objectives (whether they can perform at levels that have been previously established as criteria)

For those three kinds of circumstances, standardized diagnostic tests or teacher-made diagnostic and achievement tests can serve well. There are still other reasons for giving tests regularly. Two of them are seldom mentioned, yet they are of great importance to students:

> Students *can* enjoy tests and like the excitement that accompanies competition and self-appraisal. This condition can occur when tests are seen as something other than criteria for grades, passes, failures, and threats associated with study requirements.

> Testing experience *can* help students become "test wise" and better prepared emotionally for taking tests. Tests do remain a significant

part of most teachers' activities. Thus we can be of some service to students by giving them experiences in threat-free test taking. We can do them even greater service by helping them become test wise—by helping them look for wordings within items that sometimes point to one response over another; by helping them learn to respond to shorter, easier items first; by helping them learn to use neat handwriting and good spelling and grammar. Cheating? Hardly. You know full well that some students become test wise on their own, and can outperform other students who know as much or more. If you have been a very successful student, you probably owe part of that success to your expertise in taking tests. Why not, then, help every student learn to take tests well? That's not cheating: that's giving students a more even break.

Teacher-made tests, used without undue threat to students, serve some useful purposes. But we want to avoid holding them up as the big goals on the horizon—the shibboleths that all else points to and that mean academic life or death.

The following suggestions will help you to make better tests. They will also give hints you can pass along to students, through practice, to help them become better test takers. When you write test items, keep these hints in mind.

1. Be sure to include directions that are perfectly clear.
2. Avoid the trivial.
3. Use simple wording, language, and sentence structure—don't make it a test of reading comprehension unless that's what you intend.
4. Don't include more than one problem in any single item.
5. If possible, try to stick to items that have only a single correct answer.
6. Don't use trick statements, involved directions, or double negatives—don't let your achievement test become an intelligence test.
7. True-false items should be clearly true or false, not yes *and* no, or maybe, or sometimes.
8. Avoid using words that give hints about correct responses such as; all, always, none, never, totally, exactly, completely, and only, especially in true-false items, and a, an, singulars and plurals before blanks—"Toby rode an ＿＿＿＿＿＿, a large animal in India."
9. Be sure an item doesn't provide the answer to another item.

With those suggestions in mind, look over the following test items. Each item illustrates one or more errors often made in writing tests. See if you can identify the errors.

1. (Fill in the blank.) The Wright brothers discovered many principles that are still used in the construction of an ＿＿＿＿＿＿.
2. (Fill in the blank.) The Wright brothers did their work in ＿＿＿＿.
3. (Write the answer in the space provided.) What was the name of the Coast Guardsman who befriended the Wright brothers when they were conducting their important tests at Kittyhawk?

＿＿＿＿＿＿＿＿＿＿＿＿＿＿＿＿＿＿.

4. (Write your answer on the back of the page.) Describe how the Wright brothers made and used their wind tunnel and what the most important things were that they found out from using it.

5. (Circle the correct answer.) What was the name of the place in North Carolina where the Wright brothers conducted their important tests?

> Raleigh
> Kittyhawk
> Big Moon
> Seabreeze

6. (Circle one: true or false.) The Wright brothers worked very well as a team, and they made millions of dollars from their discoveries.

7. (Circle one: true or false.) The Wright brothers, while neither was known as a mathematical expert, nonetheless were not unsuccessful in disproving existing tables of air lift over curved surfaces.

interpreting results of teacher-made tests

Suppose you have constructed and administered a test. You have the results and you are ready to interpret them. Before you can do so with confidence, you must assure yourself that you are accurate in two assumptions:

> you must assume that your test is **valid**—that it measures what it is supposed to measure

> you must assume that your test is **reliable**—that individual students would give the same answers again if they retook the test

The test is probably valid if the items are identical (or very similar) to behavioral objectives toward which students have been working. Or it is probably valid if test items look very similar to textbook material or other subject content with which the students have worked. On the other hand, the test is probably not valid if the items appear only partially related to content and objectives, or if items are ambiguous, confusing, misleading, or otherwise poorly composed. Reliability also depends on the items being worded simply and clearly, so that students would read them the same way (and thus answer them the same way) time after time.

If you are reasonably satisfied that your test is valid and reliable, you can proceed with some interpretations that will help you do a better job of perceiving the strengths and weaknesses, abilities and disabilities of your students. You will have two important kinds of information available.

> **total test results** These are expressed as scores based on the number of correct responses to items for all the individuals in the class. This information provides a quick indication of the extent to which individual students, and the entire class, have attained overall instructional objectives.

individual test item results These tell you specifically which students responded correctly to which items. This information tells you whether specific objectives have been attained by individuals and by the entire class.

With these two kinds of information, you can make judgments in one or both of two widely recognized ways — **normative** and **criterion-referenced evaluation procedures.**

normative evaluation procedures Normative procedures let you find out how each student's performance compares with the performances of other students like him. In a way, we can say that this kind of evaluation pits students against each other in large-scale, benign competition. The better one student does, the more poorly another student is seen to do. All standardized tests are built on this concept. In fact, to say "standardized" is to say that a test has been administered to large numbers of people and the results have been compiled into "norms" that indicate the levels of performance that are typical for students of various age or grade levels.

Normative procedures are based on the concept of the gaussian or "normal" curve, a bell-shaped curve that shows the normal distribution of many human characteristics, including the scores they make on intelligence tests. Ordinarily the scores that students make on achievement tests approximate the normal curve distribution. This fact has led to the practice of "grading on the curve," or assigning the letter grades A, B, C, D, and F to scores that fall in the upper, center, and lower parts of the normal distribution.

criterion-referenced evaluation procedures A second kind of procedure commonly used in making judgments about student test performance can tell you whether, or to what extent, individual students have reached the behavioral objectives set for them. What other students do on the test is irrelevant: a student competes against a standard, not against other students. This kind of appraisal is called criterion-referenced, and it has begun to gain favor in the recent upsurge in the use of behavioral objectives.

Criterion-referenced evaluation is simply a means of checking to see whether students have reached objectives or performance criteria. While judgments are based upon fixed standards, this procedure is not identical to an earlier system of grading on the basis of absolute standards. In that older system, students took tests and received marks of 100%, 90%, 85%, and so forth; or they received grades of A, B, C, D, or F to indicate how well they performed in comparison with the established standard. Criterion-referenced evaluation, on the other hand, has only one mark. That mark is "credit," and students receive it only when they have performed the behavior stated in the objective. Until they have performed the behavior, they receive no mark at all — no fail, no incomplete, no grade of C or D.

Whether you use normative or criterion-referenced evaluation procedures, you will want to obtain information about student performance both during instruction and at the end of instruction.

Test information obtained *during* instruction is called **formative information.**

It tells you how things are going — whether instruction is succeeding, whether teaching techniques are appropriate to the students, whether learning is occurring as rapidly as expected. It helps you stay on the track, or get back on the track if things are going poorly.

Test information obtained *at the end* of instruction is called **summative information.** It indicates after instruction has ended the extent to which students achieved the objectives toward which they were striving. It helps you to evaluate students, methods, materials, grouping, and your own styles of teaching.

You use standardized tests

Descriptions of standardized tests have limited value for most classroom teachers. Teachers do not make standardized tests. That's work that requires highly specialized training and elaborate production and validation procedures. Neither do they become test officers nor directors of testing programs unless they have been trained for it. At most, teachers administer standardized tests to their students, and occasionally they participate in deciding which tests will be used in the district where they teach.

That being the case, there is fairly little you can "do" with regard to standardized tests. One thing you can do is inform yourself about the kinds of standardized tests and the significant qualities that test makers build into them. We will take note of some characteristics and uses of standardized tests in the paragraphs that follow.

To say that a test is standardized, as we noted previously, is to say that it has been administered to large groups of people — often thousands — and that the results of those administrations have been carefully summarized and converted into norms. Those norms indicate what is considered "normal" or typical performance for students of different age and grade levels. Of course, credible norms accompany only tests that have been shown to be valid and reliable.

To give you a general idea of the makeup of a standardized test, suppose the Whiz Test Bureau wanted to prepare a standardized test in mathematics. They might begin by examining math textbooks that are widely used to select test content. Next they would carefully compose and test out the items (questions) that were to be included in the test, retaining only those that had been proved valid, reliable, and of the appropriate levels of difficulty. Finally, they would select a sample of students of various ages, grades, ethnic groups, socioeconomic levels, geographic locales, and so forth to accurately represent all of the students in all of the schools in the country.

They would administer the test to those students and record and summarize the results, which would then be presented in tables of norms. The tables of norms would show test users what, for instance, the "average" sixth grader had done on the test, or possibly what the average 15-year-old had done. That would enable a teacher who later used the test to take Sally's score of 35 and check it against the norms to see whether Sally was below, at, or above the average of students at her age or grade level.

Norms are the crucial aspect of standardized tests. Both age norms and grade norms figure prominently. Grade norms often accompany achievement tests. They can tell you how the students in your class have fared on the test, as compared with students in the same grade nationwide. Age norms must accompany intelligence tests, and they show how a student compares with others of the same age, irrespective of grade level.

Further, the norms themselves may be expressed in various forms. For intelligence tests, "mental age" norms have been extensively used. A raw score of 48 on intelligence test X might represent a mental age of 12 years, although it was made by John, whose chronological (calendar) age is only 10 years. From this information one can determine that John has an IQ of 120:

$$IQ = \frac{\text{mental age (12)}}{\text{chronological age (10)}} \times 100 = 120$$

Another very common norm is called the "percentile." Susan's raw score on the intelligence test was 41. For her chronological age (suppose it is 10 years and 2 months) the norm shows that 41 falls in the thirty-eighth percentile. That means Susan did as well as or better than 38% of the students who took the test when they were 10 years and 2 months of age.

Yet another common norm is called the "stanine," a name derived from the term "standard nine." Here, the range of scores on the test is statistically divided into nine groups. The first stanine is the lowest, the fifth is average, and the ninth is highest. So if Samuel makes a raw score of 47 on a test, he might fall in the sixth stanine for his age group, which would be slightly above average.

Grade norms are stated in a different way, and chronological ages don't figure in the picture at all. Arturo, in the eight grade, makes a raw score of 102 on the math achievement test. When we check that raw score in the table of norms we find that it is the average score made by eleventh graders who took the test. We say, then, that Arturo has a grade placement in mathematics of eleven. He does as well as the average eleventh-grade student.

sample grade-level norms

raw score	grade equivalent
99	10.8
100	10.9
101	11.0
→ 102	→ 11.0
103	11.1

kinds of standardized tests

Standardized testing has become very big business in this country. Many large corporations have involved themselves in it, and their revenues run into the millions of dollars yearly. The kinds of tests they produce are varied and numerous—there are literally dozens of standardized tests available in some curriculum areas such as reading. The following summary of the kinds of standardized tests available gives you an idea of the enormity of the testing enterprise.

aptitude, prognosis, and readiness

You will find tests in:

    clerical skills
    language aptitude and readiness
    employment prognosis
    algebra readiness
    arithmetic readiness
    reading readiness

personality & interests

You can find tests to measure:

    occupational interests
    general interests
    personality traits

language arts achievement

These tests measure levels of achievement in:

    general English
    elementary English
    intermediate English
    high school English
    college English
    listening comprehension
    language and spelling
    word recognition
    reading difficulties
    reading capacity
    oral reading
    silent reading
    primary, intermediate, and advanced reading

mental ability

These tests purport to measure ability in general
problem solving and abstract thinking in:

    kindergarten
    primary grades
    intermediate grades
    upper grades
    verbal areas
    performance areas
    drawings
    vocabulary

mathematics

These tests measure mathematics achievement in
areas such as:

    algebra

tests
tests
tests
tests
tests
tests
tests
tests
tests
tests
tests
tests
tests
tests
tests
tests
tests
tests
tests
tests
tests
tests
tests
tests

tests
tests
tests
tests
tests
tests
tests
tests
tests
tests
tests
tests
tests
tests
tests
tests
tests

arithmetic
general mathematics
geometry
mathematical concepts

foreign languages

French
German
Spanish

sciences

elementary science
intermediate science
high school general science
chemistry
physics
biology
psychology

social sciences

critical thinking
arts and humanities
elementary social studies
advanced social studies
American history
world history

technical & commercial

business and economics
technical comprehension

Those are merely some of the areas you might be interested in exploring further. If there are specific test names and descriptions you would like to examine, go to the library and look at Buros' *Mental Measurements Yearbook.* That reference contains descriptions and evaluations of most of the standardized tests that are available.

using standardized test results

Suppose you have administered standardized tests to your classes. What do you do with, or in light of, the results? It is probably fair to say that most teachers do very little, and that they seldom change instruction at all because of them. Neither do school districts do much, unless the district results are uncomfortably low in comparison with national or state norms.

Scores do get recorded on students' permanent records. Sometimes teachers or administrators discuss scores and use them for assigning students to certain classes or groups. Sometimes teachers or administrators discuss the scores with parents, and sometimes teachers or counselors use the results for guidance purposes in advising students. Each of these uses could fill a fairly important function.

Records of general ability, achievement, interests, specific aptitudes, and diagnosed weaknesses could be used to good advantage by teachers in planning each student's work, provided that scores aren't used to label students or excuse their lack of progress.

Counseling with students, especially at the secondary level, requires objective data about personality traits, vocational interests, and special aptitudes.

Conferencing with parents proceeds better if teachers can mention interpretations of test data. Those interpretations should not be made in sophisticated technical terms. Rather, they should be made in terms of averages (at, somewhat above, somewhat below), in terms of special abilities, in terms of general personality traits, and in terms of areas requiring further work.

Test bureaus advise not telling parents their children's IQ's, percentile ranks, or even their specific grade equivalent scores. Such measures are not precise — they simply indicate approximations. Parents often misinterpret and misuse such "precise" (really imprecise) information. If you feel you project a more professional image by using statistical terms, use the stanine; tell the parent that stanines are nine divisions of the total group scores, and that stanines one through three are below average, four through six are about average, and seven through nine are above average. **Emphasize that these are scores the students made on tests, not innate parts of the students themselves,** and describe your plans for a positive approach to helping the student improve his performance in weaker areas. Help the parent to see that students should not be admonished for "low" test performance, but helped through positive efforts to achieve improvement in ability.

a tiny glossary of useful terms

descriptions of group scores

    mean the arithmetic average of the scores

    median the middle score, when all scores are ranked from highest to lowest

    range the distance between the highest and the lowest scores

    standard deviation a statistical indication of the spread of scores (in a normal distribution, about two thirds of the scores fall between plus one and minus one standard deviations from the mean)

evaluation judging worth or correctness

    criterion-referenced evaluation judging student and class performance on the basis of whether behavioral objectives have been met

    norm-referenced evaluation judging student and class performances by comparing them to large numbers of other students and classes

measurement obtaining samples of student performance (connotes but does not denote the use of formal tests)

necessary qualities of tests

    reliability the degree to which a test consistently measures whatever it measures

    validity the degree to which a test measures what it is supposed to measure

norms of standardized tests summaries of performances by large numbers of different students

    age norms typical performances by students at different age levels

    grade norms typical performances by students at different grade levels

percentiles the percentage of scores that fall below a certain level

stanines bands of scores obtained by statistically dividing the array of scores into nine groups

observation obtaining samples of student performance by watching and listening to students at work on instructional activities

scores

    converted score a score derived from a raw score that has a more clear-cut meaning than the raw score

    raw score the number of correct answers made by an individual on a test

standardized tests commercially prepared tests, carefully checked for reliability and validity, and accompanied by norms and directions for administration and scoring

    achievement tests tests that measure academic performance

    aptitude tests tests that measure the probability of future success in specific areas

    intelligence tests tests that measure the ability to solve problems and think abstractly

teacher-made tests tests composed by teachers, as distinct from commercially prepared tests

    essay tests tests containing items that require students to compose and write out fairly long responses

    short answers tests tests containing items that require at most one- or two-word responses: true-false, completion, multiple choice, matching.

essence

Evaluation is the process of discovering how well students are progressing toward instructional goals and, in turn, how effective their instructional activities and materials have been. This knowledge of progress and effectiveness is crucial to the improvement of instruction.

For the most part, teachers can make adequate judgments about progress and effectiveness merely by systematically observing students at work. By carefully noting skill performance and social behavior, they can record strengths, weaknesses, and objectives attained.

Occasionally, useful procedures can be served by formal testing. Teachers can learn to construct adequate tests for their own classes. They must strive for validity and reliability through attention to item content and wording.

Teachers may be called on once in a while to administer and perhaps score standardized tests. Such tests are available for measuring academic achievement, specific aptitudes, intelligence, personality, and interests, in addition to other areas. They contain tables of age and/or grade norms to aid in interpretation of results.

Results of observations, teacher-made tests, and standardized tests can be used in counseling with students, conferencing with parents, improving overall instruction, and improving instruction for individual students.

Part V

Subject matter of educational psychology

summarizes the **principles of growth and learning**
in its one chapter

Chapter 15

Psychology for the schoolhouse: content

This is a book about
the psychology of
teaching and learning.
It is for teachers,
and it has
only one purpose:

to
help
build
teaching
skills
that
are
psychologically
sound . . . . .

definitions:

teaching skills

acts performed by teachers to instruct students

psychologically sound

consistent with what psychologists and teachers know about conditions under which students learn best

The psychological content I have drawn on includes only what I believe is important for teachers. That has made the book short, agreeably so I hope. At the same time, we won't pretend it "covers the entire field" of educational psychology. And we will recognize that it does not represent the only way to describe teaching and learning. The first fourteen chapters examined learning philosophy, teaching acts, and learning conditions. Those acts and conditions were based on the content summarized in the remaining pages of this chapter.

more definitions

psychology is the study of behavior. Findings from such studies can often be used to improve learning and teaching.

experience is the interaction of an individual with the environment.

learning is the modification of behavior that results from experience. I think you will realize intuitively that learning does not include changes in behavior that result from maturation, from physical injury, or from the influence of drugs.

education refers to the process of amassing desired learnings. We usually think of those learnings as occurring under the aegis of schools, although obviously a great portion of them occur elsewhere.

educational psychology is the study of conditions that facilitate and inhibit desired learnings. It is important to teachers only insofar as it helps them do their jobs better.

Areas of endeavor

Educational psychologists do most of their work in three major areas:

characteristics of learners

correlates of learning

instructional implications

(Don't waste your valuable time memorizing the lists that follow. But do take note of them—they help to explain why certain points have been stressed in earlier chapters.)

characteristics of learners important in education include:

    physical capabilities and potentialities

    mental capabilities and potentialities

    psychological needs

    social inclinations

    emotional tendencies

    attitudes, values, and interests

correlates of learning include those things that have bearing on:

    acquisition — what, how much, and how easily people learn

    retention — what, how accurately, and how long people remember

    transfer — how well people can use what they know

some correlates of acquisition

    characteristics of learners mentioned above

    readiness

    motivation

    experiences: organization and presentation

    instructional materials

    active learner involvement

    reinforcement

    social and emotional climates

some correlates of retention

    intent to remember

    sensory involvement

    emotional involvement

    muscular involvement

overlearning

practice

mnemonics

some correlates of transfer

understanding

generalization

ability to sense relationships

similarities between tasks

practice in applying

instructional implications are hypotheses about what teachers should do to promote learning. They are deduced from a consideration of characteristics of learners, other correlates of learning, and realities of the school — educational goals, class size, available materials, and so forth. These hypotheses suggest designs, strategies, methods, techniques, and tools of teaching. And they affect every aspect of planning, instructing, and evaluating, including:

objectives

method

materials

activities

evaluation

interest

climate

interaction

discipline

to mention just a few that come readily to mind.

And so much for that, for now.

27 principles of educational psychology & what they mean for teaching

Now,

embarrassed at having lulled you to a state of somnolence through the preceding presentation of contextless lists, I hasten to present twenty-seven important principles of impeccable pedagogy. In other words, what will follow is the essence of what psychologists and teachers have discovered about students and the conditions under which they learn. I present these principles as statements. They are supported by experimentation and/or receive widespread acknowledgement from learning experts. With each principle, I present a brief suggestion as to what it means for teaching.

characteristics of learners

Most human characteristics result from the interplay between heredity and environment. Some of these characteristics are largely predetermined by genetic makeup, and they can be influenced only slightly by education. Others seem to originate mainly in experience, and they can thus be influenced greatly by education. The following categories of learner characteristics are arranged roughly in order of increasing susceptibility to environmental influence.

1. Psychological needs such as safety, acceptance, affection, and achievement seem to be characteristics of all learners. Schooling does little to change them; however, all learners seek to fulfill them.

implication Since every person's psychological well-being depends on the satisfaction of these needs, teachers must strive to see that the school experience meets each of them to the greatest extent possible.

2. Most characteristics of physical growth and development such as skeletal growth, development of organs, and maturation of the nervous system are determined by heredity. School learning has little influence on them.

implication Furniture is adjusted to students' sizes. Similarly, materials must be adjusted to the developmental levels of students' eyes, and activities must be adjusted to the length of students' attention spans.

3. Muscle growth and development are related to strength, speed, endurance, and coordination and can be influenced by experience.

implication Provide activities to develop the large muscles—running, jumping, calisthenics—and the small muscles—cutting, drawing, typing. Also, activities to develop eye-hand coordination—catching, throwing, bouncing—should be made available.

4. Some social and emotional maladjustments such as aggression, unruliness, nervousness, timidity, submission, and withdrawal can be ameliorated through school experiences.

implications Make every effort to meet your students' psychological needs—this is **crucial**. Provide clear explanations of desirable and undesirable behavior. Arrange frequent opportunities for students to practice desirable behavior. Reward desirable behavior.

5. The experiences students have influence their ability to perform cognitive/psychomotor acts.

implication Provide experiences that require students to perform a variety of acts such as perceiving, relating, reproducing, analyzing, applying, evaluating, and producing.

Experiences made available to students during their first few years of school should be built around concrete objects as often as possible. More advanced elementary and secondary school experiences can include a larger proportion of abstract activities.

As a general rule, new learnings at every level should proceed from the concrete to the abstract and from the known to the unknown.

6. Students' attitudes, interests, and values result almost entirely from experience.

implications Model, as sincerely as you can, the attitudes and values you hope your students will acquire. Students imitate teachers they admire. To develop new interests in students, provide very pleasant experiences with what you want them to become interested in, and show your own interest.

One more word: as we noted before, much learning occurs outside the school. This is particularly true of attitudes, interests, and values, so that although these characteristics are easily shaped in the school, they are also easily shaped in the home and community—often in ways at odds with those of the school.

7. A great variety of differences exists among the individuals of any group.

implication Learn what the differences are, how to spot them, and how to modify instruction accordingly.

correlates of learning

correlates of acquisition

8. Students learn best when taught at their own levels of working competence, with tasks that are challenging but possible and with procedures and materials that are of the highest interest.

implications Personalize instruction—that is, teach all students in ways that are best for them personally, with activities that interest them and materials at their levels of working ability.

9. Students cannot profit from additional or more advanced instruction until they have reached a minimal level of readiness.

implication Check for readiness. Develop readiness if possible.

note The concept of readiness includes the following general elements: experiential background, mental development, sensory-motor development, academic achievement, verbal ability, and a desire to learn. To determine readiness to learn a new act, you must identify the skill components of that act and then see whether learners possess the identified skills. If they do, they are "ready." If they do not, they will be ready as soon as they possess those component skills.

10. Students who are motivated usually learn far more than those who are not.

implications Do what you can to motivate your students. That is, do things to focus attention, to get them to begin work, and to get them to continue work. We know that students have certain needs and interests at each age level. We know they are curious about their surroundings. We can thus motivate students by providing them with opportunities to meet their needs by incorporating their interests into learning activities and by playing on their curiosity about the novel and the incongruous.

Further, we can motivate by providing sensory experiences and a variety of activities; we can provide knowledge of objectives and progress, and we can provide opportunities for success; we can allow friendly competition; and we can furnish enthusiasm, warmth, and humor.

11. Instructional materials increase active student participation and extend the range of classroom experiences.

implications Use varieties of instructional materials at every opportunity. Flat pictures and diagrams are worth far more than a thousand words. So are objects like bones, caterpillars, and rare books. Their color, movement, and novelty spark interest. Their tangibility begs manipulation. Similarly, other materials such as charts, filmstrips, transparencies, models, and motion pictures—to say nothing of excellent reference materials—permit experiences otherwise unobtainable in the classroom.

12. Active learner response is essential to learning.

implication Elicit as much student response as you can in every instructional activity. We defined learning (remember?) as behavior change resulting from experience. And experience as interaction of the individual with the environment. The greatest behavior changes occur when individuals actively seek information, when they question, manipulate, react, and respond. There is great truth in the old maxim: "We learn what we do."

13. Reinforcement speeds learning.

implication Reward students for improvements.

Reinforcement includes anything that happens to individuals after they act that makes them more likely to repeat the act. Loosely, we think of reinforcement as the supplying of a reward for desired acts. The reward comes *after* the act, not before.

Reinforcers include tangible objects such as candy or money, of course. But most often in education they are simply teacher approval, peer approval, or awareness of the correct performance on a given task.

14. The social-emotional climate of the classroom influences the degree to which students acquire self-control, ability to work with others, and willingness, enjoyment, and commitment to work.

implications Be warm, supportive, and fair with students. Involve them in planning and evaluating. Emphasize purposefulness in classwork, keep a sense of humor, and never use sarcasm. Use threats and punishment only when all else fails.

15. Students learn more and like school better in classes where there is a high degree of verbal interaction.

implication Do what you can to increase the amount of purposeful talk by and among students in the class.

16. Fatigue, boredom, and frustration inhibit learning.

implications Do your best to make every activity interesting. Change activities before students become overly tired. Be sure that the learning tasks, while challenging, are never so difficult that the students cannot complete them.

correlates of retention

17. Students remember best those materials that they consciously intend to remember.

implications Emphasize learnings that are worth remembering. Have contests to see who can remember longest. Check on students' memories of key elements periodically throughout the year.

18. Sensory involvement increases retention.

implications When possible, see that students use more than one of their five senses in what they learn. Generally, the more of their five senses the individuals use in learning, the better they remember. If they see *and* hear something, they will remember better than if they only see *or* hear it. If they can touch it, they will remember it still better.

19. Emotional involvement increases retention.

implications When possible, point out whatever

might be funny, tragic, shocking, embarrassing, delightful, or perplexing about what is being learned.

20. Muscular activity increases retention.

implications When possible and practical have students run, jump, hop, throw, sing, act out, write, draw, or talk as an integral part of their learning tasks.

21. Overlearning improves retention.

implication Arrange activities that cause students to continue practicing new learnings, even after they have reached the point of mastery.

22. Periodic practice improves retention.

implications Have students repeat some of what they have learned at various times throughout the year. Have them apply these learnings to the solution of problems.

23. Mnemonics increase students' ability to remember

implications Teach students to use varieties of mnemonics — memory aids or plans for remembering. Familiar examples are "Thirty days hath September . . .," "Every good boy does fine," and "Spring forward and fall backward." Mnemonics have been frowned upon by many people who consider them a kind of trickery. They aren't. If we really want students to remember what they learn (and how else can we justify teaching?), we should help them do so in every way possible.

correlates of transfer

24. People can make better use of learnings that are understood.

implications Strive to help students see the meaning in what they learn. Emphasize *what's, how's,* and *why's* in information learned. Have students interpret and extrapolate. When they can explain what they have learned in their own words, we may infer that they have "understood."

25. Learnings that can be generalized are more easily used.

implications Provide practice in generalizing. At the same time help learners to avoid overgeneralizing.

To generalize is to make a statement that you believe is descriptive of a whole class of objects or events. For example, if you learn that pigeons are warm-blooded, sparrows are warm-blooded, and ostriches are warm-blooded, you may generalize that birds are warm-blooded. In the same way, you may learn that salmon lays eggs, bass lay eggs, and carp lay eggs, and may then (over)generalize that all fish lay eggs.

26. One can use learnings more easily if one can sense relationships.

implications Give students practice in identifying similarities and other relationships among objects, among processes, and among events.

To transfer is to use now that which was learned in a previous circumstance. To relate means to associate one thing with another. Especially transferable from one circumstance to another are processes, or ways of doing things—describing, solving problems, painting, composing paragraphs.

27. Students learn to transfer better if they have direct practice in applying what they have learned.

implications Treat every new learning as useful. Help students recognize its usefulness through direct application. The underlying idea of education is that what we learn now must serve us somehow elsewhere. Be sure that what you teach your students can pass that test, and be sure your students know it.

that's it

That's one view of what educational psychology is all about and what it has taught us, in the main. We could just as well have begun and ended here. Except for one thing.

We learn by doing.

Remember? Dewey said that, and he spoke true. These principles of educational psychology will have absolutely no effect on you until you incorporate them into your teaching style—into the ways you operate in the classroom with students. You will learn what you do.

That's what this book has been about.

Index